THE WG&L HANDBOOK OF

SHORT-TERM & LONG-TERM FINANCIAL MANAGEMENT

EDITOR

DENNIS E. LOGUE

AMOS TUCK SCHOOL OF BUSINESS ADMINISTRATION
DARTMOUTH COLLEGE

WARREN, GORHAM & LAMONT

COLLEGE DIVISION South-Western Publishing Co.

Cincinnati Ohio

Acquisitions Editor: Christopher Will
Production Editors: Sharon Smith and Sue Ellen Brown
Marketing Manager: Denise Carlson
Cover Designer: Lotus Wittkopf

FN63AA

Library of Congress Cataloging-in-Publication Data

The WG&L handbook of short-term & long-term financial management /
    editor, Dennis E. Logue.
        p.   cm.
    Includes index.
    ISBN 0-538-84251-2
    1. Corporations—Finance. 2. Commerical credit. 3. Cash
management. 4. Budget in business. 5. Lease and rental services.
6. Capital investments. 7. Venture capital. 8. Corporations—
Valuation. I. Logue, Dennis E.
HG4026.W475   1995
658.15—dc20   94-20686
                                                                    CIP

I⦿P
International Thomson Publishing

This book is printed on acid-free paper that meets Environmental Protection
Agency standards for recycled paper.

Preface

As the editor for the W, G, & L *Handbook of Modern Finance, Third Edition,* I am happy to note that South-Western Publishing Company is publishing this series of five "break-out" readings books for use in your classroom:

The W, G, & L *Handbook of International Finance*
The W, G, & L *Handbook of Financial Markets*
The W, G, & L *Handbook of Securities and Investment Management*
The W, G, & L *Handbook of Financial Policy*
The W, G, & L *Handbook of Short-Term and Long-Term Financial Management.*

These readers make a unique contribution to the classroom in that they are written primarily from the practitioner's point of view; showing students how the principles they are learning in class can be applied to real-world financial problems.

Thus they are ideally suited to supplement courses in Corporate Finance, Investments, Capital Markets, Financial Institutions, and International Finance both at the undergraduate and MBA level. They are also ideally suited for use in an executive education program.

These readers cover virtually every major technical, analytical, and theoretical financial question likely to be raised by active, inquisitive corporate financial and business executives, strategic planners, accountants (public and private), attorneys, security analysts, and bankers. They provide your students with insights for solving day-to-day business problems as well as provide guidance in long-term planning. Institutional arrangements are explained; relevant economic and financial theory and its application are presented and described. In addition, sophisticated quantitative analyses are presented in the context of real-world examples, numerous figures illustrate textual explanations, and end-of-chapter readings direct interested readers to additional technical literature in the field. The intent has been to produce a series of readings books that will help students understand the practical applications of the theory presented in their textbooks, thus helping them become better-prepared business professionals.

The W, G, & L *Handbook of Short-Term and Long-Term Financial Management* covers short-term internal corporate financial decisions as well as financial decisions of long-term consequence. This material can be very useful in strategic problem solving. Nearly every chapter in this reader takes the student from theory to practical application with a minimum of complexity and with strong illustrations. Contributors include:

William B. Bygrave
Associate Professor and Academic Coordinator of Entrepreneurial Studies, Babson College

C. Bradford Cornell
  Financial Consultant, FinEcon

William B. Gartner
  Visiting Professor, Henry W. Simonsen Chair in Entrepreneurship, University of Southern California

James A. Gentry
  Professor of Finance, School of Business, University of Illinois

Diana R. Harrington
  Babson Distinguished Professor of Finance, Babson College

Noriko Ozawa
  Fieldstone Private Capital Group, L.P.

Sharon K. Peterson
  Fieldstone Private Capital Group, L.P.

Donald R. Reed
  President, Granite Finance Company

Andrew K. Rosson
  Fieldstone Private Capital Group, L.P.

Solomon B. Samson
  Managing Director, Standard & Poor's Corporation

Alan C. Shapiro
  Ivadelle and Theodore Johnson Professor of Finance and Business Economics, School of Business Administration, University of Southern California

Bernell K. Stone
  Professor, School of Management, Brigham Young University

Ronald A. Zanoni
  Managing Director, Kidder, Peabody & Co., Inc.

The editor wants to thank all of the authors who have worked so hard to produce highly focused chapters with a strong managerial slant. All are to be thanked and congratulated.

In addition to the authors, thanks must also go to Audrey Hanlon, who helped organize the work done by Tuck; Beverly Salbin of Warren Gorman Lamont, who brought so much to the party that she deserves much more recognition than this; and to Leora Harris and Vibert Gale, also of WGL, whose skills contributed so much to the final product.

Finally, I want to thank South-Western Publishing Company for bringing these readers to the college market.

DENNIS E. LOGUE

Hanover, New Hampshire
November 1993

Contents

9. Venture Capital
William B. Gartner and William B. Bygrave

291

10. Corporate Valuation
Bradford Cornell

331

THE WG&L HANDBOOK OF

SHORT-TERM & LONG-TERM FINANCIAL MANAGEMENT

Chapter 1
Credit Analysis

Solomon B. Samson

1.01 INTRODUCTION

Credit analysis is performed for a very specific purpose. Credit ratings assigned to fixed-income securities provide the investment community with the analyst's opinions as to whether a borrower will make principal and interest payments in a complete and timely manner. The nature and provisions of the obligation and its relative position in the event of a bankruptcy are also taken into account.

Typically, the primary determinant of a credit rating is an analysis of the creditworthiness of the borrower. This chapter focuses on the key elements that go into the analysis of the credit quality of an industrial company. The basic form of the analysis is the same whether the security to be rated is a long-term debt issue or a short-term obligation such as commercial paper (CP). Some added factors concerning CP are covered later in the chapter.

1.02 RATING METHODOLOGY

It is critical to understand that the rating process is not limited to the examination of various financial measures. Proper assessment of debt protection levels requires a broader framework, involving a thorough review of business fundamentals including judgments as to the company's competitive position and evaluation of management and its strategies. Clearly, such judgments are highly subjective; subjectivity, however, is at the heart of every rating.

Standard & Poor's (S&P) Ratings Group uses a format similar to that shown in Figure 1-1, which divides the analytical task into several categories, providing a framework that ensures that all salient issues are considered. For corporates, the first several categories are oriented to business analysis; the remainder relate to financial analysis.

However, there is no formula for combining the scores for each of these categories to arrive at a rating conclusion. Ultimately, the analytical variables are not separable; they are all interdependent.

At times, a rating decision may be heavily influenced by financial measures. At other times, business risk factors may dominate. If a firm is strong in the one respect and weak in the other, the rating will balance the different factors. Viewed differently, the degree of a firm's business risk sets the expectations for the financial risk it can afford at any rating level. An analysis of industry characteristics and of how a firm is positioned to succeed in that environment is necessary in order to establish the financial benchmarks used in to the quantitative part of the analysis.

[1] Industry Risk

Each rating analysis begins with an assessment of the company's environment. To determine the degree of operating risk that faces a participant in a given business, S&P analyzes the dynamics of that business. This analysis focuses on the strength of the industry prospects, as well as the competitive factors that affect that industry.

The many factors that are assessed include industry prospects for growth, stability, or decline and the pattern of independent business cycles. It is critical to determine the vulnerability to technological change, labor unrest, or regulatory interference. In addition, industries that have long lead times or that require fixed plant of a specialized nature face heightened risk.

FIGURE 1-1

Analyzing Business Risk and Financial Risk

Industry Characteristics		Financial Characteristics	
	Score		Score
Issuer Position			
(e.g.) Marketing	_____	Financial policy	_____
(e.g.) Technology	_____	Profitability	_____
(e.g.) Efficiency	_____	Capital structure	_____
Management	_____	Cash flow protection	_____
Composite			
Competitive position	_____	Financial flexibility	_____

While any particular profile category can be the overriding rating consideration, the industry risk assessment goes a long way toward setting the upper limit on the rating to which any participant in the industry can aspire. Specifically, it would be very difficult to imagine S&P assigning AA and AAA bond ratings or A−1+ CP ratings to companies with heavy participation in industries considered to be of above-average risk, regardless of how conservative a financial posture is maintained. Examples of some of these industries include integrated steel makers, tire and rubber companies, home builders, and most of the mining sector.

Conversely, some industries are regarded favorably. They are distinguished by such traits as steady demand growth, an ability to maintain margins without impairing future prospects, flexibility in the timing of capital outlays, and moderate capital intensity. Industries possessing one or more of these attributes include manufacturers of branded consumer products, drug firms, and publishing and broadcasting. Again, high marks in this category do not translate into high ratings for all industry participants, but the cushion of strong industry fundamentals provides helpful support. The industry risk assessment also sets the stage for analyzing more specific company (debt issuer) risk factors and the priority of these factors in the overall evaluation. For example, if an industry is determined to be highly competitive, a careful evaluation of a firm's market position is needed. If the industry has large capital requirements, examination of cash flow adequacy assumes major importance.

[2] Keys to Success

As part of the industry analysis, the key rating factors are identified: the keys to success and areas of vulnerability. A company's rating is affected crucially by its ability to achieve success and avoid the pitfalls inherent in its industry.

The nature of competition is, obviously, different for different industries. Competition can be based on price, quality of product, distribution capabilities, image, product differentiation, service, or some other factor. Competition may be on a national basis, as is the case with major appliances. In other industries, such as chemicals, competition is global, and in still others, such as cement, competition is strictly regional.

The basis for competition determines which factors are analyzed for a given company. Figures 1-2 and 1-3, respectively, highlight the factors that are considered critical

FIGURE 1-2

Rating Factors for Pulp and Paper Industry

Cost Position

Low-cost status
    Operating margins
    Return on assets
    Mill margins
    Mill cash cost per ton
    Mill cost per ton
    Worker hours per ton

Modern efficient asset base
    Capital expenditures as a percentage of net fixed assets over last 10 years
    Repair and maintenance expenditures as a percentage of net fixed assets over last 10 years
    Ratio of capital expenditures to inflation-adjusted depreciation
    Are facilities "built out," or is there room for additions?
    Are facilities integrated (on-site pulping)?
    Are machines new and in good running order?
    Mill site configuration and layout
    Process control and computer use

Mill location
    Closeness to growth markets
    Closeness to major metropolitan regions
    Closeness to deep seaports for export
    Freight advantages
    Harvest costs

Labor relations
    Union versus nonunion mills
    History of labor disruptions
    Advantageous wage rates and work rule flexibility
    Union contract expiration schedules

Customer Satisfaction

Quality, service, and customer loyalty
    Brightness, opacity, strength, runability, and printability
    Independent surveys
    Evaluation by commercial printers and publishers and customers
    Capacity utilization (although not a pure indicator of quality, service, or customer loyalty, it
      does provide some directional insight)

Product Mix

    Value-added versus commodity grades
    Sales revenue per product ton
    Diversity of mix
    Breadth of products: Full line or one-product supplier
    Consumer versus nonconsumer end markets
    Relative pricing sensitivity in key grades

Self-Sufficiency

Fiber self-sufficiency and long-term adequacy
    Fiber sources: Internal sources versus long-term private cutting contracts versus
      government contracts versus outside market purchases
    Fiber mix: Softwood versus hardwood versus recycled paper
    Reforestation programs

FIGURE 1-2 (*continued*)

Energy mix and self-sufficiency
 Fuel mix: Internal sources versus oil versus coal versus gas
 Cogeneration and hydropower
 Ability to convert or change to alternative energy source quickly

Marketing Prowess
 Gain or loss of market share
 Distribution channels
 Ratio of advertising cost to sales
 New product introductions
 Degree of influence on pricing
Forward integration
 Percent of in-house paper used by converting facilities
 Wholesale and retail distribution

---

in the pulp and paper products business and the airline industry and the specific considerations that determine a company's position in each.

For any particular company, one or more factors can hold special significance, even if that factor is not common to the industry. For example, the fact that a company has only one major production facility should certainly be viewed as an area of vulnerability. Similarly, reliance on one product creates risk, no matter how successful that product is. For example, one major pharmaceutical company has reaped a financial bonanza from a single type of medication, which continues to grow and provide the firm with exceptional profits and cash flow. The firm's debt is rated highly, but it would be viewed still more favorably were it not for the lopsided dependence on a single drug (which, after all, is subject to competition and patent expiry).

[3] Diversification Factors

When a company participates in more than one business, each segment is analyzed separately. A composite is formed from these building blocks, weighting each element according to its importance to the overall organization. The potential benefits of diversification, which may not be apparent from the additive approach, are then considered. General Electric Company, Allied-Signal Inc., and Figgie International Inc. are cases where the balance of different businesses is a major supporting factor in their ratings.

For a company to be considered diversified, no single business segment can be dominant. One major automobile company has received much attention for diversifying into aerospace and computer software. But it is not a diversified firm, since its success is substantially determined by one line of business.

Limited credit will be given if the various lines of business react similarly to economic cycles. For example, diversification from nickel into copper cannot be expected to stabilize performance; similar risk factors are associated with both metals.

Most critical is a company's ability to manage diverse operations. Skills and practices needed to run a business differ greatly among industries, not to mention the challenge posed by participating in several different industries. For example, a number of old-line industrial firms rushed to diversify into financial services, only to find themselves saddled with unfamiliar businesses they had difficulty managing.

FIGURE 1-3

Rating Factors for Airlines

Market Share

Share of industry traffic, measured by revenue passenger miles or revenue ton miles for
  airlines with significant freight operations

Share of industry capacity, measured by available seat miles or available ton miles

Share gap (share of traffic minus share of capacity): A measure of market strength

Trend of overall market share

Market share among travel agencies of computerized reservation system (CRS) owned by or
  shared by airline (travel agencies tend to book a disproportionate number of tickets on
  airlines whose CRS they use)

Position in Specific Markets

Geographic position of airline's hubs for handling major traffic flows; position of competing
  hubs of other airlines

Share of enplanements and flights at hubs

Share at major origination and destination markets; economic and demographic growth
  prospects of those markets

Strength of competition at hubs and in major markets served

Adequacy of infrastructure
  Gates
  Terminal space and other ground facilities
  Air traffic control; takeoff and landing slot restrictions

Position in international markets
  Growth prospects of markets
  Treaty and regulatory barriers to entry
  Strength of foreign and U.S. competition

Revenue Generation

Utilization of capacity, measured by "load factor" (revenue passenger miles divided by
  available seat miles)

Pricing
  Yield (passenger revenues divided by revenue passenger miles)
  Yield adjusted for average trip length (airlines with shorter average trips tend to have
    higher yields)

Unit revenues, measured by passenger revenue per available seat mile (yield times load
  factor)

Effectiveness of revenue management: Maximizing revenues by managing trade-off between
  pricing and utilization

Service reputation; ranking in measures of customer satisfaction

Productivity, measured by revenues or revenue passenger miles per employee or per dollar of
  assets

Cost Control

Operating cost per available seat mile
  Adjusted for average trip length
  Adjusted for use of operating leases

Labor
  Labor costs as a percentage of total operating costs
  Labor cost per available seat mile
  Structure of labor contracts; existence and nature of any B scales (lower pay scales for
    recent hires)
  Flexibility of work rules; effect on productivity
  Status of union contracts and negotiations; possibility of strikes
  Labor relations and morale

FIGURE 1-3 (*continued*)

Fuel costs and impact of potential fuel price hikes, given fuel efficiency of fleet and nature of routes flown

Commissions, marketing, and other operating expenses

Aircraft Fleet

Number and type of aircraft in relation to current and projected needs

Status of fleet modernization program
  Average age of fleet; age weighted by seats
  Proportion or aircraft meeting Stage III noise requirements
  Fuel efficiency of fleet
  Aircraft orders and options for future deliveries

Some firms have adopted a portfolio approach to their diverse holdings. The business of buying and selling businesses is different from running operations and is analyzed differently. The ever-changing character of the company's assets typically is viewed as a negative. On the other hand, there is often an offsetting advantage: greater flexibility in raising funds when each line of business is a discrete unit that can be sold off.

[4] Size Considerations

S&P has no minimum size criteria for any given rating level. Size becomes a rating issue when it affects a company's inability to compete. Obviously, the need to have a broad product line or a national marketing structure is a factor in many businesses. In this sense, sheer mass is not important; demonstrable market advantage is.

Market share analysis is often an important rating consideration. However, large shares are not always synonymous with market advantage or industry dominance. For instance, where an industry has a number of large but comparably sized participants, none may have a particular advantage or disadvantage. Conversely, where an industry is highly fragmented, even the large firms may lack pricing leadership potential. The textile industry is an example.

Small companies can also hold dominant market positions that give them competitive benefits. Two examples are Jostens Inc. in school rings and Sotheby's in the art business. Still, small companies are almost by definition more concentrated in terms of product, number of customers, or geography. In effect, they lack some elements of diversification that can benefit larger firms. To the extent that markets and regional economies change, a broader scope of business affords protection. This consideration is balanced against the performance and prospects of a given business. In addition, lack of financial flexibility is usually an important negative factor. Adverse developments that would simply be a setback for firms with greater resources could spell the end for small companies with limited access to funds.

There is a controversial notion that small growth companies represent a better credit risk than older, declining companies. While this is intuitively appealing, it ignores some important considerations. Large firms have substantial staying power, even if their businesses are troubled. Their constituencies, including large numbers of employees, can influence their fates. Banks' exposure to these firms may be quite extensive, creating a reluctance to abandon them. Moreover, such firms often have accumulated a large number of peripheral assets that can be sold. In contrast, the promise of small firms can fade very quickly and their minuscule equity bases offer scant protection, especially given the high debt burden some companies deliberately assume.

Fast growth is often subject to poor execution, even if the idea is well conceived. There is also the risk of overambitiousness. Moreover, some firms tend to continue high-risk financial policies as they aggressively pursue ever greater objectives, limiting any credit quality improvement. There is little evidence to suggest that growth companies initially receiving speculative-grade ratings have particular upgrade potential. A large proportion already have experienced business reverses. Many more have defaulted than have achieved investment grade. Oil exploration and high-technology firms have been especially vulnerable, even though their great potential was touted at the time they first came to market.

[5] Management Evaluation

Management is assessed for its role in determining operational success and also for its risk tolerance. The first aspect is incorporated in the competitive position analysis; the second is weighed as a financial policy factor.

For rating agencies that meet with senior management on a regular basis, subjective judgments lead to conclusions regarding each aspect of management evaluation. Opinions are formed during the meetings and, over a period of years, are as important as the company's track record. While management's track record may seem to offer an objective basis for evaluation, it is often difficult to determine how results should be attributed to management's skills. The analyst must decide to what extent the firm's performance is the result of good management, devoid of management influence, or achieved despite management.

Plans and policies have to be judged for their realism. Management credibility is also an important issue here. Stated policies often will not be followed, and the analyst should be skeptical unless management has earned credibility.

The evaluation also should be sensitive to potential organizational problems. These include the following situations:

- There is significant organizational reliance on an individual, especially one who may be close to retirement.
- The finance function and finance considerations do not receive high organizational recognition.
- The transition of management to professional and organizational from entrepreneurial or family-bound has not yet been accomplished.
- A relatively large number of changes occur within a short period.
- The relationship between organizational structure and management strategy is unclear.
- A substantial presence of one or a few shareholders exists, imposing constraints on management prerogatives.

[6] Measuring Performance and Risk

Having evaluated the issuer's competitive position and the environment in which it operates, the analysis proceeds to several financial categories. To reiterate: The company's business risk profile determines the level of financial risk appropriate for any rating category. Financial risk is portrayed largely through quantitative means, particularly by using financial ratios. (Medians for key ratios for U.S. companies are found at the end of this chapter.) Benchmarks vary greatly by industry, and several analytical adjustments typically are required to calculate the ratios for an individual company. Cross-border comparisons require additional care, given the differences in accounting conventions and local financial systems.

[a] **Accounting Quality.** Ratings rely on audited data, and the rating process does not entail S&P's auditing a company's financial records. Analysis of the audited financials begins with a review of accounting quality. The purpose is to determine whether ratios and statistics derived from financial statements can be used accurately to measure a company's performance and position relative to both its competition and the larger universe of industrial companies. The credit analysis process is very much one of comparisons, so it is important to have a common frame of reference.

Accounting policies to be reviewed include the following:

- Consolidation basis (the Financial Accounting Standards Board now requires the consolidation of even nonhomogeneous operations. For analytical purposes, it is critical to separate these and evaluate each type of business in its own right.)
- Income recognition (e.g., successful efforts versus full cost in the oil industry and percentage of completion versus completed contract in the construction industry)
- Depreciation methods and asset lives
- Inventory pricing methods
- Impact of purchase accounting and treatment of goodwill
- Employee benefits, including pensions and postretirement health benefits and employee stock ownership plans
- Various off-balance sheet liabilities, from leases and project finance to defeasance and receivable sales

To the extent possible, analytical adjustments are made to better portray reality. Although it is not always possible to recast a company's financial statements completely, it is useful to have some notion of the extent to which performance is overstated or understated. At the very least, the choice of accounting alternatives can be characterized as generally conservative or liberal.

[b] **Financial Policies.** S&P emphasizes the importance of management's philosophies and policies involving financial risk. A surprising number of companies have not given this question serious thought, much less reached strong conclusions. For many firms, debt leverage (calculated without adjustment of reported figures) is the only focal point of such policy considerations. More sophisticated business managers have thoughtful policies that recognize cash flow parameters and the interplay between business and financial risk.

Many firms that have set goals do not have the wherewithal, discipline, or management commitment to achieve these objectives. A company's leverage goals, for example, need to be viewed in the context of its record and the financial dynamics affecting the business. If a management states, as many do, that its goal is to operate at 35 percent debt to capital, rating agencies will tend to factor that into their analyses only to the extent that it appears plausible. For example, if a company has aggressive spending plans, that 35 percent goal would carry little weight, unless management has committed to a specific program of asset sales, equity sales, or other actions that in a given period would produce the desired results.

S&P does not encourage companies to manage themselves with an eye toward a specific rating. The more appropriate approach is to operate for the good of the business as management sees it and to let the rating follow. Certainly, prudence and credit quality should be among the most important considerations, but financial policy should be consistent with the needs of the business rather than an arbitrary constraint.

If opportunities are forgone merely to avoid financial risk, the firm is making poor strategic decisions. In fact, it may be sacrificing long-term credit quality for the facade of low risk in the near term. One financial article described a company that curtailed spending expressly "to become an 'A' rated company"; as a result, "the company's business responded poorly to an increase in market demand. Needless to say, the sought-after 'A' rating continued to elude the company."

In any event, pursuit of the highest rating attainable is not necessarily in the company's best interests. AAA may be the highest rating, but that does not suggest that it is the "best" rating. Typically, a company with virtually no financial risk is not optimal as far as meeting the needs of its various constituencies is concerned. A company has shareholders as well as bondholders. An underleveraged firm is not minimizing its cost of capital and is thereby depriving its owners of potentially greater value for their investment. In this light, a corporate objective of having its debt rated AAA or AA is at times suspect. Whatever a company's financial track record, the analyst must be skeptical if corporate goals are implicitly irrational. A firm's conservative financial philosophy must be consistent with the firm's overall goals or needs or otherwise must arise from the nature of its operations.

[7] Profitability

The analysis of all of the financial categories covers both historical and projected performance. Because a rating is an assessment of the likelihood of timely payment of interest and future repayment of principal, the evaluation emphasizes future performance. However, the rating analysis does not attempt to forecast performance precisely or to pinpoint economic cycles. Rather, the forecast analysis considers variability of expected future performance based on a range of economic and competitive scenarios.

Profitability actually encompasses two analytical areas. First, a company's earning power is measured. In the long run, profit potential is the most important determinant of credit protection. Second, earnings are viewed in relation to a company's burden of fixed charges. Otherwise, strong performance can be detrimentally affected by aggressive debt financing; the opposite is also true.

The more significant measures of profitability are the following:

- Return on capital
- Profit margins
- Earnings on assets and business segments

Pretax, preinterest return on average invested capital and operating income as a percentage of sales are ratios that indicate a company's performance regardless of how it is capitalized. Obviously, all else being equal, a company that generates higher operating margins and returns on capital has a greater ability to generate equity capital internally, attract capital externally, and withstand business adversity. Earnings power ultimately attests to the value of the firm's assets.

While the absolute levels of the ratios are important, it is equally important to focus on trends and to compare these ratios with those of competitors. Various industries follow different cycles and have different earnings characteristics. Therefore, what may be considered favorable for one business may be relatively poor for another. For example, the drug industry usually generates high operating margins and high returns on capital. Defense contractors generate low operating margins and high returns on capital. The pipeline industry has high operating margins and low returns on capital. Comparisons with a company's peers will influence the perception of a firm's competitive strengths and price leadership flexibility.

The two primary fixed-charge coverage ratios are pretax interest coverage and pretax coverage of interest plus total rents. If preferred stock is outstanding and material, fixed charges are adjusted to include preferred dividends. To reflect more accurately the ongoing earnings power of the firm, the reported figures are typically adjusted. The effects of last-in, first-out (LIFO) liquidations, foreign exchange gains, and unremitted equity are excluded, as are those of nonrecurring or extraordinary gains and losses. Similarly, the analyst is interested in coverage of interest payable, and adjustments are made where interest has been capitalized.

Particularly important today are management plans for achieving earnings growth. Can existing businesses provide satisfactory growth, especially in a less inflationary environment, and to what extent are acquisitions or divestitures necessary to achieve corporate goals? At first glance, a mature cash-generating company offers a great deal of bondholder protection, but S&P assumes a corporation's central focus is to augment shareholder values over the long run. In this context, a lack of indicated earnings growth potential is considered a weakness. By itself, this may hinder a company's ability to attract financial and human resources. Moreover, limited internal earnings growth opportunities may lead management to pursue growth externally, implying greater business and financial risks.

[8] Capital Structure: Leverage and Asset Protection

Ratios employed to capture the degree of leverage used by a company include the following:

- Total debt/total debt + equity
- Total debt + off-balance sheet liabilities/total debt + off-balance sheet liabilities + equity
- Total debt/total debt + market value of equity
- Long-term debt/long-term debt + equity

Traditional measures focusing on long-term debt have lost much of their significance, since companies increasingly rely on short-term borrowings. It is now commonplace to find permanent layers of short-term debt, which finance not only seasonal working capital but also an ongoing portion of the asset base. Management's reluctance to refinance during periods of high interest rates contributed to this phenomenon in recent years.

A company's asset mix is a critical determinant of the appropriate leverage for a given level of risk. Assets with stable cash flow or market values justify greater use of debt financing than do those with clouded marketability. Adjustments are made for companies with disproportionate amounts of cash, investments, or receivables. In this vein, grain and tobacco inventory and even stand-alone business entities would be viewed positively compared with assets that might be concentrated in fixed plant and equipment. Similarly, transportation equipment is viewed favorably, given its suitability for use by other companies.

Knowing the true values to assign a company's assets is key to the analysis. Highlighting materially undervalued or overvalued assets relative to book value allows asset protection to be viewed in an alternative light. S&P considers the profitability of an asset the basis for determining its economic value. Market values of a company's assets and independent asset appraisals can offer additional insights. However, there are shortcomings in these methods of valuation (just as there are with historical cost accounting) that prevent reliance on any single measure. The stock market emphasizes growth prospects and has a short time horizon; it is influenced by changes in alternative investment opportunities and can be very volatile. A company's ability to service its debt is not directly affected by such factors.

Financial statements of merged and acquired companies pose a special analytical challenge. The acquired company's assets and equity are to be written up to reflect the acquisition price. Management may want to maintain the debt ratio at preacquisition levels, but the revalued assets have only the same earnings power as before; they cannot support more debt just because a different number is used to record their value. At the time of the transaction, the analysis can take these factors into account, but down the road the picture becomes muddied, and the ability to relate to preacquisition financial values and to make comparisons with peer companies is lost.

The presence of a material goodwill account always indicates the impact of acquisitions and purchase accounting on a firm's equity base. If supported by earnings power and good prospects, intangible assets have value that is the same as or greater than that of tangible ones. But comparisons are still distorted, since other companies cannot record their own valuable business intangibles, those that have been developed instead of acquired. This alone requires some analytical adjustment before measuring leverage. In addition, analysts are entitled to be more skeptical about earning prospects that rely on turnaround strategies or "synergistic" mergers.

[a] Off-Balance Sheet Financing. Off-balance sheet items that are factored into the leverage analysis include the following:

- Operating leases
- Pension and retiree health benefit liabilities
- Debt of joint ventures and unconsolidated subsidiaries
- Guarantees
- Take-or-pay contracts and obligations under throughput and deficiency agreements
- Receivables that have been factored, transferred, or securitized
- Potential legal judgments or settlements of lawsuits

Various methodologies are used to determine the proper adjustment value for each of the off-balance sheet items. In some cases, the adjustment is straightforward. For example, the amount of guaranteed debt can simply be added to the guarantor's liabilities. Other adjustments are more complex or less precise.

Debt of a joint venture is often apportioned to the partners according to their share of ownership. However, if the venture is more critical to one of the partners' operations, the analyst may burden that partner with a disproportionate amount of the debt. Similarly, the partners' relative ability to service the joint venture debt helps determine the analytical attribution of the debt. In other cases, owners have little incentive to support the venture's debt if it is large enough in relation to their investment. In those cases, an adjustment would be made to write down the owners' investment, rather than adding debt to their balance sheets.

In the case of contingencies, an estimate can be developed. For example, in the wake of lawsuits against Union Carbide Corporation arising from the Bhopal explosion, S&P analysts estimated the cost of a likely settlement, subtracted the estimated insurance coverage, and took the present value of the remainder (considering the likely time frame for actual payment). The resulting amount was viewed as a Union Carbide liability from an analytical perspective.

The sale or securitization of accounts receivable represents a form of off-balance sheet financing. If used to supplant other debt, the impact on credit quality is neutral. (There can be some incremental benefit to the extent that the company has expanded access to capital, but there may also be an offset in the higher cost of such financing.) For ratio calculation, S&P would add back the amount of receivables and a like amount of debt. This eliminates the distorting, cosmetic effect of utilizing an off-balance sheet technique and allows better comparison with other firms that have not chosen this avenue of financing. Similarly, if a firm uses proceeds from receivables sales to invest in riskier assets and not to reduce other debt, the adjustment will reveal an increase in financial risk.

The debt equivalent value of operating leases is determined by calculating the present value of minimum operating lease obligations as reported in the annual report's footnotes. The lease amount beyond five years is assumed to mature at a rate approximating the minimum payment due in year 5.

The variety of lease types may require the analyst to obtain additional information or use estimates to evaluate lease obligations. This is needed whenever lease terms are shorter than the assets' expected economic lives. For example, retailers report only the first period of a lease written with an initial period and several renewal options over a long term. Another limitation develops when a portion of the lease payment is tied to sales, as is often the case in the retailing industry.

Traditionally, operating leases were recognized by the factor method, under which annual lease expense is multiplied by a factor that reflects the average life of the company's leased assets. This method is an attempt to capitalize the asset, rather than just the use of the asset for the lease period. However, the method can overstate the asset to be capitalized by failing to recognize the use of the asset over the course of the lease. It is also too arbitrary to be realistic.

As financing techniques become more innovative, ratio analysis becomes more complicated and more tenuous as well. The analyst must distinguish between the different hybrid debt securities based on their features.

Convertible debt is usually not considered equity until it actually converts. Many well-intentioned companies project conversion within a short time but fail to accomplish it. Conversion is subject to enough variables beyond management's control that a prediction of when it might occur becomes presumptuous. Obviously, if conversion is mandatory, the security can be viewed as equity in advance of the actual conversion.

Original issue discount debt, such as zero-coupon debt, is valued net of unamortized discount (the amount of legal liability) for purposes of capital structure analysis. However, borrowings will increase with time, and the growing amounts are taken into account in cash flow analysis. Since there is no sinking fund provision, the issue matures all at once, creating a very sizable refinancing requirement that could test a company's financial flexibility. The need to refinance a very large amount at one time can become a challenge unless prudent steps are taken to anticipate the need.

[b] Preferred Stock. Preferred stock now comes in many forms. Some preferreds clearly represent permanent equity, especially when featuring convertibility into common shares. Other preferreds are viewed as debt or equity or something in between, depending on their features and the circumstances. Any preferred that the analyst believes will be refinanced eventually with debt should be viewed as a debt equivalent, not equity, from the beginning.

There are preferred stock issues that represent merely a debt alternative for companies that are not current taxpayers and that therefore do not benefit from the tax deductibility of interest expense. Auction preferreds, for example, are "perpetual" on the surface. However, the typical issuer is not motivated to keep such preferreds permanently outstanding. Other redeemable preferred stock issues also are likely to be refinanced with debt once an issuer becomes a taxpayer. Preferreds that can be exchanged for debt at the company's option also may be viewed as debt in anticipation of the exchange.

Preferreds with sinking funds represent a hybrid, with elements of debt and equity. Sinking fund requirements are comparable to debt maturities, and rarely does a corporation finance the sinking fund payment through cash flow or with newly issued equity, common or preferred. Rather, the sinking fund payment is met through debt issuance, which results in the sinking fund preferred being just the precursor of debt. It would be misleading to view sinking fund preferreds, particularly the portion coming due in the near to intermediate term, as equity, only to have each payment convert to debt on the sinking fund payment date. Accordingly, at least the portion of the issuer's sinking fund preferreds due within the next several years should be viewed as debt. A supplementary analysis might view the entire issue as debt, since presumably it will eventually be debt.

In any event, an anticipated increase in debt burden as a result of replacing preferred with debt must be viewed in the dynamic context of prospective performance. For example, the trigger prompting a company to redeem or force exchange of its preferred likely would be a shift to tax-paying status from non-tax-paying status, a situation generally associated with improved profitability. Such a positive development could offset the added debt in the capital structure and balance the impact on credit quality.

The implications are different for the many issuers that are not marginal earners but that do not pay taxes for various other reasons, including the availability of tax loss carryforwards or foreign tax credits. For them, a change in tax-paying status is not associated with better profitability, but the incentive to turn the preferred into debt is identical.

Discussions with company management can help the analyst determine whether a given preferred stock issue is a permanent feature of the capital structure, as well as the circumstances that might lead to replacement or refinancing. Indeed, the burden of proof is often the issuer's to show that a preferred transaction represents more than pseudoequity.

Even when preferred stock does qualify for treatment as equity for the purpose of calculating capital structure ratios, preferred is not the equivalent of common equity, since the company has less flexibility to pass a preferred dividend. This is especially true in the case of auction preferreds and similar issues.

[9] Cash Flow Adequacy

Earnings may be the best long-term determinant of creditworthiness, but when an interest or principal payment date arrives, earnings are not what matters. The obligation cannot be serviced out of earnings, which is just an accounting concept; the payment has to be made with cash. Although there is usually a strong relationship between cash flow and reported earnings, many transactions and accounting entries affect one and not the other. Analysis of cash flow patterns can reveal a level of debt servicing capability that is either stronger or weaker than might be apparent from earnings.

Cash flow analysis is critical in all credit rating decisions. Lately, it has taken on added importance as the debt market has been increasingly populated by speculative-grade issues. While companies with investment-grade ratings generally have ready access to external cash to cover temporary shortfalls, junk bond issuers lack this degree of flexibility and have fewer alternatives to internally generated cash for servicing debt.

Discussions about cash flow often suffer from lack of uniform definition of terms. Figure 1-4 illustrates S&P's terminology with respect to specific cash flow concepts. At the top is the item from the funds flow statement usually labeled ''funds from operations'' or ''working capital from operations.'' This quantity is net income adjusted for depreciation and other noncash debits and credits that have been factored into it. The net change in working capital investment is subtracted to arrive at operating cash flow.

Capital expenditures and cash dividends, respectively, are backed out to arrive at free operating cash flow and discretionary cash flow. Finally, the cost of acquisitions is subtracted from the running total, proceeds from asset disposals are added, and other miscellaneous sources and uses of cash are added. The end result of these computations is prefinancing cash flow, which represents the extent to which company cash flow from all internal sources has been sufficient to cover all internal needs. The bottom part of Figure 1-4 reconciles prefinancing cash flow to various categories of external financing and changes in the company's own cash balance. In the figure, XYZ Corporation experienced a $35.7 million cash shortfall in year 1 that had to be met with a combination of additional borrowings and a drawdown of its own cash.

[a] **Cash Flow Ratios.** Ratios show the relationship of cash flow to debt and debt service and also to the firm's needs. Since there are calls on cash other than repaying debt, it is important to know the extent to which those requirements will allow cash to be used for debt service or will lead to greater need for borrowing.

Some of the specific ratios that are considered are the following:

- Funds from operation/total debt
- Total debt/discretionary cash flow = debt payback period
- (Funds fróm operation + interest)/interest

FIGURE 1-4

Cash Flow Summary: XYZ Corporation

	Year 1	Year 2
Working capital from operations	18.58	22.34
Decrease (or increase) in noncash current assets	(33.12)	1.05
Increase (or decrease) in nondebt current liabilities	15.07	(12.61)
Operating cash flow	0.52	10.78
Capital expenditures	(11.06)	(9.74)
Free operating cash flow	(10.53)	1.04
Cash dividends	(4.45)	(5.14)
Discretionary cash flow	(14.98)	(4.09)
Acquisitions	(21.00)	0
Asset disposals	0.73	0.23
Net other sources (uses) of cash	(0.44)	(0.09)
Prefinancing cash flow	(35.70)	(3.95)
Increase (or decrease) in short-term debt	23.00	0
Increase (or decrease) in long-term debt	6.12	13.02
Net sale (repurchase) of equity	0.32	(7.07)
Decrease (or increase) in cash and securities	6.25	(2.00)
	35.70	3.95

Note: Dollars in millions.

- (Free operating cash flow + interest)/(interest + annual principal repayment obligation) = debt service coverage
- Funds from operation/capital spending requirements
- Capital expenditures/capital maintenance

Interpretation of the ratios is not simple; higher values often can be indicative of problems rather than strength. A company serving a low-growth or declining market may exhibit relatively strong cash flow owing to minimal fixed and working capital needs. Growth companies, in comparison, often exhibit thin or even negative cash flow because investment is needed to support growth. For the low-growth company, credit analysis weighs the positives of strong current cash flow against the danger that this high level of protection might not be sustainable. For the high-growth company, the problem is just the opposite: weighing the negatives of a current cash deficit against prospects of enhanced protection once the current investment begins yielding cash benefits. There is no simple correlation between creditworthiness and the level of current cash flow.

Where long-term viability is more assured—i.e., higher in the rating spectrum—there can be greater emphasis on the level of funds from operations and its relation to the total debt burden. These measures clearly differentiate between levels of protection over time. Focusing on debt service coverage and free cash flow becomes more critical in the analysis of a weaker company. Speculative-grade issuers typically face near-term vulnerabilities, which are better measured by such a focus.

[b] Need for Capital. The analysis of cash flow in relation to capital requirements begins with an examination of a company's capital needs, including both working and fixed capital. While this analysis is performed for all debt issuers, it is critically important for fixed capital–intensive firms and growth companies. Companies seeking working capital generally are able to finance a significant portion of their current assets through trade credit. However, rapidly growing companies, such as small and medium-sized computer manufacturers, must place greater reliance on nontrade credit. Despite strong profitability, the dynamic growth of these companies typically involves a buildup in receivables and inventories that cannot be financed internally or through trade credit.

The key to determining the working capital requirements of a company is first to establish a projected growth rate and a turnover rate for inventory and receivables. In the last few years, improved working capital management techniques have greatly reduced the investment that might otherwise have been required. This makes it difficult to base expectations on recent trends. In any event, improved turnover experience would not be a reason to project continuation of such a trend to yet better levels.

Because companies are analyzed as ongoing enterprises, the analysis assumes that the firms will provide funds continually to maintain capital investments as modern, efficient assets. Cash flow adequacy is viewed from the standpoint of a company's ability to finance capital maintenance requirements internally, as well as its ability to finance capital additions. It is not easy to quantify the requirements for capital maintenance unless data are provided by the company.

An important dimension of cash flow adequacy is the extent to which a company has the flexibility to alter the timing of its capital requirements. Expansions are typically discretionary. However, large plants with long lead times usually involve, somewhere along the way, a commitment to completion of the project.

For many firms, capital spending needs must also include funds for acquisitions. There are companies that have cash flow adequate to the needs of the existing business but that are known to be acquisition-minded. Their choice of acquisition as an avenue for growth means that this activity must also involve a need for capital.

Management's stated acquisition goals and past takeover bids, including those that were not consummated, provide a basis for judging the prospects for future acquisition.

[10] Financial Flexibility

The previous assessment of financial factors (profitability, asset protection, and cash flow) are combined to arrive at an overall view of financial health. In addition, sundry considerations that do not fit in other categories are examined, including serious legal problems, lack of insurance coverage, or restrictive covenants that place the firm at the mercy of its bankers.

Then, the analyst evaluates the company's options under stress. In this vein, the potential impact of various alternatives to expectations is considered, along with the firm's contingency plans. Access to various capital markets, affiliations with other entities, and ability to sell assets are important factors.

Flexibility can be jeopardized when a firm accumulates bank borrowings and CP with the hope of funding out when market conditions improve. Reliance on short-term money or floating interest rate funds creates obvious risks. An unusually short maturity schedule for long-term debt and limited-life preferred stock is also a negative. There is no problem if maturing obligations can be financed with internally generated funds, but a growing business typically refunds maturing debt and preferred stock with new debt.

A firm's access to various capital markets can become an important factor in financial flexibility. A company's experience with different financial instruments and capital markets gives management alternatives if conditions in a particular financial market suddenly sour. The size of a company and its financing needs can play a role in whether it can raise funds in the public debt markets. Similarly, a firm's role in the national economy—this is particularly true outside the United States—can enhance its access to bank and public funds.

Access to the common stock market is primarily a question of management's willingness to accept dilution of earnings per share, rather than a question of whether funds are available. When a new common stock offering is projected as part of a company's financing plan, S&P tries to measure management's commitment to this financing vehicle, even at what would be less attractive prices.

Potential asset disposals add flexibility if they can be accomplished under terms acceptable to the company. However, as going concerns, companies should not be expected to repay debt by liquidating operations. Clearly, there is little benefit in selling natural resource properties or manufacturing facilities if these must be replaced in a few years. Nonetheless, a company's ability to generate cash through asset disposals enhances its financial flexibility.

Pension obligations and environmental liabilities can hinder a company's ability to sell assets, because potential buyers may be reluctant to assume the liability. Off-balance sheet items also have played a pivotal role in discouraging some managements from closing excess or inefficient manufacturing facilities. Such a closing might require the immediate recognition of future pension obligations and result in a substantial charge to equity, thus impairing the firm's financial flexibility.

When there is a major lawsuit against the firm, the analyst may use a range of estimated costs to reflect the uncertainty inherent in all litigation. Moreover, there are often intangible costs that are reflected qualitatively in an assessment of a firm's prospects. Disputes with suppliers or customers can have a long-term effect on a company's competitive position. A well-publicized product failure may cost a company far more in lost sales than the payment to any injured individual would cost. A potential liability so large that it seems to threaten a firm's solvency, such as that faced by Texaco in its dispute with Pennzoil, will often the limit the company's access to capital, at least temporarily.

1.03 INTERNATIONAL CORPORATIONS

Assessment of corporate credit quality on an international basis follows the same methodology as that employed in analysis of U.S. corporations: Industry risk and a company's competitive position are evaluated in conjunction with the firm's financial profile and policies. This fundamental analysis is performed with an eye toward the financial characteristics of the relevant industry as well as those of a specific country or region. For consistency, a global rating scale imposes a common discipline on all cross-border analysis, yet S&P recognizes the importance of assessing an issuer in its local context as well as on a global basis.

[1] Business Risk

Business risk analysis entails the assessment of an issuer's economic, operational, and competitive environment. The analysis of corporations of differing nationalities calls for an appreciation of this environment for an issuer's specific geographical and industrial mix. Demand and supply factors, both domestic and worldwide, are assessed. Industries where competition takes place on a local basis, such as retailing, are viewed differently from those that are exposed to international market forces, such as semiconductors or energy. Other industries, such as automobiles, face a combination of global and regional market considerations. Perceptions of industry risk vary from region to region.

In reviewing companies in export-oriented countries, emphasis is placed on a firm's ability to withstand local currency appreciation and the country's sentiments towards trade protectionism. Japanese manufacturers, for example, were challenged in the mid-1980s by the strong appreciation of the yen relative to the dollar. Labor conditions can also differ internationally. Where labor costs are high, an industrial company's cost structure can impair its international competitive position. Differing social attitudes toward labor make head count reductions or other forms of industrial rationalization more difficult in certain countries.

The role of regulation and legislation, actual and potential, must also be considered. In Europe, a growing number of industries are experiencing challenges to traditional arrangements stemming from new directives from the European Community (EC).

[2] Financial Risk

As with U.S. corporate ratings, key aspects of financial risk include earnings protection, cash flow adequacy, asset quality, use of debt leverage, and financial flexibility. The challenge is to compare and interpret on a single, global scale financial measures that are derived from differing accounting practices. The analyst can begin by assessing company performance based on its own accounting framework. Adjustments to the accounting data are then made to enable comparisons. A rating agency does not translate the entire financial statements to a basis of generally accepted accounting principles. Rather, analysts seek out only differences that have a material impact on the way a company operating under one reporting system compares with an international peer group.

Endeavoring to adjust measurements of international companies to common denominators, the analysis focuses on "real" stocks and flows, i.e., levels of debt, cash, and cash flow, and places less emphasis on abstract measures, such as shareholders' equity and reported earnings. Although earnings and net worth have important economic meaning if measured consistently and responsibly, this meaning is often blurred in a cross-border context. In addition, profitability norms differ on an international basis. A company generating relatively low returns on permanent capital in a country with low interest rates may be viewed more favorably than a similar company reporting higher returns in a higher interest rate environment.

Financial parameters that are increasingly viewed as relevant and reliable include coverage of fixed financial charges by cash flow and operating cash flow relative to total debt. The traditional measure of debt to capital is no longer weighted as heavily. In any event, ratios of corporations outside of the United States are not directly comparable with median statistics published for U.S. industrials.

[3] International Financial Considerations

[a] **Balance Sheet Distortion.** Treatment of goodwill offers a good example of balance sheet distortion. U.K. companies, among others, tend to write off goodwill at the outset of an acquisition, whereas companies in other parts of the world do not. The result is that U.K. companies tend to have capital structures that look weaker and earnings that look better than those of competitors from countries that capitalize goodwill and amortize it over time. To adjust, S&P adds back goodwill to shareholders' funds and makes a qualitative or quantitative adjustment for goodwill amortization in analyzing a U.K. company.

Asset valuation practices also differ from country to country, resulting in differences in both a company's reported equity base and its depreciation expense. There is no easy way to compare companies that revalue their assets with those that do not. Rather, S&P recognizes that for all companies, reported asset values often differ from market values. In discussions with management, S&P analysts endeavor to gain an appreciation of the realizable values of a company's assets under reasonably conservative assumptions.

[b] **Net Debt.** In many countries, notably Japan and Europe, local practice is to maintain a high level of debt while holding a large portfolio of cash and marketable securities. Many companies manage their finances on a net debt basis. In these situations, S&P focuses on net interest coverage and the ratios of cash flow to net debt and of net debt to capital. When a company consistently demonstrates such excess liquidity, interest income may be offset against interest expense in looking at overall financial expenses. Net debt leverage is similarly calculated by netting out excess liquidity from short-term borrowings. Each situation is analyzed on a case-by-case basis, subject to additional information regarding a company's liquidity position, normal working cash needs, nature of short-term borrowings, and funding philosophy. Funds earmarked for future use, such as an acquisition or a capital project, are not netted out.

In some countries it is not uncommon for industrial companies to establish their treasury operations as a profit center. In Japan, for example, the term "zaiteku financing" refers to the practice of generating profits through arbitrage and other financial market transactions. If financial position taking comprises a material part of a company's aggregate earnings, S&P segregates those earnings to assess the profitability of the core business. S&P also views with skepticism the ability to realize such profits on a sustained basis and may treat them like nonrecurring gains.

[c] **Earnings Differences.** Shareholder pressures and accounting standards in certain countries, such as the United States, can result in companies' seeking to maximize profits on a quarter-to-quarter or short-term basis. In other regions, it is normal practice to take provisions against earnings in good times to provide a cushion against

downturns, resulting in a long run "smoothing" of reported profits. Given local accounting standards, it is common to see a Swiss or German company vaguely report "other income" or "other expenses," which are largely provisions or provision reversals, as the largest line items in a profit and loss account. In meetings with management, S&P discusses provisioning and depreciation practices to see to what extent a company employs noncash charges to reduce or bolster earnings. Credit analysis focuses on operating performance and cash flow, not financial reports distorted by accounting techniques.

[d] **Contingent Liabilities.** Consideration of contingent liabilities also varies internationally. Off-balance sheet obligations can often be significant and subject to differing methods of calculation. For example, the practice of factoring receivables with recourse back to the company is common in Japan. While some accounting systems treat this practice as a form of debt financing, Japanese companies simply report it as a contingency.

Accounting for pension obligations also differs from country to country. Therefore, some companies report ongoing actuarial funding of established pension plans, while others report an aggregate liability of benefits accrued to employees. Most companies keep pension finances separate from consolidated accounts, whereas in some countries, notably Germany, pension assets and liabilities are included in the company's reported balance sheet. Calculation of comparative pension obligations can therefore be difficult, particularly when local accounting standards do not require detailed disclosure in a company's financial statements. Other forms of contingent liabilities, such as implicit financial support to nonconsolidated affiliated companies or projects, are also common and must be factored into the analysis.

[4] National and Regional Considerations

Generally, the country's sovereign credit rating acts as a ceiling, limiting the debt rating for a corporate issuer to the rating of its country of domicile. On the other hand, many international corporate issuers benefit from their status within the country or region of domicile. This is particularly true for corporates with significant state ownership. Other local factors that might enhance an issuer's financial flexibility include access to local banks and capital markets.

[a] **State Ownership.** Without a guarantee or other form of formal support arrangement, a state-owned corporate issuer does not intrinsically carry the same level of credit risk as its sovereign owner. Nevertheless, state ownership can bolster a company's credit profile through implicit support. Government support can take the form of facilitated access to external sources of finance or, in extreme cases, direct financial infusions.

The link between government and industry differs from country to country and, even within a country, from firm to firm. The analyst begins by considering the state's historical relationship with industry, including the degree to which governmental financial aid has been used to support state-owned firms in the past. In addition, it is important to anticipate potential changes in historical arrangements. For example, EC free trade policies have the potential to inhibit the ability of member states to freely grant economic support to industries operating in competitive sectors.

The analyst then considers the strategic importance of the firm to the country of domicile. Certain state-owned firms provide a vital service or technology, often in fields relating to defense, energy, telecommunications, or electronics. Such firms may be perceived as serving national interests more than firms engaged in more basic industries. Also, a firm's economic importance is considered in terms of employment, foreign exchange generation, and local investment. (Analysis of an issuer on a stand-alone basis allows the rating to reflect both the likelihood of the issuer's needing to seek external state support as well as the likelihood of the issuer's receiving such support.)

[b] Local Ownership Blocks. Concentration of ownership resulting in companies with cross shareholdings or common parents exists in several countries. Japan, for example, has numerous industrial groupings that combine companies across several industrial sectors. In other countries, including Canada, Sweden, and Italy, large networks of family holdings are also found.

There are both positive and negative implications of group affiliation. In many cases, a company may benefit from operating relationships or greater access to financing. Conversely, a company's group affiliation could bring responsibility for providing support to weaker group companies. The analyst assesses whether constraints, such as a minority interest position, justify rating an issuer on a stand-alone basis. If not, the analysis attempts to incorporate the economic and financial trends in the issuer's affiliate group as well.

[c] Access to Local Sources of Finance. An issuer's standing within its home financial community also must be considered. Large issuers in a relatively small country are often in a favorable position to attract financing from that country's banking system. Access to ready bank financing may be enhanced by cross shareholdings between a bank and an industrial firm. At the same time, certain issuers benefit from recognition and status within local capital markets. While access to public debt and equity cannot be assumed, particularly in times of financial stress, prominence within local markets broadens a firm's financial options. One way to determine how well a company might compete for capital is comparing its performance with that of local peers in terms of local accounting and financial norms.

1.04 PARENT-SUBSIDIARY RATING LINKS

[1] General Principles

Affiliation between a stronger and a weaker entity will almost always affect the credit quality of both, unless the relative size of one entity is insignificant. The question is how close together the two ratings can be pulled on the basis of affiliation.

In general, economic incentive is the most important factor on which to base judgments about the degree of linkage that exists between a parent and subsidiary. This matters more than covenants, support agreements, assertions by management, or legal opinions. Business managers have a primary obligation to serve the interest of their shareholders, and it should generally be assumed that they will act to satisfy this responsibility. If this means infusing cash into a subsidiary that they have previously announced stands alone or finding a way around covenants to get cash out of a protected subsidiary, management can be expected to follow these courses of action. It is important to think ahead to various stress scenarios and consider how management is likely to act under those circumstances. If a parent supports a subsidiary only as long as the subsidiary does not need it, such support is meaningless.

A weak subsidiary owned by a strong parent will usually, although not always, enjoy a stronger rating than it would on a stand-alone basis. The range of possibilities spans ratings equalization at one extreme to very little or no help from the parent's credit quality at the other. When the stand-alone rating of the subsidiary is close to that of the parent, the affiliation between the two more easily closes the gap. For the subsidiary's rating to be raised by two or more rating categories (e.g., from BB to A), much caution should be employed and the relationship between the two entities should be examined very carefully. The greater the degree of integration, the less the ability of the parent ever to consider distancing itself from the subsidiary's debt and the greater the reason for equalizing their ratings. (The parent's rating is, of course, assigned when the parent guarantees or assumes subsidiary debt. While guarantees and assumption of debt are different legal mechanisms, they are equivalent from a rating perspective. Cross-default and cross-acceleration provisions in bond indentures can also be important rating considerations. They can provide a powerful incentive for a stronger entity to support debt of a weaker affiliate, since they trigger default of the stronger unit in the event of a default by the weaker affiliate. It should be kept in mind, however, that cross-default provisions can disappear if the debt whose indentures contain them is retired or renegotiated.)

A strong subsidiary owned by a weak parent should be rated no higher than the parent. The key reasons for this are (1) the ability of and incentive for a weak parent to take assets from the subsidiary or burden it with liabilities during financial stress and (2) the likelihood that a parent bankruptcy would cause the subsidiary's bankruptcy, regardless of its stand-alone strength. In most cases, a "strong" subsidiary is no further from bankruptcy than its parent and thus cannot have a higher rating. Actual experience over most of the last decade has shown that bankrupt industrial firms file with their subsidiaries more often than not.

Consolidation in bankruptcy, sometimes referred to as substantive consolidation, occurs when assets of a parent and its subsidiaries are thrown together by the bankruptcy court into a single pool and their value is allocated to all creditors without regard to any distinction between the two legal entities. In such cases, creditors of a subsidiary may lose all claim to any value associated with that particular subsidiary. Much more often, a parent and its subsidiaries will all file, but each legal entity will be kept separate in the bankruptcy proceeding. Creditors keep their claim to the assets of the specific legal entity to which they extended credit.

It is important to recognize that for rating purposes, the risk of substantive consolidation is only a secondary issue. Since ratings primarily address default risk, the key issue is not consolidation but rather whether a bankruptcy filing will occur. Therefore, nonconsolidation legal opinions are of little use, since they address only the likelihood of substantive consolidation, not the likelihood of simultaneous bankruptcies for parent and subsidiary, the primary issue for rating purposes. The usefulness of a nonconsolidation opinion is limited to the fact that willingness to obtain such an opinion might serve as some evidence of management intent regarding a subsidiary's independence.

Protective covenants apparently protect a subsidiary from its parent by restricting dividends or asset transfers. In general, this type of covenant is given only limited weight in a rating determination. Reasons for the limited value of protective covenants include the following: (1) They do not affect the parent's ability to file the subsidiary into bankruptcy; (2) it is very difficult to structure provisions that cannot be evaded; and (3) ultimately, courts usually cannot force a company to obey the covenant. During severe financial stress, especially prior to a bankruptcy, a weak parent may have a powerful incentive to strip a stronger subsidiary. The court can, at best, only award monetary damages to a creditor that has incurred a loss (when the issue defaults) and chooses to sue.

[2] Regulated Companies

In contrast, regulated subsidiaries are generally subject to restrictions on cash or asset transfers that are more likely to be enforced (by regulatory authorities, not the courts) than covenant restrictions protecting unregulated subsidiaries. Moreover, operating banks and insurance companies are not subject to the U.S. Bankruptcy Code (Code), eliminating the risk that a bank or insurance company might be drawn into the bankruptcy of its parent. Because of these two factors, normal restrictions on rating a subsidiary higher than a parent do not necessarily apply to a regulated subsidiary. Where restrictions are sufficiently strong, the regulated subsidiary is indeed rated higher than the parent if its stand-alone strength warrants. However, corporate affiliation is never totally ignored, even where regulated subsidiaries are involved, because of the risk that the regulatory veil might not be absolute under all circumstances.

Regulated utilities are typically strong on a stand-alone basis but are often owned by firms that finance their holdings in the utility with debt at the parent company (known as double leveraging) or that own other, weaker business units. Both the credit quality of the utility on a stand-alone basis and the credit quality of the consolidated group are analyzed. The utility can routinely be rated up to a full rating category higher than the group's rating level, relying on the regulators to insulate it if the group is adjudged to be at least investment grade. To achieve a greater rating differential or to rate the utility investment-grade when the group it is part of is not investment-grade requires strong evidence, based on the specific regulatory circumstances, that the regulators will act to protect the utility's credit profile.

The analyst makes this determination case by case, since regulatory jurisdictions vary. Implications of regulation are different for companies in Wisconsin from those in Florida or those subject to the scrutiny of the Securities and Exchange Commission under the Public Utilities Act of 1935. Also, regulators might react differently depending on whether funds that would be withdrawn from the utility were destined to support an out-of-state affiliate, the parent company that needed to service its own debt, or another in-state entity, such as a cellular telephone unit. Finally, regulators may be relied on to a greater extent to support BBB or A credit quality; in most cases, there is little basis to think that regulators would insist that a utility maintain an AAA or AA profile. Their mandate is to protect provision of services, which is not directly a function of the provider's financial health. In fact, the overall cost of capital, and therefore the cost of service, can be higher when utilities have little debt in their capital structures.

There is a corollary that negatively affects the parent and weaker units when a utility is rated on its stand-alone strength. If the regulated utility is viewed as insulated from the other units in its group, it is because its cash flow is less available to support them. To the extent, then, that the utility is rated higher than the consolidated credit quality, the parent and weaker units are correspondingly rated lower than the consolidated rating level.

[3] Foreign Ownership

Parent-subsidiary considerations are somewhat different when a company is owned by a foreign parent. The foreign parent is not subject to the Code, so a bankruptcy of the parent would not in and of itself prompt a bankruptcy of the subsidiary. In most jurisdictions, insolvency is treated very differently than in the United States, and various legal and regulatory constraints and incentives need to be considered. However, in all circumstances, it is important to evaluate the parent's credit quality even if no separate parent rating exists. The foreign parent's creditworthiness is a crucial factor in the subsidiary's rating to the extent that the parent might be willing and able to either infuse the subsidiary with cash or draw cash from it.

Even when subsidiaries are rated higher than foreign parents, the gap usually should not exceed one full rating category. To permit a larger gap, it must be demonstrated clearly that even under a stress scenario the parent's interest would be best served by keeping the subsidiary financially strong rather than using it as a source of cash.

In the opposite case, even larger gaps exist between ratings of weak subsidiaries and strong foreign parents than if both were domestic entities. Sovereign boundaries tend to impede integration, making it easier for the foreign parent to distance itself in the event of problems at the subsidiary.

[4] Partial Ownership

The relationship between the ratings of a parent and a subsidiary obviously is strongest where 100 percent ownership exists. If the parent owns less than 100 percent, the ties linking the two ratings are weaker. For example, if a company owns 5 percent of the stock of a company in an unrelated business, the ownership position will generally represent a purely passive investment and ratings on the two companies would be entirely independent. On the other hand, 50 percent ownership of a company in a related business probably suggests substantial integration between the two companies and would lead to a relatively close relationship between the ratings. There is no demarcation line between a purely passive investment and an active parent-subsidiary relationship. In the case of a joint venture, the incentive and ability of the other owner or owners to support or exploit the subsidiary is also considered.

In any event, shared ownership usually implies greater independence for a subsidiary than if it were wholly owned. The subsidiary is less likely to be pulled into a bankruptcy of a parent, and there are obstacles (not necessarily insurmountable) to a parent's attempting to drain cash or assets from the subsidiary. Conversely, shared ownership also creates a disincentive for a parent to unilaterally infuse cash into a faltering subsidiary, since it would be spending money to protect the investment of outsiders in addition to its own. For these reasons, shared ownership can, in some circumstances, allow a subsidiary to be rated slightly higher than a parent. It can also lead to greater distancing, on the downside, of the rating of a weak subsidiary from that of its parent.

[5] "Smoke and Mirrors" Subsidiaries

Sometimes multibusiness enterprises controlled by a single investor or family have the following characteristics:

- Unusually complex organizational structures
- Opportunistic buying and selling of operations, with little or no strategic justification
- Cash or assets moved between units to achieve some advantage for the controlling party
- Aggressive use of financial leverage

By their nature, these types of companies tend to be highly speculative credits.

As a general rule, the approach to rating a unit of such an organization begins with some assessment of the consolidated group. Often, some of the affiliated units will be private companies; nonetheless, at least some rough assessment must be developed. In general, no unit in the group is rated higher than the consolidated group would be rated, if such a rating were assigned. Neither indenture covenants nor nonconsolidation opinions can be relied on to support a higher rating for a particular subsidiary. It is certainly inadvisable to base credit judgments firmly on the profile of any specific unit at any particular point in time.

At the same time, there is no reason for all entities in a "smoke and mirrors" family to receive the identical rating. Any individual unit can be notched down as far as needed from the consolidated rating to reflect stand-alone weakness. This reflects the probability that a weak unit will be allowed to fail if the controlling party determines that no value can be salvaged from it. Complex structures are developed in order to maximize such flexibility for the controlling party.

1.05 RATIO GUIDELINES (U.S. INDUSTRIALS)

Risk-adjusted ratio guidelines depict the role that financial ratios play in S&P's rating process, since financial ratios are viewed in the context of a firm's business risk profile. This principle has long been integral to S&P's rating methodology.

For a given rating category, expected levels of financial ratios vary with the business or operating risk of a company. A company with a stronger competitive position, more favorable business prospects, and more predictable cash flows can afford to undertake added financial risk while maintaining the same credit rating.

The guidelines for U.S. industrials displayed in Figures 1-5 and 1-6 make more explicit the linkage between financial ratios and levels of business risk as S&P perceives it. For example, for a company with an average business risk profile, cash flow coverage of 60 percent would be indicative of an A rating. If a company is below average, it would need about 85 percent cash flow coverage to qualify for the same rating. Similarly, for the A category, a firm that has a low business risk could tolerate approximately 40 percent leverage and an average firm could tolerate only 30 percent. The matrices also show that a company with only an average business position could not aspire to an AAA rating, even if its financial ratios were extremely conservative.

Data used to develop these guidelines reflect the existing rating universe, and the matrices can be used as a guide to the typical standards for the various investment-

FIGURE 1-5

Cash Flow From Operations/Total Debt Guidelines

Company Business Risk Profile	Rating Category				
	AAA	AA	A	BBB	BB
Excellent	80%	60%	40%	25%	10%
Above average	150	80	50	30	15
Average		105	60	35	20
Below average			85	40	25
Vulnerable				65	45

FIGURE 1-6

Total Debt/Capitalization Guidelines

Company Business Risk Profile	Rating Category				
	AAA	AA	A	BBB	BB
Excellent	30%	40%	50%	60%	70%
Above average	20	25	40	50	60
Average		15	30	40	55
Below average			25	35	45
Vulnerable				25	35

grade rating categories. By contrast, the ratio medians are merely statistical composites. They are not rating bench marks, precisely because they gloss over the critical link between a company's financial risk and its business, or competitive risk. Moreover, the medians are based on historical performance, while guidelines refer to expected future performance.

[1] Using the Guidelines

Application of ratio guidelines requires a great deal of discretion. While they provide insight into ratings in general, it would be a mistake to oversimplify the entire thought process behind a specific rating by relying solely on these numbers. Certainly, there are additional dimensions to consider in evaluating a firm's financial condition. For example, the nature of the asset mix is important. To the extent that assets are especially liquid—in the form of receivables, brand name inventories, or salable real estate—a higher percentage of debt financing can be supported. Other elements of financial flexibility cannot be captured quantitatively, including corporate affiliations and banking relationships. The access to funds enjoyed by a large capitalization firm can also be a factor. To make practical use of the information, bear in mind the following:

- The business risk assessment is a qualitative evaluation. Evaluation of a company's industry environment and competitive position is, by its nature, subjective. It is also relative to the entire universe of industrial firms.

- The ratios standards relate to projected financial condition, as credit ratings are assessments of a company's ability to meet its future obligations. The analyst's confidence regarding a company's ability to achieve its plans has a direct bearing on the expected level of ratios. Furthermore, the level of risk over time, rather than at any specific point in time is important. Certainly, S&P looks at performance over the anticipated course of a full business cycle and not what is viewed as a peak or trough year.

- The ratios standards do not conform to an "as reported" basis. Rather, a firm's financial figures are subject to adjustment for off-balance-sheet liabilities and distortions in asset values. For example, S&P attempts to normalize financial measures in situations where purchase accounting records current, sometimes bloated, valuation of recently acquired assets. In other cases, for companies in a tax arbitrage posture, S&P adjusts by netting out excess cash and a corresponding amount of debt.

- The guidelines are not meant to be precise. Rather, they are intended to convey the ranges which characterize the levels of credit quality as represented by the different rating categories.

- Guidelines focus on only two ratios: total debt to capitalization (leverage) and cash flow from operations to total debt (cash flow protection). These are the key measures of financial risk for differentiating among obligors of investment-grade quality. Return on capital, an especially important measure, and interest coverage, which is of somewhat lesser significance, are indicators primarily of the company's performance and business risk as opposed to its financial risk. S&P uses many other measures to round out its analysis or focus on specific issues on a case-by-case basis. Strengths evidenced in one financial measure can offset, or balance, relative weakness in another.

[2] Speculative-Grade Issuers

Analysis of more volatile speculative-grade credits does not revolve around traditional financial measures and defies the relatively patterned methodology associated with investment-grade credits. Instead, a more dynamic analysis of cash flow is used, with the emphasis on free cash flow, coverage of full debt service, and a shorter time horizon. The importance of nonquantifiable elements, such as banking relationships, debt covenants, and management opportunism, also argues for exclusion from ratio guidelines. Numbers shown in the BB column serve primarily to delineate the BBB range by way of contrast and do not necessarily represent the typical BB profile.

[3] Industrial Ratio Medians

The ratios presented in Figure 1-7 are historical medians for U.S. industrial companies by rating category. Formulas for calculating the ratios and key terms in credit analysis appear in Figure 1-8. These key ratios are used by S&P in analyzing credit strength. In addition, several other ratios and analytical techniques, including those unique to certain industries or firms, are used in the rating process.

Ratios broadly define a company's position relative to rating categories. They are not intended to be hurdles or prerequisites that should be achieved to attain a specific debt rating. Moreover, caution should be exercised when the ratio medians are used for comparisons with specific company or industry data because of major differences in the method of ratio computation, importance of industry or business risk, and impact

FIGURE 1-7

Key Industrial Financial Ratios

	Industrial Long-Term Debt: Three-Year Medians (1989–1991)						
	AAA	AA	A	BBB	BB	B	CCC
Pretax interest coverage	12.12×	8.71×	4.40×	2.70×	1.43×	0.70×	0.46×
Pretax interest coverage including rents	5.86×	4.82×	3.05×	2.00×	1.27×	0.82×	0.74×
EBITDA[a] interest coverage	14.83×	11.49×	6.39×	4.50×	2.45×	1.59×	1.17×
Funds from operations/ total debt	113.1%	73.1%	42.5%	29.7%	16.7%	8.4%	4.3%
Free operating cash flow/total debt	35.2%	23.3%	11.1%	3.2%	(0.1)%	(2.2)%	(2.2)%
Pretax return on permanent capital	28.4%	20.4%	15.4%	11.3%	9.9%	6.8%	4.8%
Operating income/sales	21.0%	16.5%	14.5%	11.9%	10.4%	9.3%	9.8%
Long-term debt/capital	10.8%	16.8%	30.0%	39.7%	48.7%	57.1%	73.6%
Total debt/capitalization including short-term debt	26.2%	28.8%	36.9%	46.7%	56.8%	65.4%	77.8%
Total debt/capitalization including short-term debt (including 8 times rents)	37.6%	39.7%	49.6%	59.6%	68.5%	78.5%	81.8%

	Industrial Long-Term Debt: Three-Year Medians (1988–1990)						
	AAA	AA	A	BBB	BB	B	CCC
Pretax interest coverage	11.08×	9.43×	4.65×	3.16×	1.91×	0.88×	0.63×
Pretax interest coverage including rents	5.46×	5.10×	3.00×	2.18×	1.54×	0.94×	0.69×
EBITDA[a] interest coverage	13.65×	11.65×	6.65×	4.97×	3.00×	1.59×	1.22×
Funds from operations/ total debt	82.9%	74.2%	45.6%	31.7%	18.7%	8.4%	7.0%
Free operating cash/flow total debt	24.8%	23.4%	8.7%	3.4%	(0.5)%	(3.4)%	(4.2)%
Pretax return on permanent capital	26.2%	21.1%	16.7%	13.0%	11.1%	7.4%	8.1%
Operating income/sales	21.6%	15.9%	14.9%	12.0%	12.5%	9.3%	12.3%
Long-term debt/capital	12.9%	16.6%	29.5%	39.4%	45.7%	63.5%	79.3%
Total debt/capitalization including short-term debt	25.1%	27.6%	37.3%	48.0%	54.8%	73.7%	85.5%
Total debt/capitalization including short-term debt (including 8 times rents)	38.2%	38.7%	50.9%	58.6%	65.5%	78.5%	87.2%

[a] Earnings before interest, taxes, depreciation, and amortization.

FIGURE 1-8

Key Terms and Ratio Formulas for Analyzing Credit Strength

Source: Standard & Poor's Creditstats (June 1993)

Pretax income from continuing operations. Net income from continuing operations before (1) special items; (2) minority interest; and (3) gains on reacquisition of debt, plus income taxes.

Eight times rents. Gross rents paid multiplied by capitalization factor of eight.

Equity. Shareholders' equity (including preferred stock) plus minority interest.

Free operating cash flow. Funds from operations minus capital expenditures and minus (plus) the increase (decrease) in working capital (excluding changes in cash, marketable securities, and short-term debt).

Funds from operations (or funds flow). Net income from continuing operations plus depreciation, amortization, deferred income taxes, and other noncash items.

Gross interest. Gross interest incurred before subtracting capitalized interest and interest income.

Gross rents. Gross operating rents paid before sublease income.

Interest expense. Interest incurred minus capitalized interest.

Long-term debt. As reported, including capitalized lease obligations on the balance sheet.

Operating income. Sales minus cost of goods manufactured (before depreciation and amortization), selling costs, general and administrative costs, and research and development costs.

Total debt. Long-term debt plus current maturities, CP and other short-term borrowings.

Formulas for Key Ratios

$$\text{Pretax interest coverage} = \frac{\text{pretax income from continuing operations} + \text{interest expense}}{\text{gross interest}}$$

$$\text{Pretax interest coverage including rents} = \frac{\text{pretax income from continuing operations} + \text{interest expense} + \text{gross rents}}{\text{gross interest} + \text{gross rents}}$$

$$\text{EBITDA}^a \text{ interest coverage} = \frac{\text{pretax income from continuing operations} + \text{interest expense} + \text{depreciation and amortization}}{\text{gross interest}}$$

$$\text{Funds from operations/total debt} = \frac{\text{funds from operations}}{\text{total debt}} \times 100$$

$$\text{Free operating cash flow/total debt} = \frac{\text{free operating cash flow}}{\text{total debt}} \times 100$$

$$\text{Pretax return on permanent capital} = \frac{\text{pretax income from continuing operations} + \text{interest expense}}{\begin{array}{c}\text{sum of (1) the average of the beginning-of-}\\\text{year and end-of-year current maturities,}\\\text{long-term debt, noncurrent deferred taxes,}\\\text{minority interest, and shareholders' equity}\\\text{and (2) average short-term borrowings}\\\text{during year per footnotes to financial}\\\text{statements}\end{array}} \times 100$$

$$\text{Operating income/sales} = \frac{\text{operating income}}{\text{sales}} \times 100$$

$$\text{Long-term debt/capitalization} = \frac{\text{long-term debt}}{\text{long-term debt} + \text{equity}} \times 100$$

^{a} Earnings before interest, taxes, depreciation, and amortization.

FIGURE 1-8 *(continued)*

$$\text{Total debt-capitalization + short-term debt} = \frac{\text{total debt}}{\text{total debt + equity}} \times 100$$

$$\text{Total debt + 8 times rents capitalization +} \atop \text{short-term debt + 8 times rents} = \frac{\text{total debt + 8 times gross rentals paid}}{\text{total debt + equity + 8 times gross rentals paid}} \times 100$$

of mergers and acquisitions. Ratings are designed to be valid over the entire business cycle, and ratios of a particular firm at any point in the cycle may not appear to be in line with its assigned debt ratings. Particular caution should be used when cross-border comparisons are made, owing to differences in accounting principles, financial practices, and business environments.

Because of technical limitations, the medians do not reflect the many analytical adjustments that are commonly made in the calculation of ratios used in the rating process. While several of the median ratios are adjusted for a few special items, they do not incorporate many key changes generally made to reported figures to exclude the impact of nonrecurring items, including write-downs and special charges, gains or losses on asset sales, litigation gains or losses, LIFO gains, and off-balance sheet liabilities. As a proxy for the operating lease adjustment, medians are included for coverage of interest plus rents and for the ratio of total debt plus eight times rents to capital.

The medians themselves are affected by economic and environmental factors as well as mergers and acquisitions. The universe of rated companies is constantly changing, and in certain rating categories, adding or deleting a few companies can materially change the financial ratio medians.

1.06 COMMERCIAL PAPER

CP consists of unsecured promissory notes issued to raise short-term funds. Typically, only companies of unquestionable credit standing are able to sell their paper in the money market, although there was some growth in the issuance of lower-quality, unrated paper prior to the junk bond market's collapse in 1989. (Issuance of CP backed by letters of credit (LOCs) from first-tier banks has become quite popular. The credit quality of such paper rests entirely on the transaction's legal structure and the credit-worthiness of the bank. As long as the LOC is correctly structured, the credit quality of the direct obligor can be ignored. The legal issues regarding LOC backing are not covered in this chapter.)

[1] Rating Criteria

The evaluation of an issuer's CP reflects S&P's opinion of the issuer's fundamental credit quality. The analytical approach is virtually identical to the one followed in assigning a bond rating, and there is a strong link between the short-term and long-

FIGURE 1-9

Correlation of CP Ratings With Bond Ratings

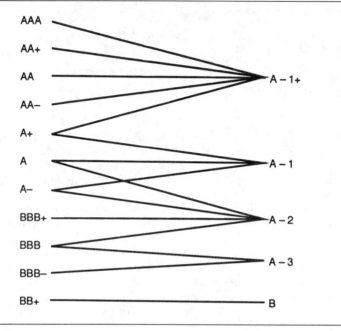

term rating systems. The correlation of CP ratings with bond ratings is shown in Figure 1-9.

In effect, the minimum credit quality associated with the A − 1 + CP rating is the equivalent of an A + bond rating. Similarly, for CP to be rated A − 1, the bond rating would need to be at least A − . (In fact, the A − /A − 1 combination is rare, and so is a combination of AA − and A − 1. Typically, A − 1 CP ratings are associated with A + and A bond ratings.) Conversely, knowing the bond rating will not in itself determine a CP rating, considering the overlap in ratings categories. However, the range of possibilities is always narrow. To the extent that one of two CP ratings might be assigned at a given level of long-term credit quality (e.g., the A level), several criteria are used to make that determination.

The overall strength of the credit within the rating category is the first consideration. For example, a marginal A credit would likely have its CP rated A − 2; a solid A would almost automatically receive an A − 1 rating.

Next come liquidity considerations, which receive greater emphasis in CP ratings than in bond ratings. The purpose and pattern of CP usage are rating elements. For example, if CP is used only to finance seasonal working capital requirements, that could contribute to a higher rating. The rating benefits because the assets liquidate in a predictable way and enable repayment of the CP.

Finally, the CP rating perspective sometimes focuses more intensely on the nearer term. The time horizon for a CP rating extends well beyond the typical 30-day life of a CP note, the 270-day maximum maturity for the most common type of CP, or even the one-year tenor used to distinguish between short-term and long-term ratings. Thus, CP ratings are likely to endure over time rather than change frequently. Nonetheless, occasionally the near-term financial condition is distinct from the long-term prospects. For example, there are companies with substantial liquidity, which provides protection in the near or intermediate term, but that also have less than stellar profitability, a long-term factor. Similarly, companies with relatively large cash holdings that may or may not be used to fund acquisitions in the future are in this category.

This distinction, in reverse, often applies after an issuer makes a major acquisition. The analyst's confidence that the firm can restore financial health over the long term is factored into its bond ratings, while the financial stress that dominates the near term may lead to a relatively low CP rating. The use of different time horizons as the basis for long-term and short-term ratings implies that either one rating or the other will change with time.

[2] Backup Policies

In the past, a key purpose of S&P's requiring bank line backup was to insure that an issuer would be able to meet its obligations in the event of a disruption to the financial markets that might inhibit the normal rollover of CP, even while the issuer's own financial condition remained strong. However, the growth of the CP market prompted a reevaluation. It is S&P's current judgment that the protection afforded by backup facilities could not be relied on with a high degree of confidence in the event of wide-spread disruption of the CP markets. A general disruption of CP markets would be a highly volatile scenario, under which most bank lines would represent unreliable claims on whatever cash would be made available through the banking system to support the market. S&P neither anticipates that such a scenario is likely to develop nor assumes that it never will. Bank line availability is emphasized as an important buttress to liquidity only in the context of normal market conditions. The change in the CP backup policy shifts the focus away from market disruption while confirming the utility of bank facilities in supporting operations of any entity that incurs short-term obligations in the normal course of business.

A substantial level of liquidity in the form of bank facilities or readily available liquid resources is prudent for virtually all issuers and will continue to be necessary to support an investment-grade rating on both CP and long-term debt. From time to time, there will be developments (e.g., bad business conditions, a lawsuit, management changes, or a rating change) that will affect a single company or group of companies and that may make CP investors nervous and unwilling to roll over the issuer's paper, even though the issuer remains creditworthy. Prearranged bank facilities are often essential in protecting against the risk of default under these circumstances.

Industrial and utility issuers typically provide 100 percent backup (excess liquid assets or bank facilities) for paper outstanding. However, companies with the highest credit quality can provide a lower percentage of coverage. A-1+ issuers need not prearrange 100 percent coverage, because they should be able to raise funds quickly even if some adversities develop. The exact amount is determined by the issuer's overall credit strength and its access to capital markets. Some AAA issuers may have as little as 50 percent backup.

Backup must be sufficient to provide the appropriate level of coverage for other maturing short-term debt, not just CP. Backup for 100 percent of rated CP is meaning-less if other debt maturities for which there is no backup coincide with those of CP.

Thus, the scope of backup must extend to Euro CP, master notes, syndicated bank notes, and other similar confidence-sensitive obligations. Banks offer various types of credit facilities that differ widely regarding the degree of the bank's commitment to advance cash under all circumstances. Ever weaker forms of commitment, which are less costly to issuers, have become increasingly common in recent years and provide banks with still greater flexibility to redirect credit at their own discretion.

At the very least, all backup lines should be in place and confirmed in writing. Preapproved or orally committed lines are viewed as insufficient. S&P is also particularly skeptical about reliance on money market lines or similar arrangements, which are little more than an invitation to do business at a future date. Payment for the lines, whether by fee or balances, generally creates some degree of moral commitment on the part of the bank. Whether a facility is specifically designated for CP backup is of little significance.

The weaker the credit, the greater the need for more reliable forms of liquidity. A – 1 + issuers have superior access to capital because of their strong credit profiles; one assumes that banks would not hesitate in honoring lines of credit to such borrowers. In contrast, S&P considers it prudent for A – 1 and A – 2, and certainly A – 3, CP issuers to have a substantial portion of their banking facilities contractually committed in the form of a revolving credit. These revolving credits should provide same-day availability of funds.

As a general guideline, an A – 1 should have sufficient revolving credit capacity to provide for the next 10 days' maturities of outstanding paper. In the case of A – 2 and A – 3 issuers, revolving credits should cover at least 15 days of maturing paper. (Usually, for A – 2 and A – 3 issuers, this translates into backup of 50 percent of total outstandings with revolving credits.) The rest of the backup should be with other committed facilities, such as compensated lines. Stronger backup may be required in some cases to provide additional protection against potential roll-over problems caused by declining market confidence in the issuer.

S&P recognizes that even revolving credit agreements, which usually represent the strongest commitment a bank can make, often include "material adverse change" clauses, allowing the bank to withdraw under certain circumstances. While inclusion of an escape clause weakens the commitment, S&P does not consider it critical or realistic for most borrowers to negotiate removal of "material adverse change" clauses. Even the strongest form of backup, a revolving credit without such a clause, does not enhance underlying credit and does not lead to a higher rating than indicated by the company's own creditworthiness. Credit enhancement can be accomplished only through an LOC or another instrument that unconditionally transfers the debt obligation to a higher-rated entity.

Banks providing issuers with facilities for backup liquidity should themselves be sound institutions with the capacity to lend funds as committed. A bank's credit rating can serve as a guide as to its soundness: Possession of an investment-grade rating should indicate sufficient financial strength for the purpose of providing a CP issuer with a reliable source of funding.

S&P criteria do not require that the bank's credit rating equal the issuer's rating, nor do they require that the bank's credit rating be AA, A, A – 1, or even A – 2 to be included in the lineup of banks supporting an issuer's liquidity. There is no reason to presume that any potential difficulties for the bank would coincide with the period during which the issuer would look to it for support. Moreover, higher credit quality of the bank does not translate into an inclination to add assets at a given point in time or to lend to a given borrower. Nonetheless, S&P would look askance at situations where most of a company's banks were only marginally investment-grade, since this would indicate an imprudent reliance on banks that might deteriorate to weak, non-investment-grade status.

Dependence on just one bank or very few banks is also viewed as an unwarranted risk. Apart from the possibility that the bank will not have adequate capacity to lend, there is the chance that it will not be willing to lend to the issuer. Having several banks diversifies the risk that any one bank will lose confidence in the borrower and hesitate to provide funds.

Concentration of banking facilities also tends to increase the dollar amount of an individual bank's participation. As the dollar amount of the exposure becomes very large, the bank may be more reluctant to step up to its commitment. In addition, the potential requirement of higher-level authorizations at the bank could create logistical problems with respect to expeditious access to funds for the issuer.

Diversification is desirable up to a point; a company must not spread its banking business so thin that it lacks a substantial relationship with any of its banks. In the end, a solid business relationship with a bank is the key to whether the bank will stand by its client. Standardized criteria cannot capture or assess the strength of such relationships. However, S&P is interested in any evidence, even subjective, that might demonstrate the strength of an issuer's banking relationships. For example, the nature of credit and noncredit services provided by the bank and the length of the business relationship often can provide some insight.

Chapter 2

Financial Forecasting and Planning

Donald E. Reed

2.01 INTRODUCTION

The chief financial goal of almost all corporations is to maximize shareholder value. To do this, companies must have a well-designed financial plan. In turn, the financial plan requires a financial forecast.

Developing a usable financial forecast has never been easy, but volatile financial markets and rapid changes in the real economy make good forecasting not only more difficult but even more important to do with as much accuracy as possible. The construction of spreadsheets, or financial forecasts, unfortunately cannot be done with great accuracy. Too much happens during the forecast period to allow the gap between actual and forecast to be persistently small. The possibility of error is, however, no reason not to do the exercise. Indeed, the wider the margin for error, the more important it is to have an idea, even if vague, of where the company is headed.

All successful companies have clearly defined goals that identify where management wants to have the firm at a certain number of periods in the future. An integral and indispensable part of defining goals is the development of fairly detailed financial forecasts, beginning at the smallest business unit within a company and then consolidating the forecasts. As part of forecasting, both internal and external financing requirements and opportunities are identified. Anticipation of financing needs is beneficial both in the area of time planning and in the identification of appropriate types and sources of funds. It is often too late, for example, to recognize near the end of a quarter that during the next quarter substantial operating capital is required. Market opportunities could be missed or capital costs could be excessive, and, as a result, the perceptions of the company in the financial marketplace as well as the value of the company to its shareholders could decline.

2.02 THE MODEL

Figure 2-1 uses a spreadsheet to present the basic forecasting process. With minor alteration, it can provide a profit and loss statement for financial accounting purposes and also derive a balance sheet on the same basis. The following sections describe the development of each line in the table and then show how the table is actually employed.

[1] Sales Forecasting

The best and often the only good way of developing a sales forecast is to have the people who actually sell the product prepare the sales outlook. Superficially, this seems fairly easy to accomplish. Most forecasts, however, tend to be straight lines with slopes that are exactly equal to the direction that sales took over the past two periods. That is, if 1993 sales were better than 1992 sales, most sales forecasts will show 1994 sales as better than 1993 sales. The reverse is true as well. If a respected economic or econometric forecast from either internal or external sources can be used as an overlay or template, the tendency to picture the immediate future may be modified.

The sales forecasting for a small, one-product company is identical to that for a very large multiproduct firm. The forecaster is charged with answering the following questions: Given that the nation's economy will grow at x rate for y years and that

FIGURE 2-1
Cash Flow Planning Sheet

	Year 1	Year 2	Year 3	Year 4	Year 5
Sales revenue					
Manufacturing cost	——	——	——	——	——
Gross margin					
Fixed costs					
Depreciation	——	——	——	——	——
Operating income					
Interest	——	——	——	——	——
Pretax income					
Tax	——	——	——	——	——
After-tax income					
Depreciation	——	——	——	——	——
Cash flow from operations					
Capital expenditures					
Dividends	——	——	——	——	——
Net cash flow	═══	═══	═══	═══	═══

consumer spending (or basic steel or machine tools, and so forth) will lead (or be concurrent with or lag) gross national product (GNP) growth, who will buy the company's product and how much will they buy? In addition, given the forecast rate of inflation and the assessment of competitive and technological forces, what price, net of customer discount, is expected to be received for each product from each customer? Will all sales be made in domestic markets, or will there be any export sales?

The sales force should be required to provide its forecast with as much detail as can be developed for two reasons. First, management may wish to amend the forecast (although this should be done with trepidation, since the sales force knows the customers best). Second, the detailed forecast forms the basis of postperiod audit. The audit can address such questions as: What happened to the sales to Company X? Were volume expectations met? Did price increases hold up? What can be done to correct a wayward situation? The requirement to develop a detailed sales forecast forces the creation of a formal marketing plan, especially if management will be looking at performance based on the salesperson's own forecast.

[2] Manufacturing Costs

There are two basic types of direct manufacturing costs: variable and fixed. Variable costs are those that are volume sensitive. For example, for every extra ton of steel, so much electricity is needed, so many hours of labor, so much ore. By breaking out the factors that compose variable costs, manufacturing costs can be forecasted.

Again, the manufacturing people should be required to provide sufficient detail in variable cost to let management assess the forecast both on a prospective and retrospective basis. Fixed manufacturing costs are partially volume sensitive but, as the title implies, will not go away unless production ceases. Part of the labor expense (e.g., supervising efforts) will remain constant at most levels of production. Other fixed manufacturing expenses include a portion of utilities (e.g., lighting, heat, and water), managers' salaries, and attendant office expenses. These costs are less sensitive to general economic conditions but cannot be blindly included in a forecast in disregard of the overall economic environment.

Gross margin or operating margin is simply sales minus manufacturing costs. For a multiproduct company, gross margin for a corporate forecast is the sum of each product line gross margin.

[3] Fixed Costs

Two groups of costs generally do not vary with volume: direct fixed costs and indirect overhead costs. Typically, the direct fixed costs include a portion of labor expense, insurance, rentals, building expense (excluding depreciation), a portion of utilities, local property taxes, and office expenses at the manufacturing location. Indirect fixed costs include wages and salaries of the corporate headquarters, which in a multiproduct company might be allocated to each operating location as a function of sales volume, employment levels, or assets employed. In addition, most corporate-level overhead expenses fall into the category of country club memberships, donations, catering, and other nondiscretionary costs that are absolutely essential to maintain the esprit de corps of the senior corporate staff.

Excluded from fixed costs is depreciation, which, because of its effect on taxation and cash flow, needs to be calculated on a consolidated basis, i.e., without regard to individual operating locations. Depreciation, on a tax basis, is included in analyses or forecasts of financial performance for operating locations where discounted cash flow or internal rate of return analyses are used to determine whether incremental investment at that location is justified.

[4] Depreciation

Depreciation is a financial representation of the deterioration, in both a physical and economic sense, of the assets used in the production of a company's goods. In the context of financial planning, it can also be viewed as a cash generator because it is a deduction from income subject to tax; in other words, for every dollar of depreciation, the taxpayer can avoid 40 cents of federal, state, and local income tax. Further, the generation of cash may occur at a level beyond the actual physical depreciation of the equipment. In the context of this forecasting procedure, all of these characteristics must be considered.

From the perspective of financial accounting, depreciation is a profit and loss item, or an operating expense; from the balance sheet perspective, the accumulation of depreciation reduces gross assets. Where depreciation is applied to producing assets, renewal capital expenditure can be estimated; that is, cash flow items that will require funding can be predicted.

At the same time, depreciation, for tax purposes, generates cash through the reduction of income taxes payable. The amount of depreciation appearing in a product line financial forecast must be adjusted for the corporation as a whole to develop the proper net income for tax purposes, and such adjustment can be substantial. In an emerging company with a fairly high level of new investment, the difference between tax basis and book basis depreciation can be substantial. In a more mature firm with a lower level of new net fixed investment, the reverse could be the case. Taxation as a percentage of net book earnings would be much greater, thus causing cash requirements beyond what would be inferred from a product line or profit center forecast of gross margin. The depreciation question should be given to the tax department or the firm's tax adviser for resolution, since the calculation of the amount of depreciation can be fairly detailed and subject to current tax regulations.

[5] Operating Income

The line for operating income in Figure 2-1 simply represents the profitability of operations, before the effect of interest, taxes, and external financing.

[6] Interest and Finance Costs

The interest line in Figure 2-1 has two elements: (1) existing interest and (2) interest and finance charges incurred as a result of new financing. The sum is derived from both this forecasting exercise and the preparation of a balance sheet. In many corporations where the borrowing or finance function is centralized, the corporate treasury staff develops the interest expense number. In any event, computing this number is one of the last calculations performed, since business results plus investments made during the immediately preceding period will be the basis for the calculation of incremental finance charges. Unlike the sales and operating forecasts, which are relatively discrete from year to year, these calculations are done in series. In addition, a change in funds required or generated early in the planning period would require a recalculation of all succeeding years.

To this point, only the volume portion of interest expense has been addressed; equally important is the price portion. Unfortunately, consistently accurate forecasts of interest rates are nearly impossible to make. Nevertheless, some attempt must be made to estimate both the direction and magnitude of change of interest rates, both short- and long-term. (See Chapter B1 in the *Handbook of Finance* and Chapter 1 in the *Handbook of Securities and Investment Management* for an analysis of interest rates.) Both categories of rates must be addressed, since it does not follow that all incremental borrowing will be either short- or long-term but rather some combination of the two, depending on the desired complexion of the balance sheet.

The farther into the distance one gazes, the greater the need for corrective lenses; when it comes to interest rates, even a radio telescope is inadequate in providing clarity after a certain point. One suggested method of forecasting interest rates is to look forward on a quarterly basis for the first year of the plan and on an annual basis thereafter. However, some forecasters shy away from even the near-term quarterly outlook and just pick an average rate for the year. Either method can be chosen because any misses in the interest rate forecast are bound to be offset by inaccuracies elsewhere in the assumptions, especially the more distant the horizon.

[7] Taxation

For the most part, it is easiest to assume a 40 percent tax rate on net income. The actual rate can be made up of federal, state, and local income taxes as appropriate.

For forecasting purposes, a flat rate of 40 percent, although not exact, is reasonable. It should be kept in mind that for a single-product company, especially one with a relatively small net income, the assumed tax rate can be dramatically different from 40 percent. There are other more complex considerations here, such as carryback or carryforward, investment tax credit, foreign tax credits, and dividend withholdings.

Possibly the best way to forecast taxes in a complex international company is to prepare a consolidated profit and loss statement, on a cash or tax basis, that can be reviewed by the company's internal tax department or an outside accountant. That person can take into account all (or most) of the tricky tax considerations and some major swings in cash generation; as a result, the financing needs of the company can be predicted more accurately. The tax-planning aspect is also important in determining the investment posture of the firm, its view toward tax-based leasing, venture capital, and other opportunities or requirements imposed on the firm. Therefore, even though the taxation part of the forecasting process is easily the most complicated, it cannot and should not be ignored.

[8] Capital Expenditure and New Investment

There are five fairly straightforward elements in capital expenditure: maintenance capital, environmental requirements, expansion capital, new product investment, and external acquisitions. In each case, an expenditure or event in the first year of the forecast will work its way through most of the cash flow categories in succeeding periods. Maintenance capital may reduce variable manufacturing costs or just keep it even in some instances, while environmental expenditures may have no profit and loss effect other than an increase in tax depreciation and a consequent reduction in taxes. Expansion capital or new product investment will have an impact on every item in succeeding years' forecasts, and external acquisitions could change the complexion of the entire forecast as well as the balance sheet configuration.

Again, these items need to be built from the bottom, starting basically in the order previously shown. Usually, all but the last category, acquisitions, can and should be developed by the operating entities.

[9] Dividends

Dividends on preferred and common stock are after-tax items. They are linked to the number of shares outstanding or, in the case of a privately or closely held company, are negotiated. Among the factors considered in computing dividends are how much the company must retain for reinvestment, how much should be paid to maintain the market price of the stock, historical dividend policy, industry practice, and cash availability. (See Chapter E3 in the *Handbook of Modern Finance* and Chapter 3 in the *Handbook of Financial Strategy and Policy* for an analysis of dividend policy.)

[10] Dynamics

The calculation of corporate net cash flow is simple arithmetic, given a reasonably consistent generation of the basic numbers. The process, however, soon leads to iterations in series, as previously mentioned. The results of year 1 need to be developed before going on to year 2, and so forth. Furthermore, if extreme accuracy is desired,

FIGURE 2-2

Forecast for Wonderful Division

	Year 1	Year 2	Year 3	Year 4	Year 5
Revenue					
Volume	1 million	1.2 million	1.2 million	1.5 million	1.5 million
Price (dollars/unit)	$ 1.00	$ 1.05	$ 1.20	$ 1.30	$ 1.42
Total revenue	$1,000	$1,260	$1,560	$1,950	$2,125
Manufacturing cost					
Variable (dollars/unit)	$ 0.25	$ 0.27	$ 0.27	$ 0.30	$ 0.35
Fixed (dollars)	$ 125	$ 125	$ 125	$ 160	$ 200
Total manufacturing cost	$ 375	$ 449	$ 476	$ 610	$ 725
Gross margin	$ 625	$ 811	$1,084	$1,340	$1,400
Fixed capital	$ 100	$ 100	$ 100	$ 110	$ 110

Note: Dollars in thousands.

iterations within each study period will also be required; for example, if a significant investment is made in the first quarter, cash required for the rest of the year and the value of short-term investments, debt, or equity will change, as will interest expense or dividends in quarters 2 through 4. A daily financial forecast would provide as much mathematical accuracy as possible, but obviously such effort would be fruitless. Monthly calculations for the three months following the forecast, then for three quarters, and then for a year should provide about as much information as can be used effectively and have some reasonable chance of being accurate.

Before proceeding from year 1 to year 2, however, financial statements on a basis compatible with those that would be published need to be prepared.

2.03 CASE STUDY

What follows is a constructive example of the first part of the forecasting process: the attempt to predict operating events and consequent financing requirements.

[1] Building the Estimates

The Zed Corporation has two divisions: Wonderful and Incredible. In November of each year, the management of each division submits its five-year forecast of the business. Figure 2-2 shows that the Wonderful division enjoys steady growth in both sales volume and price. When the president of the Wonderful division reviewed the economic forecasts he had received from both the corporate office and his own outside sources, he deduced that demand for his products would exceed the growth of the economy over the next five years. However, he also felt that his pricing policy would be determined more by the rate of inflation than by demand. Thus, with real GNP growth forecast at 5.5 percent and inflation at 4.5 percent, he forecast an annual average growth rate of 8.5 percent for sales volume, about 1.5 times that of the entire

FIGURE 2-3

Forecast for Incredible Division

	Year 1	Year 2	Year 3	Year 4	Year 5
Revenue					
Volume	2.5 million	2.5 million	2.5 million	3.1 million	3.5 million
Price (dollars/unit)	$ 5.00	$ 5.25	$ 5.10	$ 5.20	$ 5.20
Total revenue	$12,500	$13,125	$12,750	$16,120	$18,200
Manufacturing cost					
Variable (dollars/unit)	$ 1.50	$ 1.55	$ 1.55	$ 1.60	$ 1.55
Fixed (dollars)	$ 2,500	$ 2,650	$ 2,800	$ 3,000	$ 3,500
Total manufacturing cost	$ 6,250	$ 6,525	$ 6,675	$ 7,960	$ 8,925
Gross margin	$ 6,250	$ 6,600	$ 6,075	$ 8,160	$ 9,275
Fixed capital					
Maintenance	$ 300	$ 300	$ 350	$ 400	$ 500
Expansion			$ 5,000		

Note: Dollars in thousands.

economy, but only a 4.5 percent average growth rate in price, equal to the increase in the consumer price index.

He also felt that there was a need for maintenance capital over the next five years, but on a real basis, growing very slowly. Because he has adequate existing capacity to produce at his forecast sales levels, and because his plant produced absolutely no pollution, other capital expenditures were nil.

The president of the Incredible division, on the other hand, felt that her product was in a much more competitive environment, with demand more a function of price. Even though she reviewed the same economic forecasts as her golfing buddy at Wonderful, her outlook was very different, primarily because her products were much more sensitive to foreign competition. Because of these strong pressures, Incredible's president believed that within the next two to three years there would be a shake-out in the industry. Therefore, she wanted to be prepared to step in and take over that part of the market vacated by producers that she felt would eventually close their doors. She believed that business prospects were not good for the first three years of the forecast period but that in year 3 a significant expansion of capacity would be desirable. That expansion would have to be financed from the corporate funds flow, either internal or external, and would just begin to yield sizable earnings after about a year of production. In addition, ongoing maintenance capital requirements would increase slightly. Again, she ran a pristine operation, so good that it took in dirty air and water and returned them perfectly clean.

[2] Consolidating Forecasts

When the vice-president of finance of Zed received the two division forecasts (Figures 2-2 and 2-3), he started the corporate financial forecast by preparing the skeleton format for the entire company, as shown in Figure 2-1. It was fairly easy to fill in the revenue, manufacturing cost, and gross margin lines, those being nothing more than the combination of the two divisions' sales and manufacturing forecasts.

FIGURE 2-4

Projected Costs for Corporate Office

	Year 1	Year 2	Year 3	Year 4	Year 5
Fixed costs					
Salaries	$2,500	$2,500	$2,650	$3,500	$3,750
Utilities, etc.	150	150	160	200	250
Selling, general, and					
administrative expense	1,425	1,049	999	1,300	1,000
Total	$4,075	$3,699	$3,809	$5,000	$5,000

Note: Dollars in thousands.

FIGURE 2-5

Combined Fixed-Capital Requirements

	Year 1	Year 2	Year 3	Year 4	Year 5
Fixed-capital expenditures					
Maintenance	$ 400	$400	$ 450	$ 510	$ 610
Expansion	—	—	5,000	—	—
Environmental	—	—	—	—	—
Acquisition	—	—	—	—	—
Total	$ 400	$400	$5,450	$ 510	$ 610
Depreciation calculation (assuming 5-year MACRS property)					
Year 1	$ 80	$128	$ 76	$ 58	$ 58
Year 2	—	80	128	76	58
Year 3	—	—	90	144	86
Year 4	—	—	—	1,102	1,763
Year 5	—	—	—	—	122
	$ 80	$208	$ 294	$1,380	$2,087
Depreciation (tax basis)					
Existing capital	$1,000	$750	$ 500	$ 250	$ 100
New capital	80	208	294	1,380	2,087
Total	$1,080	$958	$ 794	$1,630	$2,187

Note: Dollars in thousands.

The first three lines of the corporate forecast equal the sum of the same lines from Figures 2-2 and 2-3. He then gathered his own corporate expenses (Figure 2-4) to develop the fixed-cost line.

The next part of the cash flow forecast, depreciation, required some calculation. The vice-president knew, from the previous year's forecast, the amount of depreciation (tax basis) generated by existing assets. He then took the combined fixed-capital requirements of the divisions, shown in Figure 2-5, and, since all of the fixed-capital

FIGURE 2-6

Interest and Finance Costs

	Current Year	Year 1	Year 2	Year 3	Year 4	Year 5
New Financing						
Net cash flow	NA	$ 610	$ 931	$(3,762)	$1,507	$2,165
Source of funds						
Short-term debt	NA	(350)	(150)	221	(221)	—
Long-term debt	NA	(260)	(740)	1,000	(1,000)	—
Equity	NA	—	—	2,500	—	—
Net cash position	—	—	$ 41	—	$ 286	$2,451
Existing Financing						
Short-term debt						
Amount	$ 500	$ 150	—	$ 221	—	—
Rate	0.1	0.1	0.1	0.1	0.1	0.1
Interest expense	$ 50	$ 15	—	$ 22	—	—
Long-term debt						
Amount	$1,000	$ 740	—	$ 1,000	—	—
Rate	0.12	0.12	0.12	0.12	0.12	0.12
Interest expense	$ 120	$ 89	—	120	—	—
Total interest expense	$ 170	$ 104	—	$ 142	—	—
Equity						
Shares outstanding	1,000	1,000	1,000	1,250	1,250	1,250
Dividend	$1,000	$1,000	$1,000	$ 1,250	$1,250	$1,250
Market price (dollars/ share)	$ 15	$ 12	$ 12	$ 10	$ 12	$ 15

Note: Dollars in thousands.

requirements were machinery and equipment, he used the appropriate rates for five-year modified accelerated cost recovery system (MACRS) equipment supplied by his tax manager. In addition, the tax manager estimated the timing of the usage of the benefits (in this example, the possibility of carryback or carryforward is ignored), which is a function of the date the equipment is placed in service. He assumed that all of the maintenance capital would be placed in service during the year of expenditure and would be immediately depreciable. However, the expansion capital needed by the Incredible division, because of the size and timing of the project, would not be spent until early the following year, and depreciation would not be applicable until then.

Again, these calculations, also shown in Figure 2-5, were performed simultaneously for all years of the forecast and added in to the corporate financial forecast.

[3] Dynamics

At this point, the dynamic calculations began. The vice-president knew his cost of debt capital, debt outstanding at the beginning of the period, and dividend requirements (see Figure 2-6, column 1). From these figures, he could calculate interest expense

FIGURE 2-7

Cash Flow Forecast

	Year 1	Year 2	Year 3	Year 4	Year 5
Revenue	$13,500	$14,385	$14,310	$18,070	$20,325
Manufacturing cost	(6,625)	(7,336)	(6,551)	(8,570)	(10,075)
Gross margin	$ 6,875	$ 7,049	$ 7,759	$ 9,500	$10,250
Fixed costs	(4,075)	(3,699)	(3,809)	(5,000)	(5,000)
Depreciation	(1,080)	(958)	(794)	(1,630)	(2,187)
Operating income	$ 1,720	$ 2,392	$ 3,156	$ 2,870	$ 3,063
Interest	(170)	(104)	—	(142)	—
Pretax income	$ 1,550	$ 2,288	$ 3,156	$ 2,728	$ 3,063
Tax at 0.40	(620)	(915)	(1,262)	(1,091)	(1,255)
After-tax income	$ 930	$ 1,373	$ 1,894	$ 1,637	$ 1,838
Depreciation	1,080	958	794	1,630	2,187
Cash flow from operations	$ 2,010	$ 2,331	$ 2,688	$ 3,267	$ 4,025
Capital expenditures	(400)	(400)	(5,450)	(510)	(610)
Dividends	(1,000)	(1,000)	(1,000)	(1,250)	(1,250)
Net cash flow	$ 610	$ 931	$(3,762)	$ 1,507	$ 2,165

Note: Dollars in thousands.

for year 1 of the forecast. He assumed, even though he knew that it was slightly inaccurate, that his divisions would not remit cash to corporate headquarters until the end of the year (earnings on cash are ignored). (See Chapters 3 and 4 for detailed analyses of the cash management process.) Therefore, he calculated the net cash flow for year 1 as follows. Since interest expense on outstanding debt was $170, pretax income in year 1 (Figure 2-7, column 1) was $1,550. He gave the data to his tax manager, who calculated that year's tax, as shown in Figure 2-7, column 1. The vice-president took that amount, multiplied it by 0.4 to compute the overall tax liability, calculated after-tax income, and added back depreciation (a noncash item), thus deriving cash flow from operations. Projected capital spending and dividend payments (both after-tax items) were deducted, thus producing the first year's net cash flow, $610 (all shown in Figure 2-7, column 1).

He then moved on to year 2 of the forecast. Again, the operating-income line was complete, so he had to derive the information from interest expense on down. Figure 2-6, column 2 shows this process. The vice-president assumed that he would use the $610 to pay down $350 of short-term debt and $260 of long-term debt, in order to maintain a certain balance in these categories. The new interest expense was then $104. He followed the same process in year 2 to derive net cash flow as previously described. Moving along with great dispatch, the vice-president continued the calculations for all but the last three lines of the forecast for year 3, at which time significant external funds would be required to finance the expansion at the Incredible division.

The vice-president again assumed that all events occurred at year-end, and for the sake of illustration he financed the net cash requirement from year 3 immediately at

FIGURE 2-8

Source and Application of Cash for Zed Corporation

		Key
Sources of funds		
Pretax income	$ 255	1
Depreciation and amortization	50	2
Proceeds from stock issue	500	3
Proceeds from long-term debt	300	4
Total	$1,100	
Applications of funds		
Increase in working capital	$ 125	5
Purchase of fixed assets	825	6
Payment of taxes	150	7
Payment of dividends	100	8
Total	$1,200	
Increase (decrease) of cash	$ (100)	9

Note: Dollars in millions.

the beginning of year 4. The vice-president looked at his pro forma year-end balance sheet and determined that 40 percent of the incremental funds would be derived from debt and 60 percent from a new equity issue. (The split between these two sources is arbitrary at this point in the example but is addressed more fully later.)

From this point forward, the iterative process is the same as previously described, merely working down through interest, income, tax, and so on through to the end of the forecast period.

[4] Financing Requirements

The vice-president then went to work on the second major part of his forecast, the implications of the upcoming year's activity on Zed's balance sheet. (It should be noted that the numbers in the following tables are not consistent with those presented earlier. These numbers were created for illustrative purposes only.)

Because it was a public company with both debt and equity issues trading in New York, Zed needed to be aware of the impact that ratings for both debt and equity issues would have on the company's cost of funds. Without going into great detail, debt ratings are determined by a number of things, including quality of earnings, balance sheet strength, historical and forecast growth rates, industry outlook, dividend policy, and strength of management. (See Chapter 1 for an analysis of credit ratings.) Only the balance sheet character could be influenced with any success by the vice-president, and that was his task for that afternoon.

The vice-president used all of the divisional and corporate profit and cash flow data generated thus far to put together a corporate profit and loss statement, a source and application statement (Figure 2-8), and, finally, using both of these, a balance sheet for both the recent year-end and the next year-end (Figure 2-9). (Figure 2-10 is a key or cross-reference between Figures 2-8 and 2-9). Since Zed is an industrial company subject to swings in overall economic activity and thus its earnings vary with economic

FIGURE 2-9

Balance Sheet for Zed Corporation

	Dec. 31, 1993	1994	Dec. 31, 1994
Assets			
Current assets			
Cash	$ 125	$(100)	$ 25
Accounts receivable	2,625	250	2,875
Other	82	—	82
Subtotal	$2,832	$150	$2,982
Investment in unconsolidated subsidiaries	$ 422	$ 20	$ 442
Fixed assets	1,055	775	1,830
Intangibles	120	(5)	115
Other	238	(12)	226
Total assets	$4,667	$928	$5,595
Liabilities			
Current liabilities			
Short-term debt	$ 82	—	$ 82
Accounts payable	1,007	$125	1,132
Other	128	—	128
Subtotal	$1,217	$125	$1,342
Long-term debt	$ 885	$300	$1,185
Other liabilities	222	(125)	97
Subtotal	$2,324	$300	$2,624
Stockholders' Equity			
Capital stock (20 million shares at $1 par)	$ 700	$500	$1,200
Retained earnings	1,565	128	1,693
Foreign currency adjustment	78	—	78
Subtotal	$2,343	$628	$2,971
Total liabilities and stockholders' equity	$4,667	$928	$5,595

Note: Dollars in millions.

cycles, it had to maintain liquidity and a strong equity base. A strong balance sheet was needed to provide adequate reserves to maintain the business when sales and earnings deteriorated and thus maintain the current bond and stock ratings.

From the divisions' forecasts, the vice-president knew that 1993 would not be a banner year, but he also knew that a major acquisition would take place nevertheless. His goal, then, was to try to maintain appropriate financial ratios during the year. The first thing he needed to know was the approximate size and character of the proposed acquisition. He was advised that the purchase would be of a private nature and could only be funded with cash and that the total cost would be approximately $800 million. It was immediately obvious that even a friendly banker would not be willing to fund a cash requirement of that magnitude. He also knew that such an increase in debt (preferably long-term debt, since the bulk of the purchase was for producing assets)

FIGURE 2-10
Key to Activity

Balance Sheet for 1994 Activity[a]	Source and Application Statement[b]
Changes in Assets	
Cash: Decrease of $100	Item 9 (net of all cash items)
Accounts receivable: Increase of $250	Resulting from increased sales (not shown) and reflected in item 9 (increase in working capital)
Investment in unconsolidated subsidiaries: Increase of $20	Earnings of subsidiaries during year included in item 1
Fixed assets: Increase of $775	Net of item 6 (acquisition of Alpha Corporation) and item 2 (depreciation)
Intangibles: Decrease of $5	Amortization of goodwill, included in item 1
Other: Decrease of $12	A plug item of no interest to anyone
Changes in Liabilities and Stockholders' Equity	
Short-term debt: No change	A commercial paper program—have to keep name in market
Accounts payable: Increase of $125	Resulting from increased production to support increased sales and reflected in item 5
Long-term debt: Increase of $300	Item 4, used to fund part of purchase of Alpha Corporation
Other liabilities: Decrease of $125	Reduction of deferred taxes payable; appears as item 7
Capital stock: Increase of $500	Proceeds from new issue, item 3, and used to fund part of purchase of Alpha Corporation
Retained earnings: Increase of $128	Item 1 less annual taxes (not shown) and less dividends, item 8, plus earnings from unconsolidated subsidiaries

---

[a] See Figure 2-9.
[b] See Figure 2-8.

---

would severely increase the debt-to-equity ratio at a time when he could not really afford the risk or the debt service requirements.

His plan consisted of three parts: (1) Raise equity to improve the ratios; (2) with the improved ratios, raise some long-term debt; and (3) use the proceeds of both to make the acquisition. He also knew that Zed's existing operations would be largely self-sustaining.

The question of the moment was how much equity and how much debt. From the balance sheet perspective, an equity issue of the full amount would be best. However, an $800 million issue was too big and would be very difficult to sell. The vice-president decided that if Zed could maintain its ratios during 1994, future growth, both from existing operations and from the acquired company, would enhance the balance sheet satisfactorily. With an equity issue of about $500 million and then a debt issue of about

$300 million plus forecast activity during the year, he felt that the major ratios of financial strength would be maintained as follows:

	1993	1994
Current ratio	2.3	2.2
Long-term debt-to-equity ratio	0.4	0.4
Total liabilities-to-equity ratio	1.0	0.9

There are other considerations beyond financial ratios. A look at the ratio of the market price of the stock to book value per share can be very helpful in assessing whether a large equity issue will be successful. The general industry environment should also be studied. For example, an automobile company could issue more shares at a higher price if the most recent period had been a good one for the automobile industry. There is no single formula that allows the financial executive to identify precisely the best size or price of an external (public) financing. Nevertheless, all of these elements need to be taken into consideration.

Consistent with the company's policy of requiring five-year forecasts, the vice-president continued the process previously described. He produced a profit and loss statement, funds flow statement, and balance sheet for each of the remaining years in his forecast. Once it was completed, he packaged the whole thing, put it in his bookcase, and never looked at it again.

[5] Dynamic Scenario Analysis

Given the difficulty and importance of forecasting, many companies are applying dynamic scenario analysis to their forecasts. This technique requires that forecasts be developed under very specific alternative conditions. For example, one forecast would assume rising demand and stable interest rates, while others might assume flat demand with rising rates. The technique differs from simulation analysis. It demands that the forecaster specify possible states of the world, whereas simulation analysis simply evaluates outcomes over all states of nature. Simulation analysis does not really require the forecaster to develop an internally consistent view of how the world will behave in the future. Accordingly, some output from simulation can reflect high inflation and low interest rates occurring simultaneously. This hardly ever happens in real life, however.

The advantage of dynamic scenario analysis is that it allows the forecaster to see how real possible future events affect the company. Hence, it allows the forecaster to develop planning options and to see how valuable such options may be.

The forecast discussed earlier is a best-guess forecast. It shows rising cash flows from operations and a large capital expenditure (an acquisition) in year 3 (see Figure 2-7). The forecast implies a specific timing for the sale of new debt and equity. Suppose, however, that sales rise more rapidly or grow more slowly than forecasted. This would surely have ramifications for the amount of new capital spending and would therefore also have ramifications for the amount of new debt and equity that must be sold and the timing of these sales. The knowledge associated with the financial implications of alternative but plausible specific scenarios cannot help but allow managers to do their jobs better. They will better understand what they must be prepared to do should the world be rosier or gloomier than they initially guessed it would be.

2.04 SUMMARY

Briefly, the steps to follow in preparing financial forecasts are as follows:

- ☐ Ask the people who actually do the selling to prepare sales forecasts that take into account the state of the economy, not just what happened last year.

- ☐ Ask those responsible for manufacturing operations to provide complete data on the different product costs, based on volumes from the sales forecast.

- ☐ Compute depreciation on a consolidated basis, taking into consideration existing levels plus forecast new capital expenditures.

- ☐ Use operating income to measure the effectiveness of unit management.

- ☐ Base interest costs, which are both price and volume sensitive, on published forecasts. Such forecasts are usually free and sometimes fairly accurate. Using a consensus or average from several forecasts is the simplest way to obtain a figure. Interest costs must be projected in series; year 2 can be calculated only after year 1.

- ☐ Bring in a tax expert if the standard 40 percent assumption is inappropriate.

- ☐ Do not include capital expenditures in the forecast unless it is certain that the funds will be spent.

- ☐ Look at industry dividend patterns as well as the company's history when projecting dividends.

- ☐ Be realistic in the breakdown or identification of future periods in the forecast. Monthly forecasting may be a good exercise for division management but can take more time to calculate, on a companywide basis, than its value to corporate management warrants.

- ☐ Be realistic when looking at external funding alternatives. The markets may not have as much confidence in the company as management does.

- ☐ Use the forecast to plan both prospectively and retrospectively. Comparisons of actual performance to forecast performance can be used as guidelines in determining incentive compensation.

- ☐ Finally, look at the forecast and plan periodically after it has been completed. Revise it if the environment has changed significantly.

Suggested Reading

Fransson, M.C. "How to Use Dynamic Scenario Analysis." *Journal of Corporate Finance,* Vol. 15 (Spring 1987), pp. 19–28.

Higgins, Robert C. *Analysis for Financial Management,* 2nd ed. Homewood, Ill: Dow Jones-Irwin, 1989.

Chapter 3
Short-Run Financial Management

JAMES A. GENTRY

3.01 INTRODUCTION

The purpose of this chapter is to update the state of the art of short-run financial management (SRFM). SRFM reflects a broad, dynamic perspective on managing a firm's liquid resources. In this chapter, the term "SRFM" is used to encompass all of the components that affect the inflow and outflow of cash through a firm.

It is initially useful to identify major SRFM themes. Figure 3-1 presents a three-dimensional framework that characterizes decision problems by their underlying structure. The three dimensions of the problem space are degrees of uncertainty, time dependence, and complexity. The degree of uncertainty ranges from deterministic situations where all variables are known to highly probabilistic situations where little information is available about any variable. The time dimension ranges from a static condition of no change at a specific moment to a dynamic condition that reflects changes occurring in future periods. The complexity dimension is measured in terms of the number of variables required, where the more variables involved in the analysis, the greater the complexity.

Each corner of the problem space corresponds to specific types of financial information or models. Corner 1 depicts information for a single variable that is deterministic and static. Financial ratios would be an example of corner 1 information. Moving up the plane to corner 4, the number of variables is increased, but the deterministic and static constraints are still present. From a financial perspective, corner 4 corresponds to balance sheet or income statement information.

Corner 2 reflects a deterministic, single-variable problem with a changing (dynamic) orientation. Examples of corner 2 information would be the calculation of future value or present value of an investment. The dividend valuation model is another example of a corner 2 model. Corner 7 represents several variables that are changing over time. SRFM examples would be a forecast of monthly cash budgets, monthly pro forma balance sheets, and income statements. Also located at corner 7 are linear programming models and the net present value (NPV) model, i.e., the discounted cash flow (DCF) model.

Corner 3 represents a probabilistic, static, single-variable set of information, such as the frequency distribution of a financial ratio, funds flow component or any financial variable. Corner 6 is a probabilistic, static, multivariable problem. Leading financial theory models such as the capital asset pricing model (CAPM) and arbitrage pricing theory (APT) (see Chapters B2 and D2 of the *Handbook of Modern Finance*; Chapter 2 of the *Handbook of Securities and Investment Management*; and Chapter 2 of this book) are located at corner 6.

Uncertainty and dynamic dimensions for a single variable are introduced in corner 5. Option pricing theory (OPT) (see Chapter A9 of the *Handbook of Modern Finance* and Chapter 9 in the *Handbook of Financial Markets*) is a classic example of a Corner 5 model. Using past daily cash flow information in an autoregressive integrated moving average (ARIMA) model to predict a firm's cash flow position also exemplifies a corner 5 analysis.

SRFM involves the management of real cash flows, assets, and liabilities and includes many variables that cause a firm's daily flow of cash to change continuously. These characteristics of SRFM are best represented at either corner 7 or corner 8 of the problem space. The CAPM, APT, and OPT do not focus on the management of real cash flows, assets, and liabilities and, unless modified, the CAPM and APT do not possess the dynamic features that are needed to integrate the flows related to SRFM into a total financial planning model.

Corner 8 is the most complex corner location in the problem space. All decision

FIGURE 3-1

Problem Space: Models, Authors, and Accounting Information

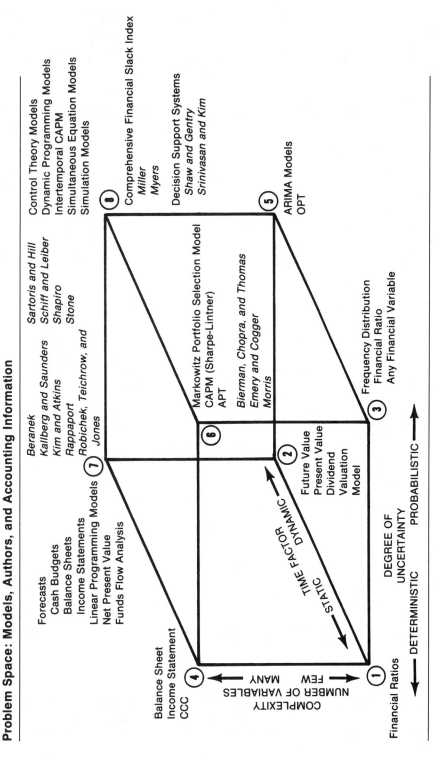

problems could be at corner 8, because it incorporates all three factors that are indispensable for a meaningful analysis. The five classes of models that incorporate all three dimensions are control theory, dynamic programming, intertemporal CAPM, simulation, and simultaneous equations. The problem space provides a structure for classifying contributions to the SRFM literature.

3.02 OVERVIEW OF SHORT-RUN FINANCIAL MANAGEMENT LITERATURE

A review of the major research themes that have motivated managerial developments sets the stage for projecting future managerial directions in SRFM. Early research used accounting information to model or focus on specific activities, such as cash management, accounts receivable management, inventory management, short-term borrowing, and cash budgeting.

   The early research in and practice of SRFM created generally unrelated pockets of knowledge and was conceptually based on balance sheet information. Early efforts did not create a theory that integrated the cash flow contributions of the SRFM variables into the total value of the firm.

[1] Integrated Theory of Value

During the 1970s, finance research emphasized the development of theories of valuation. These theories were based on the widespread belief that financial markets are economically efficient. The CAPM and the APT assume that there are a few relatively stable variables that determine the financial value of the firm in the marketplace. Furthermore, these views assumed that the internal operations of the firm are efficient and therefore neither created nor destroyed value. The long-run theories did not recognize the uncertainties created in a firm's day-to-day operations that directly affect the creation or destruction of value. In contrast, the practice of SRFM is based on a large number of real variables that are changing almost continuously. Real value is based on the success of short-run resource management.

   Integration of working capital information into a larger conceptual and managerial system was suggested by several authors throughout the 1960s and 1970s. In the early 1980s, Morris (1983) incorporated cash inflows and outflows into a modified single-period CAPM valuation framework, which highlighted the risk-return trade-off as it relates to cash. Cash outflows must be financed either from existing cash balances or with costly borrowing. A cash flow shortfall will cause a firm to borrow and thereby increase the systematic risk of the dividend payoff to stockholders at the end of the operating horizon. When operating cash inflows are greater than outflows, the firm uses the excess cash to repay the short-term debt and, if cash is available, to fund the ongoing operations of the firm or invest in marketable securities. This framework recognizes that managing cash flows is a primary activity of the firm and, furthermore, indicates that critical resources are invested in cash and/or receivables as well as in productive capital assets and inventories.

[2] Gentry and Lee Model

Gentry and Lee (1988) expanded upon the Sartoris and Hill (1983) model, which integrated short-term cash flows into an NPV framework. Gentry and Lee incorporated real variables that have a significant effect on cash inflows and outflows and, therefore,

FIGURE 3-2

Value Creation Process

	Operations	Other
Components contributing to cash inflow	Sales Collection patterns Collection effort Sales patterns Joint effects Credit terms Return on marketable securities Bad debt write-off	Short-term or long-term borrowing Sale of preferred stock Sale of common stock Sale of fixed assets
Components contributing to cash outflow	Raw materials Purchasing patterns Payment patterns Production patterns Disbursement terms Holding and ordering costs Labor costs Services Compensating balances Research expenditures Delivery and storage costs	Capital expenditures Repayment of debt Repurchase of shares

Note: $\text{NPV} = \dfrac{CI - CO}{(1 + r)} + \dfrac{CI(1 + g) - CO(1 + g)}{(1 + r)^2} + \cdots + \dfrac{CI(1 + g)^n - CO(1 + g)^n}{(1 + r)^n}$

where:

CI = cash inflows

CO = cash outflows

r = risk-adjusted cost of capital

g = growth rate

n = number of years

on the value of the firm. The model provides an overview of the numerous cash inflow and outflow components and shows how each one can create or destroy value in an NPV framework. The expanded model takes into account the interrelationships that exist among the sales and collection, purchase and disbursement, and production and inventory management efficiency effects. In addition, it incorporates forecasting error effects that cause changes in inventories.

A brief discussion of the Gentry and Lee model illustrates the integration of short-run operating cash flows into the NPV framework. The model shows that changes in SRFM policies, product demand, and costs of production can either create or destroy value. To create value, the object is to collect cash as quickly as possible and to hold onto the funds as long as possible. Therefore, cash inflows and outflows are presented as separate components. Policies or actions that increase the speed (timing) of the inflows or increase the level (amount) of the inflows enhance the value of the firm, and vice versa. There are numerous possible causes of increases and decreases in cash inflows and outflows. These are summarized in Figure 3-2.

Usually, operating flows compose the major cash inflows or outflows of a firm. Figure 3-3 shows a timeline of inflows and outflows that exist in the cash operating

FIGURE 3-3

Cash Flow Timeline

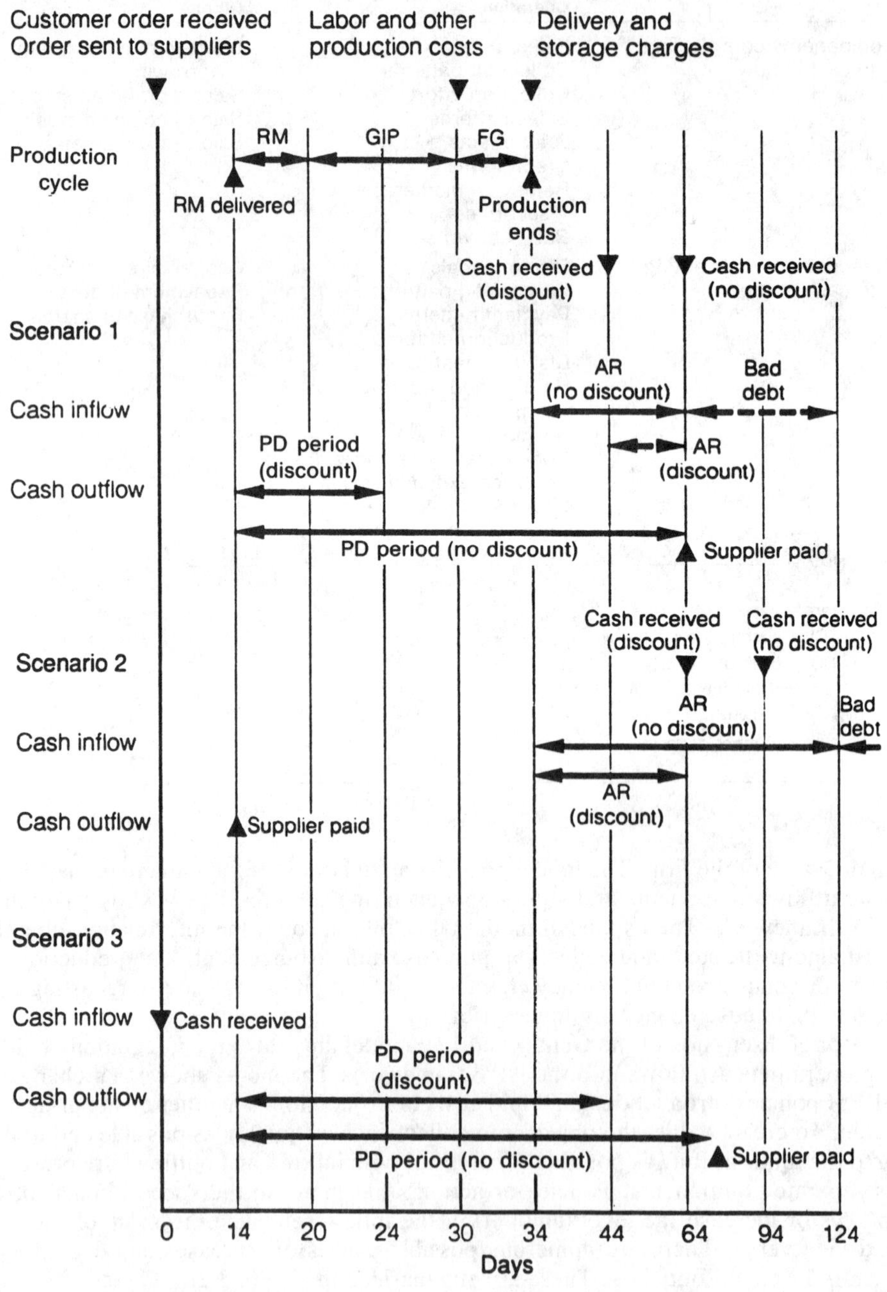

cycle. The figure highlights how a firm's competitive position in its product market affects the speed of the flow of cash into and out of the firm, which directly affects the value of the firm. It is assumed in Figure 3-3 that a firm has one division and one set of credit terms for its customers and one set for its suppliers. Also, it is assumed the terms remain constant throughout the planning period. Three scenarios are presented to illustrate how competition affects the timing of cash inflows and outflows.

The production phase of the timeline is presented at the top of Figure 3-3. It is assumed that the production cycle is identical for all three scenarios. The assumption is that the receipt of an order triggers the production process and simultaneously materials and supplies are ordered on day 1. The raw materials (RM) are delivered at the end of day 13, and production does not start until the beginning of day 20. The RM cycle is 6 days. The goods-in-process (GIP) cycle runs from day 20 through day 29, which is a 10-day cycle. The finished goods (FG) cycle is 4 days, day 30 through day 33, and encompasses the storage and delivery activities. The production and inventory cycle is the sum of the RM, GIP, and FG cycles, which is 20 days. Although it is not shown in Figure 3-3, value has been added throughout the inventory cycle, with outflows for labor and other production costs occurring throughout the GIP cycle. Additionally, there are other cash outflows not shown that affect the value of the firm because of independent billing schedules, e.g., electric power, gas, communication, insurance, and capital investment expenditures.

Scenario 1 depicts a firm that has received terms from its suppliers of 1/10, net 30. Payment to the supplier is deferred (PD period) until day 24 if the discount is taken or until day 44 if it is not taken. Cash is received from the customer on day 44 if the discount of 1/10, net 30 is taken and on day 64 if the discount is not taken. If a customer does not pay in 90 days, the account is assumed to be a bad debt, and no cash inflow occurs. The cash operating cycle is 30 days if the customer takes the discount and 50 days if the discount is not taken and payment is made on day 64. To complete the cash conversion cycle (CCC), the payment deferral period is subtracted from the operating cycle. The credit terms available and the decision to accept or reject the discount have a significant effect on the timing of the cash flows and thus the value of a firm. For example, if the discount from the supplier is taken and the customer takes the discount, the CCC is 20 days (day 44 minus day 24). However, if the customer does not take the discount, the CCC is 40 days (day 64 minus day 24). Alternatively, if the discount from the supplier is not taken and the customer takes the discount, the CCC is zero (day 44 minus day 44), but if the customer does not take the discount, the CCC is 20 days (day 64 minus day 44).

Scenario 2 exemplifies the firm that is in a weak bargaining position with both its customers and suppliers. The company has to pay the supplier cash on delivery (COD) on day 14. There is no discount when the terms are COD. Terms to the customers are 2/60, net 90. Thus, if the discount is taken, the customer pays on day 94, which is an 80-day operating cycle (day 94 minus day 14). The CCC is also 80 days, because there is no payment deferral period. If the customer does not take the discount, the CCC is 110 days.

Scenario 3 is representative of a firm that is in a strong bargaining position with both its suppliers and customers. The customer delivers a check for good funds on day 1 when the order is placed. The firm has the use of these funds until the suppliers are paid. The supplier provides terms of 2/30, net 60. If the firm takes the discount, the operating cycle and CCC are −43 days (day 1 minus day 44), which means that the firm has the use of the funds for 43 days before the supplier is paid. The CCC is −73 days if the discount from the supplier is not taken.

The three scenarios illustrate that the competitive position of the firm to its suppliers and customers has a significant effect on the timing of the cash flows, which directly affects the value of the company. Although not demonstrated in Figure 3-3, if a firm is in a strong competitive position with its customers, the quantity of goods sold should be higher than if it was not in a strong competitive position. Likewise, if a firm is in a strong competitive position with its suppliers, it could have lower costs of production, thereby reducing the cash outflow. Although the timeline in Figure 3-3 does not include all of the outflows or other revenue inflows, these also directly affect the value of the firm.

The NPV approach focuses on the effects that real variables have on a firm's cash inflows and outflows. However, NPV models do not explicitly include a financial market risk measure. Additionally, simulation, simultaneous equation, and control theory models will set the stage for building new theoretical linkages between short-run and long-run financial management that should result in a natural evolution of SRFM thought.

[3] Cash Flow Story

The concern over managing cash blossomed in the 1970s for several reasons. There was a rapid increase in inflation and interest rates that focused management attention on the need to invest idle cash balances. Simultaneously, computer technology emerged that provided commercial banks with the tools to offer cash management services to corporate customers. Microcomputers arrived in the 1980s and provided easy access to daily cash receipt and disbursement information, which resulted in a better understanding of the short-run cash flow process. The next few paragraphs briefly present the major conceptual areas of cash management.

Cash balance management encompasses short-term borrowing and investing, cash forecasting, and cash position management. Robichek, Teichroew, and Jones (1965) focused on short-term borrowing, while Orgler (1974) presented cash management as a multiperiod linear programming model. The Orgler model was designed to minimize the net cost from a cash budget through the planning horizon. Several authors have used linear programming to formulate the cash management process. Maier and Vander Weide (1978) developed a leading user-friendly linear programming model, and Stone (1973) created a financial statement simulator to determine a firm's line of credit and/or short-term investments needs.

There are numerous statistical-based cash forecasting models. A few of the leading models were created by Stone and Wood (1977), Stone and Miller (1981), Miller and Stone (1985), Beehler (1983), Kallberg and Parkinson (1984), and Homonoff and Mullins (1975). The cash-gathering process collects customer payments and deposits them into the banking system. Lockbox collection models were created by several authors (e.g., Maier and Vander Weide, and Stone).

Cash mobilization and concentration focuses on moving funds through a concentration system to desired locations where the company can efficiently utilize its resources. The principal focus is on selecting concentration banks and transferring funds among banks.

The objective of the cash disbursement process is to select optimal disbursement sites. Maier and Vander Weide developed a unified model that locates lockboxes and disbursement banks. Their model recognized that a firm may use one bank for both collecting customer payments and disbursing its checks.

Several studies have analyzed the problem of designing an optimal banking system for credit and noncredit services. A principal concern was determining how much in balances or cash to reimburse a bank for services it provided. In the design of a company's banking system, it is important to take into account the interrelationships that exist among a company's cash budget, credit requirement needs, and the bank system design.

The cash flow timeline of Ferguson and Hill (1985) was based on the principle of present value and showed that a firm's value is determined by the amount and the timing of its cash inflows and outflows. In another context, cash flow components (CFC) were used in a probit or logit model to classify and predict financial failure. However, many studies found that net operating cash flows, operating inflows minus operating outflows, are not statistically significant predictors of corporate bankruptcy.

Another important dimension of cash management is the investment of excess cash or short-term borrowing to cover a cash flow shortfall. There are numerous new products available for short-run investment, such as auction rate preferreds or Eurodollar certificates of deposits. (See Chapter A3 in the *Handbook of Modern Finance* and Chapter 3 of the *Handbook of Financial Markets* for a discussion of the money markets.) Another interesting investment opportunity is hedged dividend capture strategies. (See Brown and Lummer (1984), Zivney and Alderson (1986), and Joehnk, Bowlin, and Petty (1980).)

3.03 CASH FLOW MEASURES

[1] Cash Flow Model

One of the most useful financial tools for analyzing the performance of management is the statement of cash flows. The cash flow model integrates accounting information from the balance sheet and the income statement and provides a unique interpretation of the allocation of a firm's resources. The cash flow statement is a basic financial analysis tool for management that integrates the sources and uses of funds from the balance sheet with the inflow and outflow of funds from the income statement. Because the balance sheet reflects the measurement of assets and liabilities at a single point in time, to calculate the change in the movement of cash it is necessary to measure the change between periods. A use of cash arises when there is an increase in an asset or a decrease in a liability. A source of cash occurs when a liability is increased or an asset is decreased. These changes reflect the accounting movement of funds during the period being analyzed.

The cash flow statement has 13 major components that provide diagnostic information for analyzing chronological movement of cash inflows and outflows. Additionally, the cash flow statement provides a tool for evaluating management strategies and policies related to the allocation of resources; it also introduces an integrated financial statement that provides information for measuring and judging the overall effectiveness of management.

Gentry, Newbold, and Whitford (1985, 1990) restructured and refined the Helfert (1982) funds flow analysis statement into an integrated financial statement with 12 major CFCs. The cash flow statement is based on information from the income statement and changes in balance sheet items between 2 periods and provides cash flow information for measuring and judging the overall effectiveness of management. Recent

FIGURE 3-4

Income Statement for Year _t_

Net sales	$2,000
Cost of goods sold	(500)
SG&A expenses	(100)
Depreciation expense	(320)
Earnings before interest and taxes	$1,080
Interest income	20
Interest expense	(180)
Earnings before taxes	$ 920
Taxes	(200)
Net income	$ 720
Dividends	(300)
Transfer to retained earnings	$ 420

Note: Dollars in millions.

revisions to the total cash flow system added interest income. Thus, the current version of the cash flow model has 13 CFCs.

An example illustrates how to develop a cash flow statement and to calculate each of the CFCs. The income statement and balance sheet that provide the basic information used to create the cash flow statement are found in Figures 3-4 and 3-5, respectively. The development of a cash flow statement is found in Figure 3-6.

Figure 3-6 shows that the primary operating inflow is the $2,000 in sales. The three basic components of operating outflow are cost of sales ($500), selling, general, and administrative (SG&A) expenses ($100) and income taxes ($200). The source of the sales information as well as the cost of sales, SG&A expenses, and income tax expenses are found in Figure 3-4. The net operating cash flow (NOF) of $1,200 is the difference between operating inflow and operating outflow ($2,000 minus $800 equals $1,200).

The next step is to use the balance sheet information to determine the amount of cash outflow going to each working capital component and, alternatively, the cash inflow coming from the working capital components. Conceptually, an increase in accounts receivable (ΔAR), inventories (ΔINV) or other current assets (ΔOCA) is a cash outflow. A reduction in accounts payable (ΔAP) or other current liabilities (ΔOCL) also represents a cash outflow. Alternatively, a reduction in any of the current assets would be a source of cash or an inflow of cash, as would an increase in any current liability.

Figure 3-6 shows two of the current assets increasing, thereby using cash. Specifically, $440 million is used to support an increase in accounts receivable, and $360 million in cash is used to increase inventories. The cash inflows used to support the $800 million increase in current assets comes from a $20 million decrease in other current assets, a $200 million increase in accounts payable, and a $100 million increase in other current liabilities. Thus, the cash outflow related to net working capital is $480 million (− $800 plus $340). Figure 3-6 shows that the cash flow surplus after working capital investment is $720 ($1,200 minus $480).

FIGURE 3-5

Balance Sheet for Years *t* and *t* − 1

	t	*t* − 1	Change Inflow	Change Outflow
Assets				
Cash	$ 340	$ 500	160	
Accounts receivable	1,440	1,000		(440)
Inventories	1,860	1,500		(360)
Other current assets	100	120	20	
Total current assets	$3,740	$3,120		
Property plant and equipment	$3,720	$3,000		
Accumulated depreciation	(1,320)	(1,000)		
Net fixed assets	$2,400	$2,000		(400)
Other assets	$ 100	$ 100		
Total assets	$6,240	$5,220		
Liabilities and Equity				
Short-term debt	$ 200	$ 200		
Accounts payable	1,200	1,000	200	
Other current liabilities	300	200	100	
Total current liabilities	$1,700	$1,400		
Other liabilities	$ 200	$ 240		(40)
Long-term debt	$ 640	$ 300	340	
Preferred stock	$ 100	$ 100		
Common stock	$1,000	$1,000		
Retained earnings	2,600	2,180	420	
Common equity	$3,620	$3,180		
Total liabilities and equity	$6,240	$5,220		

Note: Dollars in millions.

The net cash outflow going to net investment represents a firm's capital expenditures. The net investment flow equals the sum of the change in net fixed assets (ΔNFA) and the depreciation expense on the income statement. The change in net fixed assets represents any capital additions less any sale or losses from the disposition of fixed assets. The depreciation expense is added to the ΔNFA because it is assumed that the depreciation expense is actually reinvested in plant and equipment. The rationale for this assumption is that the firm is an ongoing concern and the amount established for depreciation is reinvested in plant and equipment so that the firm may remain an ongoing concern. Figure 3-6 shows that net investment is $720 million, consisting of $320 million of depreciation expense from Figure 3-4 and $400 million of ΔNFA from Figure 3-5. The cash flow surplus after total investment represents the amount of NOF that remains after subtracting the investment in working capital and capital expendi-

FIGURE 3-6

Cash Flow Measurement

Type of Cash Flow	Inputs		Example
Operating			
Inflows	Net sales		$2,000
Outflows	Cost of sales ($500) + SG&A expenses ($100) + taxes ($200)		(800)
= NOF	NOF		$1,200
Working Capital			
	Inflow	**Outflow**	
Δ accounts receivable (AR)		Δ AR	$ (440)
Δ inventory (INV)		Δ INV	(360)
Δ other current assets (OCA)	Δ OCA		20
Δ accounts payable (AP)	Δ AP		200
Δ other current liabilities (OCL)	Δ OCL		100
Δ net working capital			$ (480)
Cash flow surplus after working capital investment	= NOF + Δ AR + Δ INV + Δ OCA + Δ AP + Δ OCL		$ 720
Capital Investment			
Inflow	Decrease in NFA		0
− Outflow	Increase in NFA ($400) + depreciation expense ($320)		$ (720)
= Net investment	NIF		$ (720)
Cash flow surplus after total investment expenditures	= NOF + Δ AR + Δ INV − Δ OCA + Δ AP + Δ OCL + NIF		0
Interest income	II		$ 20
Fixed Coverage Expenditures	FCE = interest paid		(180)
Cash flow surplus or deficit available for dividends	= NOF + Δ AR + Δ INV + Δ OCA + Δ AP + Δ OCL + NIF + FCE		$ (160)
Dividends	DIV		(300)
Net cash flow surplus or deficit after major cash flows	NOF + Δ AR + Δ INV + Δ OCA + Δ AP + Δ OCL + NIF + FCE + DIV		$ (460)
Financial			
Inflows	Δ LTD ($340) + Δ STB + Δ CS		$ 340
− Outflows	Δ LTD + Δ STB + Δ CS		0
= Net financial	Δ NFF		$ 340

FIGURE 3-6 *(continued)*

Type of Cash Flow	Inputs	Example
Other Assets and Liabilities		
Inflows	ΔOA + ΔOL	0
– Outflows	ΔOA + ΔOL ($40)	$ (40)
= Net other assets and liabilities	ΔNOA&L	– 40
Net cash flow surplus or deficit after 11 cash flows		$ (160)
Change in cash (ΔCASH) = (ending cash + marketable securities) – (beginning cash + marketable securities)		160
Net cash flow after all flows		0

Note: Dollars in millions. LTD = long-term debt; STB = short-term borrowing; CS = common stock; OA = other assets; OL = other liabilities.

tures. Figure 3-6 indicates that the cash flow surplus after total investment is zero, i.e., $1,200 minus $480 minus $720. In summary, the firm has used all of its operating cash to finance the expansion of its working capital and to meet its capital investment needs.

Figure 3-6 shows that interest income provided $20 million of cash inflow. The $180 million in fixed coverage expenditures (interest expense) is subtracted from the $20 million cash flow surplus. Thus, the firm has a deficit cash flow available for paying dividends of – $160 million (i.e., $20 million plus – $180). The cash outflow for dividends is $300 million. The information for dividends and interest expense is found in Figure 3-4. The amount of operating cash flow and interest income that remains after deducting net working capital, net investment, dividends, and fixed coverage expenses is called the cash flow surplus or deficit after major cash flows. In the example, the cash flow deficit after major cash flows is – $460 million (i.e., in millions, $1,200 minus $480 minus $720 plus $20 minus $180 minus $300 equals – $460).

In this example, the remaining cash flow components are the changes in net financial flows (ΔNFF), net other assets and liabilities (ΔNOA&L) and change in cash (ΔCASH). Figure 3-5 shows that the firm raised $340 of long-term debt as in inflow of cash. Additionally, this figure reveals that there is a $40 million decrease in other liabilities that represents a use of cash or a cash outflow. Taking these two transactions into account results in a cash flow deficit after the 12 CFCs of $160 million. This means that the total cash outflow was $160 million greater than the total cash inflow.

How did the firm finance this $160 million shortfall? It is offset by reducing cash or marketable securities. That is, a decrease in an asset is considered an inflow or a source of cash. Thus, the cash flow surplus or deficit after all flows are taken into account is zero because the sum of the cash outflows must equal the sum of the cash inflows. The 13 CFCs developed in Figure 3-6 are summarized at the top of Figure 3-7. The total cash inflow equals $2.04 billion, and the total cash outflow is $2.04 billion.

[2] Relative Cash Flow

A relative CFC (CFC*) represents the percentage contribution of each component to the total cash flow. The CFC* are determined by dividing each component by the

FIGURE 3-7

Cash Flow Components

Cash Inflows		Cash Outflows	
Cash Flow Components in Dollars			
NOF	$1,200	Δ receivables	$(440)
Interest income (II)	20	Δ inventory (INV)	(360)
Δ other CA	20	Fixed coverage expenditures (FCE)	(180)
Δ payables	200	Net investment	(720)
Δ other CL	100	Dividends (DIV)	(300)
Δ net financial	340	Δ net other assets and liabilities (NOA&L)	(40)
Δ cash MS	160		
Total cash flow	$2,040	Total cash flow	$(2,040)

Cash Inflows	Percentage of Total Cash Flow	Cash Outflows	Percentage of Total Cash Outflow
Relative Cash Flow Components[a]			
NOF[b]	58.8	Δ receivables[b]	(21.6)
II	1.0	Δ INV[b]	(17.6)
Δ other CA[b]	1.0	FCE[b]	(8.8)
Δ payables[b]	9.8	Net investment[b]	(35.3)
Δ other CL[b]	4.9	DIV[b]	(14.7)
Δ net financial[b]	16.7	Δ NOA&L[b]	(2.0)
Δ cash MS[b]	7.8		
	100.0		(100.0)

Note: Dollars in millions.

[a] $\dfrac{\text{Cash flow component}}{|\text{total cash flow}|}$ = relative cash flow component.

[b] Indicates relative cash flow as opposed to actual cash flow.

---

total cash flow. That is, each component is divided by |$2,040|, the total cash flow. The CFC* are presented at the bottom of Figure 3-7. A brief overview of the major components shows the proportion each component contributes to the total cash flow. Figure 3-7 shows that 58.8 percent of the total inflow came from operations, 16.7 percent was from net financing, and 9.8 percent came from payables. On the outflow side, net investment represented 35.3 percent of the total outflow, receivables 21.6 percent, inventories 17.6 percent, and dividends 14.7 percent.

In Figure 3-6, the CFCs were arranged in a hierarchical order that reflected their economic importance in evaluating the financial health of a firm, which is what financial and credit analysts use to evaluate a firm's financial strengths and weaknesses. The CFC* hierarchical structure presented in Figure 3-6 highlights the contribution each component makes to the net cash flow surplus or deficit and the contribution of each CFC* to the overall performance of the firm. An example of the hierarchy of the CFC* and the relative net cash flow NCF* (the net surplus or deficit cash flow position) is presented in Figure 3-8. This example is based on research findings of Gentry, Newbold, and Whitford (1986).

FIGURE 3-8

Example of the Hierarchy of Relative Cash Flow Components Under Various Risk Conditions

Relative Cash Flow Components (CFC*)	Company			
	Lowest Credit Risk			Highest Credit Risk
	A	B	C	D
NOF*	91%	70%	55%	15%
ΔAR*	(9)	(15)	(22)	30
ΔINV*	(11)	(17)	(18)	25
ΔOCA*	(1)	(3)	1	10
ΔAP*	7	15	17	(43)
ΔOCL*	1	7	9	(25)
NIF*	(45)	(38)	(30)	(15)
Surplus or deficit after investment expenditures	33%	19%	12%	(3)%
II*	1	1	2	0
FCE*	(3)	(7)	(9)	(16)
Surplus or deficit available for dividends	31%	13%	5%	(19)%
DIV*	(12)	(13)	(15)	(1)
Surplus or deficit after major cash flows (NCF*)	19%	0	(10)%	(20)%
ΔNFF*	(9)	7%	11	19
ΔNOA&L*	0	0	(6)	1
ΔCASH and MS (ΔCASH*)	(10)	(7)	5	0
CFC* after all cash flows	0	0	0	0

By definition, Company A has the highest credit risk, which is based on the composition of the CFC*. Figure 3-8 shows that 91 percent of Company A's cash inflows originate from operations (NOF*), which is the highest NOF* among the four credit risk classes. After deducting from NOF* the major outflows for investment, NIF* (-45 percent), the highest among the four credit risk classes, and changes in net working capital (-13 percent), the remaining cash flow surplus represents 33 percent of the total. This is the highest surplus among the four credit risk classes. The two major outflows associated with the costs of external financial capital are interest expense (fixed coverage expenditures [FCE*]) and dividends (DIV*). After adding the interest income (II*) and deducting the FCE*, which is the lowest among the four credit risk classes, the surplus cash flow available for DIV* is 31 percent. DIV* consume 12 percent of total outflows, leaving a surplus after major flows of 19 percent. The surplus cash is used to retire debt (-9 percent) and invest in marketable securities (-10 percent).

In contrast, Company D is an example of a distressed company, and it is in the highest credit risk class. Company D has 15 percent of its cash inflow coming from operations, which is the lowest NOF* among the four risk classes. After deducting cash outflows of 18 percent for the total investment (NIF* being 15 percent) and a net reduction in working capital of 3 percent, Company D has a deficit cash flow equal to -3 percent of the total cash flow. The cash outflow to NIF* and net working capital is the smallest among the four credit risk classes. The FCE* represents 16 percent of the total outflow, which leaves -19 percent to pay DIV*. The interest payment for Company D is the largest among the four credit risk classes, and the deficit to pay FCE* is the largest. DIV* adds an additional 1 percent to total outflow, the lowest among the four groups. The -20 percent deficit after major cash flows shows that Company D has used all of its cash inflows plus an additional 20 percent of the total to cover the outflows for investment, dividends, and fixed coverage expenditures. Figure 3-8 shows that the deficit was offset by an increase in financing, ΔNFF equals 19 percent, and there is a decrease in net other assets and liabilities of 1 percent.

Figure 3-8 illustrates several basic concepts that exist between the net cash flow surplus or deficit and levels of risk. First, as the percentage of cash inflows from net operations declines, the surplus after investment and after major cash flows becomes smaller or the deficit becomes larger. Second, as the surplus cash after major flows declines or the deficit increases, a firm's financial risk increases. For example, Company A has the highest surplus after deducting for the major flows, and it has the lowest financial risk. In contrast, Company D has the largest deficit after investment and after major cash flows, and it has the highest financial risk. Third, as the NOF* decreases, the relative cash outflow to capital and working capital investment decreases. That is, the percentage of cash outflow going to investment is closely related to operating cash inflows. In turn, as the FCE* increases, the outflow for DIV* decreases. Furthermore, the trend of FCE* is negatively related to NOF* and NIF*. The pattern of the interrelationships among the key cash flow components is closely associated with the financial health of a firm.

3.04 CASH CONVERSION CYCLE

The concept of liquidity is closely associated with SRFM. Many researchers place special emphasis on the inverse relationship between liquidity and profitability. Gilmer used the CAPM to show there is an optimal liquidity level for companies in selected industries. Myers (1984) and Myers and Majluf (1984) indicate that financial slack is a critical ingredient in corporate finance, but they recognize that it is a complex phenomenon that is not well understood and needs further research. Brealey and Myers (1988) suggest that the broad question related to liquidity is, How should a firm divide its total investment between relatively liquid and relatively nonliquid assets? What is needed is a theory of liquidity. Lenders are concerned with the liquid nature of inventory and receivables in the event that net cash flow is insufficient to repay a loan. Likewise, financial failure is often associated with the lack of liquidity. These examples show that measuring liquidity and interpreting its effects on the value of the firm is a primary concern of SRFM. A brief overview of the development of the many facets of liquidity follows.

The characteristics of cash inflows and outflows, such as the level and speed of cash flow as well as its stability and patterns, are important components that should be included when designing a direct measure of liquidity. Financial statement information is widely used by external analysis to create an indirect measure of liquidity. A primary example of an indirect measure of liquidity is the CCC developed by Richards and Laughlin. The CCC is an additive measure based on the length of time that cash is tied up in the production, distribution, and collection processes less the time associated with the deferral of payment to suppliers. The shorter the CCC, the more liquid the firm.

FIGURE 3-9

Unadjusted Cash Conversion Cycle

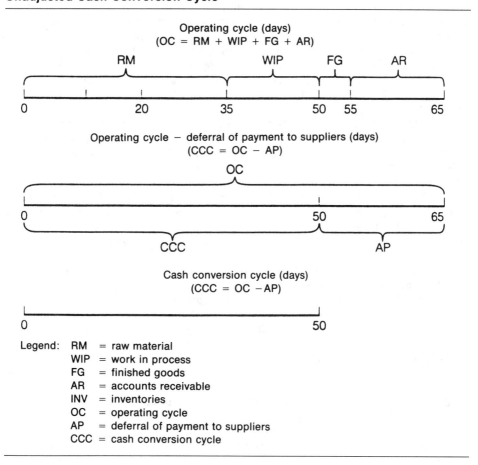

Legend: RM = raw material
         WIP = work in process
         FG = finished goods
         AR = accounts receivable
         INV = inventories
         OC = operating cycle
         AP = deferral of payment to suppliers
         CCC = cash conversion cycle

The CCC focuses only on the length of time funds are tied up in the cycle and does not take into consideration the amount of funds committed to a product as it moves through the operating cycle. A weighted cash conversion cycle (WCCC) combines the timing and the amount of funds tied up in the cycle. The WCCC determines a weight for the amount of funds committed to the production, distribution, and collection process and then combines each weight with the time component. The WCCC provides useful information for evaluating the performance of management and should be of interest to boards of directors, credit analysts, investors, and students of finance.

An overview of an unadjusted CCC is presented in Figure 3-9. The 55-day inventory cycle is decomposed into 35 days of funds committed to RM, 15 days to work in process (WIP) and 5 days to FG. Cash is not collected from receivables for another 10 days; therefore, adding the 10-day receivable cycle to the inventory cycle results in a 65-day operating cycle. However, payments to the suppliers do not occur until 15 days after the inventory is received. Subtracting the 15-day deferral in payment from the 65-day investment in inventories and receivables results in a CCC cycle of 50 days, the unadjusted CCC.

The concept underlying WCCC is developed in Figure 3-10. The area under the stairstep function that is shaded reflects the amount of funds committed to the production, distribution, and collection process. For comparative purposes, the area under the dotted line in both diagrams in Figure 3-10 approximates the unadjusted operating cycle (OC) and CCC. The white space below the dotted line and above the shaded region approximates the gap that exists between the unadjusted and weighted operating cycle. Figure 3-10 is based on information in Figure 3-9 that was used to calculate the 50-day CCC.

In the OC, shown at the top of the figure, there is a $5 million commitment to production distribution and collection for a 65-day period. The horizontal base in the figure shows that $1 million is committed to RM for 65 days. That is, funds are tied up in RM for 35 days before production actually starts. After production begins, these funds are committed for the remaining 30 days of the operating cycle. During the WIP phase, $2 million in funds were used for 15 days plus being committed for the remaining 15 days of the operating cycle. There is $0.5 million of funds committed for the 5-day FG phase, plus the remaining 10 days before cash is collected. AR represents $1.5 million due from customers in 10 days, which represents an opportunity cost to the firm.

Comparing the WCCC to the weighted OC in Figure 3-10 highlights the fact that the RM component is reduced by a 15-day payment deferral. It is assumed that the value of the AP is $1 million for 15 days. The figure highlights the time and amount components that are present in the WCCC. The WCCC graphic in the figure shows that the time component is 50 days, day 15 to 65, and the amount component is the gray area under the step function. The equations used to determine each component are in Gentry, Vaidyanathan, and Lee (1988).

The traditional liquidity measures, such as current or quick ratios, are one-dimension indicators and are located in the vicinity of corner 1 in Figure 3-1. On the other hand, a time series of monthly cash flow components combines several variables changing over time. The result is a comprehensive corner 7 information source that can be used to analyze liquidity trends. Daily cash inflows and outflows combined with qualitative information are superior financial slack measures that embody corner 8 characteristics, but these data are difficult for external analysts to acquire. Thus, the external analysts are forced to use indirect measures of liquidity combined with qualitative information as measures of liquidity.

3.05 MONITORING WORKING CAPITAL

[1] Monitoring Receivables

Monitoring the performance of receivables has received the greatest attention by researchers. Several authors have shown that changes in day's sales outstanding (DSO) in account receivables are caused by a change in sales. Therefore, DSO is not a reliable measure for explaining the cause of a change in receivables. That is, there is a negative relationship between a change in sales and a change in DSO.

Gentry and De La Garza (1985) found nine sets of conditions could be used to analyze changes in accounts receivable. Each of these nine conditions is appropriately

FIGURE 3-10

Weighted Cash Conversion Cycle

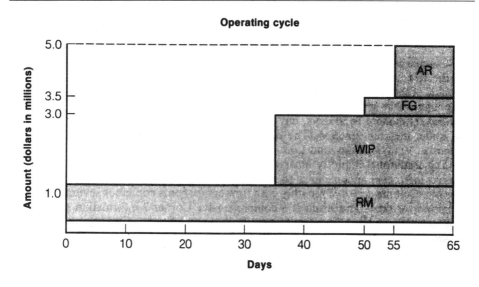

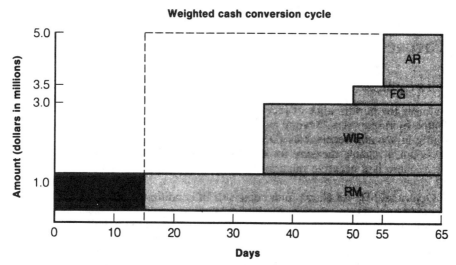

Legend:
RM = number of days $1 million committed to raw material
WIP = number of days additional $2 million committed to work in process
FG = number of days additional $0.5 million committed to finished goods
AR = number of days additional $1.5 million committed to accounts receivable
AP = number of days payments deferred to suppliers

FIGURE 3-11

Sets of Conditions Responsible for Changes in Receivables and Payables

	Sales or purchasing patterns		
	Up ($\uparrow$)	No change	Down ($\downarrow$)
Deteriorating ($\uparrow$) (CE) Lengthening ($\uparrow$) (PE)	4	2	6
No change	3	1	3′
Improving ($\downarrow$) (CE) Reducing ($\downarrow$) (PE)	7	2′	5

Collection experience (CE) or payment experience (PE)

identified and illustrated in Figure 3-11. The horizontal axis represents changes in receivables owing to changes in sales patterns. Changes in sales are in turn related to changes in the demand for a firm's products. The vertical axis reflects changes in receivables related to collection experience. These changes in collection experience are in turn related to changes in a firm's credit policies.

Changes in sales patterns refer to changes in the level of sales occurring on a month-to-month basis. The pattern and trend of sales can change because of seasonal, cyclical, or random forces. The collection experience reflects the payment behavior of a firm's customers and is related to a firm's credit policy actions. Collection experience is characterized by the fraction of credit sales in a month that remains outstanding at the end of each subsequent month. For example, if the collection pattern for March is 90-60-20, it means that 90 percent of March's sales are outstanding as receivables on March 31; 60 percent of February's sales are outstanding as receivables on March 31; and 20 percent of January's sales are outstanding on March 31.

An overview of the nine conditions shown in Figure 3-11 provides the logic underlying the revised algorithm found in Gentry and De La Garza. In condition 1, receivables do not change because there is no change in sales patterns or collection experience. Under condition 2, 100 percent of the change in receivables can be attributed to a change in collection experience. For example, receivables can increase because of lenient credit policies that result in a slowdown in customer payment patterns. Alternatively, receivables can decrease because of tightened credit policies that have no impact on sales.

Under condition 3, the opposite extreme from condition 2, 100 percent of the change in receivables stems from changes in demand for the firm's products. One case under condition 3 occurs when an increase in receivables is caused solely by an increase in sales. The other case occurs when a decrease in receivables is totally related to a decrease in sales. In condition 3, the increase or decrease in sales has not affected credit policy and collection behavior.

Condition 4 in the figure highlights the case where lenient credit policies are responsible for an increase in receivables. These policies have a spillover effect on sales, which contributes to the increase in receivables. At the same time, an increase in demand is also fundamentally responsible for an increase in sales. The demand generated by sales results in a subsequent increase in receivables, which may spill over and cause collection experience to deteriorate. An example of condition 4 is a credit card promotion that results in increased sales but also brings in new but slow-paying customers. In summary, when credit policies are lenient and sales are increasing, there are three effects responsible for a change in receivables: sales, collection, and joint.

In contrast to condition 4, there are stringent credit policies in condition 5. Tightened credit policies and procedures represent a two-edged sword that might result in lower receivables and also a reduction in sales. Simultaneously, a decline in demand is reflected in declining sales and subsequently lower receivables. The reduction in sales may also manifest itself in a tightening of credit policies. For example, if sales for a faddish product declined rapidly, the company could immediately stop extending credit and sell only for cash. A part of the decrease in receivables is caused by a joint interaction between sales and collection, because a portion of the sales decrease is related to restrictive credit policies. The interaction of improved collection patterns and declining sales creates a joint effect.

Under conditions 6 and 7, opposing forces moderate the change in receivables. Under condition 6, for example, credit policies are lenient, causing receivables to increase, but a decline in demand causes receivables to increase, and a decline in demand causes sales to decrease and receivables to decline. The size and direction of the change in receivables depends on whether the decline in demand has a greater effect than the lenient credit policy. Under condition 7, tightened credit policies result in improved collection experience and declining receivables, while increased demand causes sales and also receivables to increase. The size and direction of the change in receivables depend on whether the increase in demand is more prominent than tightened credit policy. In summary, from a sales and credit manager's perspective, condition 7 is the most preferred outcome of the seven scenarios in Figure 3-11, and condition 6 is the least attractive outcome of the scenarios.

Customer payment behavior is crucial in explaining changes in accounts receivable. The standard textbook example assumes that collection patterns are stable in the preparation of a cash budget. Kallberg and Saunders (1983) tested the stability of the payment behavior of retail customers and found that when economic conditions worsen, customers accelerate their payments in order to preserve their financial credibility with the retailers. Although untested, discovering if the payment behavior of corporate industrial customers is stable during a recession will be a significant contribution to the credit literature. Finally, evaluating the effect that changes in credit policy have on the level and flow of accounts receivable is a valuable research area in corporate finance.

Why do nonfinancial firms extend credit to their customers, and how do they establish the terms of sale? Bierman and Hausman (1970) offer a set of credit granting models that quantify the expected value of future credit extension opportunities. Bierman and Hausman capture an important dimension concerning why firms extend credit. Credit scoring models discriminate between good and bad credit risks and generate weights for various characteristics of the credit applicant. The total weighted score is used to estimate creditworthiness, which provides a foundation for establishing credit terms. Schwartz (1974) concluded that a seller with easy access to capital markets may benefit by extending trade credit to customers that do not have easy access to capital. Lewellen, McConnell, and Scott (1980) showed that trade credit cannot be used to increase firm value when financial markets are perfect. Under these circumstances, all acceptable credit terms to sellers and buyers are the present value equivalent of cash terms. They did indicate that imperfections in the financial markets may exist that would explain the presence of accounts receivable.

Emery (1984) focused on several financial market imperfections to explain why firms extend trade credit and how they establish the terms of sale, i.e., a pure financial explanation, a pure operating flexibility motive, and a pure financial intermediary motive. Emery showed that a trade credit lender is familiar with the payment behavior of its customers and can economize on lending transaction costs when extending trade credit. Additionally, the trade credit lender has an advantage over financial intermediaries related to collection costs. Finally, Emery showed that there are increasing opportunity costs to the firm for not extending trade credit and that there are financial market imperfections in the extension of trade credit. These factors establish the limits on credit policy and provide the rationale for extending trade. Based on the preceding assumptions, Emery derived an optimal level of accounts receivable for the firm.[1]

Mian and Smith (1987) analyzed the implications of the choice of accounts receivable financing policy, which ranged from internal management to subcontracted financing through a factor. Specifically, Mian and Smith showed that there were several financing alternatives. They included general corporate credit; establishing a captive finance subsidiary; financing through accounts receivable secured debt; using a credit reporting agency, credit collection agency, or credit insurance company; and using a factoring agent. They found that larger, more creditworthy firms established captive finance companies, while the smaller, riskier firms issued debt secured by accounts receivable.

[2] Monitoring Inventories

The literature related to inventory control is voluminous. In general, the inventory literature is found not in finance-related journals but rather in three separate areas. Topics related to inventory valuation are in the accounting-related journals. Inventory planning and control models are in the management science literature, while the effect that inventories have on the aggregate economy is found in the economics literature. From a financial perspective, Hall's concept of a stockless production strategy not only stands in sharp contrast to the traditional view of an optimal level of inventory

---

[1] In another article, Emery discusses the four incentives for trade credit. The incentives are financial, operating, contracting cost, and pricing motives. The theories described provided explanations concerning why and when nonfinancial firms lend money to their customers. Emery develops a positive theory of trade credit based on its use as a financial response to deterministic variations in demand. The operating alternatives to demand are modeled using results from the peak-load pricing literature.

but has profound implications for cash flow performance. Stockless production reduces WIP inventory and space needed for production, plus eliminating problems related to quality, production bottlenecks, coordination, obsolescence, shrinkage, and supplier unreliability. The financial benefit of stockless production is an increase in profitability, liquidity, and reduction in financial leverage. Likewise, the growth of global competition has changed the competitive environment and created a revolution in manufacturing operations. Johnson and Kaplan point out that the revolution was led by new practices emphasizing total quality control, just-in-time inventory systems, and computer-integrated manufacturing systems. The result is a change in inventory systems that has a direct effect on financial performance. Johnson and Kaplan emphasize that the challenge for today's environment is to develop new and more flexible approaches to the design of effective cost accounting, management control, and performance measurement systems. The development of these systems highlights the contribution that SRFM makes to the total value of the firm.

Gentry, De La Garza, Newbold, and Whitford (1992) have developed an approach to assess inventory performance by determining if production costs and inventory practices are contributing to the creation of shareholder wealth. Their model provides management with a tool for interpreting the two basic factors that cause inventories to change: trends of production costs and inventory control. They present a segmented hierarchy of inventory performance results that shows that the joint performance of production costs and inventory control can range from creating to reducing shareholder value. The underlying algorithms are developed and can be used to measure the effects that production costs, inventory control, and their joint interaction have in causing inventories to change. An empirical study shows that approximately one half of the sample industrial companies had an inflation-adjusted inventory performance that had the potential of adding value to the firm in both recessionary and nonrecessionary periods.

[3] Monitoring Payables

Gentry and De La Garza identified nine sets of conditions that were needed in order to analyze changes in accounts payable. These conditions were conceptualized in a three-by-three matrix in Figure 3-11 and are based on the trend of purchasing patterns and payment experience (CE). The horizontal axis represents changes in payables due to changes in purchasing patterns. Changes in purchases are in turn related to changes in a firm's demand for a supplier's products. The vertical axis reflects changes in payables related to the firm's payment experience. These changes in payment experience are in turn related to changes in the supplier's credit policies or the firm's own internal payment policies.

Changes in the purchasing patterns refer to changes in the level of purchases occurring on a month-to-month basis. The pattern and trend of purchases can change because of seasonal, cyclical, or random events. The firm's payment experience reflects its relationship with the supplier, the credit terms, and the collection behavior of the supplier. Payment experience is characterized by the fraction of credit purchases in a month that remain outstanding at the end of a subsequent month. For example, if the payment pattern for December is 80-25-5, 80 percent of December's purchases are outstanding as payables on December 31, 25 percent of November's purchases are outstanding as payables on December 31, and 5 percent of October's purchases are outstanding on December 31.

An overview of the nine conditions shown in Figure 3-11 provides the logic for the payable's algorithm. In condition 1, payables do not change because there is no change in the purchasing patterns or the payment experience. Under condition 2, 100 percent of the change in payables is associated with a change in payment experience. For example, payables can increase because of lenient collection practices of suppliers or because the firm stretches payments beyond the due date to its suppliers. Condition 2 is a lengthening of the payment pattern that creates value because the firm is able to finance its operations with supplier trade credit without any explicit cost for the use of the funds. This extension has no effect on purchases. Alternatively, under condition 2′, payables can decrease because suppliers tighten their collection practices or a firm pays before the due date. The result is a reduction in a firm's payment experience that has a cost and affects value because full use was not made of the credit period. This reduction has no effect on the firm's purchasing patterns.

Condition 3 is the opposite of condition 2, where 100 percent of the change in payables can be attributed to a change in the demand for goods from suppliers. Condition 3 reflects an increase in payables caused by an increase in purchases. Under condition 3′, there is a decrease in payables that is associated solely with a decrease in purchases. In condition 3 or condition 3′, the increase or decrease in payables did not affect supplier credit terms and collection behavior.

Condition 4 depicts the case where payables increase because of lenient collection practices by suppliers or the firm receiving credit stretches on its payments. These practices have a spillover effect on purchases that, in turn, is responsible for an increase in payables. Simultaneously, an increase in the demand for supplier goods contributes to an increase in purchases. The demand for additional supplier goods results in a further increase in payables, which can spill over and cause a further relaxation in collection practices by suppliers or a stretching of the firm's payments, i.e., a lengthening in payment experience. In summary, an increase in payables can be a combination of a pure purchasing effect, a pure payment effect, and a joint interaction effect between purchases and payment. Under condition 4, both the purchasing pattern effect and the payment experience effect are so positioned as to cause payables to increase. An example of condition 4 is a manufacturer that experiences an increase in demand and in turn increases its purchases from the supplier. The supplier responds by relaxing collection practices because of increased business and allows the manufacturer to delay payment for the goods. Or a supplier relaxes its collection policies, which encourages a manufacturer to increase the size and frequency of its orders for goods. The result of these two examples is an increase in payables attributable to three factors: purchasing, payment, and joint.

The circumstances under condition 5 are opposite to those in condition 4. A tightening of collection procedures by a single dominant supplier may result in the manufacturing firm's having to accelerate its payments for the goods received. At the same time, the firm may reduce its purchases from the supplier because of the shortened credit period or it may either substitute a lower-cost product or reduce the need for the supplier's product. Because both payment experience and purchasing patterns are positioned to cause payables to decline, a segment of the decrease in payables is caused by a joint interaction between payment experience and purchases. The interaction of more rapid payment and declining purchases creates a joint effect. Thus, under conditions of tightened credit practices from a supplier, payables decline because of a reduction in payment experience, a reduction in purchases, and a joint effect.

Under conditions 6 and 7, opposite forces are interacting that create a moderating influence. Under condition 6, purchases are down because of a decline in sales that results in lower payables, but lenient collection practices by the supplier cause payables to decline less rapidly than purchases or possibly to increase. These are opposing interaction effects between the two forces. The size and direction of the change in the payables is dependent on whether the decline in purchases has a greater effect than the lengthened payment experience. Under condition 7, tightened credit practices result in lower payables, but increased demand causes purchases to increase. As in condition 6, there are opposing interaction effects, with the payment experience causing the change in payables to increase less rapidly than the purchases, or possibly to decline. The size and direction of the change in payables depends on whether the increase in purchases is more prominent than the influence of the tightened collection practices of the supplier. In summary, from the perspective of the accounts payable manager and taking into account the purchase, payment, and joint effects, condition 4 is the most attractive outcome of the seven scenarios in Figure 3-11 and condition 5 is the least preferred outcome.

[4] Ranking Performance

One of the best uses of monitoring models is ranking the operating performance of payables and receivables management. The models provide a tool to analyze the performance of payables and receivables management and thereby determine the effectiveness of the operating strategies pursued by a company. The algorithms calculate the contribution of each component and thereby identify the causes of the changes in payables and receivables.

An objective of top management is to analyze and judge the performance record of payables and receivables management. Figure 3-12 is an extension of the original matrix in Figure 3-11 and shows graphically that changes in accounts payable (ΔAP) are caused by changes in purchases (ΔP) and payment experience (ΔPE) and that changes in accounts receivable (ΔAR) are related to changes in sales (ΔS) and changes in collection experience (ΔCE). Figure 3-11 provides a valuable operating framework for financial managers, analysts, and academic researchers to identify quickly the sets of conditions and variables responsible for changing the cash convertibility trend of AP and AR. Using the present value model as a benchmark, Figure 3-12 highlights the location of the best and worst sets of conditions for creating or destroying firm value through payment or collection strategies. The ranking methodology is based on the principle of creating present value.

The best strategy for receivables management is to speed up the inflow of cash. That would occur when the rate of change in receivables is below the rate of change in sales. The receivable management strategies that would speed up the inflow of cash are strategies 7, 2′, and 5 in Figure 3-12. A summary of the rankings and the underlying rationale related to sales and collection performance are presented in Figure 3-13. The worst strategy for receivable management is to slow down the inflow of cash. That occurs when the rate of change in receivables is greater than the rate of change in sales. These worst receivable management strategies are in cells 4, 2, and 6, as shown in Figures 3-12 and 3-13. Finally, strategies 3, 1, and 3′ reflect a neutral receivables strategy where the change in receivables is equal to the change in sales.

The best present values for payables management occur when there is a slowdown in the outflow of cash. Such an event happens when the rate of change in payables is greater than the rate of change in purchases, which is strategies 4, 2, and 6 in Figure 3-12. A summary of the rankings and the underlying rationale related to purchase and

FIGURE 3-12

Examples of Relationships That Cause Changes in Payments and Receivables

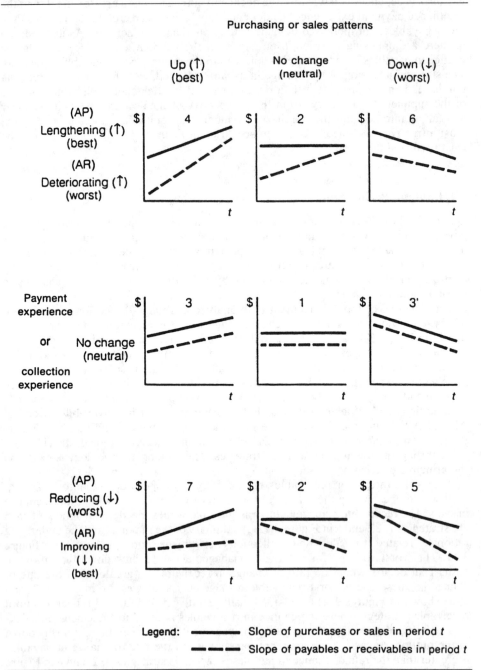

Legend: ———— Slope of purchases or sales in period *t*
        – – – – Slope of payables or receivables in period *t*

FIGURE 3-13

Ranking of Payables and Receivables Performance

	Payables			Receivables		
Rank	Cell in Figure 3-11	Purchase Performance	Payment Performance	Cell in Figure 3-11	Sales Performance	Collection Performance
1	4	Best	Best	7	Best	Best
2	2	Neutral	Best	2'	Neutral	Best
3	6	Worst	Best	5	Worst	Best
4	3	Best	Neutral	3	Best	Neutral
5	1	Neutral	Neutral	1	Neutral	Neutral
6	3'	Worst	Neutral	3'	Worst	Neutral
7	7	Best	Worst	4	Best	Worst
8	2'	Neutral	Worst	2	Neutral	Worst
9	5	Worst	Worst	6	Worst	Worst

payment performance are presented in Figure 3-13. Likewise, the worst strategy for payables management happens when there is a speedup in the outflow of cash. Figures 3-12 and 3-13 show that the worst strategies are 7, 2', and 5. Finally, strategies 3, 1, and 3' are neutral because the change in payables is equal to the change in purchases.

The performance-ranking system can be used by top management to accomplish several important tasks. First, if top management observed that either payables or receivables management were in the worst-ranking performance cells, credit policies and collection or payment procedures could be designed to either speed up the inflow of cash, causing receivables to become a smaller proportion of sales, or slow down the outflow of cash, causing payables to decrease in relation to purchases.

Second, if the synchronization of cash inflows and outflows is an important goal, management would select the best possible joint strategy for managing receivables and payables. The best synchronization would occur when the rate of cash inflow is greater than the rate of cash outflow. When sales and purchases are increasing, Figure 3-13 shows that the best strategy for the synchronization of cash flow would be cell 7 for receivables and cell 4 for payables. When sales and purchases are relatively flat, the best joint strategies for synchronizing inflows and outflows would be 2' for receivables and 2 for payables. Finally, under conditions of declining sales, the best joint strategies for the synchronization of flows would be 5 for receivables and 6 for payables. If top management observes that receivable or payable performance is not achieving the best possible joint strategy, appropriate credit terms and allocation or payment changes should be used to cause the performance to reflect the desired joint strategy.

Third, top management may wish to create a hierarchy of rewards if the performance record is deserving and creates shareholder value. For example, Figure 3-13 shows that the highest award would occur when the performance achieved is consistently at the highest level over time, which would be in cell 4 in Figure 3-12 for payables management and cell 7 for receivables management. The second-highest award would be for performance achievement that is consistently in the top three strategies over time, which would be cells 4, 2, and 6 for payables management and cells 7, 2', and 5 for receivables, as reflected in Figure 3-13.

The best way to rank the performance of payables and receivables management involves determining the length of time required to disburse cash to suppliers and collect cash from customers. Modern accounting and cash management systems can provide daily updated information on cash disbursements to each supplier and cash receipts from each customer. These data make it possible to create frequency distributions of payment patterns to suppliers and collection patterns for each customer. With these individual payment and collection pattern data, an aggregate frequency distribution can be calculated for each group. By comparing the time series trend of payment pattern data with the trend of the purchases data in period t, the strategy employed in managing payables can be determined. Comparable information related to collection patterns and sales makes it possible to determine accurately the strategy being followed in managing receivables. Internal analysts can use the proposed approach in evaluating the performance of payable and receivable management. External analysts, however, would usually not have access to the necessary information to calculate the payment and collection pattern and could not use the proposed approach. A separate approach, therefore, is presented to meet the needs of the external analyst.

As indicated in Figure 3-14, having a trend measure of purchases, payables, sales, and receivables makes it possible to determine the strategies being followed in managing payables and receivables. A recent ARIMA model by Box, Pierce, and Newbold (1987) makes it possible to use time-series data to estimate a trend of the desired variables. Quarterly information from Compustat files can be used in the Box, Pierce, and Newbold ARIMA model to estimate a trend for sales and receivables. The estimated trend of sales and receivables is used to determine the performance of receivables management. The model is extremely valuable, because it makes possible the use of quarterly time series data as opposed to using annual data. The model assigns higher weights to the more recent observation and, most importantly, takes into account seasonal effects.

The performance ranking of payables and receivables can also be obtained by calculating the growth rate of purchases, if data are available, and payables in period t and the growth rate of sales and receivables for the same time period. With the calculated growth rates, the strategy used to manage payables and receivables can be determined. Management can use this performance information to make necessary adjustments to strategies used in managing payables and receivables.

3.06 WORKING CAPITAL CONTROL

Accounts receivable, accounts payable, and inventories are the three basic working capital components. The decision to invest in capital equipment also requires an investment in accounts receivable and inventories in order for the capital investment to be operational. Thus, the investment in working capital is directly linked to the process of creating shareholder wealth. Likewise, payables provide a valuable source of financing for a firm's inventory purchases and, as such, are also linked to the process of creating shareholder wealth.

In a present value context, an increase in accounts receivables and/or inventories is an investment decision. The accounts payable offset a portion of the investment in working capital assets. Because the working capital assets are an integral part of the value creation process and can consume large quantities of cash, it is important to identify the forces that cause each working capital component to change. The objective of this discussion is to present the fundamental variables that cause accounts receivable, accounts payable, and inventories to change and to suggest how these variables affect the values of a firm.

The basic reasons for changes in accounts receivable relate to sales behavior, collection, and interaction. The increase or decrease in accounts receivable can be directly linked to an increase or decrease in sales. Also, a change in receivables is directly associated with a collection effort; that is, a substantive collection effort can cause a decline in the rate of increase in accounts receivable, or the lack of collection effort can cause an acceleration in the rate of increase in accounts payable. Mathematically, there is an interaction effect between the sales behavior effect and the collection effect.

Gentry and De La Garza (1985) have shown in a three-by-three matrix that there are nine possible outcomes associated with the factors that cause accounts receivable as shown in Figure 3-11. These outcomes include various combinations of changes in sales or purchases and changes in collection experience or payment patterns. They also show that to control the change in accounts receivable adequately, management must focus on measuring the effect of sales behavior and collection efforts on accounts receivable rather than relying on an aging schedule or an average collection period (ACP) measure to correctly identify the cause of the change in receivables. Many analysts have shown that the aging schedule and the ACP measure are directly tied to sales behavior and are not good tools for controlling accounts receivable. Understanding the collection behavior of the customer in conjunction with the trend of sales is the key to controlling accounts receivable.

In companion studies, Gentry and De La Garza (1990) and Gentry, De La Garza, Newbold, and Whitford (1992) have determined that changes in accounts payable are associated with purchasing, payment, and interaction effects, while changes in inventories are related to production, inventory control, and interaction effects. A three-by-three matrix shows that there are nine possible outcomes associated with the variables that cause accounts payable or inventories to change. Again, the outcomes have to do with various combinations of inventory usage and payment pattern. To adequately control the changes in accounts payable, management must focus on measuring the purchasing and payment effects. To monitor inventory changes, management must measure production and inventory control efficiency. Payables turnover and inventory turnover are linked to sales and introduce a severe bias that undermines management's ability to control accounts payable and inventories.

A summary of the effects that cause working capital components to change is presented in Figure 3-14.

FIGURE 3-14

Causes of Change in Working Capital Components

Working Capital Variable	Factor That Causes Working Capital Variable to Change		
Receivables	Sales behavior	Collection	Interaction
Payables	Purchasing behavior	Payment	Interaction
Inventories	Production cost	Inventory control	Interaction

3.07 FORECASTING DAILY CASH RECEIPTS AND DISBURSEMENTS

Hoque, Gentry, and Newbold (1989) have developed a general statistical approach for forecasting daily cash receipts and disbursements. The approach is an extension of the daily cash forecasting modeling efforts of Stone (1972), Miller and Stone (1985), Stone and Miller (1981, 1983, 1985, 1987), and Stone and Wood (1977). In applying the general model to the daily cash receipts and disbursements of two Fortune 500 companies, Hoque, Gentry, and Newbold found a time-series structure, which is a predictable pattern over time, to be present in the data, thus making it possible to improve the forecasts of cash receipts and cash disbursements.

[1] General Daily Cash Forecasting Model

Regression modeling is useful in cash forecasting as long as the theoretical relationships specified reflect what actually happens. The specification of the relationship between the dependent variable (the variable to be forecast) and the independent variables (the variables used to do the forecasting) is crucial to achieving accurate cash prediction. Therefore, it is necessary to identify the true relationships among the components used in daily cash forecasting.

Stone and Wood (1977) follow the single equation approach. However, because cash management components are highly interrelated and often jointly determined, a theory based on a simultaneous equation approach is most desirable. Modeling these relationships requires mathematical sophistication. The relationships are not yet well understood and the models are not developed; therefore, analysts can only attempt to specify true relationships by focusing on one segment of the forecast process. The first step in a general daily cash forecasting model, which is modeling net cash receipts as a function of time, requires application of the Stone and Wood approach.

$$y_t = \beta_1 x_{1t} + \beta_2 x_{2t} + \cdots + \epsilon_t \qquad (3.1)$$

where:

y_t = cash receipts or disbursements

x_{1t} = dummy variables for days of the week, days of the month, and holiday effects

ϵ_t = error term

Stone and Miller observe that the specification in Equation 3.1 can be improved by using a multiplicative form, i.e., allowing each variable to be multiplied by each other variable. The benefit of a multiplicative specification must be weighed against the costs of modeling effort and loss of data.

The next step in the general daily cash forecasting model is to analyze the error term in Equation 3.1 by using the ARIMA procedure. This procedure uses current values of variables to forecast the future values of the variables. Because the error term in a regression is considered to be unexplained information, the analyst must try to reduce the unexplained portion by increasing the portion of the variation of the predicted variable, as shown by Stone and Miller. In the generalized approach, the objective is to reduce the unexplained variance by expounding solid theoretical relationships and identifying a specification of the model through analysis of residuals in a time-series framework. If the error term exhibits a pattern that is related to time, the modeling in the first step is incomplete. Otherwise, the first step is adequate.

The time-series pattern can be characterized according to three models: autoregressive (AR), moving average (MA), and autoregressive moving average (ARMA). The AR model assumes that the current residual observation ϵ_t is a linear combination of the past p observations (ϵ_{t-p}) on the variable plus a random term. The following equation represents an AR structure:

$$\epsilon_t = \phi_1 \epsilon_{t-1} + \phi_2 \epsilon_{t-2} + \cdots + \phi_p \epsilon_{t-p} + e_t \tag{3.2}$$

> *where:*
>> ϕ_i's = AR coefficients to be estimated
>> ϵ_{t-i}'s = p observations of the time series for the residuals
>> e_t = random disturbance

The MA model represents the current observation as a linear combination of the past random disturbances plus a random term.

$$\epsilon_t = -\theta_1 e_{t-1} - \theta_2 e_{t-2} - \cdots - \theta_q e_{t-q} + e_t \tag{3.3}$$

> *where:*
>> θ_i's = MA coefficients to be estimated
>> e_t's = random disturbances

A generalization of the AR(p) and MA (p) models that includes both AR(p) and MA(q) models as special cases is the mixed ARMA(p, q) model:

$$\epsilon_t = \phi_1 \epsilon_{t-1} + \phi_2 \epsilon_{t-2} + \cdots + \phi_p \epsilon_{t-p} - \theta_1 e_{t-1} \tag{3.4}$$
$$-\theta_2 e_{t-2} - \cdots - \theta_q e_{t-q} + e_t$$

For the ARMA(4, 4) case, the estimated relationship is

$$\epsilon_t = \phi_1 \epsilon_{t-1} + \phi_1 \epsilon_{t-2} + \phi_3 \epsilon_{t-3} + \phi_4 \epsilon_{t-4} - \theta_1 \epsilon_{t-1} \tag{3.5}$$
$$-\theta_2 e_{t-2} - \theta_3 e_{t-3} - \theta_4 e_{t-4} + e_t$$

Focusing on a pure AR process in Equation 3.2 allows illustration of the general model.

If Equation 3.2 can be identified as statistically complete, it can be inferred that Equation 3.1 is an incomplete specification; thus, in determining the final forecast, the estimates of Equation 3.2 must be substituted into Equation 3.1. On the other hand, if no such time-series relationship can be identified, the inference is that the specification in Equation 3.1 is robust enough to generate an adequate forecast. Thus, Stone and Wood's distribution approach to cash forecasting is a special case of the general approach.

Assuming that Equation 3.2 is identified, the next step is to estimate it and obtain Equation 3.6.

$$\hat{\epsilon}_i = \hat{\phi}_0 + \hat{\phi}_1 \epsilon_{t-1} + \hat{\phi}_2 \epsilon_{t-2} + \cdots + \hat{\phi}_p \epsilon_{t-p} + \hat{\epsilon}_t \tag{3.6}$$

> *where:*
>> ^ represents estimates

Finally, Equation 3.6 is substituted into Equation 3.1 to obtain

$$y_t = \hat{\alpha} + \hat{\beta}_1 x_{1t} + \hat{\beta}_2 x_{2t} + \cdots + \hat{\beta}_n x_{nt} + \hat{\epsilon}_t \tag{3.7}$$

Our forecast then would be $\hat{y}_{t+h}$ corresponding to $\hat{\epsilon}_{t+h}$, where h is the number of periods in the future to be forecast.

In summary, the general approach to forecasting cash receipts or disbursements includes the following steps:

1. Specify and regress the cash flow component on various explanatory variables including dummy variables.

2. Identify the time-series component of the residual term.

3. Estimate, if necessary, these time-series patterns and relationships.

4. If step 3 is necessary and an appropriate ARIMA structure can be selected, use the ARIMA information with the step 1 result to determine the final forecast. If step 3 is unnecessary or no time-series structure can be found by conventional model selection criteria, use the step 1 result to determine a final forecast.

[2] Empirical Tests

Daily cash receipts and disbursements for two Fortune 500 companies were used to build and test the general daily cash forecasting model. The cash receipts and disbursements data used for Firm 1 covered a 47-month period, while the data for Firm 2 covered a 40-month period. The major predictable components of cash receipts and disbursements were removed from the data. After substantial testing and evaluation of the results and plots of the residuals, the analysts concluded that the modeling was adequate and statistically significant.

The comparison between the simple regression model, as in Equation 3.2, and the ARMA model produced mixed but promising results. There were 12 forecasts completed using the simple regression and ARMA models. Five (42 percent) of the ARMA forecasts showed an improvement over the forecast that used a simple regression of current net receipts against general explanatory variables. Four (33 percent) of the ARMA forecasts showed no change, and three (25 percent) were worse than the simple regression forecast. Therefore, on an overall basis the forecast was improved by using the ARMA model.

[3] Evaluation of the General Model

The Hoque, Gentry, and Newbold study provides a theory and an application of a model that combines regression and time-series techniques. The methodology enables users to determine analytically the adequacy of the regression approach. If the regression analysis is adequate, the cash forecast is efficient using only the regression results. In the study, the time-series structure of the residual data was found to be random for cash receipts and disbursements for both firms. Thus, the regression forecasts alone were not adequate, since the regression approach wasted information contained in the error structure. A cash flow forecast should use both techniques, even though the time-series model is statistically superior to the simple regression forecast. The combination of the two techniques eliminates individual limitations and uses the best features of each approach. The generalized methodology is thus a useful tool for ensuring an efficient cash forecast.

3.08 FUTURE DIRECTIONS

[1] Perspectives

Porter and Rappaport have developed insights that will motivate future research in the area of SRFM. Porter's competitive analysis model provides a solid anchor for designing and evaluating strategic plans. In concert, Porter's value chain and Rappaport's DCF information system show how value is created in a company and thereby make it possible to determine whether a chosen strategy will result in a company's achieving a competitive advantage. The shareholder value approach shows that SRFM decisions related to operating inflows, operating outflows, and working capital are major contributors to the value creation process. During the next decade, research that focuses on understanding the linkage between SRFM decisions and shareholder value creation will provide new discoveries, insights, and enlightenment.

[2] Valuation Models

Earlier, it was observed that the cash flow components that contribute directly to the value of the firm have been integrated into the DCF and the CAPM models. However, the CAPM is unable to capture the dynamics of the intertemporal changes that are pervasive among the SRFM cash flow components, and the DCF model does not provide a direct measure of the risk-return trade-off that is present in the CAPM. Ideally, what is needed is a valuation model that incorporates the nonlinear dynamics of the cash flow components, accommodates the simultaneous interaction effects among these components, and captures the risk-return trade-off perspective.

[3] Positive Research

In the future, it is likely that even more attention will be devoted to developing positive theories of working capital management. Many descriptive contributions have resulted from examining trade credit or cash management behavior under economic conditions of imperfect markets. One approach to a positive theory of why firms extend trade credit is that the firm extending credit has more information than the buyer of the product. This concept is referred to as information asymmetry and has provided unique insight in explaining the implications of trade credit behavior. Determining the bargaining power of the buyer and the seller provides a fruitful approach for explaining collection and payment behavior and the rationale for existing credit terms.

An undeveloped area in financial management is the management and control of inventory. One of the most critical problems facing management is predicting and controlling inventory when there are errors in forecasting the demand for a product. In turn, these forecasting errors create uncertainty in purchasing and production, which results in inefficiencies in managing inventories.

Kaplan observes that cost systems are designed to value inventory for financial and tax statements. He believes that these systems are not giving managers accurate and timely information needed to promote operating efficiencies and measure product cost. This is a critical issue facing management.

Examining decision making under conditions of uncertainty may provide a framework for enhancing understanding of collection and payment behavior. What causes risk and how firms can control the risks that are present in a credit-granting environment are chief issues. Additionally, credit is considered a market tool that directly affects the price of the product. Thus, the exploration of creating, controlling, or avoiding risk appears to be a productive approach to developing positive theories related to cash and credit management.

[4] Financial Slack

Liquidity has a unique value. According to Brealey and Myers (1988), determining the value of liquidity is one of the 10 unsolved problems in finance. They indicate liquidity is a matter of degree and the relevant strategic issue for management is "[the division of] its total investment between relatively liquid assets." There is no theory that explains how much cash a firm should hold or be able to acquire quickly without affecting its cost. In an anecdotal sense, liquidity is most appreciated during a financial crisis and it is not as important when financial stress is relatively low.

Research efforts by Miller and Stone (1992) and Sartoris, Gentry, and Whitford (1992) have focused on measuring financial slack and liquidity, respectively. Miller and Stone examine the business firm's need for financial slack resulting from cash flow uncertainty. They indicate that financial slack is liquidity held for precautionary and speculative purposes, but not for transaction purposes. Investigation of financial slack resulting from cash flow uncertainty requires analysis and modeling of the firm's cash flow management system. Miller and Stone assert that a model for the firm's cash flow management system must integrate cash concentration, disbursement funding, concentration balance control, and investment balance control. A model that integrates the components of the firm's cash flow management system can be used to determine the optimal amount of financial slack for the firm. In this model, financial slack is a buffer stock that protects the firm from the penalties associated with running out of cash and overdrawing accounts.

Sartoris, Gentry, and Whitford have focused on measuring the liquidity of companies. Traditionally, the current and quick ratios have been used to measure liquidity. However, new ways to measure the liquidity of a company are continually being suggested, and the lack of consensus about the best way to measure liquidity attests to the fact that liquidity, although an easy concept to grasp, is difficult to measure. Sartoris, Gentry, and Whitford examined the similarities and differences between several suggested measures. Since there is no definitive way to determine the true liquidity of a company, there is no direct way to determine if any one measure is more efficient than the others. Sartoris, Gentry, and Whitford use two external assessments of the short-term financial condition of the company (the commercial paper rating and the rate paid on short-term borrowing) as proxies for a market assessment of liquidity. A factor analysis of the liquidity measures examined discovered four separate dimensions of liquidity: the balance sheet dimension, the cash flow dimension, the cash conversion cycle dimension, and a measure of liquid resources relative to the uncertainty of cash flows. Emery's lambda is the strongest measure of the last dimension. Sartoris, Gentry, and Whitford plan to examine the relationship between net cash flow and excess return in the future.

A liquidity system measure should take into account the relative liquidity of each asset class, such as receivables, raw materials, finished goods, and the ability to access capital or money markets. Liquidity should be judged on a continuum, and each asset or source of funds rank should be ordered according to its liquidity characteristics. In addition, an analysis of daily cash inflow and outflow patterns provides separate components for a liquidity measure. The qualitative characteristics of a firm's assets, liabilities, and cash flows supply another component for a liquidity measure. Combining the qualitative and quantitative components would provide the information needed to create a comprehensive financial slack index. The development of a comprehensive financial slack index should lead to the evolution of a theory that integrates the dimension of liquidity into the value of the firm.

[5] Technology and Information Effects

Electronic technology has created a revolution in activities related to managing the inflows and outflows of cash and controlling inventories. There is little doubt that future growth and refinement of decision support systems and the management of information will result in changes in operating management achievements that are currently unimaginable. Corporate strategy will focus on using capital resources to improve the decision support systems and the management of information in order to gain a competitive advantage and improve operating performance. These decision support systems and the management of information are the centerpieces of short-run financial management research. Firm value is created through the building of these systems and, short-run financial management research is directly connected to the evolution of the information age. Technology and data bases discussed by Hill et al.[2] will be at the forefront of advances in short-run financial management research in the next decade. A natural relationship exists between SRFM and corporate strategic management that is based on the substantive contributions that operating cash flows make to firm value. In the future, there should be significant growth in research that explores the connection among financial information systems, financial management activities related to operations, and strategic management of the firm.

[6] Integrated Cash Management Systems

Cash management encompasses the collection and disbursement of cash and is a focal point for determining the variables that cause the value of a company to increase or decrease. The original computerized cash management systems provided a daily reporting of cash collected and disbursed. A second-generation integrated system provides information for management to determine whether changes in credit or disbursement policies produced the desired effect on cash flows; it allows management to develop a profile of customer payment behavior and monitor the stability of the profile; it provides information to develop a profile of disbursement behavior to suppliers and monitor the stability of the profile; and it uses the profile information to upgrade the quality of the inputs used in the cash budgeting process. A model of an integrated cash management system is presented in Figure 3-15.

The first-generation cash management systems are located on the left-hand side of the figure. The inflow feature uses lockboxes to collect cash, and the system reports and transfers the amount collected each day to the concentration bank. On the outflow side, the system records the dollar amount of checks presented each day to the disbursement bank. Management takes the inflow and outflow information and deter-

---

[2] See Hill, Ferguson, and Stone (1987).

FIGURE 3-15

Cash Management System

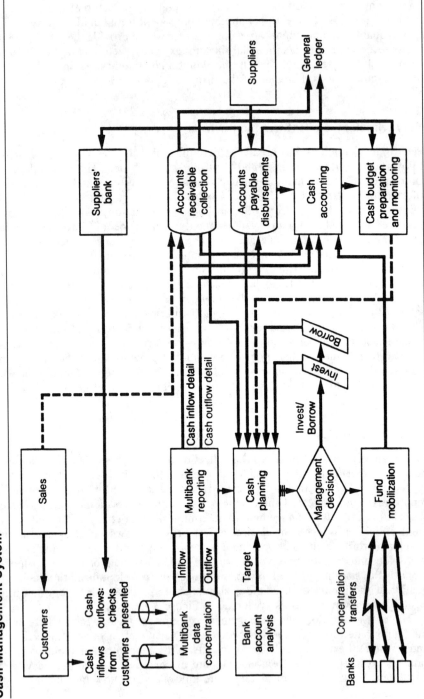

mines how much cash to invest or borrow each day. When the decision to invest or borrow is made, the necessary transfers are executed.

The integrated system would contain sales invoice information for each transaction and the time the cash receipt was received at the collection bank. By having this information for each customer in a product line, management can track the stability of the aggregate customer payment profile and evaluate the effectiveness of existing credit policies. Also, the system allows management to change credit policies and determine whether this results in a change in customer payment behavior. The system also allows management to track the payment behavior of delinquent or slow-paying customers, which could be used to initiate a delivery to that customer. The receivables segment of the system is located on the upper half of Figure 3-15. Similar profiles and information systems could be developed for tracking disbursement behavior performance.

The information profiles and the payment pattern results for each product line are a rich data source that should enhance the preparation of future cash budgets. The development of a cash management system that resembles Figure 3-15 would provide information to management that has not previously been available. Finally, it would provide a competitive advantage in the management of short-run financial variables.

[7] Daily Cash Information

Daily cash flow information is the cornerstone for building a deeper understanding of SRFM. Cash flow data files explicitly show the patterns of cash inflows and outflows, which are the foundation for determining what causes cash flow components to change and for analyzing the relationships over time among the inflow and outflow components. Although currently these cash flow data bases are not easily accessed, they are the ultimate information source for developing theoretical relationships and testing hypotheses related to SRFM. Perhaps in the future there will be an institutionalized cash flow data base equivalent to CRSP or Compustat. The availability of cash flow data bases will stimulate new research efforts and provide fresh insights into and new theoretical developments in SRFM.

In preparing cash budgets and in monitoring receivables and payables, a major problem is predicting the timing of cash inflows and outflows.[3] The timing of cash inflows and outflows is closely related to the payment behavior of a firm's customers and the disbursement behavior to its suppliers. Corporate software programs for managing and controlling receivables and payables make it possible to measure and evaluate the stability of customer payment behavior and the supplier disbursement patterns. The profiles of payment and disbursement patterns are affected by competitive factors in the industry and firm, as well as seasonal and random effects. The study of payment and disbursement behavior should lead to improved techniques and models for predicting cash inflows and outflows. A natural outgrowth of this research should be a better understanding of the relationship among customer payment behavior, disbursement behavior to suppliers, and a firm's value creation process.

Managing receivables and payables is a massive task for larger companies; therefore, a few firms are experimenting with new procedures related to purchases and payments. Where the customer and supplier have a well-established relationship and

---

[3] See, e.g., Bowen, Burgstahler, and Daley (1986); Emery (1981); Ferguson and Hill (1985).

the supplier has a record of delivering quality goods, the customer places an order with the supplier and simultaneously encloses payment without receiving an invoice. The result of this action is a substantive reduction in operating costs. In addition, some large corporations have changed to an electronic disbursement system for paying suppliers. These procedures could result in dramatic changes in cash receipt management. These and other changes in SRFM procedures can cause substantive changes in value.

Several new research developments could lead to a better understanding of the linkage between SRFM and the value creation process. As these linkages develop, SRFM will be naturally integrated into valuation models of the firm. The ultimate goal is the development of valuation models that incorporate key theoretical relationships among long-run and short-run variables.

[8] Expert Systems

Several SRFM activities are natural applications for expert systems, such as credit analysis and management, credit scoring, cash management coupled with short-term lending and borrowing decisions, management and control of inventories, and production planning and control. The information used in the knowledge-based system is frequently acquired through learning by being told. The system acquires its domain knowledge from experienced decision makers in the field, such as experienced credit or cash managers, and transforms the knowledge into the appropriate form.

Learning is an important feature of any intelligent system; therefore, more advanced artificial intelligence systems are equipped with a learning capability. The learning dimension comes into play when the system (1) learns decision rules from the knowledge base and (2) refines existing rules by observing prior problem-solving experience. Achieving these learning functions poses an important design issue related to the inductive inference techniques used in rule learning and knowledge acquisition.

The models developed for SRFM will employ production rules that represent basic knowledge of the system being created. The success of expert systems for SRFM will rest on the ability to structure the decision process being created and to design appropriate production rules that correctly represent the system being created. The economic payoff for creating expert systems is quite high in areas related to credit[4] and cash management and in production and inventory management. Within the next five years, the development of these expert systems will provide fresh insight and new perspectives related to SRFM.

[9] Risk Shifting

The need to shift risk by means of financial futures or options will experience substantial growth in the next decade. Emerging financial strategies create new financial contracts that shift a firm's risk exposure to the marketplace. The growth of the derivative securities market is closely related to SRFM and it provides a natural base for growth and development, such as financial futures and options and swaps. An interest rate

---

[4] See Shaw and Gentry (1988).

swap occurs when a company with one type of debt instrument agrees to swap interest payments with a firm that has issued a different type of debt instrument. Additionally, investment banking firms are creating new financial instruments to meet specialized corporate needs and extending the rate of return effects on the short-run portfolio. These new instruments are providing new sources of cash as well as opportunities to meet SRFM investment and borrowing needs. During the next decade, these new instruments will provide direction for future SRFM research.

There are a variety of changes occurring in the business environment that will significantly affect future developments related to SRFM. The globalization of markets introduces new control and management systems that directly change the inflow and outflow of cash, the allocation of costs, and the level of inventories, receivables, and payables. The long-run impact of financial and organizational restructuring is not understood, but it will introduce significant changes in SRFM. The need to devise short-run performance measures that are consistent with a firm's strategies and its product and process technologies will have a profound effect on the future directions of SRFM. The change to a statement of cash flows introduces a new measurement system that will significantly enhance the contributions of SRFM to the value creation process.

3.09 CONCLUSION

SRFM is closely related to the operating management of a firm and plays a key role in creating stockholder value. The theoretical linkage between cash flows generated from SRFM and strategic financial management decision making is well established. SRFM is associated with operations; hence, it does not possess the excitement of financial restructuring or the deal making related to a takeover. Nevertheless, the creation of net cash flows through SRFM decision making is how long-run value is created for stockholders.

Future research will focus on the creation of valuation models that incorporate the nonlinear dynamics of the cash flow components, accommodate the simultaneous interaction effects among the components, and capture the risk-return perspective. Liquidity is another area where future research will produce a comprehensive index that will measure financial slack. Furthermore, linking liquidity to valuation theory will be a substantive contribution to management. Corporate decision support systems and management of financial information form a new research centerpiece for SRFM. Daily or weekly cash flow data files will serve to enhance knowledge of the liquidity system. Expert system modeling, information technology expansion, risk shifting through derivative securities, globalization of markets, and devising short-run performance measures that are consistent with a firm's strategies, product, and process technologies provide the foundation for the future direction of SRFM research.

Financial research has not focused on SRFM behavioral dimensions that cause the creation or destruction of shareholder value, such as cash flow forecasting errors, customer payment patterns, supplier disbursement patterns, or inventory cost patterns. Behavioral research related to SRFM may grow rapidly in the future and provide an entirely new set of issues.

Suggested Reading

Beehler, P. *Contemporary Cash Management.* New York: Richard D. Irwin, 1983.

Benjamin, R.I., J.F. Rockart, M.S.S. Morton, and J. Wyman. "Information Technology: A Strategic Opportunity." *Sloan Management Review* (Spring 1984), pp. 3–10.

Beranek, W. *Analysis for Financial Decisions.* Homewood, Ill.: Richard D. Irwin, 1963.

Bierman, H., Jr., and W.H. Hausman. "The Credit Granting Decision." *Management Science,* Vol. 17 (Apr. 1970), pp. B519–B532.

Bowen, R.M., D. Burgstahler, and L.A. Daley. "Evidence on the Relationships Between Earnings and Various Measures of Cash Flow." *Accounting Review,* Vol. 66 (Oct. 1986), pp. 713–725.

Box, G.E.P., D.A. Pierce, and P. Newbold. "Estimating Trend and Growth Rates in Seasonal Time Series." *Journal of the American Statistical Association* (Mar. 1987), pp. 276–282.

Brealey, R., and S. Myers. *Principles of Corporate Finance,* 3d ed. New York: McGraw-Hill, 1988.

Brown, K.C., and S.L. Lummer. "The Cash Management Implications of a Hedged Dividend Capture Strategy." *Financial Management,* Vol. 13 (Winter 1984), pp. 7–17.

———. "A Reexamination of the Covered Call Option Strategy for Corporate Cash Management." *Financial Management,* Vol. 15 (Summer 1986), pp. 13–17.

Carpenter, M.D., and J.E. Miller. "A Reliable Framework for Monitoring Accounts Receivable." *Financial Management,* Vol. 8 (Winter 1979), pp. 37–40.

Casey, C.J., and N.J. Bartczak. "Cash Flow—It's Not the Bottom Line." *Harvard Business Review,* Vol. 62 (July/Aug. 1984), pp. 60–66.

———. "Operating Cash Flow Data and Financial Distress: Some Empirical Evidence." *Journal of Accounting Research,* Vol. 23 (Spring 1985), pp. 384–401.

Emery, G.W. "A Pure Financial Explanation for Trade Credit." *Journal of Financial and Quantitative and Financial Analysis,* Vol. 19 (Sept. 1984), pp. 271–285.

———. "Some Empirical Evidence on the Properties of Daily Cash Flow." *Financial Management,* Vol. 10 (Spring 1981), pp. 21–28.

Emery, G.W., and K.O. Cogger. "The Measurement of Liquidity." *Journal of Accounting Research,* Vol. 20 (Autumn 1982), pp. 290–303.

Ferguson, D.M., and N.C. Hill. "Cash Flow Timeline Management: The Next Frontier of Cash Management." *Journal of Cash Management,* Vol. 5 (May/June 1985), pp. 12–22.

Gallinger, G.W., and A.J. Ifflander. "Monitoring Accounts Receivable Using Variance Analysis." *Financial Management,* Vol. 15 (Winter 1986), pp. 69–76.

Gentry, J.A. "Integrating Working Capital and Capital Investment Processes," *Readings on the Management of Working Capital,* Keith V. Smith, ed. St. Paul, Minn.: West Publishing, 1980, pp. 585–608.

———. "Management of Information, Competitive Advantages and Short-Run Financial Management Systems," *Advances in Working Capital Management,* Yong H. Kim, ed. Reading, Mass.: Addison-Wesley, 1988.

Gentry, J.A., and J.M. De La Garza. "A Generalized Model for Monitoring Accounts Receivable." *Financial Management,* Vol. 16 (Winter 1985), pp. 28–38.

———. "Monitoring Inventories." BEBR Working Paper, University of Illinois, 1992.

———. "Monitoring Payables." *Financial Review,* Vol. 25 (Nov. 1990), pp. 559–576.

———. "Monitoring Payables and Receivables." BEBR Working Paper, University of Illinois, 1987.

Gentry, J.A., J.M. De La Garza, P. Newbold, and D.T. Whitford. "Assessing the Performance of Inventories." BEBR Working Paper, University of Illinois, 1992.

Gentry, J.A., and H.W. Lee. "An Integrated Cash Flow Model of the Firm." BEBR Working Paper, University of Illinois, 1986.

Gentry, J.A., P. Newbold, and D.T. Whitford. "Bankruptcy, Working Capital and Funds Flow Components." *Managerial Finance: Key Issues in Working Capital Management*, Vol. 10 (1984), pp. 26–39.

———. "Classifying Bankrupt Firms With Funds Flow Components." *Journal of Accounting Research*, Vol. 23 (Spring 1985), pp. 140–160.

———. "Predicting Industrial Bond Ratings With a Profit Model and Funds Flow Components." *Financial Review* (Aug. 1988), pp. 269–286.

———. "Predicting Bankruptcy: If Cash Flow's Not the Bottom Line, What Is?" *Financial Analysts Journal*, Vol. 41 (Sept./Oct. 1985), pp. 47–56.

Gentry, J.A., M.J. Shaw, and D.T. Whitford. "A Commercial Loan Risk Classification System." BEBR Working Paper No. 1,586, University of Illinois, 1989.

Gentry, J.A., R. Vaidyanathan, and H.W. Lee. "A Weighted Cash Conversion Cycle." *Financial Management*, Vol. 19 (Spring 1990), pp. 90–99.

Gilmer, R.H. "The Optimal Level of Liquid Assets: An Empirical Test." *Financial Management*, Vol. 14 (Winter 1985), pp. 39–43.

Gombola, M.J., M.E. Haskins, J.E. Ketz, and D.D. Williams. "Cash Flow in Bankruptcy Prediction." *Financial Management*, Vol. 16 (Winter 1987), pp. 55–65.

Hall, R.W. *Zero Inventories.* Homewood, Ill.: Dow Jones-Irwin, 1983.

Helfert, E.A. *Techniques of Financial Analysis*, 5th ed. Homewood, Ill.: Richard D. Irwin, 1982.

Hill, N.C., D.M. Ferguson, and B.K. Stone. "Electronic Data Interchange: An Introduction and Status Report." Working Paper presented at Financial Management Association Meetings, 1987.

Homonoff, R., and D.W. Mullins, Jr. *Cash Management.* Lexington, Mass.: Lexington Books, 1975.

Hoque, M. "Forecasting Daily Cash Receipts and Disbursements: A General Statistical Approach." Master's Thesis, University of Illinois at Urbana-Champaign, 1988.

Hoque, M., J.A. Gentry, and P. Newbold. "Forecasting Daily Cash Receipts and Disbursements: A General Statistical Approach." BEBR Working Paper, University of Illinois, 1989.

Howard, R.A. "The Foundations of Decision Analysis." *IEEE Transactions on Systems Sciences and Cybernetics*, Vol. SSC-4 (Sept. 1968), pp. 212–213.

Joehnk, M., O. Bowlin, and J. Petty. "Preferred Dividend Rolls: A Viable Strategy for Corporate Money Managers." *Financial Management*, Vol. 9 (Summer 1980), pp. 78–87.

Johnson, H.T., and R.S. Kaplan. *Relevance Lost.* Boston: Harvard Business School Press, 1987.

Kallberg, J.G., and K. Parkinson. *Current Asset Management.* New York: John Wiley & Sons, Inc., 1984.

Kallberg, J.G., and A. Saunders. "Market Chain Approaches to the Analysis of Payment Behavior of Retail Credit Customers." *Financial Management*, Vol. 12 (Summer 1983), pp. 5–14.

Kaplan, R.S. "One Cost System Isn't Enough." *Harvard Business Review,* Vol. 66 (Jan.–Feb. 1988), pp. 61–66.

Kim, Y. H., and J.C. Atkins. "Evaluating Investments in Accounts Receivable: A Wealth Maximization Framework." *Journal of Finance,* Vol. 33 (May 1978), pp. 403–412.

Lewellen, W.G., J.J. McConnell, and J.A. Scott. "Capital Market Influences on Trade Credit Policies." *Journal of Financial Research,* Vol. 3 (Summer 1980), pp. 105–113.

Maier, S.F., and J.A. Vander Weide. *Managing Corporate Liquidity: An Introduction to Working Capital Management.* New York: John Wiley & Sons, Inc., 1985.

———. "A Practical Approach to Short-Run Financial Planning." *Financial Management,* Vol. 7 (Winter 1978), pp. 10–16.

Mian, S.L., and C.W. Smith, Jr. "Accounts Receivable Management." Working Paper presented at 1987 Financial Management Association Meetings, University of Rochester, 1987.

Miller, T.W. "A Systems View of Short-Term Investment Management." Working Paper, Georgia Tech, 1986.

Miller, T.W., and B.K. Stone. "Daily Cash Forecasting and Seasonal Resolution: Alternative Models and Techniques for Using the Distribution Approach." *Journal of Financial and Quantitative Analysis,* Vol. 20 (Sept. 1985), pp. 335–351.

Miller, T.W., and B.K. Stone. "The Need for Financial Slack." Papers and Proceedings, 8th Annual International Symposium on Cash, Treasury and Working Capital Management, 1992.

Morris, J.R. "The Role of Cash Balances in Firm Valuation." *Journal of Financial and Quantitative Analysis,* Vol. 18 (Dec. 1983), pp. 533–545.

Myers, S.C. "The Capital Structure Puzzle." *Journal of Finance,* Vol. 39 (July 1984), pp. 575–592.

Myers, S.C., and N. Majluf. "Corporate Financing and Investment Decisions When Firms Have Information Investors Do Not Have." *Journal of Financial Economics,* Vol. 13 (1984), pp. 187–221.

———. "Finance Theory and Financial Strategy." *Midland Corporate Finance Journal,* Vol. 5 (Spring 1987), pp. 5–13.

Orgler, Y. "An Unequal Period Model for Cash Management Decisions." *Management Science,* Vol. 21 (1974), pp. 1350–1363.

Porter, M. *Competitive Advantage.* New York: The Free Press, 1985.

———. *Competitive Strategy.* New York: The Free Press, 1980.

Rappaport, A. *Creating Shareholder Value.* New York: The Free Press, 1987.

Richards, V.D., and E.L. Laughlin. "A Cash Conversion Cycle Approach to Liquidity Analysis." *Financial Management,* Vol. 9 (Spring 1980), pp. 32–38.

Robichek, A.A., D. Teichroew and J.M. Jones. "Optimal Short-Term Financing Decision." *Management Science,* Vol. 12 (Sept. 1965), pp. 1–36.

Sartoris, W.L., J.A. Gentry, and D.T. Whitford. "Liquidity: The Good, The Bad, and The Efficient." Papers and Proceedings, 8th Annual International Symposium on Cash, Treasury and Working Capital Management, 1992.

Sartoris, W.L., and N.A. Hill. "A Generalized Cash Flow Approach to Short-Term Financial Decisions." *Journal of Finance,* Vol. 38 (May 1983), pp. 349–360.

Schwartz, R.A. "An Economic Model of Trade Credit." *Journal of Financial and Quantitative Analysis,* Vol. 9 (Sept. 1974), pp. 643–658.

Shapiro, A. "Optimal Inventory and Credit Granting Strategies Under Inflation and Devaluation." *Journal of Financial and Qualitative Analysis,* Vol. 8 (Jan. 1973), pp. 37–46.

Shaw, M.J., and J.A. Gentry. "Using an Expert System With Inductive Learning to Evaluate Business Loans." *Financial Management,* Vol. 17 (Fall 1988), pp. 45–56.

Smith, J.K. "Trade Credit and Informational Asymmetry." *Journal of Finance,* Vol. 42 (Sept. 1987), pp. 863–872.

Smith, K.V. "State of the Art of Working Capital Management." *Financial Management,* Vol. 2 (Autumn 1973), pp. 50–55.

Srinivasan, V., and Y.H. Kim. "Credit Granting: A Comparative Analysis of Classification Procedures." *Journal of Finance,* Vol. 42 (July 1987), pp. 661–681.

Stone, B.K. "Allocating Credit Lines, Planned Borrowing and Tangible Services Over a Company's Banking System." *Financial Management,* Vol. 4 (Summer 1975), pp. 65–78.

———. "Cash Planning and Credit Line Determination With a Financial Statement Simulator: A Cash Report on Short-Term Financial Planning." *Journal of Financial and Quantitative Analysis,* Vol. 8 (Dec. 1973), pp. 711–729.

———. "Design of a Company's Banking System." *Journal of Finance,* Vol. 38 (May 1983), pp. 373–383.

———. "Design of a Receivable Collection System." *Management Science,* Vol. 27 (Aug. 1981), pp. 876–880.

———. "The Payment Pattern Approach of the Forecasting and Control of Accounts Receivable." *Financial Management,* Vol. 5 (Autumn 1976), pp. 65–72.

———. "The Use of Forecasts and Smoothing in Control Limit Models for Cash Management." *Financial Management,* Vol. 1 (Spring 1972), pp. 72–84.

Stone, B.K., and N.C. Hill. "Cash Transfer Scheduling for Efficient Cash Concentration." *Financial Management,* Vol. 9 (Autumn 1980), pp. 35–43.

Stone, B.K., and T. Miller. "Daily Cash Forecasting," *Corporate Cash Management: Techniques and Analysis,* F.J. Fabozzi and L.N. Mansonson, eds. Homewood, Ill.: Dow Jones-Irwin, 1985, pp. 120–141.

———. "Daily Cash Forecasting: A Structuring Framework." *Journal of Cash Management,* Vol. 1 (Oct. 1981), pp. 35–50.

———. "Daily Cash Forecasting With Multiplicative Models of Cash Flow Patterns." *Financial Management,* Vol. 16 (Winter 1987), pp. 45–54.

———. "Forecasting Disbursement Funding Requirements: The Clearing Pattern Approach." *Journal of Cash Management,* Vol. 3 (Oct./Nov. 1983), pp. 67–78.

Stone, B.K., and R.A. Wood. "Daily Cash Forecasting: A Simple Method for Implementing the Distribution Approach." *Financial Management,* Vol. 6 (Fall 1977), pp. 40–50.

Zivney, T.L., and M.J. Alderson. "Hedged Dividend Capture With Stock Index Options," *Financial Management,* Vol. 15 (Summer 1986), pp. 5–12.

Chapter 4

Cash Flow Management

BERNELL K. STONE

4.01 INTRODUCTION

Money flowing into and out of a company's cash pool is the essence of daily cash flow management. Regardless of whether the cash management system is check-based or electronic, cash managers face three major problems: (1) management of cash inflows; (2) management of cash outflows; and (3) management of the overall cash balance.

In addition, a company's daily cash flow management system makes extensive use of both the payment system and a variety of bank services provided to support the day-to-day corporate treasury function. A company's daily cash flow management systems also rely on a variety of internal support systems including an administrative control system, an information system, and possibly a cash forecasting system. Figure 4-1 summarizes the design and management tasks associated with major subproblems of daily cash flow management as well as cash forecasting.

Because most payments that are not coin, currency, or credit drafts are check based, the primary focus of this chapter is on check-based payment collection practices. However, the 1990s are a transition decade in which check payments and mail-voice communication are being replaced by electronic payments and electronic, computer-to-computer communication links.

4.02 CASH POSITION MANAGEMENT

[1] Daily Decisions

Cash position management is the task of managing the overall level of a company's cash balance and the closely related tasks of managing the short-term borrowing and investment positions.

On any given business day, cash inflows rarely equal cash outflows. Therefore, a company's cash balance will fluctuate from day to day unless explicit action is taken to adjust the balance level. Given a target balance, a cash manager must decide whether the discrepancy between the actual balance and the intended balance is large enough to justify an adjustment in the level of the cash balance. If an adjustment is necessary, a cash manager must decide the amount of the adjustment that should be made and the means of making the adjustment. When there is a surplus, the generic ways to reduce the cash balance are either to repay short-term borrowing or to invest in short-term money market instruments. When there is a deficiency, the generic means for increasing the balance are short-term marketable securities or short-term borrowing. Thus, the task of managing the overall cash position involves the management of both the short-term debt position and the short-term investment in money market instruments.

[2] Concentration Banking and the Central Cash Pool

The critical structuring feature of domestic cash management is the decomposition of the overall problem into the management of inflows, outflows, and the overall cash position. Once appropriate levels of cash inflows and outflows are established, a company can set balance levels at both its deposit banks and its payments banks in accordance with its balance targets and its best estimate of what the cash position will be.

FIGURE 4-1

Primary Subproblems of Day-To-Day Cash Flow Management

Problem	Design	Management
Collection system	Select lockboxes Assign receivables Select field banks	Information flow Compensation Error reconciliation
Disbursement system	Select disbursing bank Assign checks	Overdrafts Compensation Item reconciliation
Cash concentration	Select concentration bank or banks Select transfer mechanism Specify transfer initiation time	Cash transfer scheduling
Disbursement funding	Transfer mechanism	Schedule amount and timing of disbursements

Adjusted cash position
  management
	Select adjustment framework
	Select portfolio policies
	Select credit and borrowing policies
		Decide when to adjust,
		   amount, and means
		Portfolio management

Forecasting	Select framework Specify model Specify system support	Run system

At this point, managing the overall balance level is equivalent to managing the cash balance in the central cash pool.

Figure 4-2 is a simple illustration of this situation for a company with a central cash pool consisting of three collection deposit banks, two payment banks, and a single concentration bank. This example also assumes no delays in balance movement. In this situation, the overall target balance across all six banks is $15 million. The overall departure from the target before any cash transfers is simply the sum of the balances in all of the banks less the target (i.e., a shortfall of $4 million). Once $5 million is moved into the concentration bank from the three collection banks (so that balances at these banks are at their desired level) and $7 million is moved into the payment banks (so that their end-of-day balances are at their target levels), the net result is a balance in the concentration bank of $4 million, which is $4 million below target. Thus, after concentrating cash from the deposit banks and funding disbursements at the payment banks, the shortfall at the concentration bank is $4 million, the same as the overall shortfall. To remedy this overall shortfall, it is necessary to bring additional cash into the company's banking system, possibly by reducing short-term investment by $4 million or by drawing on credit lines for $4 million.

[3] Key Design Decisions

Although virtually all U.S. companies use concentration banking to reduce overall balance management to the daily management of a central balance, there are wide differences in both the system's structures for cash position management and the conceptual frameworks used for deciding on the amount and means for making daily

FIGURE 4-2

Concentration Banking

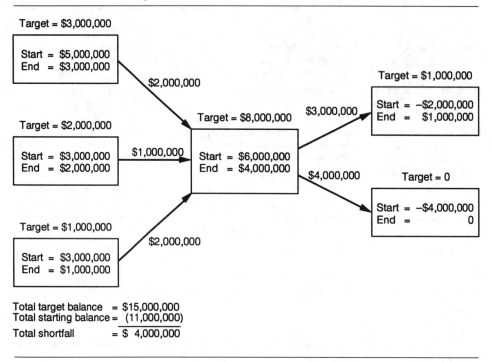

Target = $3,000,000

Start = $5,000,000
End = $3,000,000

$2,000,000

Target = $2,000,000

Start = $3,000,000 $1,000,000
End = $2,000,000

Target = $8,000,000 $3,000,000

Start = $6,000,000
End = $4,000,000

$4,000,000

Target = $1,000,000

Start = −$2,000,000
End = $1,000,000

Target = 0

Start = −$4,000,000
End =   0

Target = $1,000,000

Start = $3,000,000 $2,000,000
End = $1,000,000

Total target balance   = $15,000,000
Total starting balance = (11,000,000)
Total shortfall   = $ 4,000,000

adjustments. These decisions pertain to (1) relative reliance on short-term debt and short-term borrowing instruments; (2) bank compensation; (3) use of forecasting and its methods and systems support; and (4) the generic framework for daily balance adjustment.

[a] Relative Reliance on Short-Term Debt Financing. There are 3 broad categories of short-term debt financing decisions that in turn imply generic types of cash position management behavior: (1) always being a net short-term borrower; (2) always being a net investor in money market instruments; and (3) being a net short-term borrower for at least part of the year and a net short-term money market investor for another portion of the year. The great majority of companies are in the last category, especially those U.S. companies that are not among the 1,000 largest.

Always net short-term borrower. A company may make a conscious decision to always be a short-term borrower. This decision is most common for companies that are major issuers of commercial papers (CP), especially direct issuers. The primary reason for being an ongoing short-term borrower is to use high credit quality to lower the overall cost of debt on the assumption that the yield curve (interest rates versus debt maturity) is, on average, upward-sloping. Other reasons may pertain to trade financing, needs for flexibility in total debt levels, bridge financing, or foreign exchange exposure management.

For such a company, cash position management is reduced to managing the amount and the maturity of short-term debt. In effect, the decision is about the issuance and retirement of short-term debt. For companies borrowing exclusively from banks on a short-term line, the daily decision is merely one of amount. However, most of the companies that are net short-term debtors do at least some (and perhaps all) of their short-term borrowing through the CP market. There are both fixed and variable issuance costs that are a function of maturity.

Always net short-term investor. The opposite of always being a net short-term borrower is always being a net short-term investor. Such a company generally plans on having no short-term debt and borrows only if a cash need can be met more economically by debt than by selling a security before maturity. Since the early 1970s, very few companies have opted for such a high degree of short-term liquidity.

For such a company, cash position management is reduced to the task of managing transfers between the cash balance and the short-term investment portfolio. The decision is on the mix and maturity of short-term debt instruments, including tax-exempt securities. The goal is to increase after-tax yield while providing necessary transactional liquidity and maintaining an average cash balance sufficient to provide any compensating balances required to compensate banks.

Both short-term borrower and investor. For the great majority of companies, their business and financial situation is such that they are net short-term investors part of the year and net short-term borrowers part of the year. Because most companies face a positive spread of short-term debt costs over short-term money market returns, they seek to minimize the number of times when they simultaneously borrow and invest. Many companies in this situation are highly seasonal and rely on short-term debt to finance the seasonal buildup in their inventories and receivables but are required by banks and other institutional lenders to be free of any short-term debt for a period, such as a month or a quarter. This constraint has the effect of ensuring that short-term debt is truly seasonal financing and not a permanent part of the financial structure.

As cash flow varies over the year, the month, and possibly even the week, companies may shift from being net borrowers to net investors. Managing a cash position that involves both short-term debt and short-term investing is clearly more complex than managing either one separately, especially for smaller companies that are more constrained in their financial options and whose transactions may be small relative to unit order sizes, transaction costs, and administrative costs.

[b] Bank Compensation and Balance Targets. Companies can pay for credit lines, loans, and services with fees, balances, or a combination. Generally, the best compensation plan is a mix of fees and balances. As discussed in Stone (1975, 1983) and Hill and Sartoris (1988), the fee-versus-balance decision is a complex one that involves the following:

1. The earnings credit rate at a particular bank vis-à-vis company value for funds

2. The need for balances within a company's banking system

3. The cost of removing balances

4. Seasonality and a variety of other bank and company constraints

Once a decision on balance compensation has been made, maintaining the target level of average balances is a requirement for cash position management. For most companies, especially larger companies with a good balance management system, the target value for average compensating balances across all of the banks is much greater than the balances required for transaction purposes. Thus, the balances held for bank compensation provide a buffer that can allow the daily balance to fluctuate, since the compensating balance is based on an average computed over a month or a longer period.

[c] Daily Cash Forecasting. Whether to forecast at all is a strategic decision that companies must make. More precisely, the decision is whether to have a formal daily cash flow forecasting system. In most companies without a formal forecast, the cash manager uses an implicit forecast based on knowledge of major flows (dividends, taxes, debt repayment, payroll, and so forth), weekly and monthly patterns, and the direction of flow at various times of the year.

Companies forecast daily cash flows for a variety of reasons besides cash position management, e.g., to manage inflow transfers or disbursement funding. A daily cash flow forecast having moderate accuracy provides opportunities to improve cash position management substantially, especially for moderate-sized companies that borrow sometimes and invest at other times.

[d] Conceptual Frameworks. Figure 4-3 summarizes three generic frameworks for cash position management. Virtually all companies that engage in serious systematic cash management use one of these frameworks. The majority of the companies employ the daily target framework, which requires no formal cash forecast. However, the very largest companies, especially those that regularly issue CP or that regularly invest substantial amounts in money market instruments, employ one of the two forecast-using frameworks.

[4] Balance Adjustment Logic

In all three of the conceptual frameworks shown in Figure 4-3, the decision concerning balance adjustments is separated from decisions concerning the means to implement an adjustment. Thus, all three frameworks use some variant of the four-step procedure that follows. In fact, all three frameworks do essentially the same thing in steps 1 and 2. The differences are in steps 3 and 4 (i.e., in what action a company takes when there is a difference between the target balance and the current balance before adjustments and the way balance adjustments are implemented).

- *Step 1: Review the target balance*. The company must consider whether balance targets should be adjusted. Reasons for modifying a target balance include changes in the earnings credit rate, departures in the level of service usage from planned usage, and past balance history.

- *Step 2: Compute trial balance*. The trial balance is the starting balance in the central cash pool before any adjustments. It is the previous day's balance plus all inflows minus all outflows.

- *Step 3: Assess balance differences*. The decision whether the target balance is close enough to the actual balance is made by comparing the revised target with the trial balance. If they

FIGURE 4-3

Three Cash Position Management Frameworks

Framework	Description	Comments
Daily target	Company returns cash balance to target value each business day.	Very simple, requires no forecasting Dependent on bank balance reports Generally costly in terms of administrative effort, transaction costs, and overall borrowing costs and/or forgone return
Control-limit with smoothing	Firm keeps balance within range above and below target value of average balance and generally matches security maturities with major known cash flows.	Many variants of this basic framework Requires a forecast of major cash flows and a daily forecast of nonmajor flows out for 1 to 4 weeks Relative to daily target, can reduce transaction costs, borrowing amount or cost, and improve investment return
Dynamic target	Firm sets time-varying targets and plans periodic adjustments to reflect known patterns, trends, and forecast information. Unplanned balance adjustments occur only when there is a significant departure from the planned level of the average balance.	Used by most issuers of CP Requires forecast and custom software Greater system costs and forecasting effort are justified by lower administrative costs, lower transaction costs, reduced borrowing amounts and costs, and/or greater returns on invested funds.

are the same or nearly the same, there is no problem. If they are different, the cash manager must decide whether the difference is big enough to warrant an adjustment.

- *Step 4: Determine and implement adjustments.* If there is to be an adjustment, the cash manager must also determine the amount and the means for providing the adjustment.

[5] Daily Target Framework

The great majority of companies use the daily target framework, especially those that do not issue CP. Most balance management software is designed for the daily target framework, which does not require a formal forecast. The daily target framework relies on daily balance reports from a company's banks to keep the balance on target. The change in the balance each day is the difference between the target balance and the trial balance before adjustments. A company meets its target average balance by being on target each day.

The daily target framework involves costs, however: (1) high administrative and transaction costs; (2) higher levels of borrowing than in other frameworks (which smooth out below-target and above-target balances); and (3) forgone yields on short-term investments because of the need for extreme liquidity (e.g., investing primarily in overnight instruments).

[6] Control-Limit Framework

The control-limit framework keeps the cash balance close to the target value of the average compensating balance. Transactions occur only when there is a large departure from the target. With a short-period forecast, e.g., 5 to 10 business days ahead, a company would transact only if the departure from target was expected to continue. Moreover, the transaction amount would reflect the forecast cash flow as well as the current position.

The control-limit framework has the following advantages over the daily target framework: fewer transactions; a lower dollar volume of transactions; generally larger amounts per transaction (which can improve yield when investing and reduce the issuance costs per dollar raised when borrowing through CP); lower interest costs from a lower volume of borrowing; and a higher yield on short-term investments (from moving out of overnight and very short-term maturities, from ability to invest in less liquid instruments, and from larger investments per transaction).

The costs of a control-limit framework are the need to run a daily cash forecasting system and the need for custom software. While more complex conceptually, the control-limit framework is administratively less costly once designed and implemented. Moreover, it is much less dependent on daily balance reports from banks.

[7] Dynamic Targets

The term "dynamic target" refers to a time-varying value for the intended balance level. There are two variations. Many companies vary their target balance from month to month as part of their cash budgeting. However, for daily cash position management, dynamic targets refer to planned variations in the daily cash balance relative to a target average value, generally to reflect known patterns and cycles in their cash flow within a month. For instance, a company might have above-average balances in the first part of the month and below-average balances in the second half to reflect a known pattern of more inflows in the first half and more outflows in the second half of the month. Or, a company might have above-average values of the cash balance on Monday and Tuesday (high-inflow days), an average value on Wednesday, and below-average values on Thursday and Friday. Similarly, a company could set balance levels across the week to reflect weekly patterns in short-term interest rates or other structural features of the money market such as the weekly maturity of Treasury bills.

The dynamic target can be viewed as an extension of the control-limit models from static targets with flat limits to time-varying targets with time-varying limits that reflect only departures from the intended cash balance. Aside from planned adjustments, a company would transact only if the cumulative forecast error exceeded a specific upper or lower limit.

This system is self-correcting. At each planned transaction time, the amount transacted is adjusted to reflect the cumulative average departure from the planned balance. Thus, unplanned borrowing or investing occasions are unusual. The dynamic target framework gives a company much greater control over its short-term borrowing and investing than either the daily target or the static control-limit framework.

Dynamic targets require a daily forecast that measures weekly and monthly patterns, generally at least one month ahead. The system is complex to implement and requires custom software. However, once implemented, it is administratively simple, primarily because transactions occur less frequently and generally at planned times. This system uncouples debt position management and short-term investing from daily cash flow management. For a company with strong weekly or monthly patterns in daily cash flows, the dynamic model improves over the static control-limit model, providing lower transaction frequency and volume, lower borrowing costs, and higher investment yields.

[8] Other Frameworks and Approaches

Virtually all companies engaged in active cash position management use the daily target, the static control-limit, or the dynamic target framework. Each has many variations, especially the control-limit and dynamic target frameworks.

Other approaches have been suggested in the finance literature. It is worthwhile to examine why they are not used or are used only by very small businesses.

[a] **The EOQ Inventory Model.** Many finance texts present a cash balance replenishment model that is structured as an inventory of cash concerned with determining an economic order quantity (EOQ). The EOQ model simply does not fit the cash position management problem. First, it assumes a certain, unidirectional, and often uniform cash flow, while actual net operating cash flows are not certain, not unidirectional, and never uniform. Second, the assumed trade-off between a fixed order cost and an idle balance cost is simply not the problem. Short-term investing generally has a small fixed component and a large variable transaction cost, as reflected in bid-ask spreads and/or brokerage charges. Given earnings credits and average compensating balances, one must question the assumed idle balance cost. Finally, overall debt costs and investment returns are not even considered in the EOQ model. In sum, neither the cost nor cash flow assumptions of the EOQ model reflect the reality of the daily cash position management problem.

[b] **Scheduling Models.** Orgler (1970, 1974) and Maier and Vander Weide (1978) proposed mathematical programming frameworks for scheduling balance changes and other cash flow management using mathematical programming. While these scheduling frameworks seem more complete than the three frameworks used in practice and integrate balance level management with debt position and investment position management, they have limitations: They require too much input and therefore a high cost to use, and they require more forecast precision than is realistically attainable. Another possible disadvantage is limited practitioner knowledge of mathematical programming. Thus, the scheduling models are not practical in today's environment, even though they provide useful insights on problem structure.

[c] **Passive Management.** The daily target, control-limit, and dynamic target frameworks all assume active company management of both cash position and the associated debt and short-term investment positions. Some companies, especially smaller ones, may opt for less active management. Haag (1977, 1981) describes disbursing from an interest-bearing money market mutual fund as a way to earn some balance interest without a heavy management burden. Some banks provide automatic investment of surplus balances. The idea is to use services that provide interest on cash balances and/or provide automatic transfer to interest-bearing accounts or instruments. Compa-

nies that use this method generally obtain lower balance returns but also have much lower overall administrative costs.

4.03 COLLECTION SYSTEM OVERVIEW

[1] Cash Flow Streams

"Collection system" refers to the means and methods for receiving customer payments and for getting these payments into the company's banking system. The structure of a collection system depends on sales terms (e.g., prepayment, cash, and credit), payment instrument, the size and volume of payments, and the location of customers. Among the variables influencing collection systems, the distinction between credit and non-credit sales is especially important. Likewise, wholesale credit is very different from retail credit in terms of collection practices and the associated processing and control procedures.

The term "collection system" can be misleading to the extent that "system" implies a single, unified way for receiving payments and for getting them into a company's banks. There are many means and methods of receiving customer payments, with many associated means and methods of converting payments into value in the company's banks. Thus, a company of even moderate size and complexity typically has multiple collection systems.

"Cash inflow stream" refers to a set of cash inflows (customer payments) with sufficiently similar characteristics to permit use of the same collection methods and processing control procedures. The concept of the cash inflow stream is best illustrated by example: A cash inflow stream might be all credit sales in an amount over $1,000 that involve mailed check payments. Or it could be franchisee billings that involve advance notice of an electronic debit and then collection via an automated clearing-house (ACH) debit seven days later. Another example is cash (checks, coin, and currency) received at company stores and deposited in a local bank for subsequent concentration into the central cash pool.

Although one generally would consider a cash flow stream to characterize payments received at a particular point, it is possible that a retailer accepting both checks and credit drafts as well as coin and currency could have more than one cash flow stream. For instance, excess coin, currency, and checks could be processed by depositing them at a nearby bank, while credit drafts would go to a credit card–processing bank for collection. Furthermore, a retailer could have different streams based on the method of getting receipts to a bank. For instance, coin, currency, and checks could be deposited at a nearby bank for one store and could be picked up by an armored car for another store. At different points in time, both of these methods could be used for the same store.

The first step in designing a collection system is to identify the pertinent cash inflow streams that have different characteristics and that will be logically treated as separate components of a collection system. This chapter treats two broad categories of cash inflow streams: credit sales and noncredit sales. Noncredit sales are usually called field sales, since they usually take place at a company store, outlet, branch office, or other field sales unit and generally involve payment (value exchange) for goods or services at the point where the goods or services were received.

[2] Processing Mailed Check Payments

Most sales between companies involve extensions of trade credit, often called trade payments. Most payments for goods purchased on credit involve mailed check payments, although both electronic credits and electronic debits are emerging as important alternatives.

[a] Company Versus Bank Processing.

The basic structuring decision in processing mailed check payments is whether the receipt of the mailed payment and the processing of the check should be done by the company itself or by a third-party collection service, generally a bank-provided lockbox collection service. In making this decision, the primary issue is whether the benefits of faster collection justify the incremental collection costs. Other concerns include exceptions and variations that can complicate third-party processing, mechanisms for data capture, and control concerns, such as the speed with which a company needs information to update its accounts receivable or to track bad debts.

The standard criterion for assessing whether to use a bank lockbox collection service or company processing is the determination of a break-even receivable size. Let A denote the amount of a receivable, i, the interest rate (in days) that reflects the value of faster processing, Δt, the acceleration in collection time in days, and Δh, the net increase in processing costs. The net variable benefit (NVB) of using a lockbox collection system is the interest value of faster collection less the net cost per check paid for lockbox processing, as shown by the formula

$$\text{NVB} = iA\,\Delta t - \Delta h$$

The break-even receivable size, shown as A^*, is found by setting the NVB equal to zero in the preceding equation and solving for the associated receivable amount:

$$A^* = \frac{\Delta h}{i\Delta t}$$

EXAMPLE: Assume the quoted cost per check for a bank-provided lockbox processing service is \$0.68 but that a company reduces its own processing cost by \$0.08 so that the net cost increase per check is \$0.60. Assume further that this service accelerates collection time by two days on average and that the interest value of faster collection is 0.03 percent per day (approximately equivalent to a 10 percent annual rate). Then, the break-even receivable size is

$$A^* = \frac{\Delta h}{i\Delta t} = \frac{\$0.60}{0.0003(2)} = \$1,000$$

Thus, any mailed check larger than \$1,000 would have an interest value greater than the \$0.60 net cost with two-days-faster collection. For only one-day-faster collection and the same net cost and interest rate, the break-even formula would indicate a positive benefit for mailed checks larger than \$2,000.

In general, a company will use a third-party processing service to accelerate the collection of mailed checks for large check amounts. It will do its own processing for small checks.

The break-even receivable size with well-quantified costs and collection times can give the misleading impression that there is a clear-cut decision between internal processing and the use of an outside lockbox collection service. In fact, there are generally several alternative third-party services with a corresponding range in both average collection times and prices. Moreover, even from a given lockbox service provider, a company can obtain faster processing by paying more per item processed (e.g., evening and weekend processing or simply expedited processing with a guarantee of fast turnaround). Similarly, the company's internal processing can present a range of collection times and associated costs. For instance, the company can invest in special processing equipment; a dedicated, well-trained staff; and other procedures to accelerate collection times with internal processing. Nevertheless, once the appropriate version of internal processing and the pertinent third-party service alternative are identified, the decision fits nicely into the prototypical break-even structure.

[b] Lockbox Fixed Costs and Break-Even Volume. While in the preceding example, break-even receivable size shows the dollar amount of a check on which the interest value of faster collection will just equal the net incremental processing cost per check, there are also fixed costs associated with using a lockbox collection service. The break-even volume is the minimum number of checks per year that are required to cover the fixed costs. Let N^* be the break-even volume. The formula for N^* is

$$N^* = \frac{\text{annual fixed cost}}{\text{average net variable benefit per item}}$$

EXAMPLE: Assume that a company with an average receivable size of $1,500 expects two-days-faster collection time. With an average receivable size of $1,500, two-days-faster collection, and annual fixed costs of $3,600 the average NVB of lockbox processing per check is

$$\text{Average variable benefit per check} = 0.0003(\$1,500)(2) - \$0.60$$
$$= \$0.90 - \$0.60 = \$0.30$$

The minimum number of checks required to cover fixed costs is

$$N^* = \frac{\$3,600 \text{ per year}}{\$0.30 \text{ per check}} = 12,000 \text{ checks per year}$$

For this company, having more than 12,000 checks per year would mean that the company would cover the fixed costs of using a lockbox collection service.

An average check size of $1,000, however, is small for wholesale (company-to-company) payments. Likewise, a check volume of 1,000 check payments per month (about 12,000 checks per year) is also small even for a middle-market manufacturer. This is why most companies having wholesale receivables use lockbox collection services to receive and process mailed checks from other companies.

[c] Design of a Lockbox Collection System. For most companies extending trade credit to other companies, the question about lockbox services is not whether to use a lockbox service to collect mailed check payments but rather how many lockboxes to use, where the lockboxes should be located, and how to assign receivables (customers) to the alternative lockboxes.

FIGURE 4-4

Mathematical Program for Selecting Lockboxes and Assigning Collection Zones

---

Cost Characterizing Parameters

i = interest rate (per day) measuring value of faster collection
N_c = number of receivable payments mailed from zone c
A_c = average size of check payments from zone c
t_{ck} = collection time for a check mailed from zone c to bank k
h_{ck} = net cost of a check from zone c processed at bank k
F_k = fixed cost of lockbox service k

Decision Variables

z_k = zero-one (exclusion-inclusion) variable (is one only if lockbox service k is included in the system)
x_{ck} = zero-one assignment variable (is one only if the checks mailed from zone c are directed to lockbox k and zero otherwise)

Objective Function

To minimize: $\sum_k F_k z_k + \sum_c \sum_k (iN_cA_ct_{ck} - h_{ck})x_{ck}$

Constraints

$\sum_k x_{ck} = 1$　　　　Assign each zone to some box

$0 \le x_{ck} \le z_k$　　　　Assign only to boxes in the system

$\sum_k z_k \le MAX$　　　　Upper limit on the number of services

---

In answering the question of what checks should be assigned to what lockbox, the solution structure generally does not deal with individual customers (individual mailed checks). Rather, receivables are placed in homogeneous receivable classes and the classes are then assigned to particular lockboxes. The primary concern in identifying receivable classes is the time to collect, which is a function of the point from which the payment is mailed and the destination address. In effect, mail origination points are the primary basis for identifying receivable classes, called collection zones. In the standard collection system design, collection zones are defined by the first two digits of the postal zip code.

The collection system design task is to select lockbox processing points that minimize overall collection costs. Collection cost is the sum of the opportunity cost of dollars in the process of collection, the fixed costs of the lockbox collection service, and the variable processing cost. The problem of minimizing costs while assigning receivables can be formulated as a fixed-cost assignment location problem and structured as a mathematical programming problem. The formulation of the standard mathematical program and comments are summarized in Figure 4-4.

There are many refinements and variations on the standard formulations given in Figure 4-4. Readers interested in these are referred to Maier and Vander Weide (1974, 1976), Nauss and Markland (1980, 1981), and Stone (1980, 1986).

4.04 CASH CONCENTRATION

Cash concentration is the task of moving funds from deposit banks into a company's central cash pool. The term "concentration" reflects the fact that sales proceeds received in many locations and deposited into many different collection banks are ultimately gathered in a central cash pool that can be managed as a single balance for funding outflows, managing short-term debt, and/or managing short-term investments.

[1] Concentration Banking

The term "central cash pool" refers to the single central balance that is the difference between daily cash inflows and cash outflows. For the majority of companies (all but the 800 to 1,000 largest and most sophisticated companies), the central cash pool resides at a single bank called the concentration bank and is simply the balance at the concentration bank.

For large divisional companies and/or companies with extensive international operations, it can make sense to have the central cash pool spread over several principal banks. In this case, the central cash pool is treated as a single logical balance even though it resides at more than one bank. The ability to treat the central cash pool as a single logical balance requires an information system that tracks balances in these banks and quick, generally same-day, fund transfers between these banks.

[2] Reasons for Multiple Concentration Banks

There are several reasons why a company, especially a large multidivision company with extensive international activities, might use more than one bank in managing its central cash pool. Some of these reasons are organizational or locational, and others pertain to specialized services that some banks provide.

[a] **Bank Service Functions.** Companies may use several different banks in managing their central balance because different banks have different capabilities and/or specializations. Figure 4-5 summarizes different roles that banks play in cash concentration, cash position management, and international support.

[b] **Organizational Structure.** The primary organizational reason for using several concentration banks is parent-subsidiary structure. Many companies organize cash management for subunits of the company, especially separate subsidiaries. (In this section, the term "divisional structure" refers to a separate subsidiary, a division, or a profit center.) In a divisional organization of daily cash flow management, each of the divisional subunits can have its own divisional concentration bank that receives divisional inflows and that generally funds divisional payment banks. In addition, the company will have an overall primary (corporate) concentration bank.

Another organizational reason for multiple concentration banks is a geographical structuring of cash management to correspond to the company's geographical territories. Receipts go first to a field deposit bank and then to a geographical gathering bank. Historically, the use of a geographical gathering bank has also sped up cash concentration in terms of obtaining usable funds from deposits faster when depository transfer checks (DTCs) were the primary fund transfer mechanism for field deposits.

FIGURE 4-5

Operational Functions of Principal Banks

Manage cash concentration

Prepare depository transfers
Execute depository transfers
Balance reporting
Control services

Money market investment support

Information
Trading
Security receipt and delivery; custody
Dealer and/or market maker

Borrowing support

Lead bank in syndicated line
CP issuance
Automatic overdraft coverage

International cash management

Letters of credit
Foreign exchange
Banker's acceptances
International collection
Multilateral netting

Location-service connections

Corporate or divisional headquarters
New York City: money market facilitation
Chicago: futures trading facilitation

For checks, the availability delay was a function of time and distance; therefore, staged concentration from a local deposit bank to a regional gathering bank and then to an overall concentration bank generally meant faster fund availability than with one-stage concentration from local deposit bank directly to the primary concentration bank.

With fund transfer via the ACH, there is no geographical difference in availability time and thus no availability-based reason for having a regional gathering bank. In addition, the regional gathering bank can involve additional cost and management overhead. For these reasons, the use of regional gathering banks among national retailers has declined rapidly since 1980, although the practice still occurs. However, when major retailers use regional gathering banks today, the reason is generally not faster fund availability but rather to maintain control and regional management within historical cash gathering and concentration structures.

[3] Concentration Banking Versus Cash Concentration

It is important to understand the difference between cash concentration and concentration banking. Historically, the term "concentration banking" referred to the division

FIGURE 4-6

Lockbox Concentration Versus Field Receipt Concentration

Lockbox Receipts	Field Receipts
Few banks	Many banks

Deposit composition
  All checks
	Deposit composition
	  Coin and currency
	  Checks
	  Credit drafts

Extensive bank services
  Balance reporting
  Customized control reports
  Transfer management
  Credit lines
	Limited bank services
	  Deposit taking
	  Periodic statements

Bank compensation
  Fees or balances
  Little trouble with excess balances
	Bank compensation
	  Generally balances only
	  Excess balances common

Dollar volume
  High per bank
  Monday peak
	Dollar volume
	  Low per bank
	  Often strong cycles

Fraud theft minor concern	Fraud theft major concern
	  Uncertainty in receipts
	  Coin and currency
	  Multiple shift managers
	  Delay in problem discovery
	  Limited recovery

of the overall daily cash flow management into the management of inflows, outflows, and overall cash position. Generally, inflows were moved to a single central bank called the concentration bank. In fact, as cash concentration evolved, the responsibility for managing the movement of inflows usually resided with this central bank. In addition, most companies managed their overall cash position on the basis of the balance that resided at the concentration bank. The key point is that concentration banking implies much more than simply the concentration of deposits from collection banks to a single location. Rather, the most important attribute of concentration banking is the separation of daily cash flow management into the separate management of inflows, outflows, and the overall cash position. Thus, concentration banking must be viewed as a broad management tool and not just as the concentration of cash inflows at a single central location.

[4] Types of Cash Concentration Systems

As with collection systems, cash concentration is very different for credit sales and noncredit sales. Figure 4-6 contrasts the concentration of lockbox receipts with the concentration of field deposits.

    [a] Lockbox Receipt Concentration. Lockbox concentration is very easy compared to field concentration. The task of transferring funds from lockbox banks is often managed by the lockbox bank itself rather than the company. In this case, the company simply receives a deposit report summarizing deposits, balance levels, and funds transferred. Thus, the deposit report becomes the input into the overall cash management system, with little effort being expended by the company to actually run its lockbox concentration system.

[b] Field Receipt Concentration. In contrast, field concentration is extremely complex. This complexity arises because of the receipt of coin and currency, which are immediate good funds and must be concentrated quickly to avoid idle balances. Adding to the complexity is the absence of bank services to report on field deposits and the need to verify that all receipts are actually deposited.

In addition, complexity arises from the large number of field units and field banks. For a national retailer, there are typically more than 1,000 stores making deposits, often several deposits per day per store into 500 or more banks. Simply designing and managing an information control system to track daily cash flows from more than 1,000 units is itself a complex design and management task. In addition, the company must design and manage a system for moving funds from its field units to its field deposit banks and then to its central cash pool.

For major retailers, cash concentration is the primary daily cash management problem, with field concentration requiring the majority of the cash manager's efforts. However, there is a large payoff. Without investment in a daily information control system and daily cash forecasting, a national retailer would have excess balances in its field deposit banks. The amount of excess balances across all field banks is at least a day's deposits and often two or more days' worth of deposits above what is required to compensate field banks. Moreover, a retailer that is not engaged in designing an appropriate information control system will have exposure to and generally incur significant fraud theft losses.

The design of a retail cash concentration system is intimately related to the design of an information control system and generally involves the design and management of a daily cash forecasting system at the field unit level.

[5] Designing a Field Concentration System

The starting point in designing a system is a series of make-buy decisions about deposit reporting and bank services. A company must decide between using external services or having the company operate key aspects of its field concentration system. Two critical make-buy decisions pertain to deposit information gathering and transfer system operation.

[a] Deposit Information Gathering. Most companies use third-party deposit information gathering and reporting services to get information about field deposits from each field unit to a central location. However, since the early 1980s, there has been a trend for leading-edge national retailers to assume responsibility for managing their own deposit information gathering and to take over this function internally. Two major alternatives for a company-managed deposit gathering system reflect recent developments in information technology.

Point-of-sale deposit information gathering. To use a company's point-of-sale information system, personnel in the field unit simply record deposit amounts and pertinent deposit details at the point of sale. These data are periodically transferred with other point-of-sale data into a company's point-of-sale information system, where it is sorted and organized. Deposit information is then transferred to the corporate treasury area.

Company-operated telephone gathering. Instead of calling a third-party information service, field unit personnel may call a central company location. What differentiates this practice today from the historical company gathering of deposit information through telephone is the ability to automate the process. Technology now enables a company to automate telephone answering with a computer-based voice prompt so that touch-tone signals from field unit personnel record deposit amounts and other pertinent deposit detail. This automated information gathering drastically changes the economics of information gathering, so that the larger retailers are able to replicate the service structure of a third-party information-gathering service.

While a large retailer can cut its deposit reporting costs, the reasons for assuming company responsibility for the management of its field deposit information gathering is generally not cost savings per se but rather the faster receipt of information and tighter information control systems, especially when transfers are based on a combination of company forecast data and reports of field deposit information.

[b] Deposit Transfer Management. Cash transfers are generally initiated by a principal operational bank, which is often the primary concentration bank. Thus, for most companies, the question about deposit transfer management is not whether the transfers will be initiated by a bank but rather the roles of the company and the bank in preparing the transfers and in determining their amount and timing.

Historically, a third-party reporting service would send deposit reports directly to the concentration bank. The amount of the transfer would be the amount of the reported deposit, and the timing would be daily. The concentration bank would assume responsibility both for preparing DTCs and for entering them into the check clearing system. The role of the company in this system was passive. It simply received reports from either the third-party deposit information gathering service or from the concentration bank about what was deposited, field units that failed to report, and possibly other control information, such as deposits that were out of line with either forecasts or historical behavior. As the practice evolved, especially as transfer amounts became based on forecasts, companies have assumed progressively greater responsibility for the transfer amount.

The extreme today is a company-managed transfer system in which the company determines the amount and timing of transfers and simply sends to its operational bank a set of transfer images to be entered into the ACH. In a company-operated system, the company will prepare and update forecasts and prepare computer records of transfer amounts for every field unit (field bank) as a function of both forecasted deposits and deposit reports.

There are many variations between the extremes of a bank-operated system driven solely by deposit reports and a system in which the company does everything, including preparing the transfer images. These involve a mixture of company and bank processing and reflect competitive advantages between a company and its bank. Most systems today fall into this middle ground of joint operation of a transfer system.

[c] Transfer Mechanisms. There are three ways to move funds from deposit banks into the central cash pool: wire transfer, DTCs, and the ACH. Figure 4-7 summarizes

FIGURE 4-7

Fund Transfer Mechanisms

Mechanism	Time	Cost Range	Comments
ACH debit	1	$0.15–$0.50	Primary mechanism
DTC	0–2	$0.25–$1	Displaced by ACH debit
Wire drawdown	0	$5–$25	Quick but expensive

key features of alternative transfer mechanisms. Since the mid-1980s, virtually all national retailers have adopted the ACH as the primary mechanism for concentrating field deposits. Field concentration is the one area where checks (DTCs) have been displaced almost completely by the ACH.

A wire transfer gives same-day movement of funds. It is fast but costly. Wire transfers are generally used only for moving large dollar amounts when neither the amount nor the need to move funds can be predicted at least one day ahead of time. In field concentration, wire transfers might be used to prevent an overdraft or to move a very large unanticipated deposit.

[d] Other Design Decisions. In addition to deciding on the operation of a deposit information gathering system and the relative role in determining transfer timing, amount, and mechanism, other key interdependent design issues must be addressed, including logic for the determination of the transfer timing and amount, the design of a control system, the design of a forecasting system, and the design of an overall information support system.

4.05 OUTFLOW MANAGEMENT

[1] Payment Stream Design Issues

Each major payment class (trade, payroll, dividend, tax, and customer) involves different banking services and payment practices, as shown in Figure 4-8. For each payment stream, companies face a variety of design issues.

A company must design and manage a disbursement system for each of these payment streams. This chapter focuses on the design and management issues pertinent to trade payments, i.e., payments to suppliers and vendors, especially for purchases involving trade credit. The conventional practice for trade payments is the mailing of a check payment in response to an invoice. In addition, the paying company generally provides the billing company with a remittance advice (payment advice), which identifies the invoice or invoices being paid; discounts taken (both trade and volume); other adjustments to the amount invoiced, such as returns, damage allowances, promotional allowances, and trade allowances; and identification of any disagreements (e.g., what was received, the proper price, or other aspects of the relationship). In effect, the remittance advice is a continuation of the information exchange between the buyer and the seller that enables the selling company to update its accounts receivable and

FIGURE 4-8

Major Classes of Payments

Type	Definition	Standard Practice	Practice Variations
Trade	Payments to suppliers	Mailed check drawn on a controlled disbursement account, a concentration bank, or a local payment bank	ACH credit ACH debit Wire transfer
Payroll	Payments to employees	Check plus advice Direct deposit of payment through ACH plus delivered pointed advice	
Dividend	Payments to stockholders of record on dividend record data	Mailed check prepared by third-party dividend payment service	Company-prepared and -mailed check ACH credit to stockholders
Taxes	Payments to local, state, and federal government, including income, sales, excise taxes, and employee withholding	Varies with type of tax and government entity; often transfer to treasury account	ACH credit to government Mailed check Wire transfer
Customers		Characterized by variety	

to relate the payment to other documents and sources of information that characterize the trade transactions underlying the payment.

The central design questions concerning trade payment systems concern two interrelated items: payment instruments and the form of buyer-seller communication about payments.

[a] Payment Instruments. The primary payment instrument choices are a mailed check or an ACH payment. The ACH payment can be either a payor-initiated ACH credit sent from the payor's bank to the payee's ACH receiving bank or a payee-initiated debit drawn on a designated payor bank under a preauthorized electronic debit agreement.

[b] Buyer-Seller Communications. With check payments, standard practice is to send a printed remittance advice along with the check. It is also possible to send an electronic advice statement with the check (disk or tape) or separately (electronic computer-to-computer transmission or disk or tape). When making an electronic payment, the payor could still exchange payment information by paper document exchange; however, the primary benefit of automation is the savings in payment-related document exchange. Thus, automated electronic information exchange in standardized computer-processable formats is the best alternative to printed document exchange.

[2] Automated Trade Information Exchange

Electronic data interchange (EDI) is the exchange of information through electronic (computer-readable and computer-processible) document images that enable both the fast exchange of information without manual reentry of data and the automation of data processing. In the 1970s, a number of industry and proprietary standards emerged for electronic trade document exchange. Since 1980, there have been national standards: the ANSI X12 standards for most trade documents, including purchase orders, shipping-transportation notices, invoices, payment orders, and remittance advice.

Automating payments and the related information exchanges promise significant savings as well as improvements in both quality and certainty of payment and related information exchange and processing. Nevertheless, progress has been slow. By the end of 1992, more than 98 percent of trade payments are still mailed checks, although most major companies have started EDI programs and more than 50 percent of U.S. companies with sales over $20 million expect to be doing at least some EDI by 1995.

Among the reasons why progress in electronic trade payments and related financial EDI has been slow are (1) the need for drastic redesign of company systems and documents; (2) the complexity and effort required to recontract with suppliers; (3) concerns about security, audit trails, and fraud theft controls; and (4) the need for drastic changes in both bank services and the infrastructure of the payment industry's products and service support.

Economics, the quality movement, competitive and customer pressures, and ongoing implementation activities all indicate that most companies will be doing some electronic payment and related financial EDI by 1995. By the turn of the century, electronic trade payments and document exchange will be rapidly displacing checks and paper document exchange. Given that mailed checks are still the dominant trade payment mechanism, the following discussion of disbursement systems design focuses primarily on mailed check payments.

[3] Disbursement System Design

[a] **Controlled Disbursements.** Most companies pay their trade payments using a controlled disbursement account and a controlled disbursement service. The essence of controlled disbursement is that the bank providing the service gives the company a prompt report on all checks that were presented against the account on the prior day, generally by early morning of the following business day. Figure 4-9 summarizes key features of the standard controlled disbursement service and principal variations.

[b] **Disbursement Funding Design.** Disbursement funding is the task of moving money into a disbursement account so that a company maintains the average target balance. Two major issues that must be addressed in designing a disbursement funding system for controlled disbursement accounts are the transfer mechanism (should a company use a wire transfer, a DTC, or the ACH?) and management responsibility (should the day-to-day transfer management be performed by the company itself, or should its payment bank manage the transfers and then inform the company as to what has taken place?).

Closely related are issues about the form of bank compensation—fees, balances, or a combination—and who should manage the transfer. Cash managers must also determine whether the target balance should be zero or a positive balance should

FIGURE 4-9

Variations in Controlled Disbursement Services

Service	Account Funding	Balance	Bank Compensation
Standard company-managed funding	Company initiated wire from a concentration bank to the controlled disbursement bank	Zero	Fees
Controlled disbursement bank–managed funding: ACH	Controlled disbursement bank initiates an ACH debit drawn on a company-specified bank; the amount is that day's check presentment	Average volume of daily check presentments[a]	Fees or balances
Controlled disbursement bank–managed funding: DTC	Controlled disbursement bank creates a daily DTC drawn on a company-specified funding bank; the amount is each day's check presentment total	Average volume of daily check presentments[a]	Fees or balances
Controlled disbursement bank–managed funding: wire drawdown	CDB initiates a daily wire drawdown[b] equal to each day's check presentments	Zero	Fees

[a] This balance level reflects on average the loan implicit in covering today's checks with a fund transfer instrument that has a one-business-day delay in obtaining good funds.

[b] A wire drawdown is the transmission of wire transfer instructions to the sending bank by the receiving bank as an agent for the company, in this case under a preauthorized standing agency relationship.

be maintained on average to compensate the bank and possibly provide a buffer for fluctuations in check presentment volume.

[c] Selecting Disbursement Banks and Specifying Services. The design of a disbursement system for mailed, check-based trade payments involves the selection of disbursement banks (locations) and the specification of services to be provided by these banks.

This problem is similar to the task of designing a lockbox collection system (i.e., a fixed-cost, assignment-location problem). The task is to select disbursement banks and assign check classes to each bank. However, each disbursement bank added to the system involves a fixed cost, and, in addition, there is a cost per check.

The difference between disbursement system design and collection system design is the view of time. A longer disbursement time is a benefit to the paying company, while collection time is a cost. To the extent that it takes a longer time for checks to be received by the billing company and presented against the paying company's account, there is a period during which the company can use those funds, even though the check has been mailed.

Figure 4-10 presents the disbursement system design problem as a fixed-cost, assignment location, mathematical programming problem. This standard formulation as-

FIGURE 4-10

Check-Based Disbursement Bank System

Parameters

i = interest value of funds (days)
N_c = number of checks per region
A_c = average size of checks for region c
t_{ck} = average check clearing time for region c checks in bank k
h_{ck} = cost of region c check written on bank k
F_k = fixed cost of including bank k in system of disbursement banks

Decision variables

z_k = zero-one (exclusion-inclusion) variable (is one only if bank k is included in the controlled disbursement system)
x_{ck} = zero-one assignment variable (is one only if checks to be paid to a company in region c are written on bank k)

Objective function

To maximize the value of disbursement float less the cost of obtaining it:

$$\sum_c \sum_k (iN_cA_ct_{ck} - h_{ck}) - \sum_k F_kz_k$$

Constraints

$\sum_k x_{ck} = 1$ Each region c is assigned to some bank

$0 \le x_{ck} \le z_k$ Assign checks only to banks in the system

sumes that the mail locations for sending checks to billing companies are given; thus, the only variable that has an impact on check-clearing times is the location of the disbursement bank upon which checks are written. For this reason, only check-clearing times have entered into the objective function in the mathematical program summarized in Figure 4-10.

Since 1980, there have been significant changes in the check-clearing system, check-clearing times, and the controlled disbursement services offered by major corporate service banks. As a result, the design of disbursement systems for trade payments has also changed. In the late 1970s and early 1980s, many companies did formal disbursement system design studies using data bases of check-clearing times and optimization models. However, with changes in check collection, especially the elimination of most of the differences in check-clearing times for out-of-district checks, the design practice has changed. By the mid-1980s, most companies simply identified banks that had slow clearing times for pertinent geographical zones. Since the number of disbursement banks is typically small in an optimal solution, generally four or less, companies used rule-of-thumb selection criteria (e.g., the "four corners rule," which chose remote locations).

By 1990, the differences in collection times for alternative controlled disbursement banks were less than a half a day and decreasing. Thus, extending disbursement time had ceased to be the primary criterion by which companies chose controlled disbursement banks. Rather, the focus now is on bank services, service quality, price, and the operational efficiency of the overall system. The most pertinent issue in the eyes of many cash mangers is the quickness with which a company can provide controlled disbursement data in terms of the total volume of checks presented and the dollars that are required to fund that account for that day, so that the cash manager can intelligently manage his or her daily cash position. As the mid-1990s approach, it is almost certain that service quality, efficiency considerations, and information reporting will be the criteria on which future disbursement bank selection is based. Because the differences are narrowing, it is fairly certain that the number of controlled disbursement banks will continue to decrease. It is even conceivable that companies will do a good deal of their controlled disbursement on their concentration bank.

[d] Operational Efficiency. Once companies focus on operational efficiency in managing their disbursement systems, they logically consider alternatives to check payment, especially when there are no significant float advantages to checks over electronic payment. The major alternative is the ACH. While there are modest cost and administrative savings associated with replacing checks with ACH payments, the real efficiency opportunity is reducing the cost of financial data exchange. Realizing these opportunities requires redesigning payment practices in the context of EDI, and not merely substituting an electronic payment for a check payment.

4.06 ELECTRONIC PAYMENTS AND FINANCIAL ELECTRONIC DATA INTERCHANGE

The obvious substitute for a mailed check payment is an ACH credit. However, while the benefits of EDI (including electronic payment) depend on a company, cost studies indicate that automating check payments by simply substituting an ACH credit for a mailed check is not practical and does not provide significant benefits. The benefits of substituting an ACH credit for a check are not substantial; savings in bank costs are modest (e.g., $0.10 to $0.40 per payment), as are savings in check preparation and associated company administrative and operational costs ($0.20 to $0.50 per payment).

In addition to modest benefits, the significant barrier to simply substituting an ACH credit for a check is that in trade payments, standard practice is to provide not only a check but also a remittance advice detailing what the check payment represents. In contemporary data processing, the remittance advice is critical in reconciling the amount invoiced with the amount paid. It is the document that enables the company receiving the payment to update its accounts receivable and to credit the paying company properly. Moreover, if there are disagreements, differences between the amount invoiced and the amount paid are identified in the payment advice. Thus, it is the basic document for triggering a reconciliation of disagreements.

It is not practical to have an electronic payment without also having an electronic payment advice. Thus, to have an electronic substitute for checks, the obvious requirement is to provide an electronic payment advice as well. This capability has now been incorporated into the ACH. Figure 4-11 summarizes the corporate trade payment formats available and details their ability to send an electronic advice with the electronic payment. For example, the corporate trade exchange format not only provides for an electronic payment advice to a company but also puts the advice in a national data standard for automated advice processing (ANSI X12 payment advice standard).

FIGURE 4-11

Alternative ACH Formats for Corporate Trade Payments

Source: B.K. Stone, One to Get Ready: How to Prepare Your Company for EDI *(Philadelphia: The Core States Banks, 1988), p. 18, Exhibit 3-2*

Abbreviation and Format	Payment Record	Addendum Records
CCD (cash concentration and disbursement)	94 characters	None
CCD+ (cash concentration and disbursement plus)	94 characters[a]	One 94-character advice addendum[b]
CTP (corporate trade payment)	94 characters[a]	16 to 4,990 additional records of 94 characters
CTX (corporate trade exchange)	94 characters[a]	Variable-length addendum up to length of the CTP addendum in the ANSI X12 data standard

[a] The payment record for the CCD+, CTP, and CTX formats are all the same, that is, all of the formats are a CCD payment record plus some kind of addendum record. The differences in the addendum records are what distinguish the four formats.

[b] CCD+ is intended for short, simple advices, e.g., one payment for one invoice with no dispute. It may use a subset of ANSI X12 data standards.

[1] Cost as an Impetus for Electronic Data Interchange

Most of the costs of payment processing are not the payment per se but rather the information about the payment. Even providing the capability to send an electronic payment and advice together as a substitute for a mailed check and a paper advice is a myopic use of the EDI opportunity. Companies must do much more than merely substitute electronic messages for paper documents. Relative costs are a significant factor in making the move to EDI.

Invoice creation costs are typically about $3 for a simple invoice summarizing a single shipment or purchase. For an order for many goods or for goods delivered to multiple locations, invoice creation can be substantially more expensive. Invoice validation is possibly the most expensive part of trade data exchange. Simply validating a simple invoice for a single transaction typically costs $5 or more (if there are no errors or disputes and if the information required to validate the invoice is in a single location, ideally in a computer-processable data base accessible from a terminal). Most companies responding to surveys indicate that invoice validation typically exceeds $100 in cases where there is a dispute and supporting data must be obtained to resolve the disagreement.

Remittance advice creation and the associated costs are the mirror image of invoicing and invoice validation costs. Typical costs to create a remittance advice for a standard payment are $3 to $5 if there are no problems or errors. Costs are much higher for producing remittance advices for many invoices. Likewise, costs are higher when the company has to deal with a disagreement and cite supporting documents.

The benefits of automating payment and remittance advice by simply substituting an electronic payment and advice for a check and printed advice are limited to reduced keying, reduced delays associated with mail and paper processing, reduced keying errors associated with rekeying data, fewer check errors and reduced check storage and retrieval costs.

[2] The Need for Drastic Redesign: Illustrative Examples

Achieving the really significant benefits of financial EDI requires drastic redesign of a financial system rather than just automating payment and remittance advice delivery (i.e., simply automating the payment component of the existing financial data exchange). Space here does not permit an exhaustive treatment of either the opportunity or the need for drastic redesign, but the following sections illustrate the drastic nature of redesign that is required to capture significant operational savings and simultaneously provide dramatic quality improvements.

[a] **Evaluated Receipts Settlement.** An invoice is a redundant trade document that summarizes information in a purchase order or materials release order, shipping documents, and possibly other transportation and receiving documents. Rather than automating the creation of an invoice and subjecting the purchasing company to the very high costs of invoice validation, evaluated receipt settlement allows the receiving company to initiate payment a certain amount of time after the goods are delivered. In effect, the payer does not wait for an invoice but simply initiates an ACH credit with a remittance advice outlining the reason for payment and citing the purchase order (material release order) and appropriate transportation receiving documents. Significant cost savings are a result not only of reducing the costs of processing a document but of completely eliminating an expensive, difficult-to-automate document. However, the elimination requires a significant change in how a buyer and seller interact, including their legal contracting.

[b] **Payment on Production.** A more drastic redesign than evaluated receipt settlement is pay on production, in which payment is made following an appropriate delay after a supplier's goods are incorporated in the purchaser's product. Payment is made only for goods used. There is no payment for damaged or defective goods, nor are returns involved in payment and the associated production. Pay on production is used by Japanese automotive manufacturers and now by General Motors in its Saturn car division.

Like evaluated receipt settlement, pay on production completely eliminates invoices. It also eliminates some of the expensive business transactions inherent in invoicing, especially accounting for damaged goods, returns, and similar adjustments to the payment amount. Pay on production not only requires major changes in contracting and payment procedures but also drastically changes accounting and control.

[c] **Direct Debit by Seller.** Conventional practice is for the receiver of goods to initiate payment once goods are received. Sellers notify buyers of their obligation to pay through an invoice, and buyers then pay.

In evaluated receipt settlement and payment on production, the invoice was eliminated. However, the buyer still initiated payment. A more drastic change in conventional practice, discussed in Bielfeldt (1991), is to have seller initiate payment through an electronic debit to the buyer's bank account in accord with a preauthorized electronic debiting agreement and to send the electronic debit advice (a new information exchange that replaces the invoice) directly to the company. The debit advice would generally precede the debit initiation. It bypasses the ACH and the banking system as well.

Suggested Reading

Anvari, M. "Alternative Cash Concentration Systems in Canada: An Example of National Banking." *Journal of Cash Management,* Vol. 3 (June/July 1983), pp. 48–58.

Baumol, W.J. "The Transactions Demand for Cash: An Inventory Theoretic Approach." *Quarterly Journal of Economics,* Vol. 65 (Nov. 1952), pp. 545–556.

Bielfeldt, G.R. "EFT Disbursement: ACH Credits vs. ACH Debits." *EDI Forum,* Vol. 4 (1991), pp. 32–37.

Calman, Robert F. *Linear Programming and Cash Management: Cash ALPHA.* Cambridge, Mass.: M.I.T. Press, 1968.

Cohen, A.M. "Treasury Terminal Systems and Cash Management Information Support." *Journal of Cash Management,* Vol. 3 (Aug./Sept. 1983), pp. 9–18.

Driscoll, Mary C. *Cash Management: Corporate Strategies for Profit.* New York: John Wiley & Sons, Inc., Wiley Interscience, 1983.

Fabozzi, Frank J., and Leslie N. Masonson, eds. *Corporate Cash Management: Techniques and Analysis.* Homewood, Ill.: Dow Jones-Irwin, 1985.

Ferguson, D.M., and N.C. Hill. "Cash Flow Timeline Management: The Next Frontier of Cash Management." *Journal of Cash Management* (May/June 1985), pp. 12–22.

Ferguson, Daniel M., and Stephen F. Maier. "Disbursement System Design for the 1980s." *Journal of Cash Management,* Vol. 2 (Nov. 1982), pp. 56–69.

Fielitz, B.D., and D.L. White. "An Evaluation and Linking of Alternative Solution Procedures for the Lock Box Location Problem." *Journal of Bank Research,* Vol. 13 (Spring 1982), pp. 17–27.

———. "A Two-Stage Solution Procedure for the Lock Box Location Problem." *Management Science,* Vol. 27 (Aug. 1981), pp. 881–886.

Gitman, L.J., E.A. Moses, and I.T. White. "An Assessment of Corporate Cash Management Practices." *Financial Management,* Vol. 8 (Spring 1979), pp. 32–41.

Haag, Leonard H. *Cash Management and Short-Term Investments for Colleges and Universities.* Washington, D.C.: National Association of College and University Business Officers, 1977.

———. "Using Money Funds for Business Disbursing Accounts." *Journal of Cash Management,* Vol. 1 (Oct. 1981), pp. 51–54.

Hausman, W.H., and A. Sanchez-Bell. "The Stochastic Cash Balance Problem with Average Compensating Balance Requirements." *Management Science,* Vol. 21 (Apr. 1976), pp. 849–857.

Maier, S.F., and J.A. Vander Weide. "The Lock-Box Location Problem: A Practical Reformation." *Journal of Bank Research,* Vol. 5 (Summer 1974), pp. 92–95.

———. *Managing Corporate Liquidity: An Introduction to Working Capital Management.* New York: John Wiley & Sons, Inc., 1985.

———. "A Practical Approach to Short-Run Financial Planning." *Financial Management,* Vol. 7 (Winter 1978), pp. 10–16.

———. "A Unified Location Model for Cash Disbursements and Lock-Box Collections." *Journal of Bank Research*, Vol. 7 (Summer 1976), pp. 166–172.

Miller, T.W., and B.K. Stone. "Daily Cash Forecasting and Seasonal Resolution: Alternative Models and Techniques for Using the Distribution Approach." *Journal of Financial and Quantitative Analysis*, Vol. 20 (Sept. 1985), pp. 335–351.

Nauss, R.M., and R.E. Markland. "Development and Implementation of An Improved Lock Box Location Analysis." *Review of Industrial Management and Textile Science*, Vol. 19 (Spring 1980), pp. 61–80.

———. "Solving Lock Box Location Problems." *Financial Management*, Vol. 8 (Spring 1979), pp. 21–31.

———. "Theory and Application of An Optimal Procedure for Cash Disbursement Account and Lock Box Location Analysis." *Management Science*, Vol. 27 (Aug. 1981), pp. 855–865.

Orgler, Yair E. *Cash Management: Methods and Models*. Belmont, Cal.: Wadsworth, 1970.

———. "An Unequal Period Model for Cash Management Decisions." *Management Science*, Vol. 20 (1974), pp. 1350–1363.

Sartoris, W.L., and N.A. Hill. "A Generalized Cash Flow Approach to Short-Term Financial Decisions." *Journal of Finance*, Vol. 38 (May 1983), pp. 349–360.

Smith, Derek V. "Treasury Terminal Systems: A Vogue Out of Control?" *Journal of Cash Management*, Vol. 3 (Aug./Sept. 1983), pp. 23–27.

Smith, K.V. "State of the Art of Working Capital Management." *Financial Management*, Vol. 2 (Autumn 1973), pp. 50–55.

Stancil, J.M. Jr. "A Lock-Box Model." *Management Science*, Vol. 15 (Oct. 1968), pp. B-84–B-87.

Stone, B.K. "Allocating Credit Lines, Planned Borrowing and Tangible Services Over a Company's Banking System." *Financial Management*, Vol. 4 (Summer 1975), pp. 65–78.

———. "Cash Planning and Credit Line Determination With a Financial Statement Stimulator: A Cash Report on Short-Term Financial Planning." *Journal of Financial and Quantitative Analysis*, Vol. 8 (Dec. 1973), pp. 711–729.

———. "Design of a Company's Banking System." *Journal of Finance*, Vol. 38 (May 1983), pp. 373–383.

———. "Design of a Receivable Collection System." *Management Science*, Vol. 27 (Aug. 1981), pp. 876–880.

———. "Lock-Box Selection and Collection System Design: Objective Function Validity." *Journal of Bank Research*, Vol. 10 (Winter 1980), pp. 251–254.

———. *One to Get Ready: How to Prepare Your Company for EDI*. Philadelphia: The CoreStates Banks, 1988.

———. "The Payment Pattern Approach of the Forecasting and Control of Accounts Receivable." *Financial Management*, Vol. 5 (Autumn 1976), pp. 65–72.

———. "The Use of Forecasts and Smoothing in Control Limit Models for Cash Management." *Financial Management*, Vol. 1 (Spring 1972), pp. 72–84.

———. "Zero-Balance Banking and the Design of a Collection System in a Divisional Firm," *Advances in Mathematical Programming and Financial Planning*, John Guerard, ed. Greenwich, Conn.: JAI Press, 1986.

Stone, B.K., D.M. Ferguson, and N.C. Hill. "Cash Transfer Scheduling: Overview." *Cash Manager*, Vol. 3 (Mar. 1980), pp. 3–8.

Stone, B.K., and N.C. Hill. "Cash Transfer Scheduling for Efficient Cash Concentration." *Financial Management*, Vol. 9 (Autumn 1980), pp. 35–43.

Stone, B.K., and T. Miller. "Daily Cash Forecasting: A Structuring Framework." *Journal of Cash Management* (Oct. 1981), pp. 35–50.

———. "Daily Cash Forecasting with Multiplicative Models of Cash Flow Patterns." *Financial Management*, Vol. 16 (Winter 1987), pp. 45–54.

———. "Forecasting Disbursement Funding Requirements: The Clearing Pattern Approach." *Journal of Cash Management*, Vol. 3 (Oct./Nov. 1983), pp. 67–78.

Stone, B.K., and R.A. Wood. "Daily Cash Forecasting: A Simple Method for Implementing the Distribution Approach." *Financial Management*, Vol. 6 (Fall 1977), pp. 40–50.

Sullivan, C.F. "Multitier Zero Balancing—A Customized Implementation." *Journal of Cash Management*, Vol. 3 (Oct./Nov. 1983), pp. 57–66.

———. "Reviewing Bank Account Analysis: Ramada's Approach." *Journal of Cash Management*, Vol. 2 (Nov. 1982), pp. 24–31.

LONG-TERM

FINANCIAL MANAGEMENT

Chapter 5

Capital Budgeting

DIANA R. HARRINGTON

5.01 INTRODUCTION

Managers of U.S. firms have been soundly criticized for a short-sighted management approach.[1] Critics claim that because myopic managements failed to plan adequately for the long term, U.S. industry lost its worldwide competitive edge. Some place the blame on a preoccupation with earnings per share; others blame the techniques used to evaluate opportunities. Some who have examined the investment policies of companies in various countries believe that the problem with U.S. investment policy lies with the cost of capital: The governments of some countries artificially lower the costs of debt and equity for their industries. This capital cost advantage allows managements to invest in projects that would be unacceptable if the returns were not enhanced by government intervention. Whether any of these criticisms are justified is a matter of continuing debate.

Managers do not choose to make bad decisions; nor do they knowingly use techniques that will lead to them. While the debate continues, therefore, each manager will want to consider carefully the way in which capital investment decisions are made, and the techniques that assist in such decision making.

This chapter describes the most widely used techniques for evaluating a corporation's investment opportunities, their strengths and weaknesses, and their usefulness in making capital budgeting decisions. Wherever the techniques can be misunderstood or misused, the chapter also points out the potential problems. Each section contains real-life examples.

5.02 INVESTMENT DECISION MAKING

[1] Purpose of Capital Budgeting

Most firms have a formal capital budgeting process for two reasons: First, because a company's financial health is simply a reflection of the success of its past investments, capital budgeting is an integral part of long-term strategic planning; second, because such investments are often large and can be difficult and costly to reverse once they are made, there should be a formal review before the investment plan is implemented.

The capital investment process consists of seven steps:

1. Identifying investment opportunities

2. Estimating the costs and benefits associated with each opportunity

3. Evaluating these costs and benefits

4. Determining the relative attractiveness of each investment

5. Choosing among investment alternatives

6. Implementing the chosen investments

7. Evaluating the implemented investments

---

[1] See, e.g., R.H. Hayes and W.J. Abernathy, "Managing Our Way to Economic Decline," *Harvard Business Review* (July–Aug. 1980), pp. 67–77. For a rebuttal, see D.A. Logue and R.R. West, "Discounted Cash Flow Analysis: A Response to the Critics," *National Productivity Review* (Summer 1983), pp. 233–241. This criticism is now extended to recent changes in Japanese investment practices.

The capital investment process is an ongoing one in which these seven steps are repeated continuously by the firm. Although each step is important in ensuring that the best possible decisions are made, this chapter concentrates on those that are of most concern to the financial analyst, steps 2 through 5. In addition, because managers operate on behalf of the owners of the company, who care about the size of the returns, when they can be expected, and the extent of risk associated with their investments' net benefits, investment evaluation methods that incorporate these concerns are also discussed in this chapter.

[a] Definition of Capital Investment. A capital investment is any outlay of money from which future benefits are expected. The analyst usually distinguishes a capital investment from a corporate expenditure by treating the benefits from a capital investment as continuing for some time, generally for more than a year.

Capital investments are usually considered assets that are capitalized (recorded on the firm's balance sheet). Valued at their purchase price, such assets (e.g., a building or equipment) generally are expensed not when they are purchased but over their useful lives.[2] While capital investments such as physical plants, land, and equipment may first come to mind, firms also make investments in other firms (acquisitions), in working capital (permanent increases in inventory, accounts receivable, or cash), in advertising campaigns, in marketing programs, and in uncapitalized assets such as research and development. Even though generally accepted accounting practices in the United States do not allow some of these investments to be capitalized, they are nonetheless long-term investments of capital, and capital budgeting techniques should be used to evaluate such investments.

[b] Cost/Benefit Analysis. There is a simple rule in making capital investments: Create value for the firm's owners. In order for this to happen, the benefits from the investment must exceed all of its costs. The benefits and costs are those specific to the investment itself and are thus separate from those incurred by the company's other endeavors.

The benefits and costs are measured in a currency, e.g., dollars if the investment is in the United States. Analysts determine the benefits and costs by first looking at the effect of each investment on the company's financial position. Because most firms use accrual accounting, two important factors must be considered. In the accrual method, revenues and liabilities are recorded when made, not when money is actually received or paid. Thus, there may be a lag of several months or even years between the accrual of a revenue or liability and the receipt or disbursement of cash. Because cash is the only thing a firm can use to invest, reduce debt, or pay expenses, it is disbursements and receipts, not accrued expenses (promises of payment) or accrued revenues (promises of receipts), that are of interest in valuing an investment.

Second, many companies charge an investment with a portion of the firm's ongoing expenses, sometimes called overhead. If the investment neither increases nor decreases the overall corporate overhead, such an accounting allocation is not an incremental benefit or cost and thus should be ignored in determining whether the investment will create value. The investment analyst's job is not to forecast the revenues and expenses the firm's accountants will record but to estimate the investment's cash

---

[2] In fact, useful life may be defined less by an asset's economic value than by rules of the taxing authority under which the company operates.

FIGURE 5-1

Labeling Machine: Cash Costs

Item	Cost	Timing
Machine purchase	$85,000	Before operation (year 0)
Machine overhaul	18,000	End year 5
Operator salary and benefits	25,000	Yearly (years 1–10)
Electricity	2,000	Yearly (years 1–10)

costs and cash benefits to the company. Some investments may increase or reduce the cash flows of other parts of a business; for example, expansion of an auto dealer's service area not only will increase service profits but may also increase car sales and profits. Such "systems effects" must be included.

Forecasting costs. There are two types of cash costs (outflows): capital costs and operating costs. Capital costs include the initial costs necessary to acquire the investment, plus any subsequent expenditures that extend its life or enhance its operations. Operating costs are the recurring cash outlays required once the investment is a part of the firm's operations.

Examples of cash costs can be seen in the outflows from an investment being considered by the managers of the Fire Dragon Corporation. Fire Dragon prepares and packages horseradish for domestic consumption and is located in the northwestern United States. The company's operations are seasonal and quite labor intensive. In order to reduce this labor intensity, Fire Dragon's management is considering purchasing a labeling machine to replace the 4 full-time employees whose job it is to hand-place the labels on each jar of horseradish. The purchase price of the machine is $85,000, and the manufacturer says it will have a useful life of 5 years. The machine's life can be extended to 10 years if it has a major overhaul at a cost of $18,000 after 5 years. The cost of the machine and its overhaul are capital costs.

For tax purposes, the U.S. Internal Revenue Service (IRS) requires that Fire Dragon spread the cost of the labeling machine over what it considers is its useful life, five years for both the machine and the overhaul. For operating costs, the machine will use considerable electricity, forecast at a cost of $2,000 per year, and require one full-time operator, who will receive free training by the manufacturer in operating the machine and performing basic repairs. Yearly salary and benefits for the machine operator are expected to be $25,000. The machine will be housed in a currently unused portion of the Fire Dragon factory at no added cost to Fire Dragon. Other operating costs (e.g., glue and labels) will remain the same whether the labels are placed by hand or by machine. The incremental capital and operating costs to Fire Dragon are summarized in Figure 5-1.

Forecasting benefits. Benefits can come from four different sources:

1. Revenues from increased sales

2. Cost reductions from more efficient processes

3. Cash received when replaced equipment is sold

4. Cash received when the investment is salvaged at the end of its useful life

FIGURE 5-2

Labeling Machine: Double-Declining-Balance Depreciation

Year	Book Value at Beginning of Year	Depreciation
1	$85,000	$34,000
2	51,000	20,400
3	30,600	12,240
4	18,360	9,180[a]
5	9,180	9,180[a]

[a] Equipment lasting five years would be depreciated 20 percent per year using straight-line depreciation. The double-declining-balance rate is 40 percent per year. In the fourth year, the balance yet to be depreciated is $18,360. With two years of life remaining, the straight-line depreciation is $9,180 ($18,360 divided by 2). Since it is greater than the double-declining-balance depreciation ($7.344 in the fourth year), the switch can be made in year 4. The switch to straight-line depreciation is allowed and results in tax benefit earlier than does continuing with double-declining balance.

Fire Dragon's management expects to benefit from three of these sources.

First, the company will no longer require four seasonal workers to affix labels. The savings will be $10,250 per employee for a total of $41,000 per year. Second, the equipment currently used in the labeling operation, mainly tables, will be scrapped; management expects the equipment to be sold for $2,000. Because this equipment has been fully depreciated, taxes estimated at 34 percent will be paid: $680 on the $2,000 income.[3] Third, management expects any salvage value the new equipment may have at the end of its life to be offset by the costs of removing the equipment. No increase in revenues will result from changing to the automated label-affixing process.

Indirect cash benefits will also be received by the company; depreciation will lower the taxes the company would otherwise pay. Most tax codes allow a company to expense the equipment not when it is purchased, but over its useful life. Current U.S. tax law allows Fire Dragon to depreciate (expense) the equipment using double-declining balance, an accelerated method of depreciation offering a greater tax savings in early years, over the machine's life. As a rule, companies should choose the allowable depreciation method that produces the greatest tax savings as quickly as possible.[4] The depreciation expense is shown in Figure 5-2.

Figure 5-3 summarizes the benefits from Fire Dragon's new labeling machine; it also shows the depreciation tax shield for the original machine, as well as the depreciation tax shield on the depreciable part of its prospective overhaul.

---

[3] Different tax codes treat this income differently. Under some codes, it would be taxed at a capital gains rate, and under others, the marginal tax rate for ordinary income.

[4] To calculate the double-declining-balance depreciation, double the straight-line percentage and multiply it by the book value of the asset. Straight-line depreciation (equal amounts for each year) is used at the point where it exceeds the applicable double-declining-balance depreciation.

FIGURE 5-3

Labeling Machine: Cash Benefits

Item	Benefit	Timing	
Reduced salaries and benefits	$41,000	Yearly (years 1–10)	
Sales of old equipment			
Proceeds of sale	2,000		
Taxes (at 34%)	(680)		
Net proceeds	$1,320	Before operation (year 0)	
Depreciation that will lead to tax savings			
Labeling machine	$34,000	Year	1
	20,400		2
	12,240		3
	9,180		4
	9,180		5
Overhaul	7,200		6
	4,320		7
	2,592		8
	1,944		9
	1,944		10

For a clear picture of the net after-tax cash flows from this investment, the benefits and costs are combined in Figure 5-4, which shows a standard format for presenting an investment's cash flows. Figure 5-4 shows depreciation as a cash cost. This is merely a means of showing depreciation as an expense shielding income from taxes, and thereby reducing taxable income. Depreciation is, however, a noncash cost: The cash was spent when the equipment was acquired. To adjust for this noncash expense, the analyst can either deduct depreciation as a cash cost but add it back to the profit after taxes to determine the net cash flow or deal with it directly by adding the depreciation tax shield to the profit before depreciation and after taxes. Using the latter method, Figure 5-4 would show the net income after taxes in year 1 to be $9,240 and the depreciation tax shield to be $11,560 ($34,000 times a 34 percent tax rate) for a net cash flow of $20,800.

This analysis of costs and benefits is designed to determine whether incremental investments of cash are justified by the incremental benefits. Any costs or benefits associated with the investment before this time are irrelevant (sunk) costs. For instance, any expenditure already made on research and development, such as research to design or evaluate the labeling machine, is not a cost relevant to this project: The object is to create value from any new cash investment.[5] Note that Fire Dragon's management attempts to be neither optimistic nor pessimistic in its forecasts but as accurate as possible. The result is a description of the costs and benefits that management believes will actually result from the purchase of the equipment. It does not include any expense for the portion of the plant that will house the machine, because there is no cash cost associated with it. The forecast also includes no new revenues,

---

[5] Fire Dragon's management certainly should have analyzed all costs (including research and development) and benefits before anything was done about the labeling machine in the first place. However, once costs (or benefits) are incurred, they are irrelevant to future decisions.

because the method of affixing labels has no effect on the number of jars of horseradish sold.

Fire Dragon's case demonstrates the estimation of costs and benefits, but the example is a simple one. The costs of the machine are known (as they often are), and Fire Dragon's management believes that salary and overhead costs and benefits can be accurately forecast. That is rarely the case. The treatment of uncertain forecasts is discussed later in this chapter.

[2] Approaches to Investment Decision Making

After the cash flows have been forecast, management must decide whether the investment is attractive. There are a number of methods that can be used to help make this decision, each with advantages and disadvantages. Generally, the only theoretically correct approach is the net present value (NPV) method. This is sometimes called discounted cash flow analysis. However, many companies cling to alternative methods, even though they have serious flaws. Before considering the NPV method in detail, a brief description of several of these alternative methods is offered.

[a] **Accounting Rate of Return.** Once widely used as a measure of an investment's attractiveness, the accounting rate of return is simply the average annual profits after taxes divided by the investment's average net book value over the life of the investment. The average book value of the Fire Dragon labeling machine (and its overhead) over the 10 years is $51,500 (the sum of $85,000 and $18,000 divided by 2). This is the starting value plus the ending value divided by 2. The average profit is $2,574 per year; the accounting rate of return is 5 percent.

To decide whether the project should be accepted, management compares this figure to a bench mark that is, for the most part, subjectively determined. This method ignores the timing of benefits and costs and measures accounting returns, not cash flows. Because it fails to account for the time value of money and because it ignores the excess of cash flow relative to accounting profit, this method is a poor one.

The use of accounting rate of return is used in managerial performance evaluation. However, if managers' performance is judged on the accounting rate of return, the managers will make investment decisions based on accounting returns, regardless of the method used to analyze an investment's value. Because a reward system is so important, when a firm uses one method for performance evaluation and a conflicting method for capital budgeting, the result is predictable: The reward system will dominate. A better approach is to use the performance review and reward systems that are consistent with the capital budgeting system and to measure value creation by NPV analysis.

[b] **Benefit/Cost Ratio.** Another quick but misleading measure of an investment's attractiveness is the benefit/cost ratio. To calculate this ratio, divide the total benefits by the total costs. If the ratio exceeds 1.0, the investment is acceptable. The benefit/cost ratio for Fire Dragon's labeling machine is determined in Figure 5-5. The benefit/cost ratio for the labeling machine would be

$$\frac{\text{Benefits}}{\text{costs}} = \frac{\$128,740}{\$103,000} = 1.25 = 125\%$$

FIGURE 5-4

Labeling Machine: Cash Flow Forecast

	Year			
	0	1	2	3
Changes in Income Statement				
Salaries and benefits				
Old workers		$ 41,000	$ 41,000	$ 41,000
New labeling machine operator		(25,000)	(25,000)	(25,000)
Electricity		(2,000)	(2,000)	(2,000)
Depreciation				
Labeling machine		(34,000)	(20,400)	(12,240)
Labeling machine overhaul				
Old equipment sale	$ 2,000			
Net income before taxes	$ 2,000	$(20,000)	$ (6,400)	$ 1,760
Taxes (at 34%)	(680)	6,800[a]	2,176[a]	(598)
Net income after taxes	$ 1,320	$(13,200)	$ (4,224)	$ 1,162
Noncash Charges				
Depreciation				
Labeling machine		34,000	20,400	12,240
Labeling machine overhaul				
Annual cash flow	$ 1,320	$ 20,800	$ 16,176	$ 13,402
Balance Sheet Impacts				
Labeling machine	$(85,000)			
Labeling machine overhaul				
Net Cash Flow	$(83,680)	$ 20,800	$ 16,176	$ 13,402

[a] Positive taxes represent a tax credit used against taxes on Fire Dragon income from other investments.

For Fire Dragon's new machine, the ratio is 1.25; that is, the benefits are 125 percent of the costs. The investment has an acceptable benefit/cost ratio.

    [c] Payback. The payback method is similar to but more widely used than the benefit/cost ratio. Payback simply measures the time, in years, it takes to recover the initial investment. If the cash flows from Figure 5-4 are used, the payback for the labeling machine is 6.4 years and is calculated as shown in Figure 5-6. Note that, because the labeling machine is overhauled in the fifth year, the benefits must cover this cost as well.

    It is up to Fire Dragon's management to decide whether a payback of 6.4 years is adequate. The acceptable payback period is set by each firm's managers. In choosing among several projects with acceptable paybacks, managers generally favor investments with the shortest payback periods.

    Payback is simple to use and can be helpful in certain circumstances. For instance, payback can indicate whether a firm is expected to recover its investment in time to make another investment or a payment on outstanding debt. It is relatively useless as a measure of value, however, because it ignores all cash flows after the payback period and the timing of the benefits before the payback date. An example will make this problem clear.

			Year			
4	5	6	7	8	9	10
$41,000	$41,000	$41,000	$41,000	$41,000	$41,000	$41,000
(25,000)	(25,000)	(25,000)	(25,000)	(25,000)	(25,000)	(25,000)
(2,000)	(2,000)	(2,000)	(2,000)	(2,000)	(2,000)	(2,000)
(9,180)	(9,180)					
		(7,200)	(4,320)	(2,592)	(1,944)	(1,944)
$ 4,820	$ 4,820	$ 6,800	$ 9,680	$ 11,408	$ 12,056	$ 12,056
(1,639)	(1,639)	(2,312)	(3,291)	(3,879)	(4,099)	(4,099)
$ 3,181	$ 3,181	$ 4,488	$ 6,389	$ 7,529	$ 7,957	$ 7,957
9,180	9,180					
			4,320	2,592	1,994	1,994
$12,361	$12,361	$11,688	$10,709	$10,121	$ 9,951	$ 9,951
	(18,000)					
$12,361	$ (5,639)	$11,688	$10,709	$10,121	$ 9,951	$ 9,951

Two available investments, *A* and *B,* have the cash flow patterns shown in Figure 5-7. Both have paybacks of three years and, judged by this measure, would appear to be equally acceptable. However, most rational investors would prefer investment *A*: The investor can find other uses for the $999,900 received from investment *A* in the first year and benefit from them. Investment *B* has no such hidden benefit.

Both the benefit/cost ratio and the payback methods share this hidden value. The benefit/cost ratio treats cash received at all points in time as equivalent, yet investors certainly would prefer to receive their money sooner rather than later. Payback attempts to include the investor's timing preference but does so inadequately, because it ignores cash flows beyond the payback period, which are not irrelevant. Neither payback nor the benefit/cost ratio does enough to take into account the investor's time value of money.

[d] Discounting Techniques. Investors prefer large returns over small ones, but they also want to have cash readily available for their use. If cash is tied up in an investment, investors want to be compensated for their illiquidity or their inability to use the funds elsewhere. The analyst can take this timing preference into account and compensate the investor for waiting by determining the present value of any future cash flow. The easiest way to do this is by discounting.

In discounting, the annual cash flows that will be received in the future will be reduced to reflect their value at the present time. For example, if investors require a

FIGURE 5-5

Labeling Machine: Total Cash Flows

	Total After Tax
Benefits	
Salary and benefits	
Old process	$270,000
New process	(165,000)
Depreciation	
Labeling machine	28,900
Labeling machine overhaul	6,120
Electricity	(13,200)
Salvage value	1,320
Total Benefits	$128,740
Costs	
New machine	$ 85,000
New machine overhaul	18,000
Total Costs	$103,000

FIGURE 5-6

Labeling Machine: Payback

Year	Annual Cash Flow	Remaining Investment
0	$(83,680)	$(83,680)
1	20,800	(62,880)
2	16,176	(46,704)
3	13,402	(33,302)
4	12,361	(20,941)
5	(5,639)	(26,580)
6	11,688	(14,892)
7	10,709	(4,183)[a]
8	10,121	5,938
9	9,951	15,839
10	9,951	25,740

[a] Payback = 6.4 years ($4,183/$10,121 = 0.41 year).

FIGURE 5-7

Payback: Two Alternatives

	Net Cash Flow	
Year	Investment A	Investment B
0	$(1,000,000)	$(1,000,000)
1	999,900	0
2	0	0
3	100	1,000,000

FIGURE 5-8

Labeling Machine: Present Value Payback

Year	Present Value Cash Flow[a]		Remaining Investment
0	$-\$83{,}680/1.03^0 =$	$-\$83{,}680$	$-\$83{,}680$
1	$20{,}800/1.03^1 =$	$20{,}194$	$-63{,}486$
2	$16{,}176/1.03^2 =$	$15{,}247$	$-48{,}239$
3	$13{,}402/1.03^3 =$	$12{,}264$	$-35{,}975$
4	$12{,}361/1.03^4 =$	$10{,}983$	$-24{,}992$
5	$-5{,}639/1.03^5 =$	$-4{,}864$	$-29{,}856$
6	$11{,}688/1.03^6 =$	$9{,}789$	$-20{,}067$
7	$10{,}709/1.03^7 =$	$8{,}707$	$-11{,}360$
8	$10{,}121/1.03^8 =$	$7{,}990$	$-3{,}370$[b]
9	$9{,}901/1.03^9 =$	$7{,}588$	$4{,}218$
10	$9{,}901/1.03^{10} =$	$7{,}367$	$11{,}585$

[a] Because of differences in the methods used for discounting by different
calculators and computers, the numbers can vary slightly.

[b] Present value payback = 8.4 years ($3,370/$7,588 = 0.44 year).

3 percent rate of return to induce them to invest, the promise of $1 to be received in two years at a discount rate R of 3 percent is worth 94 percent of the value of $1 today (the present value).[6]

For discounting, with n representing the number of years, the present value of cash flows (CF) is calculated as

$$\text{Present value} = \frac{CF_n}{(1 + R)^n} = \frac{\$1}{(1 + 0.03)^2} = \frac{\$1}{(1.03)(1.03)} = \frac{\$1}{1.06} = \$0.94$$

Now the investor knows that $1 received at the end of two years is really worth only $0.94 in today's dollars. At the end of the second year, $1.06 must be received to be the equivalent to $1 today.

$$\text{Future value} = (1 + R)^n(CF_1) = (1 + 0.03)^2(\$1) = (1.03)(1.03)\$1 = 1.06(\$1) = \$1.06$$

Discounting, once a laborious process, has been made quite simple by all but the most basic handheld calculators.

Present value payback. The simplest application of discounting is to include it in the payback measure. The present value payback discounts each year's net cash flow to its present value. The payback then calculated indicates the time it takes to recover the initial investment in present value terms. The present value payback for Fire Dragon's labeling machine, 8.4 years, is shown in Figure 5-8.

---

[6] The determination of future value, known as compounding, is simply the reverse of the present value method.

$$\text{Future value} = (1 + R)^n(CF_1)$$
$$= (1 + 0.03)^2(\$1) = (1.03)(1.03)\$1 = (1.06)\$1 = \$1.06$$

While present value payback includes the time value of money, unlike the simple payback method, it also ignores cash flows beyond the payback date. Thus, it is only slightly better than payback itself. Only if management considers the investment to be temporary and a subsequent use of the funds is known should payback or present value payback be used as a measure of relative attractiveness.

There is no need to discriminate arbitrarily against projects with large but later cash benefits, as does payback. NPV takes both the time value of money and all of the cash flows into account and gives a better measure of an investment's relative value to the investor than do the methods discussed so far.

NPV. The NPV is, quite simply, the present value (the value in today's dollars) of the benefits minus the present value of the costs:

$$NPV = \frac{NCF_0}{(1 + R)^0} + \frac{NCF_1}{(1 + R)^1} + \frac{NCF_2}{(1 + R)^2} + \cdots + \frac{NCF_n}{(1 + R)^3}$$

where:

NCF = yearly net cash flow (annual benefits minus costs)

R = required rate of return or discount rate

$0, 1, 2, \ldots, n$ = years from date of initial investment

Using the Figure 5-4 cash flows and a discount rate of 3 percent, the NPV for Fire Dragon's labeling machine would be (in thousands of dollars)

$$NPV = \frac{-\$83.7}{1.03^0} + \frac{\$20.8}{1.03^1} + \frac{\$16.2}{1.03^2} + \frac{\$13.4}{1.03^3} + \frac{\$12.4}{1.03^4} + \frac{-\$5.6}{1.03^5} + \frac{\$11.7}{1.03^6} + \frac{\$10.7}{1.03^7}$$

$$+ \frac{\$10.1}{1.03^8} + \frac{\$9.9}{1.03^9} + \frac{\$9.9}{1.03^{10}} = \$11,585.74$$

This is the present value of the net worth that the labeling machine is expected to contribute to Fire Dragon's owners by the end of the machine's 10-year life. The discount rate takes the timing of the cash flows into account. Using a calculator or computer spreadsheet program with an NPV function makes calculating the NPV quite simple.

The NPV is a logical way of evaluating investments that takes both the magnitude and the timing of the cash flows into account. Acceptable investments under this method are those whose NPV is zero or greater. An NPV of zero indicates that at that discount rate, the investor's value is neither created nor destroyed; it is a sort of investment breakeven. NPVs greater than zero indicate value-creating investments. Figure 5-9 shows these relationships graphically.

The Fire Dragon labeling machine provides a return in excess of the 3 percent illiquidity (time value of money) premium; it has a positive NPV.

PVI. Some managers find the dollar expression of the NPV hard to interpret and prefer to use a ratio. The present value index (PVI), which takes the present value of all costs and benefits into account, is essentially an adaptation of the benefit/cost ratio. For the Fire Dragon labeling machine, the PVI would be (in thousands of dollars)

$$PVI = \frac{\text{Present value of net benefits}}{\text{present value of investments}}$$

FIGURE 5-9

Market Price of Risk

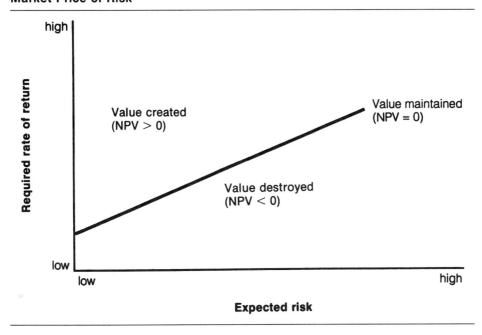

$$= \left(\frac{\$20.8}{1.03^1} + \frac{\$16.2}{1.03^2} + \frac{\$13.4}{1.03^3} + \frac{\$12.4}{1.03^4} + \frac{\$12.4}{1.03^5} + \frac{\$11.7}{1.03^6} + \frac{\$10.7}{1.03^7} + \frac{\$10.1}{1.03^8} + \frac{\$9.9}{1.03^9} \right.$$

$$\left. + \frac{\$9.9}{1.03^{10}} \right) \Big/ \$100.5 = \frac{\$112,113}{\$100,500} = 1.12 = 112\%$$

This result means that, for each dollar invested, the labeling machine is expected to return $1.12 in benefits. Note that the PVI will change if the discount rate is increased or decreased. An NPV profile for Fire Dragon's labeling machine is shown in Figure 5-10.

IRR. The internal rate of return (IRR) is an alternative discounting method to measure the average rate of return the investment is expected to yield over its life. To calculate the IRR, the formula for the NPV is used: Set the NPV equal to zero and solve for *R*, the discount rate that equates the stream of net cash flows to the initial investment.[7]

The IRR for the labeling machine is 6.1 percent. An acceptable IRR (hurdle rate) for a project with no risk would be the rate the investor requires. Because this invest-

---

[7] Solving for the rate by hand is much more difficult than calculating the NPV and is done by trial and error: Choose an arbitrary rate (*R*) and calculate the NPV; if the NPV exceeds zero, choose a higher rate to discount the cash flows; if the NPV is below zero, use a lower rate. Continue this process until the rate that yields an NPV of zero is found. Obviously, calculators and computer spreadsheet programs with the IRR function simplify the task.

FIGURE 5-10

Labeling Machine: NPV Profile

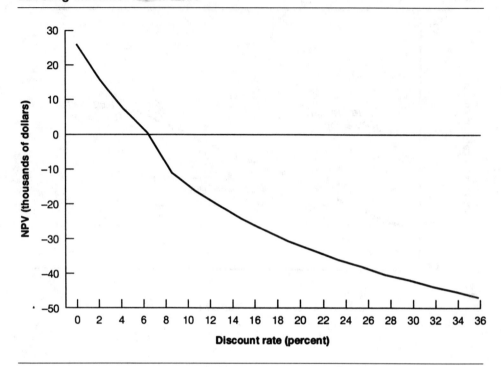

ment's IRR exceeds the rate of 3 percent used for the time value of money, the labeling machine would be acceptable.

While many believe that the IRR is equivalent to the NPV, its use can create problems. If investments compared are of different sizes, if the timing of their cash flows is different, or if there are negative and positive net cash flows alternating over the life of the project, the IRR can give results that are misleading or difficult to interpret. The labeling machine has the last problem, alternating cash flows: Because its cash flows change from positive to negative more than once, there may be more than one IRR. Most calculators and computers solve for only one IRR regardless of the fact that there may be more. Thus, the managers may believe they have adequate information on which to make an investment decision when they do not. For these and other reasons to be discussed later, the NPV is superior to the IRR in measuring value.

As noted previously, many managers find the IRR attractive, despite its limitations, because it measures value as a rate of return rather than as dollars of present value. For these managers, a graphic approach, the NPV profile, is suggested.

5.03 INCORPORATING INFLATION

Inflation is a measurement of change in the purchasing power of a currency—in Fire Dragon's case, the dollar—over time. Real cash flow forecasts (net of inflation) provide an estimate of the constant dollar costs and benefits anticipated from an investment. This estimate is not necessarily a forecast of the investment's actual outflows and inflows as they will occur. Over the life of the investment, costs and benefits may change considerably as inflation flares and wanes. For example, Fire Dragon's management forecast the salary and benefits for the new machine operator at $25,000 per year, assuming no increase in salary arising from inflation. What would change in the analysis if management expected inflation to be 5 percent per year for the next 10 years?

Figure 5-11 shows the nominal forecasts for Fire Dragon's labeling machine investment when costs and benefits are equally affected by inflation.

Obviously, the cash flows in Figure 5-11 are larger than those in Figure 5-4 and, if discounted at the 3 percent rate of return, would result in a higher NPV. However, they are not comparable. Investors want an NPV of zero or greater, after taking into account the impact of inflation on their required rate of return. Thus, the discount rate for the inflated cash flows must be increased by the expected rate of general inflation. When the appropriate discount rates are used, the NPVs of the two forecasts would be equal.

Note that the inflated cash flow forecasts in Figure 5-10 are not appropriate under the current U.S. tax code. The U.S. tax code depreciates capital investments on the basis of their original cost, regardless of the effect or potential effect of inflation on their monetary value over time. In contrast, tax regulations in high-inflation environments often revalue capital equipment each year and depreciate the new value. In periods when inflation is high and depreciation is not indexed to inflation, corporations have a smaller depreciation tax shield than they would otherwise have had. This can provide a disincentive to making investments that must be capitalized and depreciated.

To the extent that depreciation provides a smaller tax advantage as inflation increases, the net cash flows for Fire Dragon's labeling machine in Figures 5-11 and 5-12 are different. The NPV of the labeling cash flows (Figure 5-12) with 5 percent inflation (discounted at 8 percent) is $7,966.[8] If depreciation were indexed to inflation and all costs and benefits also moved directly with inflation, the NPVs with and without inflation would be $12,189.

When the IRR is used, a change to account for inflation must also be made. The nominal IRR for the labeling machine under the U.S. tax code (Figure 5-11) is 10.2 percent. To determine whether the investment is acceptable, it must be compared to the investor's required rate of return of 8 percent.

Because the rate of inflation is difficult to predict, it is critical that the forecasts for all costs and benefits be based on one explicit inflation forecast and that the forecast be incorporated into the discount rate. In this manner, all such forecasts can be adjusted in the same way to eliminate confusion as new information is received, and decision making can be based on common assumptions. Without an explicit forecast for inflation, each flow could be based on a different and unrelated inflation rate and would be useless for making decisions.[9]

---

[8] This approach is the most widely used way of including the erosive effects of inflation in the investor's time value of money. A better (but not as widely used) approach is to turn each year's nominal cash flow into real cash flow before discounting the real cash flows at the real time value of money. Because of the nature of the mechanism, the two approaches yield different NPVs. The difference is larger for long-term projects and higher rates of inflation.

[9] The use of a single inflation rate for all cash flows may be too general if inflation affects the various costs and benefits in different ways. In that case, factor-specific inflation indexes may be more appropriate. If the outlook for inflation is uncertain, sensitivity or simulation analysis may be used to evaluate its affect.

FIGURE 5-11

Labeling Machine: Cash Flow Forecast With 5 Percent Inflation Affecting All Cash Flows

	0	1	2	3	4	5	6	7	8	9	10
						Year					
Changes in Income Statement											
Salaries and benefits											
Old workers		$ 43,050	$ 45,203	$ 47,463	$ 49,836	$ 52,328	$ 54,944	$ 57,691	$ 60,576	$ 63,604	$ 66,785
New labeling machine operator		(26,250)	(27,563)	(28,941)	(30,388)	(31,907)	(33,502)	(35,178)	(36,936)	(38,783)	(40,722)
Electricity		(2,100)	(2,205)	(2,315)	(2,431)	(2,553)	(2,680)	(2,814)	(2,955)	(3,103)	(3,258)
Depreciation											
Labeling machine		(35,700)	(22,491)	(14,169)	(11,158)	(11,716)					
Labeling machine overhaul							(9,649)	(6,079)	(3,830)	(3,016)	(3,167)
Old equipment sale	$ 2,000										
Net income before taxes	$ 2,000	$(21,000)	$ (7,056)	$ 2,037	$ 5,859	$ 6,152	$ 9,113	$ 13,621	$ 16,855	$ 18,703	$ 19,638
Taxes (at 34%)	(680)	7,140	2,399	(693)	(1,992)	(2,092)	(3,098)	(4,631)	(5,731)	(6,359)	(6,677)
Net income after taxes	$ 1,320	$(13,860)	$ (4,657)	$ 1,345	$ 3,867	$ 4,060	$ 6,014	$ 8,990	$ 11,124	$ 12,344	$ 12,961
Noncash Charges											
Depreciation											
Labeling machine		35,700	22,491	14,169	11,158	11,716					
Labeling machine overhaul							9,649	6,079	3,830	3,016	3,167
Annual cash flow	$ 1,320	$ 21,840	$ 17,834	$ 15,514	$ 15,025	$ 15,776	$ 15,663	$ 15,068	$ 14,954	$ 15,360	$ 16,128
Balance Sheet Impacts											
Labeling machine	(85,000)										
Labeling machine overhaul						(22,973)					
Net Cash Flow	$(83,680)	$ 21,840	$ 17,834	$ 15,514	$ 15,025	$ (7,197)	$ 15,663	$ 15,068	$ 14,954	$ 15,360	$ 16,128

FIGURE 5-12

Labeling Machine: Cash Flow Forecast With 5 Percent Inflation Affecting All Cash Flows Except Depreciation

	0	1	2	3	4	5	6	7	8	9	10
						Year					
Changes in Income Statement											
Salaries and benefits											
Old workers		$43,050	$45,203	$47,463	$49,836	$52,328	$54,944	$57,691	$60,576	$63,604	$66,785
New labeling machine operator		(26,250)	(27,563)	(28,941)	(30,388)	(31,907)	(33,502)	(35,178)	(36,936)	(38,783)	(40,722)
Electricity		(2,100)	(2,205)	(2,315)	(2,431)	(2,553)	(2,680)	(2,814)	(2,955)	(3,103)	(3,258)
Depreciation											
Labeling machine		(34,000)	(20,400)	(12,240)	(9,180)	(9,180)					
Labeling machine overhaul							(7,200)	(4,320)	(2,592)	(1,944)	(1,944)
Old equipment sale	$2,000										
Net income before taxes	$2,000	$(19,300)	$ (4,965)	$ 3,967	$ 7,837	$ 8,688	$11,562	$15,379	$18,093	$19,774	$20,861
Taxes (at 34%)	(680)	6,562	1,688	(1,349)	(2,665)	(2,954)	(3,931)	(5,229)	(6,151)	(6,723)	(7,093)
Net income after taxes	$1,320	$(12,738)	$ (3,277)	$ 2,618	$ 5,172	$ 5,734	$ 7,631	$10,150	$11,942	$13,051	$13,768
Noncash Charges											
Depreciation											
Labeling machine		34,000	20,400	12,240	9,180	9,180					
Labeling machine overhaul							7,200	4,320	2,592	1,944	1,944
Annual cash flow	1,320	$ 21,262	$17,123	$14,858	$14,352	$14,914	$14,831	$14,470	$14,534	$14,995	$15,712
Balance Sheet Impacts											
Labeling machine	$(85,000)										
Labeling machine overhaul						(22,973)					
Net Cash Flow	$(83,680)	$21,262	$17,123	$14,858	$14,352	$ (8,059)	$14,831	$14,470	$14,534	$14,995	$15,712

FIGURE 5-13

Alternative Labeling Machines: Relative Values

	10-Year Life	7-Year Life
NPV (3% discount rate)	$11,586	$14,562
IRR	6.1%	9.6%

It is clear so far that regardless of whether there is 5 percent inflation, if Fire Dragon has the resources it should buy the labeling machine and update the label-affixing process. However, management often must choose between investments, and this analysis is a little more complex.

5.04 CHOOSING AMONG INVESTMENT ALTERNATIVES

Fire Dragon's management has just found an alternative labeling machine. This labeling machine can be purchased for $20,000 less than the one already analyzed but will last only seven years. No renovation would be needed in the fifth year, but all other cash flows for the seven years are identical to those of the first machine, apart from the depreciation aspect. A comparison of the two labeling machines is shown in Figure 5-13.

The choice appears obvious. The shorter-lived machine is better. Or is it? Actually, the two machines cannot be compared because the shareholder's capital will be at risk for ten years with the more expensive labeling machine but for only seven years with the cheaper labeler.

In order to choose between investments, the analyst must first be sure that the two investments are quite similar in terms of such things as their expected lives, risks, and costs. Otherwise, quite different strategies for using capital will be erroneously compared. For instance, the seven-year machine will affix labels for a shorter period, leaving Fire Dragon without a labeling machine for the last three years. In order to have a fair comparison, management must specify its plans for affixing the labels during years 8 through 10 or its plans for the capital if the seven-year machine is purchased. If there is no explicit assumption, the implication in the first case is that Fire Dragon will not label its products during that time, and in the second case that the funds will remain idle for three years. Because neither is likely, management's plans for the funds during those three years must be explicitly stated.

[1] Different Lives

Whenever the lives of two alternative investments are not equal, they cannot be directly compared. There are two ways to create artificially equal-lived investments: Shorten the life of the longer-lived alternative or extend the life of the shorter-lived investment. For example, to make the life of the 10-year labeler shorter, the analyst must assume that management stops using the labeler after 7 years. At that time, management might put the labeler aside, scrap it, or sell it. Most of these possibilities carry with them some benefit or cost. If management normally sells retired equipment, the analyst must forecast the price management will receive when the labeler is sold. If the machine's book value is $6,480, and it is sold for this sum at the end of the seventh year, the NPV of the cash flows would drop to a loss of $6,091. (The cash flow forecasts are shown in Figure 5-14.) This loss results from losing the final 3 years of cash flows that Fire Dragon would have earned on the savings and on the costs associated with the new labeler. However, if the labeler has held its value, it might be sold for the present value of the cash flows that Fire Dragon would have earned in years 8–10. To make this estimate, discount the last 3 years of cash flows from Figure 5-6 for 3 years.

$$\text{Value of cash flows for years 8–10} = \frac{\$10,212}{1.03^1} + \frac{\$9,901}{1.03^2} + \frac{\$9,901}{1.03^3} = \$28,200$$

Since this is the value of the last 3 years of cash flows at the end of the seventh year, add $28,200 to the cash flow in the seventh year, and discount all of the cash flows to the present. The NPV of these cash flows is $11,586, the same as the net present value of the 10-year machine if it is operated for 10 years. This is only because the analyst forecasts that management can sell the machine in the seventh year for the present value of its remaining cash flows. The value ascribed to the labeler at the end of 7 years depends on the analyst's best judgment of what the sales price might be at that time.

These 2 adjustments have been made to the cash flows of the longer-lived machine. The analyst could decide that management would require a new labeler when the shorter-lived labeler's life ends. In this case, the analyst would forecast the cash costs and benefits associated with a new labeler acquired at the end of the seventh year. A variety of labeling machine alternatives might exist: a new machine lasting 7 years, returning to hand affixing, or some other machine. The cash flows associated with these alternatives would be discounted, ensuring that the lives of the 7-year machine and its replacement do not exceed the 10-year life of the longer-lived machine. If they do, the analyst would have to make a further adjustment.

There is one final method for equalizing the lives of unequal investments: terminal net worth. To use this method, the analyst assumes that any funds freed from the shorter-lived investment are invested for a period equaling the life of the longer-lived investment. To use this method, the analyst must forecast what funds become available from the shorter-lived investment and at what rate they could logically be invested. Use the seven-year labeling machine as an example. Each year the labeling machine produces a cash flow. If the cash flow is positive, the cash could be invested; if the cash flow is negative, the cash would be borrowed. Assuming that management believes that it can invest any excess cash flows at 6 percent, the terminal net worth analysis, shown in Figure 5-15, would have an NPV of $16,078.

Which method is right? The one that best reflects management's judgment of the economic benefits and costs of the expected investment strategy. The mechanics are really the easy part; managerial judgment is critical.

[2] Different Sizes

The problem of equivalent investment strategies extends to investment size. To be comparable, the size of investments must be equal. For instance, comparing the NPV of an investment of $120 million to that of an investment of $84 million assumes that

FIGURE 5-14

Fire Dragon Labeling Machine: Cash Flow Forecast for 10-Year Machine Adjusted to 7-Year Life

				Year				
	0	1	2	3	4	5	6	7
Changes in Income Statement								
Salaries and benefits								
Old workers		$41,000	$41,000	$41,000	$41,000	$41,000	$41,000	$41,000
New labeling machine operator		(25,000)	(25,000)	(25,000)	(25,000)	(25,000)	(25,000)	(25,000)
Electricity		(2,000)	(2,000)	(2,000)	(2,000)	(2,000)	(2,000)	(2,000)
Depreciation								
Labeling machine		(34,000)	(20,400)	(12,240)	(9,180)	(9,180)		
Labeling machine overhaul							(7,200)	(4,320)
Old equipment sale	$ 2,000							
Net income before taxes	$ 2,000	$(20,000)	$(6,400)	$ 1,760	$ 4,820	$ 4,820	$ 6,800	$ 9,680
Taxes (at 34%)	(680)	6,800	2,176	(598)	(1,639)	(1,639)	(2,312)	(3,291)
Net income after taxes	$ 1,320	$(13,200)	$(4,224)	$ 1,162	$ 3,181	$ 3,181	$ 4,488	$ 6,389
Noncash Charges								
Depreciation								
Labeling machine		34,000	20,400	12,240	9,180	9,180		
Labeling machine overhaul							7,200	4,320
Annual cash flow	$ 1,320	$ 20,800	$ 16,176	$ 13,402	$ 12,361	$ 12,361	$ 11,688	$ 10,709
Balance Sheet Impacts								
Labeling machine	(85,000)							
Labeling machine overhaul						(18,000)		
Terminal value								6,480
Net Cash Flow	$(83,680)	$20,800	$16,176	$13,402	$12,361	$(5,639)	$11,688	$17,189

FIGURE 5-15

Terminal Net Worth of Seven-Year-Life Labeling Machine

Year	Net Cash Flow	Value in Year 7 at 6% Rate
0	$(63,680)	$(95,751)
1	15,554	22,064
2	13,750	18,401
3	12,462	15,732
4	11,541	13,746
5	11,158	12,537
6	11,158	11,827
7	11,158	11,158
Total net worth in year 7		$ 9,713

the firm leaves $36 million of its resources idle.[10] Because inequality is unlikely, the problem is handled similarly to the time-adjusting method: assuming a rate of investment for the unused funds from the smaller project. Again, Fire Dragon's alternative investments—the labeling machine and a new product—are used to demonstrate the approach.

Management has decided it can invest either in the 10-year labeling machine or in a new product suggested by Grandmother Trevi, horseradish-laced cookies. Management believes that the cookie would appeal to consumers concerned with their health. The cost of this alternative investment would be $120,000 to adapt an unused portion of a plant and equip it for production. The relevant measures of value for the cookies and the labeling machine are compared in Figure 5-16. Which investment should management make? Again, there is not enough information to make a decision because the investment sizes are so different.

This analysis cannot be complete until the sizes are equalized. In Figure 5-17, the cash flows from the labeling machine (the smaller investment) are subtracted from the new product's larger cash flows. The last column, the incremental cash flows, represents the cost and benefit differences between the two cash flows: NPV of the incremental cash flows is $29,337, and the IRR is 13.5 percent. In essence, Fire Dragon spends an extra $38,255 the first two years to secure a rate of return of 13.5 percent.

To decide whether the extra investment is appropriate, Fire Dragon's management must ask itself whether investing the larger sum in the new product is the best use of these funds or whether they could be invested in another project to create greater shareholder value. Since this return is better than those generally received by Fire Dragon and it creates value, investing the extra capital in the new product is the more attractive alternative.

This is a somewhat laborious and apparently arbitrary approach to dealing with different-sized investments. However, it is the best method. None of the measures of value previously described can give the manager adequate information on which to base a decision without this kind of adaptation.

---

[10] Resources can be cash or debt capacity.

FIGURE 5-16

Summary of Measures of Value

	Labeling Machine	Cookies
Accounting rate of return	5.00%	12.90%
Benefit/cost ratio	1.24	1.64
Payback	7.40 years	6.60 years
Present value payback	9.40 years	7.20 years
NPV		
No inflation[a]	$11,586.00	$40,922.00
5% inflation[b]	$ 7,967.00	40,922.00
PVI	1.13	1.56
IRR		
No inflation	6.10%	9.20%
5% inflation	10.20%	14.20%

[a] Discount rate of 3 percent.
[b] Discount rate of 8 percent.

FIGURE 5-17

Incremental Net Cash Flows: Labeling Machine and New Product

Year	Labeling Machine	Cookies	Incremental Cash Flows
0	$(83,680)	$(120,000)	$(36,320)
1	20,800	18,865	(1,935)
2	16,176	18,865	2,689
3	13,402	18,865	5,463
4	12,361	18,865	6,504
5	(5,639)	18,865	24,504
6	11,688	18,865	7,177
7	10,709	18,865	8,156
8	10,121	18,865	8,744
9	9,901	18,865	8,964
10	9,901	18,865	8,964

NPV = $29,337
IRR = 13.5%

[3] Different Risks

So far, the assumption has been that the discount rate is 3 percent and none of the investments are risky. Value depends on three things, however: the size of the expected returns, the timing of those returns, and the risk taken to gain those returns. Risk cannot be ignored.

Risk in this context is the possibility that the expected cash flows have been either overestimated or underestimated, which would result in returns that are more or less than expected. Investors do not take risks unless they are paid to do so; the higher the risk, the larger the expected return must be. In fact, there is a direct trade-off between risk and return, as was shown in Figure 5-9.

Of all the problems facing the manager in analyzing an investment, risk is the most troublesome. There is no ideal way of incorporating risk into the estimation of value, but several methods are used. The most widely applied method adds a penalty for risk to the time value of money discount rate. Note that the discount rate used so far, 3 percent, is far below the standard used in evaluating most corporate investments. This is because the 3 percent rate incorporates no risk premium, not even a premium for the risk of inflation.

While the analyst can directly estimate the risk of any investment and derive some appropriate scale for the return required for each level of risk, most analysts prefer to make the task as easy as possible by assuming that the risk of every investment is the same as the risk of the firm itself (i.e., that the cash flows are equally predictable). If that assumption is accepted, the company's investors' required return can be used as an indication of its fair return for risk. Most analysts use this rate for their analysis.[11]

5.05 ESTIMATING THE DISCOUNT RATE

Because new investment opportunities are being analyzed, the company's marginal required rate of return (the cost of raising new money in the capital markets) is used as the discount rate. Thus, the returns required by the company's lenders and share-holders and their relative proportions to be used in financing the firm are needed to estimate the company's after tax required rate of return. Fire Dragon can be used to demonstrate the estimation of the after-tax required rate of return.

[1] Marginal After-Tax Required Rate of Return

Fire Dragon is owned by members of the Trevi family. In order to determine their required return (which is also the cost of equity for Fire Dragon), the family members could be asked the following question: "What rate of return would be sufficient to prevent you from selling but not induce you to invest more in Fire Dragon?" The answer would be the shareholders' required rate of return and thus Fire Dragon's marginal required return on equity.

Estimating the required return on equity for a publicly held firm, however, is more difficult. It changes as market and firm circumstances change. Furthermore, the share-holders of a broadly held firm cannot be asked for their required return at any point in time. Thus, methods that rely on capital market data have been derived and are widely used.

An estimate of the marginal after-tax required return on debt could be obtained from Fire Dragon's bankers or by inference from the yield to maturity on any publicly traded bonds that Fire Dragon or companies comparable to it might have. The marginal after-tax required return on capital for the company is the weighted average of the cost of the after-tax required return on all forms of capital. If Fire Dragon's sharehold-

---

[11] Since capital markets arbitrage risk, they are the best source of current estimates for the market value of risk.

FIGURE 5-18

Fire Dragon: Marginal Cost of Capital

	Cost	Proportion	Weighted Cost
Debt	7.9%[a]	40%	3.2%
Equity	15.0	60	9.0
Marginal cost of capital			12.2%

[a] 12% pretax cost $\times$ (1 $-$ tax rate), where tax rate is 34%.

ers require a 15 percent return on equity, its bankers are willing to lend new funds at a cost of 12 percent, and management expects to have 40 percent of its capital from debt sources, the after-tax marginal required return on capital (with a tax rate of 34 percent) for Fire Dragon would be 12.2 percent, as shown in Figure 5-18. The 12.2 percent required return on capital rate is higher than the 3 percent discount rate used in analyzing Fire Dragon's two investments. Two reasons might account for the difference: The 3 percent rate is both risk free and inflation free, and the 12.2 percent rate is neither.[12]

The inflation estimate included in the cash flow forecasts must be both explicit and consistent with the inflation forecast included in the required return. If riskless debt (perhaps proxied by a Treasury bond) was yielding 8 percent and the estimated real, inflation-free rate was 3 percent, one might infer that investors were anticipating a 5 percent rate of inflation. Thus, if a 12.2 percent discount rate was used, the cash flows would have to include the effects of a 5 percent rate of inflation. Alternatively, management could estimate an inflation-free required rate of return for use with real cash flows. Most managers prefer, however, to include inflation both in the required return on capital and in the cash flows. Many fail to make the inflation forecasts consistent, however, rendering the resulting data useless for decision making.

With Fire Dragon's marginal required return on capital of 12.2 percent as the discount rate for the inflated cash flows from Figure 5-12, the NPV for the labeling machine is $6,110. The IRR is 10.2 percent, but now it must be compared with the 12.2 percent required return to determine its acceptability. Using the same approach with the new cookie product results in NPV of $13,379 and IRR of 14.2 percent. Using this data, can Fire Dragon's managers conclude that the only acceptable alternative is the cookies? Maybe not.

[2] Risk-Adjusted Required Return

In using the corporate required return on capital as a discount rate, the analyst assumes that the two investments carry the same risk, equal to the risk of Fire Dragon's current business. But Fire Dragon's two investments are neither risk-free nor equally risky;

---

[12] The 3 percent was used as a risk-free and inflation-free rate for the purposes of illustration, although there is some disagreement among academics and managers about the size of the real risk-free rate. Estimates for the real rate begin at a low of 0.

FIGURE 5-19

Risk-Adjusted Required Return on Capital

Category	Level of Risk	Hurdle Rate
New products and lines of business	Higher than average	A rate higher than the firm's marginal required return
Plant expansion	Average	Marginal cost of capital
Cost reductions	Low	A rate lower than the firm's marginal required return

the returns from the horseradish cookies, while potentially larger, are obviously less certain.

With a new product, managers often have little or no relevant experience to make forecasts. To gain more confidence in their forecasts, they often seek help. In addition to various experts inside the firm, one data source that is often used is the historical experience of others in similar businesses. Statistical data about other companies are available from marketing research firms. The data are aggregate, however (i.e., about firms or industries rather than products), and thus may not be as useful when a new venture is being undertaken.

A second source of data is the models and methods for determining product-market potential that have come into vogue over the last 10 years. Models such as Profit Impact of Market Strategy, from the Marketing Science Institute, and the Boston Consulting Group's product-market matrix, Porter analysis, and experience curves can provide some information about the experiences of others in similar situations or the effect of a particular technology, market position, or relative competition on expected revenues and costs.

The manager's job is to gather data and create the best forecasts possible, not to be too conservative (overestimate cost and underestimate revenues) or too optimistic, but to be as accurate as possible in forecasting an unknown future. The forecasts will help the manager make decisions as long as they contain the best estimates of the marginal cash flows the firm will incur if the investment is made.

However substantial the outside information gathered by management in considering the cookies, a new project is still risky. To compensate for risk, managers often arbitrarily change the required return on capital to a rate they believe better reflects the investment risk. Many firms have a standard system for doing this, an example of which is shown in Figure 5-19. Managers of firms using such methods for risk-adjusting hurdle rates believe that all new products are risky and that all cost reductions are less risky than average. If Fire Dragon's management used this scheme, they might choose to discount the labeling machine's cash flows at 2 percent less than the corporate required return (10.2 percent) and discount those from the new product at a higher rate, e.g., 14.2 percent.

	Nominal IRR	Hurdle Rate	Excess Return
Labeling machine	10.2%	10.2%	0
New product	14.2	14.2	0
Corporate average	NA	12.2	NA

FIGURE 5-20

Risk-Return Analyses

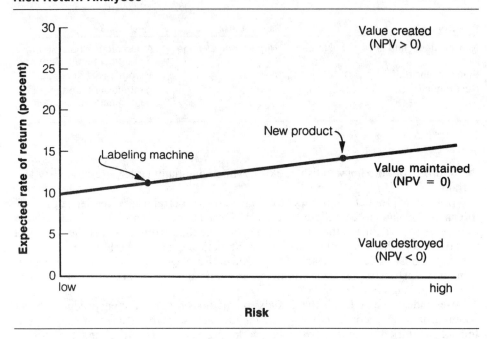

The resulting risk-return trade-off for these two products for Fire Dragon is shown in Figure 5-20. The return in excess of that required for the risk is each investment's contribution to the value of the firm. Stock market analysts call it an excess risk-adjusted return, or alpha. Shareholders call it value.

Conceptually, this approach is appealing. It separates investments on the basis of their risk and eliminates the assumption that all projects with the same returns are equally attractive. The use of this method requires a measurement of the risk of the project or, at the very least, a measurement of the return required for the risk. Basing this required return on the kind of scheme shown in Figure 5-19 creates problems. The method is arbitrary in two ways: It assumes that all investments in a given category are of equal risk and that a risk-adjusted rate can be estimated. Neither is true.

It is difficult to determine the risk-adjusted discount rate for a project. Unfortunately, some managers set such high rates for risky projects that they virtually exclude them from consideration. Because a firm's future depends on the investments it makes today, particularly in new products, processes, or services, the implementation of such an implicit strategy may not be consistent with the firm's explicit strategy (e.g., growth in product markets). Thus, a better method of incorporating risk is required.

[a] Divisional Hurdle Rates. There are two other common risk-adjustment methods: divisional and investment-specific hurdle rates. Managers of firms using divisional or line-of-business hurdle rates believe that such rates reflect the risks of that business better than does a corporatewide rate, the firm's cost of capital. A divisional rate may

FIGURE 5-21

Risk and Time

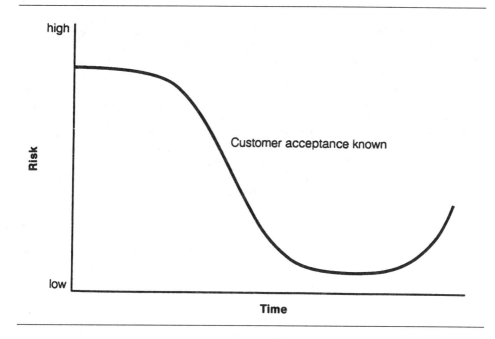

be better in firms with diverse business interests, but a divisional or line-of-business required return on capital is even more difficult to estimate than a corporate rate. This is particularly true because a division has no public investors to help determine the return they would require. Thus, managers are often forced to turn to publicly traded firms in similar businesses as proxies for the division or line of business. If, for example, Fire Dragon's management was considering opening bake shops to sell their horse-radish-based baked goods, companies such as Mrs. Smith's Cookies, David's Cookies, and Dunkin' Donuts might provide adequate proxies. While a required return linked to the risk of each project is most appropriate, more managers find it easier to estimate and substitute a less project-specific required rate of return. The divisional rate is one such approach.

[b] Other Problems With Risk-Adjusted Hurdle Rates. A single risk-adjusted rate assumes that risk increases over time, i.e., that the investor requires increasing returns as time goes on, partly to compensate for illiquidity (time value of money). The risk of an investment may not, however, keep increasing over time; new products may be quite risky until customer acceptance is known, but at that point, risk may dramatically decline. The product is either accepted by consumers or not, but the outcome is known. Later, as competition increases, risk increases again. The risk profile of such a product might be similar to that in Figure 5-21. The use of a single risk-adjusted discount rate to offset the new product's risk is not consistent with this risk profile.

The changing level of risk over time is only one of the number of problems encountered when risk-adjusted discount rates are used. New and more explicit methods of incorporating risk analysis into capital budgeting are continually being developed. Risk is currently an important part of determining relative value but has not yet been dealt with satisfactorily.

One method of analysis that is promising is the option analysis. Using this approach to consider projects that have upside potential but limited downside loss allows managers to think of investments using a different perspective and to value them using a more appropriate method. Investments such as those in research and development, new products, and exploration lend themselves to such an analysis: They have significant potential for profit, but losses can be stopped by discontinuing the development. The binomial option-pricing methodology, a variation on a decision tree, usually is the most appropriate method for valuing corporate capital investments.

After all this analysis, how will Fire Dragon's management decide between the new product and the labeling machine? If sufficient capital, management time, plant space, and so on exist, this choice may not be necessary. Management may forecast that both projects are acceptable. Obviously, the Fire Dragon example was designed to give both investments the same risk-adjusted return, an NPV of zero, as shown in Figure 5-21. This risk-adjusted return is a contribution to the value of the firm, and the choice between the labeling machine and the new product rests solely on the risks the owners are willing to take. If Fire Dragon's owners are conservative, they are likely to prefer the labeling machine. If they are risk takers, they may prefer the new product.

5.06 FINANCING INVESTMENTS: RETURN TO EQUITY

The attractiveness of an investment is analyzed based on one additional assumption: that the investment decision can be made without regard to how it is financed. Put another way, the investment evaluation analysis assumes that while the returns from a project change over time (as a result of changes in socioeconomic and political conditions), the firm's required return on capital does not. Much of the time, for many firms, this assumption is reasonably close to reality. However, there are times when it is potentially wrong: During the late 1970s and early 1980s, as the returns from the business went down, some firms' capital costs went up. This phenomenon was especially true for firms that had debt written with floating interest rates or had obtained short-term debt and subsequently rolled it over in an environment of increasingly volatile rates. The interrelationship between financing costs and investment returns is coming under increasing scrutiny, but until more research is done and experience gained, management generally will use a method of analysis that accepts the obviously erroneous assumption that investment decisions can be made without regard to financing decisions. One method explicitly includes capital costs and changes in the capital structure: return to equity.

The return-to-equity method includes any cash outflows or inflows associated with the investment's financing. The resulting net cash flows belong to the firm's owners and are discounted at the shareholders' required return on equity.

To demonstrate this process, the analysis of Fire Dragon's labeling machine can be reexamined. Figure 5-21 shows that the project is expected to break even for Fire Dragon's owners even without special financing. However, if the project has special debt financing available (e.g., because it is located in a disadvantaged area and could use development bond financing), the analysis would change. The principal of the debt would be a cash inflow to the company at the beginning of the investment, and the interest and principal repayments would be cash outflows over the project's life. In essence, the reduced cost of debt is an added benefit for the labeling machine. To demonstrate, if Fire Dragon could obtain special financing of $50,000 for five years at a cost of 5 percent, the equity NPV (at a discount rate of 15 percent) given the special financing would be $6,084. The IRR would be 21.2 percent. The full cash flow forecast is shown in Figure 5-22. This NPV contrasts with the value of the project financed in Fire Dragon's traditional capital mix (a 12.2 percent required return on capital with 60 percent equity and 40 percent debt) of −$6,110.

The special financing makes the investment acceptable. However, because any form of financing has its costs and benefits, the special financing should be carefully evaluated. Depending on the features of the debt or equity, the financing's costs and benefits could reduce or increase the return to the equity holders.

5.07 CORPORATE INVESTMENTS IN A GLOBAL ENVIRONMENT

All of this analysis has assumed that the company analyzing the investments operates in one country. However, few companies are unaffected by the increasing globalization of business, and many companies' managements must decide between investments in different countries or investments that involve cash benefits and/or costs in a variety of different currencies.

Some simple rules apply when such investments are evaluated. First, evaluate the investment's cash benefits and costs in the currency in which they actually will be received, with the exchange rate expected to be in existence. While this is a simple rule, it is often violated for no reason other than the fact that investors know their own currency best and are more comfortable with it.

For example, Fire Dragon management is considering investing in a horseradish-processing operation in another country. The Trevi family which owns the plant, has little experience in operating such a processing facility and they believe that they could benefit from Fire Dragon management's expertise. Fire Dragon would provide a cash investment for which it would own 50 percent of the business and receive 50 percent of the dividends in the future. For the management consulting, Fire Dragon would be paid annually at a contractually determined amount.

The analyst making forecasts for this investment might forecast all of the corporate cash flows from processing and selling horseradish and the consulting fees translated into dollars, since Fire Dragon is a U.S. company. The inclination is correct if the analyst can be certain that any of the following three conditions will prevail:

1. The payments made to Fire Dragon are made in dollars.

2. The payments made to Fire Dragon are made in local currency and exchanged by Fire Dragon for dollars. The exchange rate used in the cash flow forecasts is the one that is expected to be available the day the transaction is expected to take place.

3. The analyst forecasts the dividends that will be paid to Fire Dragon, the date that they will be paid, and the exchange rate expected to be available at the time of the transaction.

Common errors in such forecasts include translating cash flows at the time the company, rather than the investor, receives them and translating cash flows into dollars

FIGURE 5-22

Return on Equity for Labeling Machine: Cash Flow Forecast

						Year					
	0	1	2	3	4	5	6	7	8	9	10
Changes in Income Statement											
Salaries and benefits											
Old workers		$43,050	$45,203	$47,463	$49,836	$52,328	$54,944	$57,691	$60,576	$63,604	$66,785
New labeling machine operator		(26,250)	(27,563)	(28,941)	(30,388)	(31,907)	(33,502)	(35,178)	(36,936)	(38,783)	(40,722)
Electricity		(2,100)	(2,205)	(2,315)	(2,431)	(2,553)	(2,680)	(2,814)	(2,955)	(3,103)	(3,258)
Depreciation											
Labeling machine		(34,000)	(20,400)	(12,240)	(9,180)	(9,180)					
Labeling machine overhaul							(7,200)	(4,320)	(2,592)	(1,944)	(1,944)
Old equipment sale	$2,000										
Interest		(2,500)	(2,500)	(2,500)	(2,500)	(2,500)					
Net income before taxes	$2,000	$(21,800)	$(7,465)	$ 1,467	$ 5,337	$ 6,188	$11,562	$15,379	$18,093	$19,774	$20,861
Taxes (at 34 %)	(680)	7,412	2,538	(499)	(1,815)	(2,104)	(3,931)	(5,229)	(6,151)	(6,723)	(7,093)
Net income after taxes	$1,320	$(14,388)	$(4,927)	$ 968	$ 3,522	$ 4,084	$ 7,631	$10,150	$11,942	$13,051	$13,768
Noncash Charges											
Depreciation											
Labeling machine	0	34,000	20,400	12,240	9,180	9,180					
Labeling machine overhaul							7,200	4,320	2,592	1,944	1,944
Annual cash flow	$ 1,320	$ 19,612	$15,473	$13,208	$12,702	$13,264	$14,831	$14,470	$14,534	$14,995	$15,712
Balance Sheet Impacts											
Labeling machine	(85,000)										
Labeling machine overhaul						(22,973)					
Principal change	50,000					(50,000)					
Net Cash Flow	$(33,680)	$19,612	$15,473	$13,208	$12,702	$(59,709)	$14,831	$14,470	$14,534	$14,995	$15,712

Note: Inflation of 5 percent, no depreciation impact.

at a time before they are moved outside the country. Since there often is considerable uncertainty about exchange rates, in addition to uncertainty about the actual cash flows, cross-border investments lend themselves to "what-if" or simulation analysis, also called multiple scenario or significant factor analysis.

In addition to having problems in estimating cash flows, many analysts have difficulty in estimating the appropriate required rate of return to discount the cash flows because most of the methods used to estimate the required return on equity were developed in the United States from U.S. data. Many of the problems experienced by analysts come from a narrow interpretation of the way that the methods are used. For instance, the required return on equity estimating methods are usually interpreted as resting on historic data from the U.S. stock market. This is a narrow interpretation and not appropriate in a more integrated world. The question of how much return investors require for their investment can be asked in any country. The less developed the economy, the more the estimate will rely on the analyst's expertise in that economy and its investors. An analyst who believes that rigidly defined approaches work in a changing world is almost certain to err.

5.08 SUMMARY

The process of forecasting the future cash flows from an investment can be, to say the least, a frustrating one. Nevertheless, because investments are made for the shareholders and their future benefit, the probable effects of current actions must be examined. Capital investments are large and often commit the firm to rather inflexible courses of action; thus, methods have been developed to look to the future when considering the relative value of an investment. These techniques have gained widespread acceptance among managers for two reasons. First, in the process of forecasting what might occur, assumptions about the future are made explicit. Such explicit assumptions can expose poor judgment and strategies. Second, managers seek to create value for their shareholders and thus seek ways to measure it. Formal and systematic analyses help in ranking and choosing projects according to their value creation.

The methods can be misused, however, in several ways:

1. Cash flows can be incorrectly estimated. The manager, in an effort to be conservative, may underestimate benefits, overestimate costs, or arbitrarily shorten the true economic life of a project. Such conservatism creates bad forecasts. The manager's job is to forecast what he or she believes will be the investment's effect on the firm. Risk, the driving force behind conservatism in cash flow forecasting, must be dealt with in other ways.

2. Risks can be overestimated. Arbitrary adjustments to the required returns (hurdle rates) for investments can add unnecessarily high penalties for risk. Inflation in the early 1980s encouraged some firms to use hurdle rates as high as 25 percent without incorporating the same long-term inflation forecast into the cash flows. When the discount rate reflects an inflation forecast that is inconsistent with that reflected in the cash flow forecasts, the resulting analysis is useless.

   In addition to inflation, discount rates should be tailored to each investment and must reflect the return required for the risk of that investment. Finding a scheme to categorize smaller investments (divisional or project-type required returns) is useful and logical; the scheme must correctly reflect the risk if it is to provide adequate information for making informed decisions.

3. Some investments may be excluded. Investments in hard assets, assets that will be capitalized, are frequently the only investments whose relative value is analyzed. Investments in working capital, noncapitalized assets (e.g., research and development or advertising), and acquisitions are often analyzed using very different methods, which should not be so. They are investments of capital, even if accounting practice does not capitalize them on the balance sheet. Thus, their economic implications must not be ignored.

When one reflects on this chapter discussion, it should be noted that there is no inherent short-term bias in the method of investment analysis; bias creeps in through misuse. The techniques are flexible tools for exploring the potential of alternative courses of action.

Suggested Reading

Bierman, Harold, Jr., and Seymour Smidt. *The Capital Budgeting Decision,* 7th ed. New York: Macmillan, 1988.

Bower, R.S., and J.M. Jenks. "Divisional Screening Rates." *Financial Management* (Autumn 1975), pp. 42–49.

Brealey, Richard, and Stewart Myers. *Principles of Corporate Finance,* 4th ed. New York: McGraw-Hill, 1991.

Harrington, Diana. *Corporate Financial Analysis in the Global Environment,* 5th ed. Plano, Tex.: Business Publications Inc., 1993.

———. *Modern Portfolio Theory, The Capital Asset Pricing Model and Arbitrage Pricing Theory: A User's Guide,* 2nd ed. Englewood Cliffs, N.J.: Prentice-Hall, Inc., 1987.

———. "Stock Prices, Beta and Strategic Planning." *Harvard Business Review* (May–June 1983), pp. 157–164.

Harrington, Diana, Frank Fabozzi, and H. Russell Fogler. *Analyzing the Stock Market.* Chicago, Ill.: Probus Publishing Co., 1989.

Hertz, D.B., "Risk Analysis in Capital Investments." *Harvard Business Review* (Sept.–Oct. 1979), pp. 169–181.

Hull, J.C., *The Evaluation of Risk in Business Investment.* Elmsford, N.J.: Pergamon Press, 1980.

Levy, Haim, and Marshall Sarnot. *Capital Investment and Financial Decisions.* Englewood Cliffs, N.J.: Prentice-Hall, Inc., 1990.

Madura, Jeff, *International Financial Management,* 2nd ed. St. Paul, Minn.: West Publishing Co., 1989.

Rappaport, Alfred, *Creating Shareholder Value.* New York: The Free Press, 1986.

Rappaport, A., and R.A. Taggart, Jr. "Evaluation of Capital Expenditure Proposals Under Inflation." *Financial Management* (Spring 1982), pp. 5–13.

Shapiro, Alan, *Modern Corporate Finance.* New York: Macmillan, 1989.

———. *Multinational Financial Management.* Needham Heights, Mass.: Allyn & Bacon, 1989.

Sharpe, William F., *Investments,* 4th ed. Englewood Cliffs, N.J.: Prentice-Hall, Inc., 1990.

Stoll, Han, and Robert Whaley. *Futures and Options.* Cincinnati: Southwestern Publishing Co., 1993.

Weston, J.F., "Investment Decisions Using the Capital Asset Pricing Model." *Financial Management* (Spring 1973), pp. 25–33.

Weston, J. Fred, and Eugene F. Brigham. *Essentials of Managerial Finance,* 8th ed. Hinsdale, Ill.: The Dryden Press, 1988, ch. 16.

Chapter 6

Capital Structure and Financial Strategy

ALAN C. SHAPIRO

6.01 INTRODUCTION

The collection of assets in which a firm invests generates a stream of cash flows. In an all-equity-financed firm, these cash flows belong to the shareholders alone. Alternatively, the firm can split these cash flows into two components: (1) a relatively safe stream that it sells to debt holders and (2) a riskier stream that it sells to shareholders.

From this perspective, choosing the firm's capital structure, the combination of debt and equity financing used, is a marketing problem. It involves deciding the share of future cash flows to repackage as debt; the rights to the residual cash flows are sold as equity claims. Given the objective of maximizing shareholder wealth, the key issue in determining capital structure is, Can the firm create value by judiciously selecting its debt-equity combination?

There are two schools of thought. One says that capital structure is irrelevant: Firm value is determined by the yield on the company's real assets, and juggling the claims on those assets does not change their total value. The second school says that because of taxes and other factors, an optimal degree of financial leverage, the ratio of debt to equity, does exist, and firms can boost their market value by adding debt to the capital structure up to a certain point.

This chapter examines the issue of whether an optimal capital structure exists by exploring the nature and consequences of financial leverage and the alternative theories of capital structure and its effects on the market value of the firm. Unfortunately, however, although these theories provide some clues regarding an appropriate capital structure, their assumptions are unrealistic and ignore many of the relevant factors that are likely to influence the trade-off between more debt and more equity. Hence, the analysis must be extended to include additional factors, primarily taxes, incentive effects, and costs of financial distress, that are likely to make firm value dependent on the degree of financial leverage. Finally, the chapter examines the ways in which companies can use financial strategy and structure to increase shareholder value and the unique aspects of financing growth companies.

6.02 FINANCIAL LEVERAGE, RISK, AND RETURN

[1] Nature of Financial Leverage

The capital structure controversy centers on whether an unleveraged firm can lower its cost of capital and increase its market value per share by replacing some of its equity with debt, that is, by employing financial leverage. Operating leverage, the substitution of fixed for variable operating costs, magnifies a given change in sales into a relatively larger change in earnings before interest and taxes (EBIT), also known as net operating income. Financial leverage refers to the substitution of fixed-charge financing, primarily debt (interest and principal payments) but also preferred stock (preferred dividend payments) and leases (lease payments), for common stock with its variable dividend payments. These fixed financing charges have the same magnification effect on the firm's earnings per share (EPS) as fixed operating costs have on its EBIT. Financial leverage, therefore, adds to the risk faced by the firm's stockholders. Inasmuch as a portion of this added risk is company-specific, it is irrelevant to well-diversified shareholders. Still, financial leverage magnifies the firm's systematic risk, thereby raising the required return on leveraged shares.

FIGURE 6-1

Relationship Between the Risk of Equity Capital and Financial Leverage

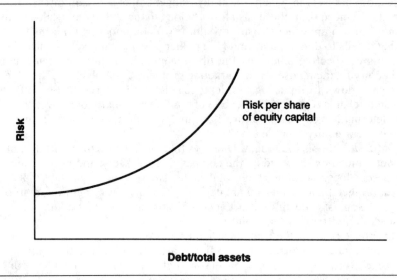

In the all-equity-financed firm, fluctuations in EPS are due solely to the firm's business risk, the inherent variability in its operating earnings. Substituting debt for equity concentrates this business risk onto a smaller number of equity shares, thereby increasing the risk that equity holders must bear. This added risk is known as financial risk. For example, suppose a firm with $1 million in assets starts with 100,000 shares valued at $10 apiece. If half this equity is replaced by riskless debt, then the remaining 50,000 shares must bear all the firm's business risk. Hence, each share is now twice as risky as before.

Figure 6-1 shows how the amount of risk per share changes with the debt ratio, the ratio of debt to total assets, assuming that the risk of default on the debt is nil. As debt replaces equity, each dollar of equity capital must bear a correspondingly greater proportion of the business's risk. Even in the absence of default risk, financial leverage increases the risk of equity.

Financial leverage also affects the expected level of EPS and return on equity (ROE). To see specifically how financial leverage affects the expected ROE, the following terms must be defined:

r_A = return on assets before financing costs = $\dfrac{\text{EBIT}(1 - t_c)}{\text{assets}}$

t_c = corporate tax rate
i = after-tax cost of debt
D = amount of debt in the capital structure
E = amount of equity in the capital structure

The linkage between financial leverage and the ROE starts with the definition of ROE:

$$\text{ROE} = \frac{\text{profit after tax}}{\text{equity}} = \frac{\text{EBIT}(1 - t_c) - iD}{E}$$

Using simple algebra, ROE can be rewritten as

$$\text{ROE} = r_A + \frac{(r_A - i)D}{E} \tag{6.1}$$

Equation 6.1 reveals that if the return on assets (ROA) before financing charges exceeds the after-tax interest rate on debt, then financial leverage (measured here as D/E) will increase the ROE and, therefore, the EPS of the firm's stock. On the other hand, if the ROA falls below the after-tax cost of debt, then financial leverage will decrease both ROE and EPS.

Because the expected ROA invariably exceeds the required yield on debt, financial leverage has two opposing effects on equity valuation: It increases the expected ROE, while simultaneously raising the variability of those returns. It is the trade-off between these two effects that largely determines whether financial leverage will increase, decrease, or leave unchanged the value of the firm.

[2] Consequences of Financial Leverage

To illustrate the consequences of financial leverage, suppose that Hi-Tech Running Shoes, Inc. requires $5 million in assets to support its sales efforts. It is considering two different financing plans: all-equity financing and equal proportions of debt and equity. The all-equity financing option is issuing 500,000 shares of common stock priced at $10 apiece. Alternatively, Hi-Tech could issue 250,000 shares of equity at $10 per share and fund the remaining $2.5 million with 10 percent debt.

Hi-Tech's earnings before interest and taxes are expected to be $1 million annually. However, these earnings are not guaranteed; they could be as low as $200,000 or as high as $2 million in any given year. The effects of financial leverage on EPS and the ROE under several alternative earnings scenarios are shown in Figure 6-2 for the two financing alternatives. Income is assumed to be taxed at a rate of 50 percent.

Figure 6-2 shows that financial leverage has a significant impact on EPS and ROE. For example, with 50 percent debt financing, if EBIT is $1 million, EPS and ROE will be 50 percent greater than what they are with no leverage. Alternatively, in bad years, leverage causes EPS and ROE to be negative, whereas they are positive with all-equity financing. The general conclusion is that when more leverage is used, EPS and ROE rise more in good years and fall more in bad years. When EBIT is increasing, added leverage causes EPS and ROE to increase more rapidly, and vice versa when EBIT is falling.

The benefits of leverage depend on the return the firm earns on its assets and the cost of debt. If Hi-Tech can issue debt at 10 percent and earn 20 percent with certainty on its assets ($1 million on assets of $5 million), it should do so; the more it borrows, the more favorable the effect of leverage will be. However, if EBIT is $500,000, yielding a pretax ROA of 10 percent, the same as Hi-Tech's cost of debt, there is no advantage to debt financing. Under the worst-case scenario, in which Hi-Tech's ROA is less than its cost of debt, the effect of leverage is unfavorable; Hi-Tech is in a loss position, and its EPS and ROE are negative.

These results are shown graphically in Figure 6-3, which displays the results of plotting EPS against EBIT for the two financing alternatives. The EBIT-EPS chart

FIGURE 6-2

Effect of Leverage on Hi-Tech's EPS

	States of the World			
	Bad	Mediocre	Normal	Good
1. No leverage; 500,000 shares at $10/share				
EBIT	$200,000	$500,000	$1,000,000	$2,000,000
Less: Interest at 10%	0	0	0	0
Equity income	$200,000	$500,000	$1,000,000	$2,000,000
Less: Tax at 50%	100,000	250,000	500,000	1,000,000
Equity income after tax	$100,000	$250,000	$ 500,000	$1,000,000
EPS	$0.20	$0.50	$1.00	$2.00
ROE (%)	2	5	10	20
2. 50 percent debt; 250,000 shares at $10/share; $2.5 million in debt at 10% interest				
EBIT	$200,000	$500,000	$1,000,000	$2,000,000
Less: Interest at 10%	250,000	250,000	250,000	250,000
Equity income	$ (50,000)	$250,000	$ 750,000	$1,750,000
Less: Tax at 50%	(25,000)[a]	125,000	375,000	875,000
Equity income	$ (25,000)	$125,000	$ 375,000	$ 875,000
EPS	$(0.10)	$0.50	$1.50	$3.50
ROE (%)	(1)	5	15	35

[a] It is assumed that losses can be carried forward or backward for tax purposes.

shows the EPS that would result from a given level of EBIT for the two financing plans. Line *A*, which represents the all-equity financing plan, shows that a given percentage change in EBIT will result in the same percentage change in EPS.

Plan *B*, which uses 50 percent debt financing, is represented by line *B*. The slope of line *B* is steeper than that of line *A*. The practical import of this is that a given percentage change in EBIT will result in a more-than-proportionate percentage change in EPS. Thus, financial leverage magnifies the effect on EPS of fluctuations in EBIT. This is beneficial in good times but is harmful in bad times.

The level of EBIT at which EPS are equal under the two plans is called the EBIT-EPS indifference point, or the break-even EBIT, and it occurs when the ROA just equals the interest cost of debt. Graphically, break-even EBIT ($500,000 for Hi-Tech) is the point in Figure 6-3 at which the two lines intersect. If EBIT is below the indifference point, common stock financing will be preferred; above that point, the substitution of debt for equity financing will result in higher EPS. Although EBIT-EPS indifference analysis will not tell a company how much debt to use, it can help assess the risk-return trade-off associated with adding more debt to the capital structure.

The indifference point can also be found algebraically between two financing plans A and B by solving Equation 6.2 for EBIT*:

FIGURE 6-3
EBIT-EPS Relationship and Financial Leverage

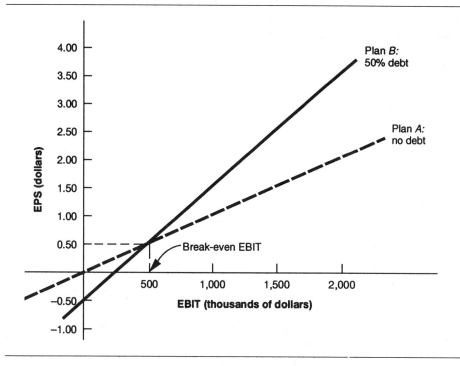

$$\frac{[(\text{EBIT}^* - I_A)\,(1 - t_c) - P_A]}{N_A} = \frac{[(\text{EBIT}^* - I_B)\,(1 - t_c) - P_B]}{N_B} \qquad (6.2)$$

where:

EBIT^* = EBIT-EPS indifference point
I_A, I_B = interest expense under financing plans A and B
P_A, P_B = preferred stock dividends under plans A and B
t_c = corporate tax rate, as defined earlier
N_A, N_B = number of shares issued under plans A and B

If preferred stock is used, its dividends must be subtracted from after-tax income because they are not tax deductible.

Equation 6.2 can be used to determine the indifference point between financing plans A and B for Hi-Tech.

$$\frac{(\text{EBIT}^* - 0)\,(0.50)}{500,000} = \frac{(\text{EBIT}^* - 250,000)\,(0.50)}{250,000}$$

or

$\text{EBIT}^* = \$500,000$

In this example's worst-case scenario, Hi-Tech's earnings will be insufficient to pay all of the interest owed. Should this happen, Hi-Tech will not necessarily be forced into bankruptcy; it can draw down its cash (including that generated by depreciation) and other liquid assets and even sell some of its fixed assets. Hi-Tech can also try to raise funds by selling more debt and equity securities or by borrowing more money from a bank. If all else fails and Hi-Tech exhausts its ability to meet its debt payments, it will default and enter bankruptcy. In the extreme case, the firm will be liquidated, meaning that all its assets will be sold off and the proceeds given to its creditors. The shareholders will divide up anything that remains after the creditor claims are met in full. Usually, though, if it comes to a forced liquidation, debtholders are not paid in full, and so shareholders get nothing.

The preceding analysis can be summarized as follows:

1. When the ROA exceeds the interest cost of debt, financial leverage raises both EPS and ROE. Leverage reduces EPS and ROE when the ROA is less than the cost of debt. Thus, in normal and good years, when the ROA exceeds the cost of debt, financial leverage is beneficial, but when the bad times come, leverage multiplies the firm's problems.

2. Financial leverage increases the variability of EPS and ROE. This financial risk is caused by the fixed nature of creditor claims. No matter what happens to the firm's earnings, a fixed amount of interest must be paid. When EBIT falls, the entire earnings decline is subtracted from the amount going to equity. On the other hand, when EBIT rises, the entire increase in earnings goes to the shareholders.

3. Financial leverage usually increases the expected levels of EPS and ROE. Therefore, substituting debt for equity should increase expected EPS and ROE, but because financial leverage also increases the variability of EPS and ROE, a financing plan that maximizes expected EPS or ROE is also likely to maximize financial risk. Thus, financial leverage involves the familiar trade-off between risk and return. Focusing on expected EPS or ROE alone in selecting a financing plan is inappropriate because it ignores risk and the effect of that risk on the stock price.

6.03 ALTERNATIVE THEORIES OF CAPITAL STRUCTURE

Does the fact that there are positive and negative aspects to financial leverage mean that an optimal capital structure exists, in which the benefits of added debt just offset its costs? Answers to this question have been set forth in the form of alternative theories of capital structure.

Historically, there have been two extreme positions concerning the effects of financial leverage on the market value of the firm: (1) the net income approach and (2) the net operating income approach.

[1] Net Income Approach

According to the net income approach, both the cost of debt (k_d) and the cost of equity capital (k_e) are independent of the capital structure; that is, they are constant regardless of how much debt the firm uses. So, for example, if a firm with no debt has an equity capitalization rate of 20 percent and can issue bonds at 12 percent, k_d and k_e will remain constant at 12 percent and 20 percent, respectively, no matter how much debt it issues. Hence, the optimal capital structure if the net income approach is correct will be 100 percent debt financing because this is the point at which the market value of the firm is maximized.

This result is patently absurd. With 100 percent debt financing, the bondholders bear all the risk of the business, the same risk as that borne by the shareholders in the all-equity firm. Why should bondholders bear this risk for a 12 percent expected return, 8 percentage points less than the 20 percent return that stockholders demand? The net operating income approach addresses this question.

[2] Net Operating Income Approach

Consider again the individual who holds all the firm's debt and equity securities. Regardless of the firm's degree of financial leverage, the individual's expected return and the riskiness of that return are identical; the individual receives the entire net operating income of the firm. In the absence of taxes, whether that return is called dividends or interest is irrelevant. Thus, it is difficult to understand why the value of the firm, or its overall capitalization rate, should vary with the degree of financial leverage. This is the fundamental insight conveyed by the net operating income approach to valuation. Essentially, this approach says there is no magic in financial leverage: The value of the firm and its weighted average cost of capital are independent of the firm's capital structure.

[3] Traditional Approach

Between these extreme positions lies what has come to be known as the traditional approach. According to this approach, a moderate degree of financial leverage can lower the firm's overall cost of capital as cheaper debt is substituted for more expensive equity and thereby increase the total value of the firm; the initial increase in the cost of equity capital is more than offset by the lower interest rate on debt capital. As leverage is increased, however, shareholders begin exacting a higher and higher penalty in the form of a more rapidly rising k_e until a point is reached at which the advantage of lower-cost debt is more than offset by more expensive equity. Consequently, the weighted average cost of funds, k_0, declines at first and then rises. The rise in k_0 is reinforced after a while by an increasing cost of debt as lenders become concerned about the firm's excessive borrowing.

The result of these opposing trends is an optimal degree of financial leverage at the point that k_0 attains its minimum value. This is the point—L^* in Figure 6-4—at which the lower cost of debt financing is just offset by the resulting higher cost of equity. Some argue that the cost of capital curve is saucer shaped, or flat bottomed, so that there is a range of optimal capital structures, but proponents of the traditional view all agree on one thing: An optimal capital structure exists, even in the absence of taxes.

[4] Modigliani-Miller Position

Determining which of the three conflicting views of capital structure in a taxless world is correct, and under what conditions, requires a theory of capital structure that is

FIGURE 6-4

Required Returns and Financial Leverage: The Traditional Approach

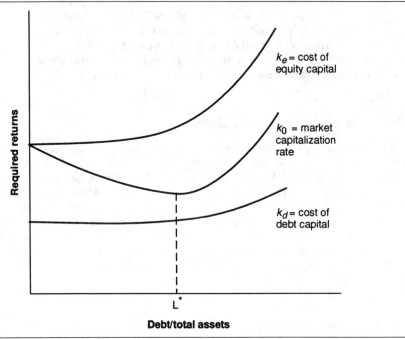

based on wealth-maximizing behavior by investors, something that was conspicuously absent in the arguments provided by supporters of the different approaches. This changed with publication of the classic article on capital structure by Modigliani and Miller (1958).

In what justly may be considered the most important paper in modern finance, Modigliani and Miller demonstrated that capital structure does not matter in a world without taxes, transaction costs, or other market imperfections. This is Modigliani and Miller's proposition 1: *The value of the firm is independent of its capital structure*. Proposition 1, which is identical to the net operating income approach, is based on an arbitrage argument that says that, in equilibrium, identical assets must sell for identical prices, regardless of the manner in which the assets are financed. This is a straightforward application of the law of the conservation of value. It says that no matter how a set of cash flows is packaged and repackaged, its value remains the same. If there are two cash flow streams, *A* and *B*, the present value of *A* + *B* will equal the present value of *A* plus the present value of *B*. Otherwise, an arbitrage profit can be earned.

Suppose, for example, that two identical firms are selling for different prices, with the unlevered firm *U* selling for less than the levered firm *L*. Modigliani and Miller argue that the possibility of arbitrage will not permit this situation to persist. By investing in firm *U*, in part with borrowed money, shareholders in firm *L* can increase their expected investment income without increasing their financial risk. This will lead them to sell off their shares in *L* and buy shares in *U*. The result will be a decline in the price

FIGURE 6-5

Required Returns and Financial Leverage: Modigliani and Miller's Proposition 2 Versus the Traditional View

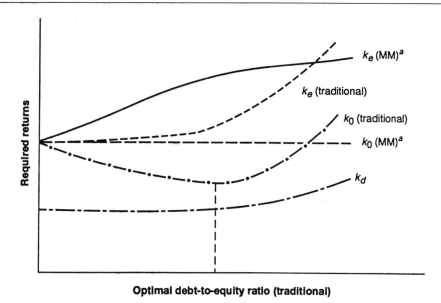

^{a} Modigliani and Miller.

of firm L shares and a rise in the price of firm U shares. These arbitrage transactions will continue until the market values of both firms are equal; that is, the value of the unlevered firm, V_U, must equal the value of the levered firm, V_L. At this point, there will be no further arbitrage opportunities.

For financial leverage to be irrelevant, the overall cost of capital, k_0, must remain constant, regardless of the amount of debt employed. In order for k_0 to be constant, the cost of equity capital must rise in a deterministic manner as leverage increases. Specifically, holding k_0 constant, the expected ROE must conform to Equation 6.3:

Expected ROE = expected ROA + risk premium for financial leverage (6.3)

$$k_e = k_0 + (k_0 - k_d)\frac{D}{E}$$

This represents Modigliani and Miller's proposition 2: *The cost of equity capital for a levered firm equals the constant overall cost of capital plus a risk premium that equals the spread between the overall cost of capital and the cost of debt multiplied by the firm's debt-to-equity ratio.* The contrast between Modigliani and Miller's proposition 2 and the traditional view is shown graphically in Figure 6-5.

Figure 6-5 implicitly assumes that at low levels of financial leverage, there is virtually no chance of default. Thus, k_d is independent of the debt-to-equity ratio, and the cost of equity capital increases linearly with the firm's debt-to-equity ratio. Once bankruptcy becomes a possibility, however, the cost of debt begins rising with leverage, and this leads to a slowdown in the rate of increase in k_e. Why does this happen? Because as the firm borrows more, debt holders bear a larger share of the firm's business risk, thereby offsetting some of the increased financial risk that shareholders must bear at higher debt levels.

6.04 CAPITAL STRUCTURE AND TAXES

In the perfect capital markets environment posited by Modigliani and Miller, the argument that capital structure is irrelevant is unassailable. Absent market imperfections, no matter how corporate cash flows are divided up between debt and equity claims, their total amount remains fixed. The risk attached to these cash flows taken as a whole also remains fixed because it just depends on the firm's basic business risk. Thus for capital structure to matter, there must be market imperfections that cause changes in financial leverage to change the amounts or riskiness of the firm's cash flows. Perhaps the most important market imperfection is the existence of taxes, both corporate and personal, and the asymmetric tax treatment of different forms of capital costs and income.

[1] Corporate Taxes

Under current law, debt has an important advantage over equity: Interest payments on debt are tax deductible, whereas dividend payments and retained earnings are not. The importance of this can be seen by examining how capital structure affects the amount of money the firm has available after tax to pay its investors.

Consider again the two firms introduced in the previous section that are identical in all respects except capital structure. Firm U is unlevered, whereas firm L has debt in its capital structure. Expected EBIT and risk are identical for both firms. Assume too that EBIT is expected to remain constant over time and that the amount of debt, D, used by firm L will stay constant over time. Then, if the firm's EBIT is not affected by capital structure, the annual operating cash flow available to firm U's shareholders, CF_U, is

Unlevered firm's cash flow to investors = dividends   (6.4)
$$CF_U = EBIT*(1 - t_c)$$

where t_c is the marginal corporate tax rate. On the other hand, the cash flows available to L's investors, CF_L, are

Levered firm's cash flow to investors = dividends + interest
$$\begin{aligned} CF_L &= (EBIT - k_d D)(1 - t_c) + K_d D \\ &= EBIT(1 - t_c) + t_c k_d D \\ &= CF_U + t_c k_d D \end{aligned}$$
                                                                            (6.5)

In other words, the combined cash flows available to investors increases with leverage by an amount equal to the value of the tax deduction on interest. The loser is the government, which collects less tax. This affects the relative market values of U and L.

The value of the unlevered (all-equity-financed) firm, V_U, is found by capitalizing its annual operating cash flows after tax, $\text{EBIT}(1 - t_c)$, at its cost of equity capital, k_e, or

$$V_U = \frac{\text{EBIT}(1 - t_c)}{k_e} = \frac{\text{EBIT}(1 - t_c)}{k^*} \tag{6.6}$$

where k^* is the capitalization rate for an all-equity-financed firm.

The value of the levered firm, V_L, is similarly found by capitalizing both parts of its annual after-tax cash flow, CF_U and $t_c k_d D$. Because the first cash flow component is precisely as risky as the cash flows to firm U's shareholders are, it should be capitalized at the same all-equity rate, k^*. On the other hand, the tax savings associated with debt financing, known as the interest tax shield, will be realized as long as the firm pays interest on its debt. Hence, the tax shield is exactly as risky as the debt itself and should be capitalized at k_d. Adding these two capitalized cash flows yields the market value of L:

$$V_L = \frac{\text{EBIT}(1 - t_c)}{k^*} + \frac{t_c k_d D}{k_d} = \frac{\text{EBIT}(1 - t_c)}{k^*} + t_c D = V_U + t_c D \tag{6.7}$$

Thus, the value of the levered firm equals the value of the unlevered firm plus the present value of the levered firm's interest tax shield, where

$$\text{PV(interest tax shield)} = \frac{\text{corporate tax rate} \times \text{interest paid}}{\text{interest rate on debt}} \tag{6.8}$$
$$= \frac{t_c(k_d D)}{k_d} = t_c D$$

According to Equation 6.8, the incremental value added to shareholder wealth with an amount of debt financing D is $t_c D$. This, of course, assumes that the firm will borrow an amount of debt, D, in perpetuity and will always be able to use the tax shield supplied by the debt. If either of these conditions is violated (e.g., the firm goes bankrupt and no longer has income to shield from taxes), the present value of the tax shield will be reduced.

To the extent that the firm has other tax shields, such as depreciation and investment tax credits, or has highly uncertain cash flows, the value of the interest tax shield for a given amount of debt is reduced. Similarly, as financial leverage increases, the firm becomes less likely to be able to utilize fully the resulting higher interest tax shield, lowering the tax advantage of adding debt to the capital structure. These problems become more severe at high levels of financial leverage, moderating the firm's incentive to substitute debt for equity.

[2] Capital Asset Pricing Model

According to MM, the cost of equity capital rises with leverage even when default risk is absent. This is because financial risk, as represented by the volatility of returns to shareholders, increases with the debt-to-equity ratio. The best way to see this is to employ the capital asset pricing model (CAPM). According to the CAPM, the cost of equity capital equals the risk-free rate plus the company's measure of systematic risk (beta or β) times the market risk premium, which is the expected return on the market less the risk-free rate. Analytically,

Cost of equity capital = risk-free return + risk premium

where the equity risk premium equals

Equity risk premium = equity beta × market risk premium

To see the effect of debt financing on the cost of equity capital, one must distinguish between the firm's asset beta and its equity beta. The asset beta, β_a, is the beta for the firm's existing assets, whereas the equity beta, β_e, is the beta for the firm's common stock. These betas will be equal only if the firm finances its investments on an all-equity basis. In this case, common stockholders face only the business risks borne by the firm's investments.

Most firms, however, finance their investments with both debt and equity. This means that the returns on corporate assets must be split among the debtholders and equityholders. Because debt holders have first claim on the firm's cash flows, the riskiness of the residual flows to equity holders is magnified. Thus, shareholders bear both the business risk of the company's real assets and the financial risk associated with the use of debt financing. Consequently, the firm's equity beta will exceed its asset beta.

The formula for the levered equity beta, the asset beta adjusted for debt financing, can be found using Equation 6.9:

$$\beta_e = \beta_a \left[1 + (1 - t_c) \frac{D}{E} \right] \tag{6.9}$$

To see the effect of leverage on the cost of equity capital, suppose the risk-free rate is 7 percent, the market risk premium is 8 percent, and the asset beta is 0.65. Then, the cost of equity capital before the use of leverage, using the CAPM, is 12.2 percent:

Cost of equity = 0.07 + 0.65(0.08) = 0.122

Now suppose the company substitutes enough debt for equity in its capital structure to raise its debt-equity ratio to 0.9. Then its tax-adjusted equity beta, assuming a 34 percent marginal corporate tax rate, rises to 1.036:

Levered beta = 0.65[1 + (1 − 0.34)0.9] = 1.036

The levered cost of equity capital, using the tax-adjusted beta, is now 15.3 percent:

Levered cost of equity capital = 0.07 + 1.036(0.08) = 0.153

If the corporate tax rate were 0, the levered beta would instead be 1.235 and the levered cost of equity capital would be 16.9 percent. Hence, the effect of the tax deductibility of interest payments is to lower the levered cost of equity capital relative to what it would otherwise be. It also lowers the cost of debt.

Taking the preceding material at face value, in the presence of corporate income taxes, additional borrowing will always increase the value of the firm. Thus, the logical conclusion of the original Modigliani and Miller argument, adjusted for corporate taxes, is that firms should be 100 percent debt financed. Indeed, in a correction to their original paper, Modigliani and Miller (1963) point out this implication. But this beautiful theory has no takers, except for firms in bankruptcy. If adding value is as easy as the theory seems to indicate, why don't we see firms with virtually all debt in their capital structures? In reality, most successful firms (e.g., Coca-Cola, Merck, and Microsoft) have very little debt in their capital structures. Moreover, corporate debt ratios are not much higher today than they were before World War II, when corporate taxes were virtually nonexistent.

There is always the possibility that firms do not take full advantage of financial leverage because of management stupidity or cupidity, but because firms like Coca-Cola and Microsoft do not appear to be shortchanging their shareholders in other ways, analysts can probably rule out these explanations for the observed pattern of less than 100 percent debt financing. Instead, it is more likely that the advantages of borrowing are less compelling in practice than they are in theory. Two possible reasons are the following:

1. The personal tax disadvantage of debt negates its corporate tax advantage.

2. Borrowers incur costs, such as bankruptcy and agency costs, that largely offset the value of the interest tax shield.

[3] Corporate and Personal Taxes

Thus far, this chapter has implicitly assumed that the presence of personal taxes does not affect the corporate tax advantage of borrowing and, therefore, the choice of capital structure. This is only the case, however, provided that the returns on debt and equity both are subject to the same personal tax rate.

Under the current system of taxation, the assumption that income to debt and equity investors is taxed at the same personal tax rate is questionable. For example, capital gains are taxed at a maximum rate of 28 percent, whereas the rate on dividends and interest is as high as 39.6 percent. Moreover, the capital gains tax is deferred until the stock is sold and the gain is actually realized. In the case of a firm that pays no dividends and investors that plan never to sell their stock, the effective personal tax rate on equity returns is zero.

What matters in establishing a capital structure are the total taxes, both corporate and personal, paid on operating income. To see the effect of financial leverage on the after-tax income to debt and equity investors when the personal tax rate on interest income, t_{pD}, differs from the personal tax rate on equity income, t_{pE}, examine the tax consequences of paying out \$1 of EBIT either as interest or as a return to equity.

Because the company pays no tax on interest payments, the after-tax value of \$1 in interest income received by a bondholder will be

$$\$1(1 - t_{pD})$$

If equity investors receive this dollar instead, both the firm and the stockholders will have to pay taxes on it. The amount left after paying corporate plus personal taxes is

$$\$1(1 - t_c)(1 - t_{pE})$$

From the standpoint of tax minimization, corporate borrowing will be preferred if the after-tax value of a dollar paid out as interest exceeds the after-tax value of a dollar paid to shareholders. Thus, debt financing is preferred if

$$1 - t_{pD} > (1 - t_c)(1 - t_{pE})$$

Equity financing will be preferred if the inequality is reversed. Corporate debt policy is irrelevant from a tax minimization standpoint if, and only if,

$$1 - t_{pD} = (1 - t_c)(1 - t_{pE})$$

The problem in figuring out which debt policy minimizes total taxes paid is that there is no such thing as "the" personal tax rate on interest income or "the" personal tax rate on equity income. Some investors, such as pension plans or charitable foundations, are tax exempt; others pay taxes but are in widely varying tax brackets.

[a] Miller's Model. In his article "Debt and Taxes" (1977), Miller supplied a controversial answer to the issue of optimal debt policy when investors are in different tax brackets. He proposed that the original Modigliani and Miller proposition 1 that financial leverage is irrelevant in a tax-free world also holds in a world with both corporate and personal taxes.

The key to Miller's argument lies in his assumption that the personal tax rate on equity income is zero: Either equity income comes in the form of unrealized and hence tax-exempt capital gains, or investors borrow against their dividend-paying stock and deduct the resulting interest expenses from their dividend income, thereby avoiding personal tax on dividends.

Suppose firms are initially all-equity-financed. As long as there are tax-exempt investors around ($t_{pD} = 0$), companies can increase their value by t_c for each dollar of debt they add to their capital structure. As firms borrow more, however, they will eventually exhaust their tax-exempt clientele; further debt must be sold to investors in higher tax brackets. To persuade taxable investors to switch from stocks (whose income is assumed to be tax-exempt) to bonds (whose interest income is taxable) firms must increase the interest they pay by an amount equal to the personal tax cost to the marginal investor in debt. If k_e is the risk-adjusted expected ROE, then the risk-adjusted expected return on debt must be at least equal to $k_e/(1 - t_{pD})$ to compensate investors for the personal tax cost of debt.

[b] Implications of "Debt and Taxes." Miller argues that the equilibrium supply of corporate debt is that aggregate amount at which the tax bracket of the marginal debtholder just equals the corporate tax rate. Otherwise, firms can earn tax arbitrage profits by rearranging their capital structures. In particular, if the marginal personal tax rate exceeds the corporate tax rate, companies will issue no debt; if it is less than the corporate tax rate, firms will finance entirely with debt. Therefore, the supply curve is perfectly horizontal at a risk-adjusted interest rate of $k_e/(1 - t_c)$.

Because investors are willing to hold more debt as companies offer them a higher before-tax expected return on debt, the demand curve for debt is upward sloping. How steep the slope is depends on the funds available to investors in different tax brackets; the more funds that are available to investors in tax brackets below the corporate tax rate, the less steep the slope will be. The result is an economywide optimal debt-to-equity ratio at the point at which the supply and demand curves for debt intersect. That point is at L^* in Figure 6-6. As the amount of minimally taxed funds falls, the optimal debt ratio will fall, to L'. Conversely, as the corporate tax rate rises relative to personal tax rates, the optimal debt ratio will rise to L''. However, no one firm can gain a tax advantage from financial leverage.

Of course, to the extent that a firm can issue tax-exempt debt, it should do so; according to Equation 6.8, each dollar of such debt will add t_c to the firm's value, because t_{pD} is zero in this case.

[c] Compromise Position. Most financial managers and financial economists believe that there is a tax advantage to issuing debt. Before Miller's paper, they had

FIGURE 6-6

Determination of the Economywide Optimal Debt-To-Equity Ratio

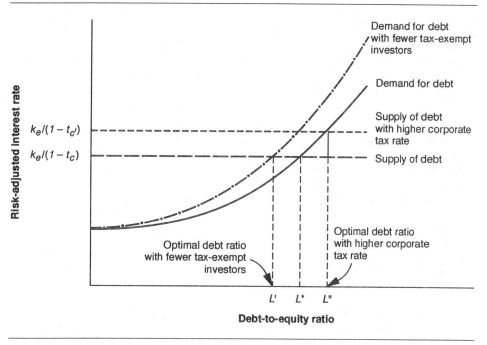

calculated the value of the tax shield on D dollars of debt as t_cD. It is now widely accepted that the effect of personal taxes is to lower this estimate. But by how much? We have already seen some evidence on this question, that supplied by the relative yields on taxable and tax-exempt debt. Masulis (1980, 1983) and others have studied the effects on firm value of recapitalizations, in which companies exchange one type of security for another. These studies suggest that a crude estimate of the net tax effect of debt is around 20 percent; that is, the net tax benefit to a firm that adds $1 in debt to its capital structure and is almost certain to use the resulting tax shield is about $.20.

The qualifier is an important one because many companies are unlikely to be able to utilize fully their interest tax shields. DeAngelo and Masulis (1980) point out that the loss of the interest tax shield results from properties of the tax code that rule out negative taxes (subsidies) and thereby limit the amount of tax shields that a firm can use. Companies that are likely to be subject to these limits include those that have (1) highly variable incomes; (2) large amounts of other tax deductions, such as depreciation and depletion allowances and lease payments; or (3) large tax loss carryforwards. Examples of firms that fit into one or more of these categories include airlines, steel companies, auto manufacturers, petroleum refiners, and tire companies. The common denominator among these firms is that they are in capital-intensive and/or cyclical industries.

On the other hand, companies with fairly stable or predictable incomes and relatively few other methods to shield their income from taxes are likely to realize most of the net tax benefit from debt. Examples include consumer goods firms, utilities, some computer manufacturers, and packaged foods companies.

To summarize, the existence of corporate tax shield substitutes for debt leads to a situation in which leverage affects the value of the firm; personal and corporate taxes do not fully offset each other. The effect of personal taxes is to reduce the net tax advantage to borrowing to somewhere in the neighborhood of $0.20 for each $1 of debt for those firms that are fairly certain of being able to use the interest tax shield. This may become a moderate tax disadvantage for those firms that are unlikely to utilize fully the interest tax shield on additional debt.

[d] Impact of TRA 1986. Miller's argument implicitly relies on the highest marginal tax bracket for investors being at least equal to the federal corporate tax rate. Under the Tax Reform Act of 1986 (TRA 1986), however, the highest individual tax rate was 28 percent, whereas the corporate tax rate was (and still is) 34 percent. During the brief period when this tax regime was in effect (1987–1990), the marginal corporate tax rate *always* exceeded the marginal personal tax rate, meaning that no matter how much debt companies issued, there was still a tax advantage for debt financing. Thus, based on tax considerations alone, the optimal capital structure was 100 percent debt.

The tax advantage of corporate debt was reinforced owing to TRA 1986's elimination of many nondebt tax deductions and credits. Tax reform also enhanced the use of corporate leverage relative to personal leverage. The tax shelter due to borrowing at the corporate level was 34 percent, but it was limited to 28 percent for individual investors.

In 1990, the highest individual rate was boosted to 33 percent (taking into account the loss of tax deductions as income rises) and it is all but certain that individual rates will rise still further. This signals a return to the pre-1987 situation, in which the marginal personal tax rate exceeds the corporate tax rate.

6.05 ESTABLISHING A CAPITAL STRUCTURE

The theoretical models discussed previously are of limited help to the financial manager who must choose a capital structure. Although they provide some clues regarding an appropriate capital structure, these models are unrealistic and ignore many of the relevant factors that are likely to influence the trade-off between more debt and more equity. However, because the importance of the different factors varies from one firm to another, there is no one solution to the capital structure problem.

Even if personal taxes moderate the tax advantages of financial leverage, the evidence presented previously suggests that for many firms the value of the interest tax shield is significantly positive. For these firms, the optimal capital structure would appear to contain mostly debt financing. Yet the most likely candidates for high degrees of financial leverage, companies like Microsoft, Coca-Cola, and Merck, have very low debt ratios. Because these firms seem to be intent on maximizing shareholder wealth, there must be potential costs to debt financing that sooner or later come to outweigh its tax advantages.

Some of the additional costs to financial leverage include the adverse incentives that shareholders have to undertake risky projects when financed primarily with debt (an agency problem), the harmful effects of financial distress on firm sales and costs, and the potential loss of financial flexibility if heavily leveraged.

FIGURE 6-7

Optimal Debt Ratio Trades Off the Interest Tax Shield Against the Costs of Financial Distress

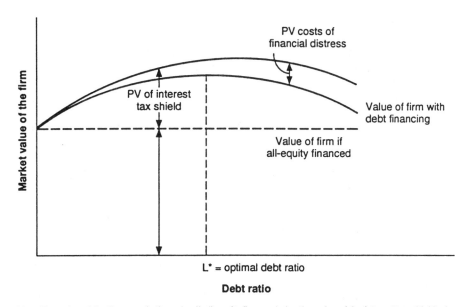

Note: The value of the firm equals the value if all-equity financed plus the value of the interest tax shield minus the costs of financial distress. The value of the interest tax shield may decline if financial leverage becomes too great and the company's ability to take advantage of the tax shield becomes questionable.

[1] Financial Leverage and Financial Distress

Financial distress occurs when a firm has difficulty in meeting its contractual obligations. In the extreme case, the firm defaults on its obligations and enters bankruptcy, a formal legal proceeding under which a company that has overextended itself is placed under the protection of the bankruptcy court, allowing it to keep operating while a plan is developed to pay off creditors in an equitable manner. Generally, the term "financial distress" refers to any weakening of a company's financial condition. All forms of financial distress involve costs to the firm and, therefore, are reflected in a reduced price for the shares of leveraged firms. Because more highly leveraged firms have more financial commitments outstanding, they are more likely to encounter financial distress. Thus the expected costs of financial distress—the probability of distress times the actual costs—will rise with financial leverage.

    Figure 6-7 shows that—ignoring other factors—the optimal debt ratio involves a trade-off between the tax advantage of additional debt and the higher expected costs of financial distress. At low levels of debt, the probability, and hence the expected costs, of financial distress are minimal, but as more debt is added to the capital structure, both the probability and the expected costs of financial distress increase, eventually exceeding the present value of the interest tax shield. The firm becomes less certain of being profitable enough to take advantage of the interest tax shield as its debt ratio rises, so the tax shield's value may decline. The optimal debt ratio, L* in Figure 6-7, is reached when the tax advantage of another dollar of debt just equals the added costs of financial distress. (See Chapters E7 and E8 in the *Handbook of Modern Finance* and Chapters 7 and 8 in the *Handbook of Financial Strategy and Policy* for a discussion of closely related issues.)

[a] Probability of Bankruptcy. All else being equal, the higher the business or operating risk facing a firm, the greater will be the probability, and hence the expected costs, of financial distress at any given level of debt financing. Determinants of business risk include the following:

1. *Operating leverage.* As the degree of operating leverage rises, income fluctuates more with a given change in sales. Steel, auto, and petrochemical firms are very capital-intensive and thus are inherently risky. Service firms are typically less capital-intensive.

2. *Cyclical variations.* The sales of some products stay relatively constant over the business cycle, whereas changes in national income greatly affect the sales of other products. The former category includes pharmaceutical companies, fast food companies, and producers of other nondurables, such as cigarettes and alcohol. The latter category includes steel and automobile companies and capital equipment manufacturers.

3. *Competition.* The more competitive the industry is, the greater the business risks will be. Personal computer firms, oil companies, and firms in commodity businesses face a great deal of competition. On the other hand, regulated industries, such as utilities, and companies with strong brand franchises, such as soft drink producers, have less competition and fairly stable earnings.

4. *Relative price fluctuations.* The prices of certain products, especially basic commodities such as copper and wheat, fluctuate greatly, increasing the business risks of companies dealing in those products. The prices of manufactured goods typically are more stable, lowering the business risk of their producers.

5. *Firm size and diversification.* Larger firms are typically better diversified, and hence less risky, than smaller firms.

6. *Stage in the industry life cycle.* Products often go through a life cycle. In the early stages, when the industry is just getting underway and growing rapidly, there is a lot of sorting out and high failure rates. Similarly, when the industry begins its decline, competition is intense, and failure rates are again high—witness the steel industry. In between, during the mature phase, firms that have survived the growth phase probably face the least business risk.

[b] Bankruptcy Costs. With limited liability, stockholders have a valuable option; they can default on the firm's obligations with no further responsibility to the creditors. They will exercise this option and throw the firm into bankruptcy when the value of the firm's liabilities exceeds the value of its assets. Bankruptcy is not costless, however. In the event of bankruptcy, the firm must bear certain direct costs in the form of various legal, accounting, and administrative expenses. The firm may also have to sell off some of its assets at "fire sale" prices to meet creditors' claims.

The possibility of bankruptcy and its attendant costs lowers the value of creditor claims. Understanding this, lenders build into their required interest rate the expected costs of bankruptcy. This reduces the market value of equity claims by a corresponding amount. The end result is that stockholders must bear the ex ante costs of bankruptcy. Because the probability of bankruptcy rises with financial leverage, the more a firm borrows, the higher its expected costs of bankruptcy and the lower the market value of its equity will be.

The direct costs of bankruptcy, however, do not seem to be the reason for the minimal amounts of debt in many corporate capital structures. In a study of 11 railroad bankruptcies, Warner (1977) estimated the average of the resulting legal and administrative expenses to be about 5.3 percent of the total market value of the railroads' debt and equity securities just before bankruptcy. The corresponding figure for bankruptcy costs relative to the firm's total market value five years before bankruptcy was estimated to be just 1.4 percent. These figures are relatively insignificant when measured against the estimated value of the interest tax shield. Although these data apply only to railroads, the complexity of such bankruptcies makes it unlikely that legal and administrative costs are a larger fraction of market value for other types of firms.

[c] Costs of Financial Distress. Far more important to explaining the observed pattern of capital structures are likely to be the indirect costs of financial distress. These costs, which increase with the probability of bankruptcy, arise from the deterioration in the firm's operating performance brought on by financial distress. Part of this deterioration is the result of management's focusing its attention and energy on keeping creditors at bay rather than on running the firm. More important, a company's prospects are not independent of the perceptions of its noninvestor stakeholders regarding its longevity and viability. According to Shapiro and Titman (1985), financial distress weakens the bonds between the firm and its stakeholders, reducing the expected cash flows that will be generated by the unique factor and product market franchises the firm has developed.

Texaco's travails provide an example of the costs imposed by financial distress. On November 19, 1985, a Houston jury found that Texaco had improperly interfered with Pennzoil's plan to buy Getty Oil and directed Texaco to pay Pennzoil $11.1 billion in damages plus interest. In the seven trading days following the verdict, the market value of Texaco dropped by $1.8 billion, while the market value of Pennzoil rose only $600 million. After the judge upheld the award, Pennzoil stock rose further, and Texaco slumped. From November 19 through December 11, the first day of trading following the judge's decision, Texaco lost $2.58 billion in market value, while Pennzoil's market value rose by just $780 million. Overall, for every $1 that the market value of Pennzoil rose, the market value of Texaco fell $3.31. One explanation for the $1.8 billion wedge ($2.58 billion − $780 million) is the cost of financial distress. Specifically, customers, suppliers, and business partners were no longer willing to do business with Texaco on the same terms. For example, Atlantic Richfield, which both buys and sells crude oil and refined products with Texaco, sent a letter to its staff in early December urging them to use "prudence" in doing business with Texaco.

The inverse relation between financial leverage and expected cash flows arises, in part, because financial distress creates management incentives that conflict with the best interests of the individuals that do business with such firms. The negative effect of these adverse incentives on sales and operating costs is compounded by the risk aversion of customers, managers, employees, suppliers, and other corporate stakeholders.

[d] Adverse Incentive Problem. Financial distress, or the threat of bankruptcy, affects management behavior in four fundamental ways:

1. Managers are more likely to select certain high-risk projects that benefit shareholders, but at the expense of bondholders.

2. Managers may pass up projects with positive net present values because most payoffs will go to bondholders.

3. Managers have a tendency to exit lines of business or liquidate the entire firm under conditions when they would otherwise continue to operate.

4. Managers may have an incentive to produce goods of inferior quality and provide a less safe work environment for their employees.

Because both stockholders and managers have strong incentives to avoid bankruptcy and premature liquidation, they may do things under the threat of financial distress that they would not otherwise do. For example, a firm having difficulty raising cash may be tempted to lower its product and service quality, as well as cut corners on employee safety. These temptations will be especially strong in cases in which quality or safety is difficult to observe ahead of time. Other problems associated with financial distress also have their origin in the emphasis on maximizing short-run cash flow. A firm facing financial distress may be tempted to conserve cash by cutting back on research and development, advertising and promotional expenditures, and various forms of working capital such as inventory and receivables. These are dangerous moves, however, because the firm will be gaining short-run profits at the expense of its reputation for providing quality products and reliable service and, ultimately, its longer-run ability to remain competitive. A financially healthy firm, therefore, has a strong incentive to produce high-quality products and to take other actions that will ensure its long-term viability.

These incentives are likely to change if the firm is suffering financial distress. Under the threat of bankruptcy, long-term profit considerations may be less important than generating enough cash to meet current debt-servicing charges. The cost savings associated with cutting quality levels may be particularly attractive to firms facing creditors threatening to take over and possibly liquidate the firms.

Potential customers and other stakeholders, anticipating these incentive changes, will be reluctant to do business with firms in financial distress, as well as with high-risk firms likely to face financial distress in the future. This will adversely affect the firms' future sales, operating costs, and financing costs. Simply put, financial distress will reduce the value of stakeholders of doing business with a risky firm. As a result, customers will lower the price they are willing to pay for the firm's products, and other stakeholders will raise the prices they charge the firm for their goods and services. These effects of financial distress reduce the firm's market value and, hence, the market value of the firm's equity; that is, the costs of financial distress are borne by the firm's stockholders.

Firms selling products that are highly differentiated are likely to have far higher costs of financial distress than is a commodity-oriented producer because product differentiation requires a large investment in organizational assets. As defined by Cornell and Shapiro (1987), these intangible assets take a variety of forms: managers and others with firm-specific knowledge and skills, a network of outside distributors and suppliers, strong brand names, and a reputation for quality and reliability. One way to view these organizational assets is to recognize that they equal the present value of all future profits that the firm expects to earn from them.

An important attribute of the firm's stock of organizational capital is that it cannot be separated from the firm as an ongoing operation. It is this inseparability that differentiates organizational capital from other capital assets. If the firm gets into financial trouble, it can sell physical assets, but it cannot liquidate its organizational capital. These intangible assets disappear along with the firm. Because the value of a firm's intangible assets largely depends on the firm's staying power, a strong financial posture is important to firms that have large amounts of these assets.

These considerations imply that firms with large amounts of organizational assets will have the highest costs of financial distress. Therefore, such firms should deliberately choose to present a low-risk profile to the public. This helps explain why firms such as Apple Computer and Coca-Cola, with substantial amounts of intangible assets, voluntarily choose to have less debt in their capital structures.

[2] Characteristics of Firms With High Expected Costs of Financial Distress

Based on the preceding discussion, it is possible to identify specific characteristics of firms for which financial distress is especially costly or highly likely. These firms should, therefore, choose to maintain low debt ratios. Some of these characteristics are industry-specific, based on product type, yet others are firm-specific, based on certain unique factors. Industry-specific product characteristics include the following:

1. *Products that require repairs.* This is illustrated by Lee Iacocca's response to suggestions that Chrysler go bankrupt: "Our situation was unique. . . . It wasn't like the cereal business. If Kellogg's were known to be going out of business, nobody would say: 'Well, I won't buy their cornflakes today. What if I get stuck with a box of cereal and there's nobody around to service it?' "[1] Financial distress is costly here because demand drops as potential customers begin to worry about buying products that cannot be serviced should the firm exit the business.

2. *Goods or services whose quality is an important attribute but is difficult to determine in advance.* An example is air transportation. In fact, airline companies in financial difficulty have been hurt by the common belief that they are more likely to cut corners on safety, thereby increasing the risk of an accident. In general, customers become concerned that a company in financial distress will reduce product quality and so will prefer to stick with a healthier company, unless given a substantial price discount.

3. *Products for which there are switching costs.* Such products—for which customers must bear large fixed costs to switch suppliers—include computers and office and factory automation equipment. Rather than be stuck with obsolete equipment if a financially distressed firm exits the business, customers will prefer to buy products from a financially strong firm. For example, many customers of Wang Laboratories, the pioneer of word processing computers, were frightened away by reports of its financial troubles. According to *The Wall Street Journal,* "Wang's customers are data processing managers who want to be sure that their suppliers are stable, well-run companies that will be around to fix bugs and upgrade computers for years to come," and doing business with Wang was too risky for many of them.[2] By the time Wang filed for bankruptcy in 1992, its stock market value had shrunk from $5.6 billion to $70 million.

---

[1] *Fortune* (Nov. 16, 1984, p. 224.

[2] *Wall Street Journal* (Oct. 18, 1989), p. B1.

4. *Products whose value to customers depends on the services and complementary products supplied by independent companies.* Many firms, such as computer manufacturers and auto companies, require third parties to distribute, sell, service, upgrade, and otherwise add value to their products. Being a low-risk firm helps persuade independent firms to enter such a symbiotic relationship.

Firm-specific factors arguing for low debt ratios include the following:

1. *High growth opportunities.* Firms having more positive net present value projects available than they can finance with internally generated funds should not jeopardize their access to outside financing by the appearance of being risky. Otherwise, prospective investors could be scared off by the previously discussed management incentive problems, and the firm will be unable to capitalize on its growth options, which are the opportunities that a firm may have to increase the profitability of its existing product lines and to benefit from expanding into new products or markets. Further, the problem of asymmetric information is likely to be more severe for a firm in financial distress, as investors figure that the company is covering up even more severe financial troubles.

2. *Substantial organizational assets.* Firms whose principal assets are intangible—in the form of managers and employees with firm-specific human capital, outside distributors, suppliers, brand names, a reputation for quality and reliability—will have higher costs of financial distress than firms with mostly physical assets. These intangible assets will rapidly depreciate in value if the firm experiences, or seems likely to experience, financial distress. As the firm's risk increases, the value of a reputation for quality products diminishes, and managers and other stakeholders are increasingly likely to sever their ties with the firm.

   Conversely, the fact of bankruptcy, or other form of financial distress, should not detract much from the value of assets like oil, factories, or hotel rooms. Therefore, firms whose principal assets are physical—for example, an oil company, a firm producing bulk steel, or a hotel—should be willing to carry higher debt ratios.

3. *Large excess tax deductions.* Companies such as Texas Air and General Motors cannot take full advantage of their available tax losses, much less the interest on additional debt. Thus, they have less incentive to load up on further debt.

An illustration of what can happen when a firm selects a capital structure that is inconsistent with its basic business strategy is provided by the events at Concurrent Computer. Concurrent Computer makes superminicomputers, extremely fast machines that crunch a great deal of data coming from different sources. Concurrent's promising product line includes tote machines for horse race tracks and state lotteries, and space shuttle flight simulators, with sales totaling about $200 million and earnings of $10 million. Concurrent specialized in proprietary, rather than open, systems, meaning that customers were locked into Concurrent hardware and software. However, many customers wanted equipment that would work on open systems, so in 1988, Concurrent decided to acquire MassComp, known for its open systems technology, with sales of $76 million and earnings of about $3 million. The agreed-on price was $240 million, which Concurrent decided to finance with debt rather than equity. This was an unfortunate choice, because high debt and high technology do not mix well. Concurrent relies heavily on customer perceptions of its long-term viability because it specializes in systems whose benefits can only be realized if Concurrent stays in business long term. As a result, customers look at Concurrent's financial leverage when deciding whether to purchase one of its systems. A high debt load calls into question Concurrent's ability to service, repair, and upgrade its products in the future.

Creditors may also impose covenants that limit Concurrent's operating and financial flexibility. Concurrent needs this flexibility to capitalize on its potential growth options and to cope with the shift from proprietary to open systems. With the rapidly changing technology, Concurrent will likely need to make substantial new investments in research and development (R&D) and marketing to protect its existing market position and take advantage of its new growth opportunities. In addition, such changes mean more business risk, which is magnified by more debt.

The move to open systems also reduces Concurrent's ability to differentiate its products. The systems sold by Concurrent are turning into more of a commodity. Commodity products typically have narrow profit margins and a more transient customer base that leads to more volatile earnings. Until Concurrent can differentiate itself in this new environment, its low margins will probably not be able to support a large debt load. Even at current margins, at a price of $240 million and with Concurrent plus MassComp earnings of $13 million, earnings will fail to cover any reasonable interest payment. For example, at an interest rate of 12 percent, the after-tax interest expense will be $19 million (0.12 × 0.66 × $240). By financing this deal with debt, Concurrent puts itself in a position of possible financial distress, calling into question its ability to meet its customers' expectations. Customers are therefore likely to desert Concurrent, increasing the strains on its financial position. Since most of Concurrent's assets are intangible, primarily its engineers, sales force, skilled managers, and credibility in the marketplace, they are likely to disappear in the event of financial distress. Based on all of these considerations, equity was clearly the appropriate financing approach for this deal.

However, Concurrent financed this deal with debt. When its growth projections did not pan out, it found itself on the verge of bankruptcy. The new chairman spent more than half of his time reassuring customers, who were drifting away, yet Concurrent lost even more sales. Concurrent fired over 900 employees, cut R&D spending, and consolidated facilities. Although Concurrent has managed to survive so far, it undoubtedly hurt its future growth prospects in the process of shrinking the organization and losing customers. By leveraging up, Concurrent has also faced competitors emboldened by its heavy debt load. They are engaging Concurrent in a battle for market share—through price cuts, heavy advertising, and so on—knowing that with its huge debt servicing charges, Concurrent's ability to respond is greatly limited.

[3] Agency Costs and Capital Structure

The modern corporation has no "owners" in the traditional sense. Instead, it is an interrelated set of contracts among a variety of stakeholders: shareholders, lenders, employees, managers, suppliers, distributors, and consumers. These stakeholders share a common interest in the firm's success. But conflicts of interest may also arise among the stakeholders (e.g., in the case of financial distress). The emphasis here is on how these potential conflicts of interest, particularly among classes of security holders, affect the firm's financial strategy.

[a] Stockholder-Manager Conflicts. Although management is legally bound to act as the shareholders' agent, the separation of ownership and control in the modern corporation may result in a conflict between the two parties. According to Jensen and Meckling (1976), the agency conflict between managers and outside shareholders derives from two principal sources. The first is management's tendency to consume some of the firm's resources in the form of various perquisites. A good example is the decision by Occidental Petroleum Corporation in 1985 to spend $500,000 of corporate funds to subsidize the publication of two highly laudatory books chronicling the life of its 86-year-old chairman, Armand Hammer. It seems safe to say that shareholders could find better uses for their money than to support these books, one of which was edited and the other written by the late Dr. Hammer.

The second important conflict arises because managers have a greater tendency to shirk their responsibilities as their equity interest falls. They are less willing to make the hard, though necessary, choices in managing employees. Most managers have little stomach for eliminating jobs, closing unprofitable operations, and slashing overhead spending. They also tend to shy away from the difficult task of measuring performance and disciplining those who fail to measure up. Managers, like most people, prefer to avoid the emotionally draining experience of constantly operating on the razor's edge of efficiency. This is especially true if the costs of underperforming employees and other operating inefficiencies are borne by others.

Moreover, managers may be unduly risk-averse, passing up profitable opportunities that the firm's shareholders would prefer to invest in. Even if managers are major shareholders in the firm, they still extract considerable wealth from their salaries. Hence, they are tempted to pursue a suboptimal risk strategy in order not to fail or to be seen as failures. Thus, as outside equity accounts for a larger share of corporate ownership, there is a corresponding decrease in managerial incentive, resulting in more shirking and higher costs to shareholders.

[b] Stockholder-Bondholder Conflicts. Agency conflicts also exist between stockholders and bondholders. The market value of any firm equals the market value of its bonds plus the market value of its stock. This means that managers can create shareholder wealth either by increasing the value of the firm or by reducing the value of its bonds. The latter possibility is at the root of stockholder-bondholder conflicts.

An important characteristic of corporate debt is that bondholders have prior but fixed claims on a firm's assets, whereas stockholders have limited liability for the firm's debt and unlimited claims on its remaining assets. If the firm is heavily leveraged, the limited liability of shareholders, which gives them the choice of turning over the firm's assets to its creditors instead of repaying its debts, means that bondholders must bear most of the risk while shareholders gather most of the potential rewards.

According to the Black-Scholes option-pricing model, this option becomes more valuable as company cash flows increase in variability. All else being equal, therefore, the value of equity rises and the value of debt declines in line with the volatility of corporate cash flows. The result is a transfer of wealth from bondholders to shareholders. An intuitive explanation of this wealth transfer is that the risk of default has risen but bondholders are not compensated for the added risk.

The bottom line is that increasing the risk of the firm will redistribute wealth from bondholders to shareholders. Other things being equal, therefore, shareholders have an incentive to engage in risk-increasing activities (e.g., highly risky projects) that have the potential of big returns. If these investments pay off, the owners will gain handsomely; if the investments are unsuccessful, the bondholders will bear most of the costs. Similarly, management can also reduce the value of preexisting bonds and transfer wealth from current bondholders to stockholders by issuing a substantial amount of new debt, thereby raising the firm's financial risk.

Of course, as pointed out previously, raising the corporate risk profile could cause corporate cash flows to decline, but even if a risky action reduces the value of the firm, the value of equity claims could still rise. This would happen if the reduction in the value of corporate debt associated with the greater risk exceeded the reduction in the value of the firm.

[c] Postcontractual Opportunism and the Issue Price of Securities. The net result of these agency problems is that the amounts and riskiness of future cash flows are not independent of the firm's ownership structure. As long as investors anticipate these agency problems, which they do in efficient markets, it is the firm and its managers, and not outside investors, that will bear the wealth effects of this divergence of interests. The settling up between the firm and its outside investors for the possibility of opportunistic (unprincipled) behavior ex post will take place ex ante, when the firm goes to raise capital. Recognizing that the firm will at times make decisions at variance with their best interests, outside investors will take into account these future departures from optimality (as they define it) by discounting the prices they are willing to pay for the firm's security issues. In this way, the firm, and not outside investors, bears the costs of all anticipated departures from the objective of shareholder wealth maximization.

Because the costs associated with agency problems are borne by management, either alone or in conjunction with shareholders, firms wishing to raise capital in an efficient market have clear-cut incentives to evolve mechanisms to assure the market that they will not engage in postcontractual opportunism, and they have incentives to provide these assurances at the lowest possible cost. These mechanisms include providing managers with incentives, such as stock options, to act in accordance with shareholder wealth maximization; bearing monitoring costs in the form of audits, specific reporting procedures, and other surveillance methods; and including various restrictive covenants in bond and bank loan agreements. If the firm violates any of these covenants, it can be declared in default on its debt, and the loan will become payable immediately. If it does not pay up or renegotiate the loan, the firm can then be forced into bankruptcy and possible liquidation by its creditors. This possibility provides a strong incentive to obey the covenants.

Although the constraints imposed by lenders can avoid many of the potential agency problems associated with debt financing by limiting management actions that may be harmful to bondholders, they can also prove costly to shareholders by greatly reducing the firm's operating and investment flexibility. For example, lenders may veto certain high-risk projects with positive net present values because of the added risk they would have to bear without a corresponding increase in their expected returns. The opportunity cost associated with the loss of operating flexibility is likely to be especially high for firms with substantial growth options.

The costs of these monitoring and control procedures, as well as the costs of any residual divergence from firm value maximization, are known collectively as agency costs. Resources will be expended on these various monitoring activities up to the point at which the marginal costs of such activities just equal their marginal expected benefits. As the percentage of outside equity or debt in the capital structure rises, so do the associated agency costs. Consequently, it pays the firm to expend more resources to monitor corporate management. Ignoring other factors, the optimal capital structure for a given amount of outside financing is achieved when total agency costs are minimized.

[d] Agency Costs of Debt. The agency costs of debt include the monitoring and control expenditures to ensure that bondholders are not exploited by shareholders, as well as the discount at which the bonds of more highly leveraged companies sell. They also include the costs arising from the restrictive loan covenants, which are a consequence of the firm's reduced operating and investment flexibility. All else being equal, therefore, the agency costs associated with the conflicts of interest between shareholders and bondholders reduce the desirable amount of debt in the firm's capital structure, because the conflicts and their costs become more severe as financial leverage increases.

[e] Agency Costs of Equity. Because the agency costs of equity also grow more severe as the proportion of outside equity increases, there is a trade-off between the desire to reduce the agency costs of debt and to reduce the agency costs of outside equity. As noted earlier, the problem with adding more outside equity to the capital structure is that management's interest in the firm diminishes along with its stake in the firm. At the extreme, if management goes from owning 100 percent of the firm to having no ownership interest, its willingness to put forth the effort and to take the risks necessary to maximize shareholder welfare is likely to be altered dramatically.

Yet, forcing management to increase its equity interest in the company—by means of stock options, profit-sharing plans, or large stock holdings—can lead to other agency problems. In particular, it defeats the risk transfer function of outside equity; by issuing stock to outsiders, managers are able to transfer some of the risks of the firm's operations to others. Because outside investors are able to diversify away much of this risk, they will charge only for bearing the systematic portion of risk. But a manager with a large fraction of her wealth tied up in the company must bear the total risk. Thus, risk-averse managers may be unwilling to undertake risky but profitable projects if they are forced to hold a large equity stake in the company.

Jensen (1986) pointed out another agency cost of equity—the incentive managers have to expand their firms beyond the point at which shareholder wealth is maximized. Growth increases managers' power and perquisites by increasing the resources at their command. It also tends to increase their compensation, because changes in compensation are positively related to sales growth.

Given these considerations, managers have strong incentives to reduce the payout of cash to shareholders. By retaining funds internally, rather than paying them out, managers seeking to expand their domains can bypass the capital markets and avoid the monitoring costs associated with the capital acquisition process. Jensen observed that conflicts of interest between shareholders and managers over payout policy are especially severe in companies that generate substantial amounts of free cash flow. Free cash flow is cash flow in excess of that required to fund all positive net present value (NPV) projects. Shareholder wealth maximization dictates that free cash flow be paid out to shareholders. The problem is how to get managers to return excess cash to the shareholders instead of reinvesting it in substandard projects and overpriced acquisitions or wasting it on organizational inefficiencies.

[f] Debt as One Solution to the Agency Costs of Equity. One answer to the problem of agency costs of equity is greatly expanded leverage. According to Jensen, by issuing large amounts of debt and using the proceeds either to pay a big dividend or to buy back stock, management is committed to using corporate cash flows for principal and interest payments. Because the value of equity equals the value of the firm less the value of its debt, using excess cash to make debt payments effectively returns this cash to shareholders. Any expansion must henceforth be financed with new capital, subjecting management's investment plans to the exacting discipline of the market.

But why should managers take on such large amounts of debt and reduce their discretion over free cash flow when they were unwilling previously to return the cash directly to the shareholders? Because companies that waste large amounts of resources become subject to hostile takeovers. A raider can offer shareholders a price for their shares that exceeds the current market price and still make money by running the company more efficiently.

[g] Leveraged Recapitalizations. Managers fearing a hostile takeover can promise to mend their spendthrift ways and pay out free cash flow to shareholders, but such a promise will not be credible unless something is done to ensure that managers who dishonor their promises incur a large penalty. Announcing a dividend increase is not adequate because managers can always cut the dividend later without penalty. A leveraged recapitalization, by contrast, can effectively bond managers' promises to pay out free cash flow. (See Chapter E8 in the *Handbook of Modern Finance* and Chapter 8 of the *Handbook of Financial Strategy and Policy* for further discussion.) In this transaction, a company boosts its debt and shrinks its equity, either by paying a huge one-time dividend to stockholders or by repurchasing a large amount of stock. The pressure to make debt payments is usually adequate to keep management honest; if the firm reverts to its old ways and is forced into bankruptcy, managers will most likely lose their jobs. Lenders also have a strong incentive to scrutinize internal investments and ensure that resources are not wasted. Added leverage, therefore, reduces the scope of management discretion, changes the process by which management's actions are monitored, and thus changes managers' motivation.

Of course, leverage has its own costs: As leverage goes up, the agency costs of debt also rise, as well as the costs of financial distress. Managers of a highly leveraged firm have to persuade suppliers to continue to sell on credit; suppliers may rightly wonder whether the company will be able to pay its bills. Customers can get the jitters as they worry about continuity and quality of service. Employees are also concerned that companies will cut staff and sell or close facilities in order to pay back the large amount of debt they are now saddled with. The optimal debt-to-equity ratio is the point at which the marginal costs of debt just offset the marginal benefits. This is the point at which the value of the firm is maximized.

[4] Estimating a Firm's Debt Capacity

Leverage is a two-edged sword that increases the expected ROE, while making those returns more risky. In effect, a firm that "levers up" is placing a bet on the future. If things turn out well, shareholders will benefit; if not, they will lose. The trade-offs in such a gamble were illustrated in the EBIT-EPS analysis presented previously. Therefore, part of the capital structure decision comes down to the question of whether management has better information about the firm's future prospects than the market does. The answer seems to be a qualified yes.

[a] Market Responses to Higher Leverage. Many managers feel that their company's stock is undervalued. In effect, such managers are saying that their company's future stream of cash flows justifies a higher price than the stock market is willing to accord it. To capitalize on this situation, management can buy back its own shares. For example, on January 11, 1993, Merck announced a $1 billion stock repurchase program. An analyst cited in *The Wall Street Journal* called the program "a real sign of optimism" on the part of Merck management and said this "implies the financial folks at Merck think their stock is attractively priced."[3] If management is correct, each $1 spent on share repurchases will buy more than $1 in value, leaving stockholders who retain their shares with more wealth per share than they started with. Thus, one way to address the question of whether managers have better information than the market does is to examine the evidence on voluntary stock buybacks.

The evidence seems decisive. Subsequent to the share repurchase, shareholders in the buyback companies earned returns that far exceeded those accruing to investors as a whole. Generally, research (summarized by Smith (1986)) on the market response to transactions representing pure financial structure changes documents the following: (1) The market responds positively to announcements of leverage-increasing transactions and negatively to announcements of leverage-decreasing transactions and (2) the larger the change in leverage is, the greater the price reaction will be. In the case of the Merck buyback, its shares rose about 2 percent over the next two days.

Despite this record, firms that issue debt and thereby bet that their version of the future will manifest itself could turn out to be spectacularly wrong. Management must trade off the benefits to be realized if their optimism proves to be well-founded against the value that will be lost if financial trouble occurs instead.

Further, management must be careful in interpreting the evidence on the favorable market response to leveraging up as supporting managerial optimism. In addition to signaling the market that they think their firm is undervalued, managers who lever up may also be reducing the agency costs of equity. A share repurchase often makes management more austere when it comes to running the company. If so, recapitalizations may boost stock prices, not because the company was previously undervalued, but because management is now operating the company more efficiently. Another way to interpret the evidence on share buybacks, therefore, is that they are used by managements prepared to change their behavior in order to realize their companies' potential.

[b] Setting Debt Policy. In setting their debt policy, many firms solicit the opinions of investment bankers and commercial lenders. They also pay attention to the yields and ratings on their existing debt, because this gives them direct evidence on how the market perceives their current risk profile. Firms also rely on industry standards in deciding how much debt to issue.

Each of these approaches is useful because it gives the firm access to potentially valuable information on what a normal debt ratio would look like, but relying too heavily on the opinions of lenders or industry standards does not take into account the unique attributes of a particular firm. In many cases, there are no firms whose business breakdown and product market strategy are similar enough to be directly comparable. Even where there is a well-defined industry and industry debt standard, the other companies may not have reached their current debt ratios by considered judgment. Indeed, there is strong evidence that individual debt proportions are to a large extent a product of random historical events. Moreover, management often has

---

[3] *Wall Street Journal* (Jan. 12, 1993), p. A5.

a better idea of the potential costs of financial distress than do outsiders. If these costs are high enough, the fact that lenders are willing to provide additional funds does not mean that the firm should borrow more.

This is where the notion of debt capacity comes in. As first defined by Donaldson (1961), debt capacity is the amount of debt in the capital structure that is optimal from the standpoint of shareholder wealth maximization. Thus, it is the amount of debt a firm should use, and not the amount it could use.

In assessing debt capacity, a key issue is the firm's ability to assume additional debt servicing charges. Such an analysis must be concerned with the more general problem of the company's capacity to service fixed charges of any type. These charges include principal and interest on debt, lease payments, and preferred dividends. In addition, some firms may perceive large costs to cutting common stock dividends and will, therefore, treat these as a fixed cost. Strategic factors also enter here. Firms with substantial growth opportunities often prefer to use some of their capacity to bear fixed charges to maintain a continuous research and development program, to fund substantial advertising and other marketing expenditures, and so on, in good times and bad.

Of these fixed charges, principal and interest payments are the most important, because the inability to meet them may lead to financial insolvency and, ultimately, to bankruptcy. Thus, the principal focus of a debt capacity analysis should be on the risk of cash insolvency, the probability of running out of cash, given a particular amount of debt in the capital structure. Balance sheet ratios of debt to equity are of minimal value in performing such an analysis. After all, the same amount of debt on the balance sheet could result in very different fixed charges, depending on the maturity of the debt and its repayment schedule. For example, the annual cash outflow associated with $10 million in debt on the balance sheet could vary from $1 million (interest only at 10 percent) to $1.333 million (interest plus principal repayable over 30 years) to $2 million (interest plus principal repayable over 10 years). Moreover, if the principal on the interest-only loan is due in one year, the cash outflow of $1 million this year will rise to $11 million next year. Despite the value of analyzing debt capacity in terms of cash flow, the difficulty of performing a thorough cash flow analysis leads many firms to limit themselves to using rules of thumb based on various coverage ratios. (See Chapters 1 and 2 for further analysis of related issues.)

[c] Coverage Ratios. Debt coverage ratios essentially measure the relationship between a firm's income and its fixed debt charges. The simplest and most popular of these ratios is times interest earned, defined as

$$\text{Times interest earned} = \frac{\text{EBIT}}{\text{interest payments}}$$

Suppose that a company had operating earnings for the previous year of $5 million and that interest payments on its various debts were $2 million. Times interest earned would be 2.5. Therefore, EBIT could drop by 60 percent, and the firm would still be able to meet its interest payments, but this tells nothing about the company's ability to make the principal repayments on its debt.

Failure to pay back principal could result in bankruptcy just as surely as could failure to make interest payments. Therefore a second coverage ratio, for the entire debt service burden, is generally computed as well. Known as the debt service coverage ratio, it is the ratio of operating income to the total amount of annual interest plus principal repayment. Specifically,

$$\text{Debt service coverage} = \frac{\text{EBIT}}{\text{interest} + \dfrac{\text{principal payments}}{(1 - t_c)}}$$

where t_c is the firm's marginal tax rate. The principal repayment is grossed up for tax effects. This is because EBIT is before-tax earnings, whereas principal payments are paid out of after-tax income; they are not tax deductible. Thus, $1 in EBIT will support only $1 - t_c$ dollars in principal payments. This means that it takes $1/(1 - t_c)$ dollars in EBIT to pay $1 in principal. If principal payments in the previous example were $1 million per annum and the firm's marginal tax rate were 40 percent, the debt service coverage ratio would be

$$\text{Debt service coverage} = \frac{\$5,000,000}{\$2,000,000 + \dfrac{\$1,000,000}{(1 - 0.4)}} = 1.36$$

This coverage ratio means that if EBIT drops by more than 9.9 percent, it will be insufficient to service the debt.

One problem with all such measures based on EBIT is that the net earnings figure found in the income statement is not the same thing as net cash inflow. Even if noncash charges such as depreciation are added back in, there is still a discrepancy between earnings and cash flow. It is necessary to take account of changes in working capital that affect cash flows but not earnings, as well as any capital or other expenditures that, like maintenance and advertising, should be made or, like insurance, must be made.

[d] Worst-Case Scenario. Coverage ratios do not tell a financial manager what is most important: the probability of cash insolvency associated with alternative capital structures. This requires a series of cash budgets prepared assuming (1) different economic conditions and (2) different capital structures. To do this properly, the financial manager must specify a range of likely future economic scenarios and how the firm's cash flows would be affected by these developments, with a probability attached to each scenario. Moreover, it is necessary to determine other possible sources of cash besides the cash flow from operations, including liquid assets that could be drawn down, accounts payable that could be stretched, expenditures that could be deferred, and assets that could be sold (and possibly leased back). The end result is a series of net cash flows that are or can be generated under each of the different economic scenarios. Based on the associated probabilities, the financial manager can then examine these cash flows and see whether a particular capital structure exposes the firm to too much financial risk.

A useful place to begin in assessing debt capacity is to analyze what happens to a firm's cash flows under a "worst-case scenario." This is usually taken to mean a general or industry recession when sales are severely depressed, but it could be any combination of adverse circumstances. In a widely cited and highly regarded work, Donaldson (1961) provided a framework for performing such an analysis. He recommended that the firm calculate net cash flows under depressed conditions, which he took to be a recession, and, from this, compute the cash balance the firm could reasonably expect to have at the end of the recession. Specifically, this means estimating

$$CB_r = CB_0 + NCF_r$$

where:

CB_r = cash balance at the end of a recession
CB_0 = cash balance at the start of a recession
NCF_r = net cash flow during the recession

Donaldson advocated doing this for a range of possible net recessionary cash flows and then using this information to construct a probability distribution of the ending cash balance, CB_r. This is analogous to using sensitivity analysis when evaluating a proposed project.

The next step in assessing its debt capacity is for the firm to compare these cash flows to the fixed debt charges associated with adding more debt to its capital structure. For each increment of debt, the firm can then determine the probability of cash insolvency, based on the probability distribution of CB_r.

Suppose that a firm normally maintains $1 million in cash and marketable securities. This is the cash balance that would be on hand at the start of a recession or other adverse circumstance. Assume that such an economic decline, when it comes, will last for two years. If the firm borrows an additional $5 million, with annual debt servicing charges of $1.5 million, then its cash balance at the end of the economic decline net of debt servicing charges, CB'_r, will be

$$
\begin{aligned}
CB'_r &= CB_r - \text{debt servicing charges} \\
&= \$1,000,000 + NCF_r - 2 \times \$1,500,000 \\
&= -\$2,000,000 + NCF_r
\end{aligned}
$$

Hence, the probability of cash insolvency under this financing plan equals the probability that net cash flow under adverse conditions will fall below $2 million. Management must then decide how high a probability of cash insolvency it is prepared to tolerate. This judgment should not be based on its own risk preferences alone but, rather, on what would add the most value to shareholders. In practice, management's preferences do matter, if only because shareholders have limited ability to control management decisions.

[e] Debt Capacity and Cash Inadequacy. Thus far, the analysis of debt capacity has been in terms of the probability of cash insolvency, but long before reaching this point, the firm could be in serious financial trouble. Furthermore, this financial distress can prove very costly for certain types of firms, especially those with substantial amounts of organizational assets.

Recognizing this possibility, Donaldson (1971) extends his analysis to deal with the case of cash inadequacy, which is defined as the inability to fund all desired, but not absolutely essential, expenditures. This category includes items such as dividends, a research and development program, expenditures to upgrade plant and equipment, and advertising and other marketing costs. By this point, the company is cutting into muscle and bone, and this will affect its ability to sustain whatever competitive advantage it has. The result will be lower expected future operating cash flows, which will be reflected in a lower stock price today.

Figure 6-8 shows the various ways in which firms can mobilize financial resources in the event of a liquidity problem, along with the length of time mobilization would take and the amount of money available from each source for a hypothetical firm.

FIGURE 6-8

Inventory of Financial Resources

Source: Gordon Donaldson, Strategy for Financial Mobility *(Homewood, Ill.: Irwin, 1971), p. 72*

	Available for Use Within		
Resources	1 Quarter	1 Year	3 Years
Uncommitted reserves			
Instant reserves			
Surplus cash	$1,500		
Unused line of credit	2,000		
Negotiable reserves			
Additional bank loans	1,200		
Issue of long-term debt		$ 4,000	
Issue of new equity			
Preferred stock		1,000	
Common stock		3,000	
Reduction of Planned Outflows			
Volume related			
Change in production schedule	600		
Scale related			
Marketing program		500	
R&D budget		200	
Administrative overhead		600	
Capital expenditures		2,000	
Value related			
Dividend payments		200	
Liquidation of Assets			
Sale of assets			
Land and real estate		3,000	
Equipment		700	
Accounts receivable		600	
Inventory		400	
Sale of business units			$ 7,000
Total financial resources available	$5,300 →	5,300	
		$21,500 →	$21,500
			$28,500

Note: Dollars in thousands.

These financial resources can be categorized into uncommitted reserves, reductions of planned expenditures, and liquidation of assets.

The first category includes excess cash and marketable securities, unused lines of credit, and other sources of liquidity. In the example shown in Figure 6-8, the firm can readily access $4.7 million. Within a year, the firm can raise another $8 million through security sales. If these sources prove insufficient, the firm can then begin cutting certain nonessential expenditures. Of these cuts, $600,000 can be made within three months, with another $3.5 million that can be made within a year. Provided the firm is already operating efficiently, these cuts will trade off future cash flows for current cash. Otherwise, these expenditures should be cut regardless of the firm's financial situation. Nonetheless, a financial crisis often triggers a closer look at the firm's operations and results in eliminating some fat that may have crept in during better times.

Finally, the firm can sell off some of its assets, $4.7 million within one year and another $7 million within three years. Again, if the firm is already being run in a lean manner, these asset sales will harm future profitability. Often, however, firms accumulate unnecessary, low-yielding assets, and a financial crisis becomes a time of general housecleaning. A dramatic increase in leverage can prompt this housecleaning before the onset of a financial crisis. The total resources available from all sources over a three-year period to this company are $28.5 million.

[5] Other Factors Influencing Financial Structures

Once the firm has completed the cash flow analysis and determined its capacity to bear fixed charges, it can turn its attention to several other factors that could have a significant, though nonquantifiable, effect on its capital structure decision. This emphasizes the point made in the introduction to this chapter that there is no set of quantitative or other techniques that can solve the capital structure problem. Rather, there are a series of factors, many of them qualitative and any one of which may be given predominant weight at any point in time, that act in concert to determine the firm's actual and preferred capital structure.

[a] **Financial Flexibility and Corporate Strategy.** Although a cash flow analysis might indicate that a firm is able to handle additional fixed charges without significantly increasing its probability of bankruptcy, this does not necessarily mean that more debt is optimal. Such a conclusion would be warranted only if the future were fairly certain and the scenarios considered in the analysis represented the true range of adverse possibilities. Because this is not the case, it is wiser to maintain some degree of financial flexibility to allow for error. Adverse economic events could severely damage a highly leveraged firm's competitive position and its stock of organizational assets.

Moreover, the more highly leveraged the firm is, the more subject it will be to restrictive debt covenants that further constrain management's choice of operating, financial, and investment policies and reduce its capacity to respond to changes in the business environment. The reduction in operating and financial flexibility will prove especially costly to firms competing in continually changing product and factor markets. These include firms whose markets are undergoing deregulation, high technology firms, and firms facing competitors scattered around the world. By contrast, firms operating in stable markets can afford more debt because their competitive stance will be less compromised by the restrictions and delays associated with high financial leverage.

In recognition of these costs, many companies, especially those with large amounts of organizational capital or those operating in unstable markets, maintain substantial financial resources in the form of unused debt capacity, large quantities of liquid assets, excess lines of credit, and access to a broad range of fund sources. This financial flexibility helps preserve operating flexibility. A firm that has left itself with financial reserves for contingencies can respond to an adverse turn of events based on long-term considerations. Alternatively, a firm with a high debt-to-equity ratio, minimal liquid assets, and few other financial resources might have to alter its commercial strategy to meet adverse circumstances, with a detrimental effect on its future competitive position.

The ability to marshal substantial financial resources also signals competitors that the firm will not be an easy target. Consider the alternative, a firm that is highly leveraged, with no excess lines of credit, or cash reserves. A competitor can move into the firm's market and gain market share with less fear of retaliation. In order to retaliate—by cutting price, say, or by increasing advertising expenditures—the firm will need more money. Because it has no spare cash and cannot issue additional debt at a reasonable price, it will have to go to the equity market. Firms issuing new equity are suspect, however, because of the asymmetric information relationship between investors and management (is the firm selling equity now because it knows the stock is overpriced?). The credibility problem is particularly acute when the firm is trying to fend off a competitive attack. Thus, a firm that lacks financial reserves faces a Hobson's choice: Acquiesce in the competitive attack or raise funds on unattractive terms.

Similarly, when opportunity knocks, a firm with substantial financial resources will be better positioned to take advantage of it than will a firm with few financial resources that faces tightly drawn debt covenants. Thus, firms with valuable growth options should also place a high priority on financial flexibility. To summarize, the opportunity cost of being highly leveraged can be considerable.

The desire for financing flexibility requires firms to perform a balancing act, which can be viewed in the context of the financing pecking order framework suggested by Myers (1984). Consider the three major financing sources in Myers's pecking order: internal funds, issuing debt, and issuing equity. Assuming that information and transaction costs make it more expensive to use financing sources at the top of the pecking order (equity), a firm that needs to raise funds faces an intertemporal trade-off. If sources low on the pecking order (internal funds and debt) are used in this period, current financing costs will appear to be low, but the firm will face the hidden opportunity cost of being pushed up the pecking order by being forced to issue more expensive equity in the future. On the other hand, if new equity is issued in this period and the funds are held as cash, current costs will be high, but by moving down the pecking order to internal funds and debt the firm will have a cheaper source of funds in the future. For this reason, firms that have substantial organizational assets and growth options should be predominantly equity financed and hold relatively large cash balances.

The trade-off from the standpoint of investors is that companies with substantial financial resources are more insulated from the discipline exerted by the financial marketplace. In well-run firms, such as those with valuable organizational assets or growth options, this is not a problem. But for many companies, particularly those with substantial amounts of free cash flow, the advantages of financial flexibility may be more than offset by the greater opportunity to indulge their spendthrift habits.

[b] Value of Financial Reserves. Although financial reserves can prove beneficial, there are limits to these benefits. First, financial reserves cannot save a failing business; they can only tide a company over temporary adversity. Second, even in the case of temporary adversity, financial reserves are beneficial only to the extent that the firm cannot or will not issue new equity to restore its solvency. Corporate debt is reversible; a company in financial distress can rearrange its capital structure by issuing new stock to retire debt. Thus, as long as the business is basically healthy and the firm has access to the equity market on fair terms, a big debt load need not be a crippling burden.

The real danger for companies with a heavy debt load is that the market may undervalue their stock when they are forced to issue new equity. If a company could always issue new equity at a fair price, it would need to hold minimal financial reserves. A fair price, it must be stressed, refers to a price that fully reflects the company's long-run prospects without placing undue emphasis on its short-term financial difficulties; it does not mean a high price.

If markets were always efficient, undervaluation would not be a problem, but the problem of information asymmetry may lead the equity market to unduly discount a company's stock. This problem stems from the well-documented fact that managers, as insiders, have better information about the firm's prospects than do outside investors. Rational behavior on the part of management would be to exploit this information asymmetry by issuing securities when management judges that the market price of the firm's securities exceeds their true value. Because sophisticated investors understand management's ability and incentives to exploit them by issuing overvalued securities, the mere act of announcing a new issue will lead them to revise downward their estimates of the firm's value.

This is the same adverse selection (lemons problem) that confronts the buyer of a used car: If the car is such a good deal, why is the owner selling it? The potential buyer's fear is that the current owner wants to get rid of the car because he knows that it is a lemon. Fearing that she will get stuck with a lemon, the potential buyer will offer less than she would otherwise for the used car.

With regard to security sales, the problem of potential insider information is most acute in the case of common stock offerings, because equity is the residual claimant (but less acute for utility offerings than industrials because the regulatory process reduces the potential for information disparity between management and outsiders). By contrast, because debt and preferred stock have more senior claims to a firm's cash flow, their values should be least sensitive to adverse information about the firm's future prospects. The values of equity-linked securities, such as convertible debt and convertible preferred, should be more sensitive to changes in anticipated firm value than straight debt or preferred, but less sensitive than common stock.

Having financial slack allows the firm to finance its investments without being forced to sell financial claims at a discount to a less informed market. Thus, those companies most prone to a credibility gap in their dealings with the financial markets are the ones that should maintain the largest financial reserves.

Bhide (1988) points to some company characteristics that should affect the size of financial reserves:

1. Credibility is less likely to be a problem for large, closely followed New York Stock Exchange companies than for smaller, younger companies that are unlisted. Hence, well-established firms can take fuller advantage of their available debt capacity.

2. Privately held companies that cannot raise equity financing quickly should use less debt in their capital structure, other things being equal. For these companies, the time-consuming nature of the equity-raising process (consider the protracted negotiations between existing and prospective shareholders as well as the creditors that are likely to follow) can prove an expensive proposition, especially if noninvestor stakeholders are focusing on corporate staying power.

3. Small companies whose stock is thinly traded are more susceptible to a credibility problem and hence should maintain more financial reserves.

4. Companies that the market has difficulty valuing are most prone to the credibility problem. These companies should, therefore, maintain more financial reserves. Here are some clues that the market may be having trouble valuing a company: There are large swings in the stock price in the absence of major changes in the business environment; the stock price fell much more than management believes was justified the last time the company faced business difficulties; and stock analysts have difficulty grasping the company's investment needs. The latter situation may arise if the company cannot give outsiders the necessary information to analyze its investments properly, because to do so would jeopardize the company's competitive position.

5. The market is also likely to have difficulty valuing firms, such as Genentech and Microsoft, with substantial amounts of growth options. Unlike companies whose value depends primarily on familiar, straightforward projects, the value of a growth company depends on expectations about future profits from novel market niches (e.g., Federal Express at its inception) or yet-to-be-developed products whose potential applications have not been fully defined (e.g., Genentech and Microsoft). The lack of an objective basis for assessing the profitability of these companies 10 years from now may make their stock prices more prone to extreme swings. The danger for a heavily leveraged growth company is that it might be forced to come to the equity market at a time when its stock is overly discounted. Again, competitive pressures may preclude the company's sharing inside information with investors.

[c] Financing Pecking Order. Thus far, capital structure has been viewed as if it were the end product of a series of conscious trade-offs among tax factors, the desire for financial flexibility, agency costs, and the costs of financial distress. By contrast, the financing pecking order story, which describes management's preference for internal versus external finance and debt versus external equity, suggests that observed corporate debt ratios at any one time may instead reflect its cumulative requirements for external finance. Highly profitable firms will tend to use lots of internal equity in the form of retained earnings and have low debt ratios, whereas less profitable firms will tend to have high debt ratios.

The credibility problem helps explain the strong corporate preference for internal, as opposed to external, finance. It also explains why firms that must raise external finance prefer to issue securities in ascending order of riskiness: first debt, then hybrids such as convertible bonds, with equity only as a last resort. Specifically, this pattern of financing preferences reduces the security price discount imposed by investors when companies raise new capital. By using internal funds, the firm can bypass the capital markets altogether. If the company must issue new securities, the credibility problem is less severe for safer securities—those with more senior claims—and, hence, the discount applied to them by investors fearful of buying lemons is smaller.

This set of financing practices has two results: (1) It minimizes the amount of new equity that must be raised and (2) it forces companies to issue equity only when necessary. By limiting management's discretion over when to issue new equity, adherence to the financing pecking order reduces investors' suspicion that management is simply trying to time the market and unload overpriced stock.

Shareholders benefit from management's preference for internal finance because it reduces transaction costs and the problems associated with information asymmetry, as long as management performs as expected. At the same time, however, management's preferences are limited by the capital markets and their business strategies. For example, the oil companies, which began with virtually no debt, are now awash in debt. Similarly, fast-growing companies that must raise external funds, while simultaneously trying to assure customers and other stakeholders of their staying power, tend to raise equity capital. It is only highly profitable companies, with few requirements for external finance, that seem to be able to stray far from what appears to be an optimal capital structure. Yet, even these companies will be subject sooner or later to the discipline of the financial marketplace if they stray too far from a policy of shareholder wealth maximization.

6.06 MARKET IMPERFECTIONS AND VALUE CREATION

Both equity and debt come in as many varieties and flavors as does ice cream. Each variety, flavor, and combination presents a different financing option with different implications for the firm's future operating and financing flexibility and economic health. This makes the long-term financing decision even more complicated than already appears to be the case.

Even if corporate cash flow is unaffected by financial policy, it may be possible to sell claims to a given cash flow pie at a higher aggregate price by cleverly packaging these claims. Viewed in this way, corporate financing is largely a marketing problem. The firm needs money to finance future investment projects. In lieu of selling some of its existing assets to raise the required funds, it will sell the rights to the future cash flows generated by its current and prospective projects. It can sell these rights directly and become an all-equity-financed firm, but the firm may get a better price for the rights to its future cash flows by dividing up and repackaging those rights before selling them to the investing public. Because the price of a security varies inversely with the security's required return, this objective translates into raising funds at a below-market rate. Put another way, the firm is trying to create positive net present value financing arrangements.

Raising funds at a below-market rate is easier said than done, however. Although numerous firms have demonstrated the ability to consistently create positive NPV investment projects, the necessary conditions for developing positive NPV securities are usually not present. When it comes to capital investments, the firm often has some type of competitive edge, either a patent, a well-known brand name, special marketing skills, or unique production know-how.

By contrast, a company selling securities is competing for funds on a global basis, not only with other firms in its industry, but also with all firms, foreign and domestic, and with numerous government units and private individuals as well. The fierce competition for funds makes it much less likely that the firm can endow its securities with special advantages.

Nonetheless, there are two situations in which repackaging of financial claims may add to firm value. First, because different securities are taxed in different ways, repackaging can reduce the government's share of the cash flow pie and thereby increase the cash flow available for sale to investors. Second, total revenue from the sale of the cash flow pie may be increased if securities can be devised for which specific investors are willing to pay a higher price. There are four circumstances in which investors may pay more in the aggregate for claims to the cash flow pie:

1. The securities are better designed to meet the special needs and desires of a particular class of investors.

2. The securities are designed to be more liquid.

3. The securities reduce transaction costs.

4. The security structure reduces the credibility gap between management and potential investors that exists whenever companies raise capital from outside sources.

[1] Tax Factors in Financing

The uneven tax treatment of various components of financial cost, such as the tax deductibility of interest payments but not dividend payments, introduces the possibility of reducing after-tax financing costs by reducing the government's share of the cash flow pie. For example, many firms consider debt financing to be less expensive than equity financing because interest expense is tax deductible whereas dividends are paid out of after-tax income, but this comparison is misleading for two reasons. First, it ignores personal taxes. Second, it ignores the supply response of corporations to potential tax arbitrage. In the absence of any restrictions, the supply of corporate debt can be expected to rise as long as corporate debt is less expensive than equity. As the supply of debt rises, the yield on this debt must increase in order to attract investors in progressively higher tax brackets. This process continues until the tax rate for the marginal debt holder equals the marginal corporate tax rate. At that point, there is no longer a tax incentive for issuing more debt. The high supply elasticity ensures that this point will occur very quickly.

This process illustrates a key insight: The supply of securities in the capital markets is almost infinitely elastic. As soon as there is a small advantage to issuing one type of security rather than another, alert financial managers and investment bankers quickly alter their behavior to profit from this discrepancy. They will continue to issue the cheaper security until the discrepancy disappears. For this reason, opportunities to create value through the issuance of new securities are small and unlikely to persist.

Only in rare instances will a tax advantage persist at the margin. The example of zero-coupon bonds illustrates one such case. In 1982, PepsiCo issued the first long-term, zero-coupon bond. Although they have since become a staple of corporate finance, zero-coupon bonds initially were a startling innovation. Zeros do not pay interest but are sold at a deep discount from par. For example, PepsiCo's $1,000 par value, 30-year zeros sold for around $60 each. Investors' gains come from the difference between the discounted price and the face value they receive at maturity.

These securities appeal to those investors who like to be certain of their long-term return. The locked-in return means that investors know the maturity value of their investment, an important consideration for pension funds and other buyers who have fixed future commitments to meet. Normal bonds do not provide that certainty, because the rate at which their coupons can be reinvested is unknown at the time of issue, but despite the potential market for such bonds, they were nonexistent until PepsiCo's 1982 issue.

The pent-up demand for its $850 million face value offering gave PepsiCo an extraordinarily low cost of funds. The net borrowing cost to the company was under 10 percent, almost four percentage points lower than the yield at that time on U.S. Treasury securities of the same maturity, but zero-coupon bonds did not remain such a low-cost source of funds for long. Once firms saw these low yields, the supply of zero-coupon debt expanded rapidly. In addition, clever Wall Street firms discovered how to manufacture zeros from existing bonds. They bought Treasury bonds, stripped the coupons from the bonds, repackaged the coupons, and sold the coupons and the principal separately as a series of zero-coupon bonds.

The increase in the supply relative to the demand for zeros resulted in a jump in their required yields, negating their previous cost advantage, but the tax advantage that is associated with any original issue discount debt (OID) remained. The tax advantage to a firm from issuing deep discount debt rather than current coupon debt stems from the tax provision that allows companies to amortize as interest the OID expense over the life of the bond. The firm benefits by receiving a current tax write-off for a future expense. By contrast, if it issues current coupon debt, the firm's tax write-off and expense will occur simultaneously. The tax advantage from OIDs, which is maximized by issuing zero-coupon bonds, translates into a reduction in the company's cost of debt capital.

These tax savings don't tell the whole story, however. Investors must pay tax on the amortized portion of the discount each year even though they receive no cash until the bond matures. Thus the tax advantage to the firm from issuing OIDs is offset by the higher pretax yields required by investors to provide them with the same after-tax yields they could earn on comparable-risk current coupon debt. As a result, corporations issuing OIDs will realize a tax benefit only to the extent that the marginal corporate tax rate exceeds the marginal investor tax rate. At the extreme, if these marginal tax rates are equal, the tax advantage to an issuing corporation will be completely eliminated by the tax disadvantage to the investor.

The initial purchasers of zero-coupon bonds and other OIDs were primarily of two groups: (1) tax-exempt institutional investors such as pension plans and individual investors (for their tax-exempt individual retirement accounts) who sought to lock in higher yields and (2) Japanese investors, for whom the discount would be treated as a nontaxable capital gain if the bonds were sold prior to maturity. Selling to the tax-exempt segment of the market yielded maximum benefits to the issuers of OIDs, because the disparity in marginal tax rates was at its greatest.

The supply of tax-exempt institutional money, however, is limited. Furthermore, the Japanese government has ended the tax exemption for zero-coupon bond gains; Japanese investors have accordingly demanded higher yields in order to compensate for their possible tax liability.

The reaction by the Japanese government to the proliferation of zero-coupon debt illustrates another key point: If one devises a legal way to engage in unlimited tax arbitrage through the financial markets, the government will change the law. More limited tax arbitrage, however, may persist for some time if

1. The firm can issue a security that reduces its taxes without increasing the investors' tax liability commensurately.

2. The firm can issue a security that reduces investor taxes without increasing corporate taxes commensurately.

These conditions can be met by issuing tax-exempt debt or selling securities to investors in marginal tax brackets below 34 percent. Examples of securities in the respective categories are industrial development bonds, which are tax-exempt securities issued on behalf of private companies by states and municipalities. (See Chapter A6.) Moreover, companies with tax losses or excess tax credits can sell preferred stock to other corporations and thereby reduce investor taxes without a corresponding increase in their taxes. The reason is that corporate investors can exclude from taxable income 70 percent of the preferred (or common) dividends they receive. This means that a corporate investor in the 34 percent tax bracket faces an effective tax rate of only 10.2 percent (0.3 × 34%) on preferred dividends. In turn, corporate investors are willing to accept a lower yield on preferred stock than on comparable debt securities. Hence, companies in low tax brackets (who are unable to fully utilize the interest tax write-off) should be able to raise funds at a lower after-tax cost with preferred stock instead of debt. Similarly, leasing enables low-tax-bracket companies to raise funds at a lower cost by passing along the depreciation tax deduction to investors in higher tax brackets in return for a lower effective interest rate.

[2] Financial Innovation

The dizzying pace of securities innovation in recent years has created an overwhelming abundance of financing alternatives. To a person schooled in marketing, the reasons for such variety are obvious. The vast array of securities in the marketplace exists for the same reasons that M&Ms come in more than one color and that Fords, Chevrolets, and Volkswagens coexist with one another and with Mercedes-Benzes and Rolls Royces. People have different tastes, preferences, and wealth levels, and whether the market is for cars or financial securities, the better designed the product is and the more closely it is tailored to the particular needs and desires of its potential customers, the higher the price it can command. Moreover, as the environment changes, whether in the form of higher oil prices, new tax laws, or more uncertain inflation, opportunities arise for astute managers to design new cars or securities that fit the new needs of the marketplace.

Furthermore, as Baskin-Robbins has successfully demonstrated, even though vanilla may be the most popular ice cream flavor, there is also a market out there for peanut butter ice cream. This suggests a potential source of value creation: To the extent that the firm can design a security that appeals to a special niche in the capital market, it can attract funds at a cost that is less than the market's required return on securities of comparable risk.

However, as in the case of zeros, such a rewarding situation is likely to be temporary, because the demand for a security that fits a particular niche in the market is not unlimited. On the other hand, the supply of securities designed to tap that niche is likely to increase dramatically once the niche is recognized.

As one example of this process, major investment banks are currently trying to create value by exploiting what they perceive as profitable niches in the mortgage market. Firms like First Boston, Salomon Brothers, and Goldman Sachs have been purchasing mortgages and repackaging their cash flows into complex securities that offer unique risk-return combinations. To the extent that such unique securities are desirable to investors, the investment banks can sell them for more than the cost of the mortgage. Once a particular security structure proves to be profitable, however, other firms aggressively enter the business and drive profits down.

In general, the high elasticity of supply means that repackaging a security's payment stream so that it reallocates risk from one class of investors to another is unlikely to be a sustainable form of value creation. The only niche that is likely to persist as a profitable opportunity in the face of competitive pressure is a niche that involves the government. If the government is willing to substitute its credit for the credit of the issuer, then investors will pay a higher price for the securities.

However, even these governmental niches are not free from competition. For instance, when the government makes subsidized loans available to small business, it produces an incentive for firms to restructure to satisfy the criteria for being "small." Furthermore, the government severely restricts the supply of securities that can take advantage of these loan subsidy programs.

[3] Increasing Liquidity

Liquidity or marketability is an important attribute of a financial security. One measure of a security's marketability is the spread between the bid and ask prices at which dealers are willing to satisfy buyers' or sellers' demands for immediate execution of their trades. Amihud and Mendelson (1986) provide substantial empirical evidence that investors are willing to accept lower returns on more liquid assets. Conversely, investors discount the prices of assets with lower liquidity in order to compensate themselves for the added trading costs they must bear. Other things being equal, therefore, a firm can increase its market value by increasing the liquidity of the claims it issues.

There are several ways in which firms can increase the liquidity of their claims. Some commonly observed means include going public, listing on organized exchanges, and standardization of securities.

Because most liquidity-enhancing measures entail significant costs (e.g., legal and underwriting fees and reporting costs), the firm must trade off the benefits of increased liquidity with the costs. The trade-off can best be understood by means of a simple model. Consider a firm with a perpetual cash flow equal to E. By enhancing the liquidity of its claims, the firm's cost of capital will decline from r to r_1, and its value will rise from E/r to E/r_1. At the same time, the investment in liquidity entails an initial cost of C_0 and an annual cash outflow of c, for a total cost of $C_0 + c/r_1$. The NPV of liquidity-enhancement V_{LE} then equals

$$V_{LE} = \frac{E}{r_1} - \frac{E}{r} - \left(C_0 + \frac{C}{r_1}\right) \tag{6.10}$$

Setting $\Delta r = r - r_1$, we can approximate Equation 6.10 by

$$V_{LE} = \left(\frac{E}{r}\right) \times \frac{\Delta r}{r} - \left(C_0 + \frac{C}{r_1}\right) \tag{6.11}$$

According to Equation 6.11, the advantages of liquidity enhancement tend to be greatest for large firms and for firms whose securities are already highly liquid. The latter implication follows from the observation that low-liquidity assets tend to be held by investors willing to hold assets for longer periods. Thus, liquidity is less valuable to them than to investors in more liquid assets.

At the same time, the cost of achieving a given improvement in liquidity may be lower when liquidity is low. So it may also pay small firms to invest in increasing liquidity.

[4] Reducing Transaction Costs

By reducing transaction costs associated with raising money, the firm can increase its net proceeds. Similarly, any cost savings associated with administering a loan will flow through to the borrower. The use of investment bankers to underwrite new security issues and shelf registration under the Securities and Exchange Commission's (SEC) Rule 415 are ways in which the costs of raising money can be reduced. Similarly, the use of secured debt and leasing can reduce administrative costs by giving a lender or lessor clear title to the pledged or leased assets. Because the costs associated with repossessing assets are more likely to be incurred the higher the probability of bankruptcy, companies in shakier financial positions will find this particular benefit of leasing or secured financing more valuable than those companies in better financial shape.

[5] Bridging the Credibility Gap

One of the key costs associated with issuing new securities is due to information asymmetry. By reducing the information asymmetry problem, companies can get better prices for their securities. A common approach to dealing with the problem of information asymmetry is to employ underwriters, who certify to outside investors that the securities are fairly valued. They do this by putting their reputation on the line with investors when pricing new issues. To protect their reputation, and the fees that accrue to it, investment bankers investigate and audit the activities of issuing firms, thereby certifying for investors that the issue is fairly priced. This certification process reduces the discount applied by investors fearful of buying lemons. The discount can also be avoided by using internal funds and bypassing the capital markets altogether.

6.07 FINANCING GROWTH COMPANIES

This section illustrates the application of the various concepts discussed so far by focusing on the unique aspects of financing growth companies. It begins by discussing the distinctive features of a growth company and then suggests how these features affect the choice of financial policy.

[1] Characteristics of Growing Companies

The most obvious characteristic of a rapidly growing company is that it has a large appetite for cash. Even though income rises along with sales, cash flow is generally negative because the investment required to finance the growth in sales typically exceeds the ROA. A company or its division usually becomes a "cash cow," generating free cash flow, only when its business matures and sales growth slows. Therefore, the ability to locate potential sources of external funds and to arrange them in an attractive financial package are major factors affecting corporate growth. The absence of free cash flow also reduces the likelihood that this will be a source of manager-shareholder conflict.

The second characteristic of growing companies is less obvious but critical nonetheless in devising a financial plan. For a company to grow in value, not just in size, it must have access to investment opportunities with positive NPVs. These opportunities may be thought of as growth options, and include the possibility of increasing the profitability of existing product lines and expanding into profitable new products or markets. Growth options are typically the primary source of value in rapidly expanding firms. Such firms often have few tangible assets in place; their assets consist primarily of specialized knowledge and management skill. For example, Genentech, a gene-splicing company, had a stock market value of over $3 billion in late 1986 even though earnings for the year were only $11 million, giving it a price/earnings ratio of over 270:1. Clearly, the market was valuing Genentech's future ability to capitalize on its research in areas such as anticancer therapy and blood clot dissolvers for heart attack victims. Moreover, these growth options are likely to be difficult to value.

Information asymmetry is likely to be pronounced in the case of a growth company because management will often have unique information about the future profitability of undeveloped products and untapped market niches. This increases the opportunity to profit from selling stock when management believes that the company's growth options are overvalued by the market and, thus, increases the amount by which investors will discount the price of new corporate securities to compensate for their informational disadvantage. The natural response—to provide investors with additional information—is often not credible (rather it is seen as self-serving) or practical, because providing outsiders with the necessary information to properly analyze its investments would jeopardize the company's competitive position.

Investors must also cope with the existence of imperfect information about management abilities and effort. The problems of managerial shirking and misrepresentation of abilities, which exist in all firms, are especially critical in growth companies because the value of growth options is especially dependent on the performance of management. The higher the percentage of value accounted for by growth options, the more severe these problems will be.

Bondholders' fears of being exploited are also magnified in the case of growth companies. Because growth options involve contingent projects, a large fraction of the investment choices made by growth companies cannot be specified in advance. Moreover, other things being equal, the riskier an investment, the more valuable is an option on it. Taken together, these factors increase the risk to bondholders of opportunistic behavior on the part of shareholders of companies with substantial amounts of growth options.

Stockholders and bondholders are not the only parties for which asymmetrical information can be an important problem. Noninvestor stakeholders such as customers and suppliers must make firm-specific investments whose returns are dependent on management's ability to effectively exploit growth options. If the firm fails in its effort to expand and develop new products, those parties that chose to do business with the firm will suffer. To reassure these stakeholders, management must do more than simply promise to honor their implicit claims; it must develop some mechanism to bond those promises. These bonding mechanisms are particularly important for growth companies because in most instances management has not had the time to develop its reputation or the reputation for the firm's products.

[2] Financial Strategy for Growth Companies

There are two basic approaches that the financial manager can take to maximize the vaule of the firm. The first approach is to increase value by dividing up and repackaging

FIGURE 6-9

Financing Checklist

1. Ways to Divide the Cash Flow Pie to Increase Value
   - Minimize total taxes
   - Design innovative securities
   - Increase liquidity
   - Reduce transaction costs
   - Reduce information asymmetry

2. Ways to Increase the Cash Flow Pie to Increase Value
   - Reduce management's ability to exploit free cash flow
   - Increase managements' incentive to maximize value
   - Reduce the costs of stockholder-bondholder conflicts
   - Reduce the likelihood of financial distress

the rights to the cash flow pie in order to sell these rights at a higher price to the investing public. The second approach is to increase the cash flow pie by using financing to reduce various conflicts of interest. Figure 6-9 summarizes the various ways in which companies can pursue these two approaches.

Taxes, for example, are primarily of concern to companies in the highest effective tax bracket. Ex ante, companies with fairly stable or predictable incomes and relatively few other methods to shield their income from taxes know that they will be in the highest corporate tax bracket each year. Examples include consumer goods firms, utilities, some computer manufacturers, and packaged foods companies. Conversely, growth companies are typically unsure of their tax bracket since it is unclear whether they will have net taxable income in any given year. On average, therefore, the effective tax rate for these companies is significantly below the maximum corporate rate. Moreover, since the variability of profit is likely to be higher for a growth company, there is a lower probability that they will be able to make full use of the interest tax shield, particularly at high levels of debt. This means that the tax advantages of debt are less valuable for growth companies than for mature companies.

There is another reason why the tax advantage of debt is unlikely to be significant for a growth company. Recall that Miller has argued that debt will be issued in aggregate until the tax advantage at the corporate level of issuing more debt is fully offset by the higher returns demanded by investors who must pay tax on their interest receipts. Even if some tax advantage to debt remains, Miller's argument implies that only those firms that face the highest effective tax rates are likely to benefit from issuing more debt. Growth companies are unlikely to fall into this category.

Although growth companies are unlikely to be able to benefit from the tax advantages of debt, taxes may still play a role in their financing strategy. Specifically, low-tax-bracket growth companies may be able to use financing to transfer certain tax benefits to other companies that can more fully utilize them in return for a lower effective cost of funds. For example, low-tax-bracket companies may be able to raise funds at a lower after-tax cost with preferred stock instead of debt. Similarly, leasing enables a growth company that is not sufficiently profitable to make current use of all its depreciation deductions to transfer these deductions to investors in higher tax brackets in return for a lower effective interest rate.

There are two reasons for designing innovative securities. One is to satisfy unmet market demand for a particular security with a unique risk-return trade-off. The second, which relates to increasing the cash flow pie, is to solve specific incentive problems and resolve potential conflicts. Only the second reason is likely to be a source of value creation for growth companies. As noted earlier, unmet demands for new securities are unlikely to persist for long in a competitive financial marketplace. Furthermore, a growth company may have a comparative disadvantage in introducing innovative securities. Because of the relatively high degree of information asymmetry that exists with growth companies, investors are likely to be especially wary of new securities from such companies that promise unique risk-return trade-offs. Fearing that these securities may be designed to exploit their ignorance, investors are likely to discount them more heavily, thereby negating the benefits of innovation.

Increasing liquidity and reducing transaction costs are potentially useful ways to increase the value of a firm. However, the benefits of these actions are apt to be smaller for growth companies. Growth companies are likely to attract investors who are more interested in long-run capital appreciation. Such investors typically follow a buy-and-hold strategy, so that the benefits of increasing liquidity or reducing transaction costs are minimal. When weighed against the costs of increasing liquidity or lowering transaction costs, therefore, such measures appear to be less beneficial for growth companies than for more mature companies.

[a] Credibility Gap and the Problem of Financing Growth Companies. The growth company has no comparative advantage in creating value by dividing up the cash flow pie. Indeed, it is likely to have a comparative disadvantage. By contrast, measures designed to overcome the problem of information asymmetry are likely to be particularly valuable for growth companies; both investor and noninvestor stakeholders will probably be more uncertain about the future prospects of a growth company than about the prospects of a more mature firm. Measures that the firm can take to resolve this uncertainty can simultaneously raise the price that investors are willing to pay for its securities and reduce potential conflicts among the various corporate stakeholders.

The problem of information asymmetry is so pervasive that it affects all aspects of financing growth companies, including some of the issues that are included under the category of increasing the cash flow pie. Perhaps the best way to introduce the problem is to consider a growing firm that needs new funds to exercise a growth option. Assume the firm is making a straightforward choice of debt or equity. To make the example concrete, suppose the option is the development of a new software package for word processing.

If the firm goes to the equity market today to finance development of the product, information asymmetry will be a serious problem. How are investors to know exactly what the product will look like, whether management will be capable of producing the product on schedule, effectively marketing it, and enhancing and supporting it? The firm has an incentive, therefore, to delay exercising its growth option until investors become more adequately informed.

Consideration of competitive conditions, however, provides an incentive for early exercise. Because these options are (1) often shared with other competitors and (2) not generally tradable, a company that waits to exercise a shared growth option, such as the chance to enter a new market or to invest in a new technology, may find that competitors have already usurped the opportunity. For instance, a software firm that delays developing its new word processing program may find that by the time the program ships, customers are committed to a competing product. The problem is analogous to deciding whether to exercise an option on a dividend-paying stock before maturity.

The implication is that companies must structure their financing to remain flexible enough to exercise growth options at the opportune time. In this regard, future flexibility may be as important as current flexibility; many strategically important investments—such as investments in research and development, factory automation, a brand name, or a distribution network—are often but the first link in a chain of subsequent investment decisions. The company must be prepared to exercise each of these related growth options in order to fully exploit the value of the initial investment. Moreover, stakeholders will condition the price they are willing to pay for the company's implicit claims today on the company's financial capacity to exercise these growth options in the future and provide them with the services and products that will enhance their firm-specific investments.

If the firm in the example decides it must have the funds today to retain its flexibility, then it must issue equity at a big discount or go to the debt market. As noted earlier, the discount on debt will be much smaller because the cash flows received by creditors are less sensitive to the performance of the firm. However, there is a cost to issuing debt that is likely to be particularly great for growing firms.

The problem is that creditors of growing firms will require detailed covenants to protect themselves against opportunism and potential management incompetence. These covenants are likely to be especially stringent for highly leveraged growth companies because these companies have the greatest ability to engage in high-risk activities and to undertake high-risk projects. Although restrictive loan covenants avoid many of the potential conflicts associated with debt financing by limiting management actions that are potentially harmful to bondholders, they are costly to shareholders because they constrain management's choice of operating, financial, and investment policies and reduce its capacity to respond to changes in the business environment. For example, lenders may veto certain high-risk projects with positive NPVs because of the added risk they would have to bear without a corresponding increase in their expected returns.

The opportunity cost associated with the loss of operating and investment flexibility will be especially high for firms with substantial growth options because such firms must be able to respond quickly to continually changing product and factor markets. All else being equal, therefore, the high costs associated with resolving the conflicts of interest between shareholders and bondholders reduce the desirable amount of debt in a growth firm's capital structure. In contrast, firms operating in stable markets can afford more debt since their competitive stance will be less compromised by the restrictions and delays associated with high financial leverage.

Faced with this unsatisfactory trade-off between the steep discount on new equity and the restrictive covenants associated with issuing straight public debt, growth companies are well advised to look elsewhere for funds. One place to start is with a commercial bank.

[b] Role of Bank Loans in Financing Growth Companies. A banking relationship may solve many of the problems associated with public debt. The potential advantages of a bank credit are twofold. First, the firm can more readily custom-tailor a set of terms and conditions in face-to-face negotiations with its bankers than by trying to deal with a large number of smaller investors. Second, renegotiating certain covenants in response to changing circumstances is less cumbersome with a bank loan. The flexibility, discretion, and durability of these arrangements is what is termed a banking relationship.

As Goeltz (1984) notes, a banking relationship solves many of the problems associated with public debt:

> There is an important advantage in dealing with individual bankers rather than an amorphous capital market. One can explain a problem or need to account officers at a few institutions. Direct communications with the purchasers of [bonds] are almost impossible. These investors, as is the case for most public issues, have little feeling of commitment to the borrower or sense of continuity. . . . If the borrower can modify the terms and conditions of the former more easily and inexpensively than the latter, then the bank loan will be less costly, even if the effective interest rates are identical.

The advantages of a banking relationship to a growing company stem from the personal nature of the relationship between borrower and lender. Presumably, bankers, who deal directly with the borrower, have lower costs of monitoring client activities than do bondholders, who are anonymous (in the case of bearer bonds) or are not interested in a long-term relationship with the borrower, as is a bank. Recent research on banks tends to bear out this assumption.

A basic theme of recent research on the role of banks in credit markets is that banks play the part of delegated monitors that check on the behavior of the firm's managers. Their ability to perform this role depends on the information-gathering and monitoring process associated with commercial bank lending. Specifically, it is claimed that banks have a comparative cost advantage in information gathering and monitoring relative to other financial institutions. This comparative advantage arises in part from banks' ongoing deposit history with the borrower and from the short-term repeat lending activity in which banks specialize.

When a firm is unable to make interest payments on time or when its financial statements indicate problems, the banker's first response is to examine the firm's condition more closely. Such examination is particularly valuable for growth companies because much of their value arises from options that will be lost if the firm cannot get financing on sufficiently flexible terms. If the banker finds that the firm's future prospects are promising, he can reschedule the firm's payments, waive a covenant, or even increase the amount of the bank's loan.

The relationship with a bank can also reduce the asymmetrical information problem with other investors. The view that bankers, as insiders, have better information about the firm's prospects than outsiders and are better able to supervise its behavior implies that the loan approval process should convey two pieces of positive information about the borrowing firm to outside investors: (1) The bank believes the firm is sound and (2) the bank will supervise corporate management to ensure that it behaves properly. The empirical evidence supports this conjecture. When a firm announces a new offering of debt or equity, the firm's stock price falls. Yet James (1987) has found that when a firm announces it has signed a loan commitment with a bank, the firm's stock price rises.

Unfortunately, these results offer no completely satisfactory explanation of the particular unique service or attribute of bank loans vis-à-vis private placements. Although James suggests that the special role of bank loans may derive from the information generated by the deposit relation that a bank has with a borrower, the issue of why bank loans are unique remains unresolved.

Another important aspect of a banking relationship is provision of continuous access to funds. In the typical commercial banking relationship, the bank can be viewed as writing options for its loan customer. Through such devices as credit lines or lending commitments, the borrower can choose the timing and the amount of the loan; the borrower can often prepay or refinance the loan at a nominal fee. Most important, the bank makes an implicit and sometimes explicit commitment to provide funds in times when the borrower finds them difficult to obtain from other sources. This flexibility is critical for growth companies because the timing of their investment program is so difficult to forecast.

Despite the advantages of bank debt, banks cannot supply all the financing required by growth companies. The difficulties are threefold. First, bank debt is still debt, which retains many restrictive features. Second, like any form of debt, bank loans increase the probability of financial distress, with all its adverse consequences for firms trying to sell implicit claims. Third, from the standpoint of the creditor, financing high-risk investments such as growth options is not attractive. The creditor bears all the downside risk, without sharing in the upside benefits. Growth options also make poor collateral; their value in liquidation is usually nil. In the case of start-ups, whose assets are composed primarily if not entirely of growth options, bank loans are virtually unobtainable.

[c] Role of Venture Capital in Financing Growth Companies. Venture capital has evolved as a solution to these problems. In effect, venture capitalists provide private equity, but, in return, they demand a much closer relationship, more control, and a high expected rate of return. Venture capitalists also demand a financial structure that shifts a great deal of risk onto company management.

Ideas often sound good on paper, but putting them into practice is a risky proposition, especially since so much depends on management's willingness to devote an extraordinary amount of effort to implement their ideas. In order to ensure that the founders remain committed to the business, Sahlman (1988) points out that venture capital firms try to structure the deal so that management only benefits if the firm succeeds. This usually involves minimal salaries for managers, with most compensation tied to profits and the appreciation in the value of the stock they own. Moreover, the venture capitalist usually buys preferred stock convertible into common shares when and if the company goes public. The venture capitalist, therefore, has a prior claim on the assets of the firm in liquidation, ensuring that the founders will not be able to liquidate the company at this point and abscond with their share of the venture's cash. By investing in the form of preferred stock, the venture capitalist also has a prior claim on the firm's earnings; the preferred coupon entitles the venture capitalist to a certain amount of dividends each year before the founders receive anything.

The obvious reason for using preferred stock instead of straight equity is to improve the venture capitalist's reward-to-risk ratio. However, this is probably not the primary reason because the founders are unlikely to give something away for nothing; if the founders have to bear more risk, they will raise the price to the venture capitalist of acquiring a given stake in the firm.

The more likely reason for using a financial structure that shifts a major share of the risk to the founders is to accomplish two objectives:

1. The venture capitalist is trying to force the founders to signal whether they really believe the forecasts contained in their business plan. If they believe their new business will be only marginally profitable, the founders have little incentive to go ahead with the deal proposed by the venture capitalist.

2. The venture capitalist wants to increase the founders' incentive to make the company succeed. By structuring the financing in this way, the founders will benefit greatly only if they meet their projections.

By their willingness to accept this deal, the founders increase the investor's confidence in the numbers contained in the business plan. The venture capitalist, therefore, is willing to pay a higher price for its equity stake. The financial structure also motivates management to work harder and thereby increases the probability that a favorable outcome will occur. This example illustrates an important point about financing: The value created by a company often depends critically on how the company's financing is structured.

To limit their downside risk, venture capitalists rarely give a start-up company all the money it needs at once. Typically, there are several stages of financing. At each stage, the venture capitalists will give the firm enough money to get it to the next product or market development milestone. By staging the commitment of capital, the venture capitalist gains the option of abandoning the project or renegotiating a lower price for future purchases of equity in line with new information. In return for this option, the venture capitalist is willing to accept a smaller ownership share for a given investment. The founders are amenable to this financing structure since it means giving up a smaller share of ownership for the needed funding. If the venture progresses according to plan, the founders will be able to bring in future capital with less dilution of their ownership share. Staged financing, therefore, provides the founders with the option to raise capital in the future at a higher valuation.

In the absence of staged financing, the deal would probably not get done. For example, suppose that to actually bring its product to market, a new venture estimates that it requires total outside funding of $4 million. Consider the problems if a venture capitalist had to put up all this money at once. Even if a venture capitalist were willing to consider such a deal—and there is little likelihood of that—the enormous risk means that the venture capitalist would have demanded such a large share of the firm that the founders would have had little incentive to proceed.

The knowledge that the company will run out of cash in the relatively near future also has a powerful motivating effect on management. Its energies are focused on getting the most out of limited resources. By treating cash as a scarce resource, management will behave in a way that redounds to the benefit of both it and the venture capitalist.

The risks borne by the founders are magnified by the fact that most venture capitalists are prepared to pull the plug and reorganize or liquidate a new venture that does not make the milestones set for it. If problems arise and the founders insist on going it alone, they will find it difficult to get second-stage financing. New outside investors know that they have less information than the original investors and will take it as a bad sign that the latter refused to provide further financing.

All of these financing arrangements should be viewed as means of overcoming the credibility gap that confronts all growth companies in raising capital.

[d] Role of Private Placements in Financing Growth Companies. If the room for discretion on the part of the bank over the years reduces the implicit cost of a bank credit compared with a bond, then the same logic should apply when judging a private placement and publicly issued bond. Privately placed debt is sold directly to a limited number of institutional investors like pension funds or life insurance companies. Such placements are especially valuable to firms with unusual requirements because of the ability to deal directly with the ultimate investor. By contrast, a public debt issue is sold to a potentially large number of unknown investors. Such issues usually contain fairly straightforward terms and conditions, thereby reducing the need for direct negotiation with the investor.

In deciding whether to use the public or private market to raise the additional debt, the choice largely depends on how highly the firm values the benefits provided by each form of financing. Publicly issued debt gives the firm flexibility in the form of call provisions and less restrictive covenants. Investors may also be willing to accept a lower expected return in exchange for liquidity. Those firms that value these features will prefer publicly issued bonds.

However, those covenants that a public offer does contain are apt to be difficult to renegotiate. Even though private placements are more restrictive, it is easier to renegotiate their terms and conditions. Thus, firms that foresee the possible need to substantially alter debt covenants in the future are likely to prefer private placements over publicly issued bonds. This suggests that private placements are particularly well suited for growth companies.

Unfortunately, there is one major complication that arises when growing firms attempt private placements. Because privately placed securities are difficult to sell prior to maturity (although the SEC's Rule 144A has greatly increased the liquidity of the private placement market), investors will want to be assured at the outset that payments will be made over the life of the security. It is just such assurances that are difficult for growth companies to provide. This produces an incentive for the creditors to protect themselves with restrictive covenants and thereby leads to the same problem with publicly-issued debt.

[e] Role of Convertible Securities in Financing Growth Companies. As an alternative to straight debt and its restrictive covenants designed to constrain the propensity to engage in high-risk gambles, companies can issue bonds convertible to stock at the bondholder's option. Such securities may provide relatively low-cost solutions to problems that are likely to arise when a growth firm is attempting to issue conventional securities. Consider a speculative company that tries to issue debt. Potential investors face two possible problems: (1) It might be very costly to assess the projects that the firm will invest in and (2) the firm might be tempted to use the issue's proceeds to invest in a risky venture and thereby increase the value of the equity call option.

The usual means of coping with these problems, by charging a higher interest rate or setting more restrictive covenants, could be counterproductive. Shareholders may be able to pay back a high interest rate loan only if they engage in high-risk, high-potential return projects; more tightly drawn protective covenants could hamper the firm's ability to respond to a rapidly evolving competitive environment, thereby decreasing the value of its growth options and increasing the probability of financial distress. Even if investors are willing to lend under these circumstances, shareholders will bear the expected agency costs, which are likely to be high.

An alternative is to issue convertibles or bonds (preferred stock) with warrants. These securities offer investors participation in the high payoffs to equity in states of the world in which the value of the firm is high, while simultaneously offering them the downside protection of a fixed-income security in those states of the world in which the value of the firm is low. This way, if the firm does undertake riskier projects, holders of convertibles or warrants will see the value of their equity claim rise even if the value of their fixed-income claim drops. Thus, holders of these securities will share in the gains as well as the losses and should be willing to provide funds on more favorable terms.

Because the effects of risk have offsetting impacts on the value of the debt and equity portions of convertibles, the value of an appropriately designed convertible should be relatively insensitive to the risk of the issuing company; if risk rises, the straight debt portion of the convertible falls in value but the conversion rights rise in value. Brennan and Schwartz (1982) point out that this feature of convertibles is particularly valuable when investors and management disagree over the risk of a company. Suppose investors think that the firm is high-risk, but management believes it is medium-risk. Facing a coupon rate of 12 percent, when companies that management deems of comparable risk are paying only 10 percent, management may decide that straight debt is too expensive. Even though a convertible at, say, 8 percent will also appear expensive, relative to the 7.75 percent that management believes is reasonable, the effect of the divergence in risk assessment is much less for the convertibles than for the straight debt. The smaller interest differential with a convertible is due to the fact that, if the market overestimates the risk of the company (and thereby undervalues the company's straight debt), it will simultaneously overvalue a convertible's call option feature.

In such a situation, management will find it more economical to issue the convertible. Note that this benefit of convertibles holds even if management and investors agree that the company's stock is correctly priced. A convertible issue may also provide more advantageous financing terms if management believes the market is undervaluing the company's stock.

One additional observation is also relevant. The lower coupon payment or preferred dividend when an equity "sweetener" is attached will reduce the debt service burden and, therefore, the likelihood of financial distress. This feature will be especially beneficial to growth firms with heavy investment requirements along with substantial amounts of intangible assets; the value of these assets would suffer greatly in the event of financial distress.

[f] Importance of Equity in Financing Growth Companies. Capitalizing on growth options involves more than developing a new product or exploiting a new market niche. The company must develop relationships with customers, suppliers, and distributors, all of whom make firm-specific investments when they do business with the company. In making these commitments, customers and other stakeholders are in effect purchasing implicit claims for timely delivery, product support, future enhancements, and the like. The prices they pay for these claims depend on how confident they are that the company will be able to honor them.

If customers, suppliers, and distributors feel that the firm is so financially weak that its longevity is in question, they will not make the investment required to develop a relationship with the firm. Without such commitment from these noninvestor stakeholders, the firm is likely to fail before it can fully develop its growth options. For this reason, a growing firm must demonstrate that it has financial strength and flexibility. Thus, the analysis points to one unavoidable conclusion: A growth company needs a good deal of equity up front (despite the steep discount at which it might be forced to issue its securities); debt is to be used with care and moderation.

6.08 CONCLUSION

The choice between debt and equity financing affects income per share, risk, control, and flexibility. Adding debt to the firm's capital structure, all else being equal, increases the expected level of EPS but at the same time increases the riskiness of those earnings. Financial leverage trades off higher expected EPS for higher variability of EPS.

The issue of capital structure is one of the most studied and debated in all of finance. It boils down to whether firms can increase their market value by repackaging their cash flows into different combinations of debt and equity securities. Traditionalists argue in the affirmative. Their position is that judicious use of debt financing can indeed increase the market value of the firm. In their seminal contribution to the logic of financial decision making, Modigliani and Miller showed that in a world without taxes and other market imperfections, the value of the firm is independent of its capital structure.

Once taxes are taken into account, the picture becomes cloudy. In the presence of corporate taxes, the interest tax shield creates a substantial advantage to debt financing. However, the tax advantage to the issuing firm may be completely eliminated by the tax disadvantage to the investor. This would be the case if personal tax laws are such that equity income can be received tax free, whereas interest income is fully taxed. However, the presence of nondebt tax shields, such as depreciation and depletion allowances, will once again lead to a situation in which leverage is relevant. Firms with substantial amounts of substitute tax shields are likely to prefer less debt, whereas those with few alternative tax shields will prefer more debt.

TRA 1986 enhanced the advantages of debt financing for two main reasons. First, the maximum corporate tax rate exceeded the maximum personal tax rate, so that the tax advantage of debt at the corporate level could not be fully offset by the tax disadvantage to the investor. Second, the elimination of many nondebt tax shields made the interest tax shield more valuable. With individual tax rates again on the rise, and higher than corporate tax rates, there is once again no clear tax advantage to corporate debt financing.

At the same time, using debt instead of equity financing may foreclose the option of using additional debt financing at a later date, especially considering the information asymmetry problem. Alternatively, equity financing leaves a firm in a more flexible financial position for later years. Thus, any decision should be part of a long-term financial plan that recognizes the probable requirement for a sequence of capital issues.

A key question is whether the firm can service the added debt in the event of adversity. This is based on the basic business risk of the firm, as well as on the firm's degree of financial leverage. A firm with growth opportunities can substantially amplify the growth rate of its earnings per share by replacing equity with debt in its capital structure. In this case, the firm is gambling on the future.

When borrowing reaches a point that financial distress becomes a real possibility, the self-interest of management as well as the interests of the shareholders will probably restrain the firm from adding more debt to the capital structure. Even if this proves not to be the case, the firm will find it difficult to lever itself to such a dangerous degree. When the leverage ratio increases to the point that there is a real danger of insolvency, banks will simply refuse further loan requests, and investment bankers will strongly suggest that the firm issue equity for its next round of financing.

There are other reasons that the firm might not want to push its debt ratio to the limit of its debt capacity. Prudence usually dictates that the firm maintain some reserve borrowing power in the event a sudden need for funds arises and the time is not

218

propitious for a new equity offering. The capital structure selected on the basis of these considerations is usually referred to as the target capital structure.

The target capital structure is a function of the agency costs associated with debt, the costs of financial distress, and taxes. The costs of financial distress rise with the firm's organizational assets. These intangible assets are primarily in the form of a reputation for quality and service and skill at coordinating and communicating with corporate stakeholders. The distinguishing characteristic of these intangible assets is that they are inseparable from the firm as an ongoing operation. Thus, their value in liquidation is zero. Firms with substantial amounts of organizational capital will protect these assets by adopting a low-risk profile, as reflected in a low debt ratio.

Perhaps the best way to summarize these observations is to note that without agency costs, in markets as efficient and competitive as financial markets appear to be, any opportunities to create value by modifying capital structure are likely to be arbitraged away. This suggests that in a well-run firm, in which agency costs are minimal, the emphasis of financial policy must be on supporting the commercial strategy of the firm, because it is here that shareholder wealth is created. For a growing company, in particular, the primary role of finance should be to preserve the growth options that are its principal source of value.

For many companies, however, the separation of ownership and control and the conflicts between bondholders and stockholders may influence the optimal amounts of debt and equity. As outside investors hold a larger fraction of equity, conflicts between owners and managers increase. Similarly, bondholder-stockholder conflicts rise with the degree of leverage. On the other hand, added leverage may mitigate some of the owner-manager conflicts by reducing management's discretion over the reinvestment of free cash flow. In the extreme cases of leveraged recapitalizations and leveraged buyouts, managerial incentives seem to be aligned in a way that enhances the firm's productive efficiency.

These are the complex factors that determine capital structure in practice. Putting them all together to come up with the "optimal" debt-to-equity ratio is not possible currently. The best companies can do is to be aware of these considerations and try to balance them as well as possible in a particular set of circumstances.

Suggested Reading

Amihud, Y., and H. Mendelson. "Liquidity and Asset Prices: Financial Management Implications." *Financial Management* (Spring 1988), pp. 5–15.

Barnea, Amir, Robert A. Haugen, and Lemma W. Senbet. *Agency Problems and Financial Contracting*. Englewood Cliffs, N.J.: Prentice-Hall, 1985.

Berlin, M. "Bank Loans and Marketable Securities: How Do Financial Contracts Control Borrowing Firms?" *Business Review* (July/Aug. 1987), pp. 9–18.

Brennan, M., and E. Schwartz. "The Case for Convertibles." *Chase Financial Quarterly* (Spring 1982), pp. 27–46.

Campbell, T., and W. Kracaw. "Information Production, Market Signalling, and the Theory of Financial Intermediation." *Journal of Finance* (Sept. 1980), pp. 863–882.

Cornell, B., and A.C. Shapiro. "Corporate Stakeholders and Corporate Finance." *Financial Management* (Apr. 1987), pp. 5–14.

——. "Financing Corporate Growth." *Journal of Applied Corporate Finance* (Summer 1988) pp. 6–22.

DeAngelo, H., and H. Masulis. "Optimal Capital Structure Under Corporate and Personal Taxation." *Journal of Financial Economics* (Mar. 1980), pp. 3–29.

Donaldson, Gordon. *Corporate Debt Capacity*. Boston: Division of Research, Harvard Business School, 1961.

——. *Strategy for Financial Mobility*. Homewood, Ill.: Irwin, 1971.

Goeltz, R.K. "The Corporate Borrower and the International Capital Markets." Manuscript dated March 6, 1984.

James, C. "Some Evidence on the Uniqueness of Bank Loans." *Journal of Financial Economics,* Vol. 19 (1987), pp. 217–235.

Jensen, M.C. "Agency Costs of Free Cash Flow, Corporate Finance, and Takeovers." *American Economic Review* (May 1986), pp. 323–329.

Jensen, M.C., and W.H. Meckling. "Theory of the Firm: Managerial Behavior, Agency Costs and Ownership Structure." *Journal of Financial Economics* (Oct. 1976), pp. 305–360.

Kensinger, J.W., and J.D. Martin. "The Quiet Restructuring." *Journal of Applied Corporate Finance* (Spring 1988), pp. 16–25.

Masulis, R.H. "The Effects of Capital Structure Change on Security Prices: A Study of Exchange Offers." *Journal of Financial Economics* (June 1980), pp. 139–177.

——. "The Impact of Capital Structure Change on Firm Value." *Journal of Finance* (Mar. 1983), pp. 107–126.

Miller, M.H. "Debt and Taxes." *Journal of Finance* (May 1977), pp. 261–276.

Modigliani, F., and M.H. Miller. "The Cost of Capital, Corporation Finance and the Theory of Investment." *American Economic Review* (June 1958), pp. 261–297.

——. "Taxes and the Cost of Capital: A Correction." *American Economic Review* (June 1963), pp. 433–443.

Myers, S.C. "Determinants of Corporate Borrowing." *Journal of Financial Economics* (Nov. 1977), pp. 138–147.

——. "The Capital Structure Puzzle." *Journal of Finance* (July 1984), pp. 575–592.

Ross, S.A. "The Determination of Financial Structure: The Incentive-Signalling Approach." *Bell Journal of Economics* (Spring 1977), pp. 23–40.

Sahlman, W.A. "Aspects of Financial Contracting in Venture Capital." *Journal of Applied Corporate Finance* (Summer 1988), pp. 23–36.

Shapiro, A.C. "Guidelines for Long-Term Corporate Financing Strategy." *Midland Corporate Finance Journal* (Winter 1986), pp. 6–19.

Shapiro, A.C., and S. Titman. "An Integrated Approach to Corporate Risk Management." *Midland Corporate Finance Journal* (Summer 1985), pp. 41–56.

Stewart, G.B., III, and D. Glassman. "The Methods and Motives of Corporate Restructuring." *Journal of Applied Corporate Finance* (Spring 1988), pp. 85–99.

Titman, S. "The Effect of Capital Structure on a Firm's Liquidation Decision." *Journal of Financial Economics,* Vol. 13 (1984), pp. 137–183.

Chapter 7

Leasing Capital Equipment

SHARON K. PETERSON

NORIKO OZAWA

ANDREW D. ROSSON

7.01 INTRODUCTION

The term "lease" means different things to different people. Because there are many forms of leases, many people are confused about the technical vocabulary of leasing and often misuse the terms. It is therefore important to know whether "lease" is being used in an accounting or a tax context.

The accounting profession defines "lease" as an agreement conveying the right to use property, plant, or equipment from one party (the lessor) to another (the lessee). Generally speaking, if the form of the agreement is a lease, it is a lease for accounting purposes.[1] The conclusion that an agreement constitutes a lease for accounting purposes, however, communicates very little about the correct accounting treatment. Often, the question of interest for lessees is whether the lease is an operating lease (off-balance sheet) or a capital lease (on-balance sheet). For lessors, the accounting question is usually whether the lease is an operating lease (that is, the asset that is "booked" is a physical asset), a sales-type lease, a direct financing lease, or a leveraged lease (in each case, the asset that is "booked" is a financial asset). Sales-type leases, direct financing leases, and leveraged leases are often referred to as capital leases. To complicate matters, as explained later in this chapter, a lease may be an operating lease from the lessee's point of view and, a capital lease from the lessor's point of view.

Independent of the accounting profession, the Internal Revenue Service (IRS), and therefore the tax legal community, have their view of what constitutes a lease. In order for a transaction to be a lease for tax purposes (a true lease), the lessor must be the owner of the leased property for tax purposes; that is, the lessor must have the benefits and burdens of ownership of the asset. With the exception of a few statutorily excepted cases, the determination of lessor tax ownership is made on a case-by-case basis and is largely influenced by the retention by the lessor of significant incidences of ownership. The form of the transaction is not determinative from a tax point of view. It is therefore possible for a transaction to be a lease from an accounting point of view and not from a tax point of view, and vice versa.

Among many forms of leases, the main economic distinction lies in which party has the burdens and benefits of owning the asset. In non-tax-oriented leases, the lessee is a tax owner, whereas in tax-oriented leases, the lessor is a tax owner. This chapter first distinguishes accounting leases (non-tax-oriented leases) from true leases (tax-oriented leases) and then focuses only on true leases, with an emphasis on leveraged leasing. The lessor's perspective is presented first because the lessee's economics reflects the lessor's perspective, whether it is tax, accounting, or economic, and, therefore, the lessee should understand the lessor's concerns.

7.02 ACCOUNTING LEASES VERSUS TRUE LEASES

[1] Non-Tax-Oriented Leases

Non-tax-oriented (accounting) leases are of two types: (1) capital leases from the lessee's point of view, also known as conditional sales agreements and (2) operating

---

[1] The converse, however, is not true. There are agreements that are, in form, executory contracts that substantively convey the right to use and are therefore leases for accounting purposes.

leases from the lessee's point of view, often called fake leases, off-balance sheet loans, and walk-away leases. In both cases, the lessee is the owner for tax purposes.

A conditional sale, which in form appears to be a lease, is actually a secured loan. In a typical conditional sale, the lease payments made by the lessee to the lessor are identical in amount to those that would have been made had the lessor loaned the lessee the full purchase price of the asset and the lessee made principal and interest payments in amounts that fully repaid the loan. The feature that distinguishes a conditional sale from a secured loan is that during the life of the transaction, the lessor in a conditional sale holds the legal title to the asset as owner rather than as a secured party. At the end of the agreement, the lessee typically has the right to purchase the asset for $1. These transactions are accounted for by the lessee as capital leases (that is, the asset and liability are on the lessee's balance sheet, and the payments are accounted for in the same manner as principal and interest).

Fake leases, off-balance sheet loans, and walk-away leases have four elements in common:

1. The initial term of the "lease" is typically short relative to the asset's economic useful life.

2. The present value of the payments required to be made by the lessee never exceeds 90 percent of the fair market value of the asset.

3. At the end of the initial term, the lessee has a purchase option at a fixed price equal to the expected fair market value, a renewal option at preset rentals, or both. These options fully repay the lessor the fair market value of the asset at a market interest rate.

4. If the option is not exercised, the asset is sold and the lessee is responsible for a substantial first loss payment.

The transaction is designed to minimize the lessor's residual exposure to a point at which, as a practical matter, it is nonexistent. The lessee should be the tax owner because all of the upside in the value of the asset is available to the lessee through the option and all of the practical downside in the value of the asset is borne by the lessee through the first loss payment.

Often, these transactions work better on paper than in practice. Balancing the lessor's exposure to declining asset values against the present value of rent is often more difficult than it first appears. In addition, obtaining the designed accounting treatment of off-balance sheet for the lessee often entails convincing the accountants that it is reasonable for the company not to exercise its option. For certain types of assets that are critical to the company's operations, walking away is sometimes not feasible.

[2] Tax-Oriented Leases

Tax-oriented leases (true leases) are leases where the tax ownership rests with the lessor. These leases are structured either as single-investor leases or leveraged leases. Single-investor leases involve only a lessee and a lessor that advances 100 percent of the asset cost. Leveraged leases involve three parties: a lessee, a lessor that advances only a portion (15 percent to 40 percent) of the asset cost, and a lender that lends the lessor the remaining asset cost.

In a typical tax-oriented lease financing, the user of the asset (the lessee) does not own the asset for U.S. tax purposes. Instead, the asset is purchased by an investor (the lessor), which leases it to the lessee for a term that is shorter than the useful life of the asset. The lessor is entitled to use the tax benefits associated with owning the asset (typically depreciation and sometimes the investment tax credit) and receives rent during the term of the lease. The lessee retains full operational control and obtains a lower-cost financing than can otherwise be obtained through a conventional debt financing. At the end of the lease term, the lessee usually has the option to renew the lease, purchase the asset, or terminate the agreement and return the asset. The main difference between these true lease structures and accounting lease structures is that in a true lease structure, the upside and downside risk in the value of the leased asset at the end of the lease term is borne by the lessor rather than the lessee.

U.S. law, however, contains no statutory provisions for determining whether a transaction should be characterized as a lease, putting aside for the moment certain specialized types of tax leases. Instead, the courts have made this determination on a case-by-case basis after analyzing all of the facts and circumstances. Guidance is provided by previous court cases and IRS rulings and procedures.

[a] **Single-Investor Leases.** Generally, for nonleveraged (single-investor) leases and real estate leases, the criteria used to determine whether they are true leases are as follows:

- Does the transaction have economic substance? The lessor must maintain meaningful benefits and burdens of ownership. At the end of the lease, it is expected that the lessor should enjoy the benefits of and bear the risks of variations in the asset's value. If (1) the lessee has an option to purchase the property at a nominal or bargain price; (2) the lease is for the property's entire expected useful life such that the lessor's expected residual value is nominal; or (3) the lessor can put the asset to the lessee, thereby passing all of the downside risk in the asset's value to the lessee, it is likely that the transaction will be characterized as a loan rather than a lease by the IRS.

- Is the transaction a bona fide arm's-length transaction between two independent and unrelated parties? If the transaction has been influenced by factors that ordinarily would not enter into a transaction of this type (e.g., other business agreements or the relationship of the parties), the transaction or portions of the transaction may be recharacterized to reflect the business realities.

- From the lessee's point of view, does the transaction involve a bona fide business purpose and does the lessor have a reasonable expectation of profit independent of tax benefits? If, for example, the rent plus the expected residual value at the end of the lease term is less than or equal to the lessor's investment in the property plus all costs of entering into the transaction, in the absence of tax benefits it is difficult to see why a rational businessperson would enter into such a transaction. If this were the case, it is likely that the IRS would view the transaction solely as a tax avoidance mechanism and disallow the lessor's tax benefits.

In addition, for the transaction to be characterized as a true lease, the lessee should not hold the legal title to or have an equity interest in the property. If the lessee has an equity interest in the property, the transaction will probably also violate, at least to some degree, one or more of the previously described criteria.

[b] **Leveraged Leases.** A similar, but more specific, set of criteria apply to leveraged leases of equipment. While single-investor leases involve two parties (a lessee and a

lessor), leveraged leases involve three parties (a lessee, a lessor, and a lender). In a leveraged lease, the lessor funds only a percentage (15 percent to 40 percent) of the necessary capital, becomes the owner of the assets, and is entitled to 100 percent of the tax benefits. The remainder of the necessary capital is funded by a nonrecourse loan from a long-term lender, which receives a security interest in the leased property and an assignment of the lease. The rent payable by the lessee is sufficient to pay all principal and interest payments under the long-term loan. Accordingly, the cost of the nonrecourse borrowing depends on the credit standing of the lessee, and the lease rate varies with the interest rate on the debt.

This addition of a third party to the structure complicates the determination of tax ownership. In a single-investor lease, there are only two possible candidates for tax ownership, the lessee and the lessor. In a leveraged lease, the extent to which the lender bears the benefits and burdens of ownership is also relevant. For example, if the lender were to lend the lessor, on a nonrecourse basis, 100 percent of the funds necessary to acquire the equipment, it is difficult to see what risks the lessor would be taking. Therefore, the question arises whether the lender or the lessor owns the equipment for tax purposes. Because of this ambiguity, in the early years of leveraged leasing, the parties to a transaction often sought an advance ruling from the IRS that the lessor was in fact the owner. Because of the proliferation of advanced ruling requests, the IRS issued Revenue Procedures 75-21, 75-28, and 76-30 (collectively known as the Guidelines), which outline the criteria used by the IRS to determine that the lessor is the owner of equipment for tax purposes. If a transaction meets all of the criteria set forth in the Guidelines, the parties can be confident without applying for a ruling that the transaction is a true lease and the lessor is entitled to the tax benefits.

As a result, few transactions are now submitted to the IRS for a ruling; investors rely instead on opinions of tax counsel. In some cases, a transaction structure may violate one or more of the Guidelines and still receive a strong favorable opinion from U.S. tax counsel. This is because the Guidelines are in fact guidelines and describe a transaction structure that the IRS will not question, rather than rules that, if not followed, automatically result in the failure of true lease status. Because the question of tax ownership is a benefits and burdens test, it is sometimes possible to violate a Guideline but not violate the benefits and burdens tests that have been created through case law. In addition, although commonly referenced in transactions involving real estate and, to some extent, single-investor leases, the Guidelines specifically refer only to leveraged leases of equipment.

The following is a summary of the key provisions of the Guidelines:

- *Residual value.* At the commencement of the lease, the estimated fair market value of the leased asset at the end of the lease term must equal or exceed 20 percent of its original cost, without taking into consideration the effect of inflation or deflation and after all costs of removal and redelivery to the lessor have been subtracted.

- *Useful life of asset.* The asset must have an expected economic useful life of at least 125 percent of the lease term, including any interim term or fixed-rate renewal term.

- *Purchase and sale rights.* The lessee may not have a right to purchase the asset for a price that is less than its fair market value at the time of sale. In addition, at the time the asset is first placed in service, the lessor may not have a right to cause any party to the lease to purchase the asset. Any provision for the lessor to abandon the asset in favor of any party will be considered a right to cause that party to purchase the asset.

- *Lessee loans and lessee guarantees.* No member of the lessee group (a broadly defined term that includes almost any affiliated entity) may lend to the lessor any of the funds necessary to acquire the asset or guarantee any indebtedness that may be incurred in conjunction with the purchase of the asset. However, the lessee and its parent or affiliates may guarantee the payments of rent. Third-party guarantees of the debt or lease obligations (letters of credit, for example) are not prohibited by the Guidelines, although the IRS has not formally approved them.

- *Minimum unconditional at-risk investment.* At all times during the lease term, the lessor must have a minimum unconditional at-risk investment equal to at least 20 percent of the original cost of the leased asset.

- *Profit requirement for lessor.* The lessor must be able to show that the transaction was entered into for profit, apart from tax benefits resulting from the transaction.

- *No investment by lessee.* Neither the lessee nor any member of the lessee group may make an investment in the leased asset either at the time of the lease commencement or at any time during the lease term. The lessee may pay for additions and improvements to the asset if they are readily removable without causing damage to the asset. More detailed rules covering lessee additions and modifications are set forth in Revenue Procedure 79-48. (Additions, improvements, and modifications are explained in detail later.)

- *Uneven rents.* There are two uneven-rent tests; one or the other must be satisfied.
  —Test 1: Each annual rent may not vary from the average annual rent by more than 10 percent.
  —Test 2: The annual rent for at least the first two thirds of the lease term may not vary from this period's average annual rent by more than 10 percent, and in the remainder of the lease term each annual rent must be (1) no greater than the largest annual rent in the first period and (2) no less than 50 percent of the average annual rent for the first period.

- *Limited-use property.* The lessor must be able to demonstrate that at the end of the lease term, the asset could be used by a party other than the lessee in a commercially feasible manner.

In addition to these issues, the following are some additional observations on the structuring of single-investor and leveraged lease transactions in the United States:

- *Rules governing purchase options.* The Guidelines allow the lessee to have a purchase option only if the option price is no less than the asset's then fair market value. However, it is common for the lessor to grant the lessee a fixed-price purchase option at a price estimated by an appraisal at the commencement of the lease to be at least equal to the asset's estimated fair market value at the time the option is exercisable. Most tax practitioners believe that if the option is exercisable prior to the end of the noncancelable lease term, the lessor must also be able to demonstrate that the lessee is not economically compelled to exercise the option (i.e., that it is not substantially cheaper for the lessee, on a present-value basis, to exercise the option than to continue to pay rent and purchase the asset at the end of the lease term).

- *Restrictions on types of assets subject to lease.* There is no restriction on the type of equipment that can be leased, as long as the useful-life, limited-use, and residual-value standards can be satisfied.

- *Restrictions on sale-leasebacks and used equipment.* There are no restrictions on sale-leasebacks or the leasing of used assets. Different statutory rules, however, may apply in determining the applicable depreciation method in these transactions. Moreover, in sale-leaseback transactions of assets involving real estate (e.g., many facility leases), in accordance with the accounting rules set forth in the Financial Accounting Standards Board's Statement of Financial Accounting Standards No. 98 (SFAS No. 98), *Accounting for Leases,* the lessee may not have a purchase option, whether for a fair market value or a fixed price, if the lessee desires an off-balance sheet treatment of the lease.

- *Restriction on early termination.* U.S. leases may contain two types of voluntary early terminations: a termination after which a third party owns the asset (third-party sale) and a termination after which the lessee owns the asset (early purchase option). In either case, it is customary for the lessee to protect the lessor's downside in the event that the lessee exercises its option. Because this downside protection occurs only in events outside of the control of the lessor, it is not of much concern to the tax specialists. In the case of third-party sale, there are no legal or tax restrictions; however, as a matter of business negotiations, such a termination is generally allowed only after a minimum period has passed and the lessee has declared the asset uneconomic and/or technologically obsolete. There may be other conditions that generally support the lessee declaration (e.g., that if the lessee is operating a similar asset, it must sell the other asset before the leased asset). In the case of an early purchase option, there are no statutory restrictions, provided the option price is not less than the fair market value price and the lessee is not economically compelled to exercise it. However, some counsel become concerned that if the lessee has too many rights (or a continuous right) to purchase the asset (i.e., if the lessee has too many purchase options), the lessor may not have control of the asset and therefore may not own the asset. As a matter of business negotiations, many lessors will resist early purchase options because they feel that such options reduce the chance that the transaction will result in an upside.

- *Use of floating-rate debt.* There are no restrictions on the use of floating-rate debt. It is frequently used in leasing transactions, with rent being adjusted to reflect periodic interest payments actually made. For purposes of the uneven-rent test described previously, the fact that the rent floats with changes in interest rate is ignored.

[c] Special Types of Tax-Oriented Leases. There are a few types of specialized leveraged leasing that are beyond the scope of this chapter; however, because of the confusion surrounding the vocabulary of leasing, it is important to mention their existence.

FSC leases. In addition to conventional leveraged leases, there are leveraged leases involving foreign sales corporations (FSCs, pronounced "fisks"). A FSC, generally an offshore special-purpose subsidiary of a U.S. taxpayer, is a tax-favored vehicle designed to promote the export of U.S.-manufactured products. In general, using a FSC in a transaction reduces the rate of tax on taxable income generated by the transaction to 70 percent or 85 percent of the rate ordinarily applicable to corporate taxpayers. When a FSC is used in a leveraged lease structure, the goal is to subject as much of the lessor's taxable income (i.e., rent and residual proceeds) as possible to the lower tax rate while subjecting as much of the lessor's taxable deductions (i.e., interest deductions and, in the case of commission foreign sales corporation leases (CFSCs), depreciation deductions) to the normal statutory tax rates. These structuring techniques magnify the tax benefits otherwise available and enable the lessor to pass increased benefits to a lessee in the form of lower rents.

There are two forms of FSC transactions: CFSCs and buy-sell or ownership FSC leases (OFSCs). CFSCs are used primarily in transactions involving U.S.-based lessees for assets that, for FSC purposes, are used predominantly outside of the United States, and OFSCs are used primarily in transactions involving non-U.S.-based lessees.

Foreign leases. Tax-oriented leases are not unique to the U.S. lease market. Some major European and Asian capital markets, e.g., the United Kingdom, Germany, France, Sweden, Ireland, Japan, Hong Kong, and Australia, have developed lease markets in the last decade. These non-U.S. lease markets provide tax-oriented leases for resident and nonresident lessees. Transactions involving a lessor and a lessor's tax base in a country other than the primary jurisdiction of the lessee are commonly referred to as cross-border leases.

In most of the major non-U.S. markets, the rules that determine tax ownership are different from U.S. rules. Most non-U.S. countries rely much more on the form of the transaction to determine tax ownership than the United States does. The opportunity therefore exists to create a transaction in which a non-U.S. party owns the asset for non-U.S. tax purposes and a U.S. party owns the asset for U.S. tax purposes. Most foreign leases to U.S. users and many U.S. leases to foreign users are structured in this manner. These transactions are often referred to as double-dip leases. A typical OFSC transaction is a cross-border lease and may or may not be a double-dip lease.

In addition, there are a few types of U.S. leases that, except for specific statutory allowances, would violate the benefits and burdens tests that define U.S. tax ownership. These are described briefly.

TRAC leases. TRAC leases are single-investor leases for licensed over-the-road vehicles that contain a terminal rental adjustment clause. A TRAC provides that if, upon sale of the equipment at the end of the lease term, the lessor does not receive proceeds equal to a stated dollar amount (usually the expected fair market value), the lessee's final rental payment will be adjusted to make up the shortfall. Typically, the lessee has a purchase option for the same stated amount. Except for specific statutory relief, these transactions would not be true leases, as the lessee bears all of the risk and enjoys all of the benefit in the value of the assets at the end of the lease term.

Tax benefit transfers. The Economic Recovery Tax Act of 1981 created a type of lease commonly referred to as a tax benefit transfer (TBT). These transactions were structured as leveraged leases except that the loan to the lessor was typically provided by the lessee, rent generally equaled debt service, and the lessee had a $1 purchase option at the end of the lease. TBTs were therefore a method of selling accelerated tax benefits without selling or affecting any of the other incidences of ownership of the leased asset. As might be expected, since lessees did not have to give up the attributes of ownership and lessors took no asset risk and only limited credit risk, TBTs proved to be very popular transactions. After several large corporations filed their 1981 tax returns reporting tax losses resulting from purchasing tax benefits and requesting refunds from the government, TBTs became perceived as abusive, and the law permitting these transactions was for the most part repealed in 1982. Many corporations, however, still have TBT transactions on their books.

Finance leases. Finance leases (not to be confused with direct finance leases for accounting purposes) were another short-lived tax phenomenon that existed during the transition phase between TBTs and the true leases that exist today and have existed for most of the history of leasing. During this short period, lessees and lessors could opt to enter into a leveraged lease that contained a bargain purchase option (but no less than 10 percent) and less-accelerated tax benefits than were available in a conventional leveraged lease. These leases were defined as finance leases by the IRS. U.S. tax laws no longer permit new finance leases, but old transactions still exist on the books of corporations.

7.03 LESSOR PERSPECTIVES

Theoretically, a decision to invest in leases, like any financial investment, should be based on an analysis of a risk-adjusted return on the investor's resources. In most financial investment decisions, cash, or the invested amount, is the resource. In a company decision to enter into the leasing business, this reasoning is generally valid because corporations have very few alternative discretionary uses for their tax base. In other words, tax base is typically an underused asset. Corporations whose tax base is more constrained than the dollars available for investment tend to favor investing in single-investor leases rather than leveraged leases, even though the market returns on dollars invested tend to be lower. Implicitly, these companies are seeking to maximize their return on available tax base. If the tax base is unconstrained, sheltering taxes is viewed as one of the goals to be accomplished, and companies naturally skew their investment decisions toward leveraged leasing where return on dollars invested is maximized.

[1] Lessor's Advantages in a Tax-Oriented Lease

Whether considering single-investor or leveraged leasing, the most attractive benefit of leasing investments for more companies is the competitive economic return compared with the return on other financial investments. There are, however, two other principal reasons companies invest in leasing. First, a U.S. tax-oriented lease, which is a capital lease from the lessor's point of view, generates favorable book earnings. Although the lessor owns the asset for tax purposes, the asset is recorded on its books as a financial asset (that is, there is no depreciation expense recorded for accounting purposes). In a single-investor lease, the balance sheet and income effect are the same as if the rent and expected residual were loan payments of principal and interest. The tax deferral arising from the tax depreciation is recorded in the deferred tax account. Accounting for leveraged leasing is even more beneficial, because the added return from the tax deferral is recognized in calculating accounting income. Second, a lease permits companies to participate in an inflation-hedged investment, the future value of the leased asset.

[2] Lessor Economics

A lessor's economics are relatively straightforward in a single-investor lease. The lessor purchases the leased property, resulting in an outflow of cash. Thereafter, the lessor will receive an after-tax inflow each year consisting of the after-tax value of the rent received or residual proceeds plus the after-tax value of any available tax benefits. The lessor's after-tax return is simply an internal rate of return (IRR) calculation.

In contrast, in a typical leveraged lease, the lessor invests a portion (15 percent to

40 percent) of its own cash, borrows the remainder of the purchase price, and purchases the asset. Most of the lease payments paid by the lessee are used to pay principal and interest on the borrowed funds. The lessor receives only small amounts of the rent paid by the lessee, and typically most of this lessor's cash is received in the last half of the transaction. In the early years of a leveraged lease, the lessor has tax losses because rent received will be less than the sum of interest deductions and depreciation deductions. In the later years, the asset will already have been fully depreciated for tax purposes, and rent received will exceed all available deductions (primarily interest), resulting in taxable income.

In a typical leveraged lease, the lessor's after-tax cash flows are as follows:

1. An outflow of cash that represents the lessor's initial investment in the leased asset plus certain fees and expenses of the transaction.

2. Several years of inflows equal to de minimis amounts of lessor's cash (i.e., the portion of rent in excess of debt service) plus the value of the tax losses (primarily from accelerated depreciation) arising from the transaction. The payback period for the lessor's initial investment is typically a little shorter than the depreciation period.

3. Several years of outflows equal to the amount by which taxes arising from the transaction exceed the lessor's cash.

4. An inflow representing the after-tax proceeds from the sale of the residual.

Figure 7-1 contains a bar graph depicting lessor cash flows based on the simplified lease cash flows that are shown in Figure 7-2. This simplified case assumes level lease payments and level debt service payments resulting in a level amount of lessor's cash. In practice, lease-pricing models create optimized rent, debt service, and lessor's cash schedules. (For ease of illustration, however, it is easier to ignore the complexities of lease optimization.) Because this pattern of cash flows does not produce a unique yield when an IRR analysis is employed, the leasing industry has developed certain conventions for analyzing this pattern of cash flows, referred to as the multiple investment sinking fund (MISF) method.[2]

To understand the MISF method, it is helpful to think of the investment in a leveraged lease as any other financial investment; that is, cash flows received as a result of the investment generally are thought, first, to be applied to the earnings and, second, to pay back the invested amount. In a leveraged lease, the issue that arises is that the lessor continues to receive cash after its investment plus earnings have been paid back. The MISF model assumes that the lessor deposits these excess funds in a theoretical non-interest-bearing account called a sinking fund. In the later years of the lease, the lessor uses the funds in the sinking fund to pay its taxes. The sinking fund is entirely depleted during the lease term, and the lessor continues to pay taxes and thereby make a secondary investment in the lease. The secondary investment earns at the same yield rate as the initial investment. At the end of the lease term, the lessor's secondary investment equals the after-tax booked residual.

In the calculation of the MISF yield, cash flows in and out of the sinking fund are ignored and the lessor's cash flow pattern is viewed as having two distinct phases.

---

[2] The IRR is the rate that, when used to discount all of the cash flows, results in a net present value of zero. There may be more than one discount rate which creates this result. For each sign change (i.e., change in cash flow from negative to positive or from positive to negative), there is an additional resulting IRR.

FIGURE 7-1

Lessor Cash Flow

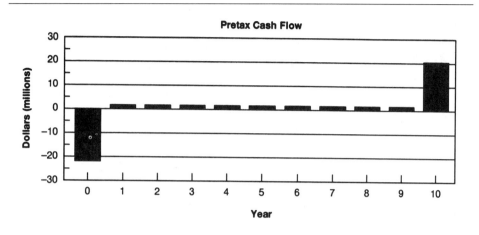

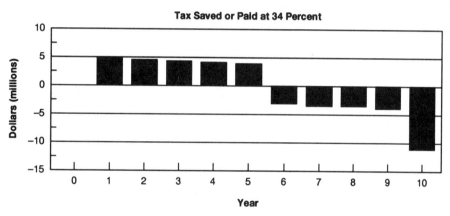

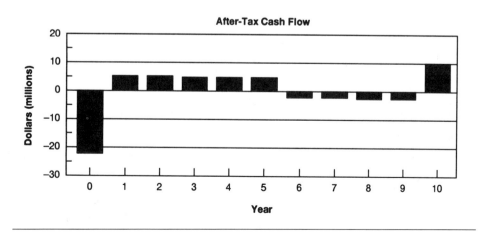

FIGURE 7-2
Simplified Lease Cash Flow

	Pretax Cash Flows			Debt			Tax Calculations				
	A	B	C	D	E	F	Noncash Deductions				
							G	H	I	J	K
Year	Initial Equity, Rents, and Residual	Debt Service	Pretax Cash Flows	Nonrecourse Debt Balance	10% Interest Payment	Principal Payment	Depreciation	Fee	Taxable Income (A-E-G-H)	Taxes Saved or Paid at 34%	After-Tax Cash Flows
0	$ (22.00)		$(22.00)	$80.00					$(14.20)	$ 4.83	$(22.00)
1	14.00	$ 13.02	0.98	74.98	$ 8.00	$ 5.02	$ 20.00	$0.20	(13.70)	4.66	5.81
2	14.00	13.02	0.98	69.46	7.50	5.52	20.00	0.20	(13.15)	4.47	5.64
3	14.00	13.02	0.98	63.39	6.95	6.07	20.00	0.20	(12.54)	4.26	5.45
4	14.00	13.02	0.98	56.70	6.34	6.68	20.00	0.20	(11.87)	4.04	5.24
5	14.00	13.02	0.98	49.35	5.67	7.35	20.00	0.20	8.86	(3.01)	5.02
6	14.00	13.02	0.98	41.27	4.94	8.08	0	0.20	9.67	(3.29)	(2.03)
7	14.00	13.02	0.98	32.38	4.13	8.89	0	0.20	10.56	(3.59)	(2.31)
8	14.00	13.02	0.98	22.60	3.24	9.78	0	0.20	11.54	(3.92)	(2.61)
9	14.00	13.02	0.98	11.84	2.26	10.76	0	0.20	32.62	(11.09)	(2.94)
10	34.00	13.02	20.98	0	1.18	11.84	0	0.20			9.89
Total	$138.00a	$130.20	$ 7.80b		$50.20	$80.00	$100.00	$2.00	$ 7.80	$ (2.65)	$ 5.15

Note: All figures based on asset cost of $100.
a Total rent = $140.
b Lessor's cash = $9.80 ($0.98 × 10); residual = $20.

FIGURE 7-3

MISF Yield Calculation

Year	A Return on Investment Balance (After-Tax Earnings)[a]	B After-Tax Cash Flows[b]	C Ending Investment Balance[c]	D Sinking Fund Balance	E MISF on First Investment Balance (IRR)[d]	F MISF on Second Investment Balance (IRR)[d]
0		$(22.00)	$22.00		(22.00)%	
1	$1.35	5.81	17.54		5.81	
2	1.08	5.64	12.98		5.64	
3	0.80	5.45	8.33		5.45	
4	0.51	5.24	3.60		5.24	
5	0.22	5.02	0	$1.20	3.82	
6	0	(2.03)	0.84	0		(0.84)%
7	0.05	(2.31)	3.20			(2.31)
8	0.20	(2.61)	6.01			(2.61)
9	0.37	(2.94)	9.32			(2.94)
10	0.57	9.89	0			9.89
Total	$5.15	$ 5.15			6.145%	6.145%

Note: All figures based on asset cost of $100.

[a] Figures are equal to the preceding ending investment balance figures in column C times 6.145 percent and represent accrued after-tax earnings on the investment.

[b] Figures are after-tax cash flows from Figure 7-2.

[c] The preceding investment balance (column C) or sinking fund (column D) plus after-tax earnings for the current period (column A) minus the after-tax cash flow (column B) equals new investment balance (column C). Investment balance is never negative. A negative value represents a sinking fund balance.

[d] Columns E and F separate the cash flows applicable to the two investment phases. Note that amounts going into the sinking fund ($1.20 in year 5) are not part of the initial investment phase ($5.02 − $1.20 = $3.82), and amounts taken out of the sinking fund ($1.20 in year 6) are not part of the secondary investment phase (−$2.03 + $1.20 = −$0.84).

The first phase involves only an initial outflow and subsequent inflows from the value of some of the tax benefits and, possibly, the lessor's cash. The second phase involves net outflows arising from the obligation to pay taxes and a final inflow at the end of the lease, the after-tax booked residual value.

Calculating the MISF yield is essentially a trial-and-error process of finding the rate that is the common IRR for the initial phase and the secondary phase. Figure 7-3 shows the MISF calculation for the after-tax cash flows shown in Figure 7-2. In columns A through D in Figure 7-3, it is assumed that the lessor initially invested $22 in the transaction. This initial investment balance earns at an after-tax rate of 6.145 percent until the after-tax cash flows completely repay the initial investment with after-tax earnings in the fifth year. Amounts left over are deposited in the sinking fund. Upon the first negative cash flow in year 6, the sinking fund balance is depleted and the reminder of the negative cash flow represents a secondary investment in the lease. This secondary investment also earns at the 6.145 percent rate and continues to increase with additional negative cash flows until the after-tax proceeds in the last year of the lease reduce it to zero. If, in the trial-and-error process, the final year's cash flow does not exactly pay off the final investment balance, the wrong rate has been chosen. Columns E and F demonstrate that if the final year's cash flows does exactly pay off the final investment balance, the IRR on the first investment balance equals the rate of return on the second investment balance.

The MISF method follows the convention required by U.S. accounting rules that an interest rate of zero on funds in the sinking fund is assumed. Therefore, the closest IRR of the after-tax cash flow is always higher than the MISF yield. The MISF yield is a conservative yield calculation.

Actually solving for the MISF yield, rental structure, and debt structure is complex and is performed using a constrained optimization program. The lessee economics are determined by a variety of factors put into the program, including the lease term, the lessor's tax parameters, the lessor's yield and book accounting requirements, the lessor's residual assumption, the debt rate, and IRS constraints. Given a number of pricing parameters, the program generates optimized rent and debt schedules that achieve the lessor's anticipated economics and at the same time minimize the cost to the lessee. The optimization theory in lease pricing is beyond the scope of this chapter.

The lessor's actual return may vary from the calculated value depending on its actual tax position. The Tax Reform Act of 1986 (TRA 1986) requires U.S. taxpayers to maintain two sets of tax calculations: one applying their regular federal tax rate (34 percent for most corporations) and the other applying the 20 percent alternative minimum tax (AMT) rate. In the process of calculating the AMT, certain adjustments (including stretching out depreciation benefits) are made, usually increasing the taxable income (or decreasing the tax shelter) for AMT purposes. Thus, the tax calculated by applying the 20 percent rate may be greater than the tax calculated by applying the 34 percent rate. Taxpayers are then required to pay the higher of the two taxes. In the context of U.S. leasing, unexpectedly becoming an AMT taxpayer could result in the lessor's losing the anticipated return on the investment if such return is based on the full use of the tax benefits associated with ownership of the asset. Since making leasing investments increases the chance that a company will be subject to AMT, the AMT provision effectively limits the volume of leasing transactions into which most lessors can enter. The application of the AMT has changed the universe of lessors; some former lessors have left the business, and some new lessors have emerged.

[3] Lessor Lease Accounting

One of the attractions of leasing to lessors is the favorable accounting provided by SFAS No. 13 for what are commonly referred to as capital leases. SFAS No. 13 actually classifies leases from a lessor's point of view as direct financing leases, sales-type leases, or operating leases. Sales-type lease accounting is available only when (1) the leased asset is on the lessor's book prior to entering into the lease or the lessor is also the dealer in the leased property and (2) the fair market value of the property is greater or less than the book amount or the dealer-lessor's cost. This difference occurs most often when the manufacturer and the lessor are the same party. Sales-type lease accounting enables manufacturers to book the profit they would have booked if they had sold rather than leased the property to the user. Otherwise, a lessor using sales-type lease accounting accounts for the lease in the same manner as a third party using direct financing lease accounting (other than leveraged lease accounting). Both sales-type leases and direct financing leases are commonly referred to as capital leases.

Capital lease treatment for the lessor provides that for book purposes, the lessor records "rent receivables plus residual" on its balance sheet, and periodically records lease income in a manner similar to interest income on its profit and loss statement. This accounting treatment means that provided everything happens as planned (e.g., no lease defaults, and residual is recognized), the transaction throws off only book income, never losses. Under operating lease treatment for the lessor, however, for book purposes, the lessor records the physical asset (as adjusted for accumulated depreciation) on its balance sheet and periodically records lease income and depreciation expenses in its profit and loss statement. Because depreciation expense is a non-cash expense, it is common for an operating lease, while cash flow positive, to throw off book losses. For this reason, operating lease treatment for most corporate lessors is unacceptable.

On the lessor's books, leases are classified as direct financing leases or sales-type leases (capital leases) if the lease meets any of the following four criteria:

1. The lease transfers ownership of the property to the lessee by the end of the lease term.

2. The lease contains a bargain purchase option.

3. The lease term is equal to 75 percent or more of the estimated life of the leased property.

4. The present value, at the beginning of the lease term, of the minimum lease payments equals or exceeds 90 percent of the fair market value of the leased property to the lessor at the inception of the lease, reduced by any related investment tax credit retained by the lessor and expected to be realized by the lessor.

In addition to meeting any of these criteria, the lessor must determine that *both* of the following will be met (otherwise, the lessor must use operating lease accounting):

5. The collectibility of the minimum lease payments is reasonably predictable.

6. No important uncertainties surround the amount of unreimbursable costs yet to be incurred by the lessor under the lease.

The first four criteria also apply to lessees in determining whether a lease qualifies as an operating lease or as a capital lease. In the same lease, it is most likely that the lessor and the lessee arrive at the same conclusions as to whether the criterion is met with respect to criteria 1, 2, and 3. The lessor and the lessee, however, often derive different conclusions with respect to criterion 4 because the lessor and the lessee may use different discount rates. The lessor uses a rate equal to the "implicit rate." The implicit rate is essentially the IRR produced from an outflow equal to the fair market value of the leased property (reduced by any investment tax credit) and inflows equal to the minimum lease payments and the lessor's expected residual proceeds. Typically, this IRR calculation results in a relatively low discount rate. When this rate is used to discount the minimum rents, the lessor will meet criterion 4, resulting in capital lease treatment, provided that the residual assumption is not too high and not too close to commencement of the lease.

If the lessee knows the lessor's implicit rate, the lessee must also discount the minimum rents at this rate. Fortuitously, the lessee is generally unable to learn this rate (more specifically, the lessor's residual assumption), in which case the lessee is required to use its incremental borrowing cost; therefore, while the lessor meets criterion 4, resulting in capital lease treatment, the lessee often cannot meet criterion 4, resulting in operating lease treatment for the same transaction. The result of these differing lease classifications is that the physical asset appears on neither the lessor's nor lessee's balance sheet, and book depreciation expenses appear on neither the lessor's nor lessee's profit and loss statement. Most long-term leases are specifically structured to accomplish this beneficial result.

For example, using the simplified lease cash flows in Figure 7-2, the present value of minimum lease payments using the debt rate (i.e., 10 percent) as the discount rate equals 86.02 percent of the asset cost, while the present value of minimum lease payments using the implicit rate (i.e., the IRR using an outflow of $100 and inflows of the minimum lease payments plus a $20 residual or 8.64 percent) as the discount rate equals 91.27 percent of the asset cost. Therefore, assuming that the lease meets none of criteria 1, 2, and 3 but meets criteria 5 and 6, the lessor can classify the lease as a capital lease by meeting criterion 4, and the lessee can classify the lease as an operating lease by failing to meet criterion 4.

SFAS No. 13 provides for a fourth classification of leases, leverage leases. A leveraged lease is a direct financing lease that meets the following four criteria:

1. The lease involves a lessee, a long-term creditor, and a lessor.

2. The long-term creditor's financing is nonrecourse to the lessor.

3. The long-term financing provides the lessee with substantial leverage.

4. The lessor's net investment declines in the early years and rises in later years. (Although this is an accounting requirement, this pattern is a result of the cash flow pattern of a true lease.)

Leveraged lease accounting allows the lessor to receive off-balance sheet accounting for the debt. The leveraged lease lessor therefore books only the equity investment on balance sheet. (Except for the consolidation rules, leveraged leasing is the only type of financing that does not require on-balance sheet treatment of nonrecourse debt.) For earnings purposes, the lessor in a leveraged lease records after-tax earnings in accordance with the MISF calculation. Column A in Figure 7-3, in addition to representing the after-tax economic return, also represents the after-tax earnings in the simplified lease. Pretax earnings are recorded by "grossing up" (dividing by one minus the tax rate) the after-tax earnings. Figures 7-4 and 7-5 show the lessor's earnings and balance sheet for the simplified lease. As can be seen from Figure 7-4, leveraged lease accounting results in a relatively front-loaded earnings pattern.

Because the balance sheet and income statement effects are so favorable for leveraged leases, leases are often structured in this manner. Lessors often try, though it is not possible, to structure a sales-type lease (and recognize a manufacturer's or dealer's profit up front) as a leveraged lease for accounting purposes. Leveraged lease accounting is only available if the transaction is a direct financing lease, although for tax purposes, both direct financing leases and sales-type leases are referred to as leveraged leases.

[4] Lessor Exposure in a Leveraged Lease

Exposure tends to be the most confusing aspect of leveraged leasing because it is unlike most other financial investments, in which the earning asset is also the amount exposed to loss in the case of a payor default. In a leveraged lease, the earning asset (investment balance) is only a portion of the exposed amount. It is probably easiest

FIGURE 7-4

Lessor's Earnings Report

| Year | Earnings | Components of Income | |
| | A | B | C |
	Allocated to Income at 6.145%[a]	Pretax Income[b]	Accounting Taxes on Pretax Income[c]
0			
1	$1.35	$2.05	$0.70
2	1.08	1.63	0.56
3	0.80	1.21	0.41
4	0.51	0.78	0.26
5	0.22	0.34	0.11
6	0	0	0
7	0.05	0.08	0.03
8	0.20	0.30	0.10
9	0.37	0.56	0.19
10	0.57	0.87	0.29
Total	$5.15	$7.80	$2.65

Note: All figures based on asset cost of $100.

[a] Figures in column A are the same as figures in column A of Figure 7-3.

[b] Figures in column B are equal to figures in column A divided by (1 − 0.34). Note that the total pretax income for accounting purposes of $7.80 equals the total pretax income for tax purposes (column I of Figure 7-2).

[c] Figures in column C equal figures in column B minus figures in column A.

to understand this concept by comparing exposure in leverage leasing to a model with which most people are familiar: exposure under a loan.

The initial exposure under a loan is the amount invested. Thereafter, as time passes, exposure is increased for accrued interest as these earnings are credited to income. From time to time, cash is received by the lender and the exposure is reduced. Exposure under an equity investment in a leveraged lease acts in much the same manner. Exposure begins at the amount invested and increases over time as earnings are credited to income. However, as cash flow is received, the earning asset, the investment balance (also called the net investment in leveraged lease) is reduced; exposure is not necessarily reduced, however.[3]

---

[3] In a leveraged lease, so much after-tax cash flow may be generated in the early years that the investment balance may be temporarily reduced below zero. A negative investment balance (sinking fund) is reflected on the accounting books as a net investment in leveraged lease of zero and a cash balance equal to the sinking fund amount. In theory, cash is placed in the sinking fund to pay taxes generated by the deal over the course of the transaction.

FIGURE 7-5

Lessor's Balance Sheet

| Year | Assets | | | | Liabilities and Net Worth | | Deferred Tax Calculation | | |
	A Pretax Rent Receivable[a]	B Pretax Estimated Residual Value[b]	C Less Unearned and Deferred Income[c]	D Investment in Leveraged Lease[d]	E Deferred Tax[e]	F Net Investment in Leveraged Lease[f]	G Taxes for Tax Purposes[g]	H Taxes for Accounting Purposes[h]	I Deferred Tax
0	$9.80	$20.00	$7.80	$22.00	0	$22.00	0	0	0
1	8.82	20.00	5.76	23.07	$ 5.52	17.54	$(4.83)	$0.70	$ 5.52
2	7.84	20.00	4.12	23.72	10.74	12.98	(4.66)	0.56	10.74
3	6.86	20.00	2.91	23.95	15.62	8.33	(4.47)	0.41	15.62
4	5.88	20.00	2.14	23.74	20.14	3.60	(4.26)	0.26	20.14
5	4.90	20.00	1.80	23.10	24.29	(1.20)	(4.04)	0.11	24.29
6	3.92	20.00	1.80	22.12	21.28	0.84	3.01	0	21.28
7	2.94	20.00	1.72	21.22	18.02	3.20	3.29	0.03	18.02
8	1.96	20.00	1.43	20.53	14.53	6.01	3.59	0.10	14.53
9	0.98	20.00	0.87	20.11	10.79	9.32	3.92	0.19	10.79
10	0	0	0	0	0	0	11.09	0.29	0

Note: All figures based on asset cost of $100.

[a] Figures in column A are equal to the starting balance (sum of periodic lessor's cash; see Figure 7-2, column C and note *b:* $0.98 × 10 = $9.80) reduced by periodic lessor's cash received over time.

[b] Figures in column B are equal to lessor's booked residual reduced to zero when it is received at the end of the lease.

[c] Figures in column C are equal to lessor's total pretax income (see Figure 7-4, column B) reduced by periodic pretax income earned over time.

[d] Figures in column D are equal to the sum of figures in columns A and B minus figures in column C.

[e] Figures in column E (column I) are equal to cumulative taxes for accounting purposes minus cumulative cash tax expenses (e.g., $0.70 − (−$4.83) = $5.52; see columns G, H and I).

[f] Figures in column F represent lessor's investment balance or sinking fund balance (Figure 7-3, column C or D). Sinking fund balance is expressed as a negative value.

[g] Figures in column G represent cash tax expenses in column J of Figure 7-2. The negative values represent tax savings.

[h] Figures in column H are equal to figures in column C of Figure 7-4.

238

In a leveraged lease equity investment, the lessor's cash over the life of the deal plus the lessor's booked residual will exactly equal an amount that will pay back the lessor's initial investment and provide pretax accounting earnings. In addition, the lessor will receive additional cash flows over the life of the deal equal to the after-tax value of the depreciation and amortization benefits. The depreciation benefits (including amortization benefits) will equal the cost of the asset plus the transaction expenses that the lessor funds (the sum of the initial equity investment plus the initial debt balance). The lessor will incur taxable revenue that is not offset by a deduction matching in time and amount (generally, rent minus interest) over the life of the deal equal to the sum of the following:

1. The initial debt balance (this occurs as rent is used to pay principal and is often referred to as phantom income)

2. The initial equity investment (this amount of taxable income occurs as lessor's cash and booked residual are received)

3. Total pretax earnings in the deal (this amount of taxable income occurs as lessor's cash and booked residual are received)

If x (the amount described in items 1 and 2) equaled not only the amount but also the timing of the depreciation and amortization benefits and y (the amount described in item 3) equaled not only the amount but also the timing of the accrual of pretax income, the exposure in a leveraged lease equity investment would act exactly like the exposure in an investment in a loan. However, because the lessor receives the depreciation tax benefits prior to the accrual of taxable income described in items 1 and 2 and because the timing of pretax accounting income is generally earlier than the receipt of pretax cash, exposure in a leveraged lease consists of not only the current investment balance (net investment in leveraged lease) but also a deferred tax component.

The accounting for an equity investment in a leveraged lease reflects these similarities and differences between leveraged lease equity and loans. The balance sheet accounting for leveraged lease investment is as follows:

Total rent receivable	(Total lessor's cash in the deal)
Plus: booked residual	(Residual booked for yield purposes)
Less: unearned income	(Total pretax earnings in the deal)
Investment in leveraged lease	Asset on books (also equal to investment balance (or net investment in leveraged lease) plus deferred taxes)

If the accounting for a loan investment is forced to mirror that of a lease, the analogous accounting for the loan would be as follows:

Total debt service	(Analogous to total rent and residual)
Less: Pretax interest receivable	(Analogous to unearned income in lease)
Principal balance	Asset on books

In each case, if there was a total loss, the asset on books would be written off, an accounting tax benefit would be recorded, and an after-tax accounting loss (equal to the economic loss) would be recognized.

FIGURE 7-6

Termination Value Schedule

Year	A Termination Value[a]	B Debt Portion of Termination Value[b]	C Equity Portion of Termination Value[c]
0	$102.00	$80.00	$22.00
1	98.05	74.98	23.07
2	93.18	69.46	23.72
3	87.33	63.39	23.95
4	80.45	56.70	23.74
5	72.45	49.35	23.10
6	63.39	41.27	22.12
7	53.59	32.38	21.22
8	43.13	22.60	20.53
9	31.95	11.84	20.11
10	20.00	0	20.00

Note: All figures based on asset cost of $100.

[a] Figures in column A are the sum of figures in columns B and C.

[b] Figures in column B represent the portion of termination value payable to the long-term lender to keep it whole.

[c] Figures in column C represent the portion of termination value payable to the lessor to keep it whole. Figures in column C are the sum of figures in columns E and F in Figure 7-5, except that the sum at the end of year 10 of Figure 7-5 shows the result immediately after payment of the residual, while the equity portion of terminal value represents the lessor's exposure immediately prior to payment of the residual.

The difference between a leveraged lease equity investment and a loan is that in the case of a loan, the recognition of accounting tax expense (and benefit in the case of a write-off) generally occurs at the same time and in the same amounts as the actual cash tax expense (or benefit). In a leveraged lease equity investment, this does not occur. In the early years of a leveraged lease equity investment, there is a cash flow benefit, while for accounting purposes a tax expense is recorded. The cumulative cash flow tax benefit in a leveraged lease therefore precedes (and in the case of a write-off, may exceed) the available accounting tax benefit. This earlier (and/or excess) cash flow tax benefit creates an entry on the liabilities side of the balance sheet in the deferred tax account. This deferred tax account will automatically be reversed through a series of accounting entries and/or cash payments.

Tax-oriented leases almost always contain a schedule that defines the termination value that must be paid by the lessee in the event of an early termination of the lease. The termination value schedule based on the simplified lease is presented in Figure 7-6. Conceptually, termination value is the amount that, if paid, would keep the debt and equity "whole" and is equal to the debt balance plus the sum of the equity's investment balance and deferred tax account (or the debt balance plus the equity's investment in leveraged lease). If the asset is effectively sold for a termination value, the deferred tax account will reverse because the equity will incur taxable income and therefore a tax bill exactly equal to the amount necessary to amortize the deferred tax account. In addition, the equity investor will receive cash sufficient to pay the resulting tax bill and retire the investment balance.

The other extreme case occurs only in a default situation, when the asset is sold for the debt balance or less. In this case, any cash generated by the sale will be used to retire debt and no cash will be received by the equity investor. The equity investor will have taxable income (or loss), however, equal to the debt balance in excess of the undepreciated tax basis and will owe taxes (or receive a refund) equal to its tax rate times the excess of the debt balance over the undepreciated tax basis.[4] This cash payment (or refund) of taxes will only partially reverse (or increase) the deferred tax account. The remainder of the deferred tax account will be reversed when the equity investor writes off the pretax asset that is on the books and recognizes the accounting tax benefit on the loss. The pretax asset that is written off is equal to the maximum default exposure (or the equity portion of termination value). This write-off is analogous to the loss recognized when a loan loss occurs. In the case of a loan loss, the loan balance is written off, a tax benefit is recognized for accounting purposes, and the net loss consists of an after-tax amount. In the case of a loan, the economic loss is equal to the after-tax write-off. In a leveraged lease, the economic loss is equal to the (positive or negative) investment balance increased for any taxes owed or decreased for any tax refunds. This amount also equals the after-tax accounting write-off.

If the asset is sold for an amount that is more than the debt balance but less than termination value, the equity investor will receive some cash and will suffer a pretax accounting loss that is less than maximum default exposure and that reduces the economic loss.

Using the simplified lease, the following examples more fully illustrate the concept of lessor exposure. (Rounding errors are ignored in the calculations.)

EXAMPLE: On the closing date, the lessor borrows $80 on a nonrecourse basis and makes an equity investment equal to $22, consisting of its investment in the asset plus payment of transaction expenses. This investment is recorded on its books as follows:

Accounting Entries		*Notes*
Rent receivable	$9.80	Rent receivable equals the sum of all of lessor's cash (rents minus the sum of principal and interest payments) in the deal (Figure 7-2, column C: $0.98 × 10 = $9.80). This amount will be reduced as lessor's cash is received.
Booked residual	$20.00	(Figure 7-2, column C and note.)

[4] Even if the sale price of the asset is less than the debt balance, the equity investor recognizes taxable revenue equal to the debt balance. To the extent of any sales proceeds, the equity investor will recognize income as such. To the extent that these proceeds are insufficient to pay off the debt, the equity investor recognizes income equal in amount to the forgiven debt.

Less: Unearned income	$7.80	Unearned income is equal to total pretax accounting income in the deal (Figure 7-4, column B: $7.80). Unearned income is also equal to the sum of total after-tax earnings (total after-tax cash in the deal) (Figure 7-2, column K) grossed up ($5.15/ (1 − 0.34)). Over time, this amount will be booked as pretax earnings during periods when there is a positive net investment in leveraged lease.
Investment in leveraged lease	$22.00	The sum of the total of lessor's cash ($9.80) plus the lessor's booked residual ($20) is always equal to the lessor's initial equity investment ($22) plus total pretax earnings ($7.80) (Figure 7-2, columns C and I). Recall that total taxable income always equals total pretax accounting income. Investment in leveraged lease of $22 is the amount that appears on the asset side of the balance sheet.
Deferred tax	$ 0.00	This number appears on the liabilities side of the balance sheet.
Net investment in leveraged lease	$22.00	Net investment in leveraged lease is also called investment balance.

EXAMPLE: During the first year, the lessor received after-tax cash flows equal to $5.81, which arose from the value of $20 of depreciation, $0.20 of fee amortization and the lessor's cash of $0.98 (Figure 7-2). In addition, since the lessor had a positive net investment in the lease, $2.05 of pretax income was booked to earnings (Figure 7-4, column B). At the end of year 1, the lessor's financial statements appear as follows:

Accounting Entries		Notes
Pretax income	$2.05	Pretax income equals the after-tax earning grossed up (see net income).
Tax expenses	$(0.70)	This expense is accrued for accounting purposes but has not been paid ($2.05 × 0.34).
Net income	$1.35	This amount is calculated by applying the after-tax yield to the investment balance (net investment in leveraged lease) (Figure 7-3, column A).
Rent receivable	$ 8.82	This number is reduced by lessor's cash received in the first year ($9.80 − $0.98) (Figure 7-2, column C).
Booked residual	$20.00	
Less: Unearned income	$5.76	This number is $2.05 less than the original booked number reflecting the earned pretax income in the first year ($7.80 − $2.05).

Investment in leveraged lease	$23.06		The original investment in leveraged lease ($22) increased by pretax income of $2.05 and decreased by lessor's cash of $0.98.
Deferred taxes	$5.52		This number consists of the cash tax actually saved by the lessor of $4.83 and $0.70 of noncash accounting tax expense ($2.05 pretax income × 0.34).
Net investment in leveraged lease	$17.54		

At the end of the first year, the lessor's exposure is equal to the following:

Net investment in leveraged lease	$17.54
Deferred taxes	$5.52
	$23.07

At the end of the first year, termination value is equal to $98.05 ($23.07 plus the debt balance of $74.98).

If the asset was sold for termination value of $98.05, the lessor would receive $23.07 cash proceeds (after paying off the debt), which is exactly enough to remove all the related entries from its books. First, the lessor would increase cash by the amount received ($23.07) and remove investment in leveraged lease from the asset side of the balance sheet. The lessor would then pay taxes on the sale ($5.52). The taxes payable by the lessor are exactly equal to the balance in the deferred tax account. Thus, cash proceeds that the lessor receives would be sufficient to pay the resulting tax bill and retire the investment balance.

Calculation of the tax bill is as follows:

Original tax basis (Figure 7-2)	$102.00
Less: Depreciation plus amortization (Figure 7-2)	$20.20
Remaining tax basis	$81.80
Termination value (Figure 7-6)	$98.05
Less: Remaining tax basis	$81.80
Taxable income	$16.25
Taxes at 34%	$5.52

Implicit in these entries is the fact that the earnings credited in the first year are preserved. The cash received and the investment in leveraged lease of $23.07, which was removed from the lessor's books, consisted of its original investment of $22 plus pretax earnings of $2.05, reduced by the lessor's cash of $0.98 received in the first year. All else being equal, the higher the yield (and therefore earnings), the higher the termination value.

In the case where the asset was sold for the debt balance, the lessor would receive no pretax cash from the sale and would write off the $23.07 asset on its balance sheet, resulting in a pretax loss of $23.07. The lessor would record an accounting tax benefit of $7.84 ($23.07 times 34 percent), resulting in an after-tax accounting loss of $15.23. The accounting tax benefit of $7.84 would reverse the deferred tax account on its books of $5.52 (since this amount will not become payable) and would reflect the $2.32 tax refund resulting from the sale.

Calculation of the tax bill is as follows:

Assumed sales proceeds (forgiven indebtedness)		$74.98
Original tax basis	$102.00	
Less: Depreciation plus amortization	$20.20	
Remaining tax basis		$81.80
Taxable income		$(6.82)
Tax refund at 34%		$2.32

The lessor's economic loss is equivalent to the economic loss generated from an accounting write-off of $23.07. The lessor would lose its investment balance of $17.54 reduced by a tax refund of $2.32, or $15.23. Note that a pretax loss of $23.07 less an accounting tax benefit of $7.84 also equals an after-tax loss of $15.23.

EXAMPLE: Using the same lease to examine the lessor's exposure at the end of the fifth year, the process is the same as previously shown. From the lease commencement through the end of the fifth year, the lessor received a cumulative net tax benefit of $22.26 (Figure 7-2, column J) and lessor's cash of $4.90 ($0.98 × 5). From the lease commencement, $6.01 of pretax earnings has been booked to income (Figure 7-4, column B). At the end of the fifth year, the remaining tax basis is equal to $1 ($102 − $101) (Figure 7-2, columns G and H) and the remaining debt balance is equal to $49.35 (Figure 7-2, column D). As of the end of the fifth year, the lessor's financial statements appear as follows:

Accounting Entries		Notes
Cumulative pretax earnings to date	$6.01	(Figure 7-4, column B.)
Tax expense charge to date	$(2.04)	($6.01 × 0.34.)
Increase in retained earnings from transaction	$3.97	
Rent receivable	$4.90	This number is less than the original rent receivable by an amount equal to the cumulative lessor's cash ($9.80 − $4.90).
Booked residual	$20.00	
Less: Unearned income	$1.80	This number is $6.01 less than the original booked number reflecting the earned pretax income for 5 years ($7.80 − $6.01).
Investment in leveraged lease	$23.10	This number represents the pretax exposure. It is equal to the original investment in leveraged lease ($22) increased by cumulative pretax income of $6.01 and decreased by cumulative lessor's cash of $4.90. Only receipt of lessor's cash and residual reduce exposure.
Deferred taxes	$24.29	This number consists of the cash tax actually saved by the lessor of $22.26 and $2.04 of noncash accounting tax expense ($6.01 cumulative pretax income × 0.34).
Net investment in leveraged lease (sinking fund balance)	$(1.20)	

At the end of the fifth year, the lessor's exposure is equal to:

Deferred taxes	$24.29
Less: Cash sinking fund balance	$(1.20)
	$23.10

In the case where the asset is effectively sold for termination value of $72.45, the lessor would receive exactly enough cash to remove all the related entries from its books, as was the case in the second example. Cash would increase by the amount received ($23.10), resulting in a cash balance of $24.29 ($23.10 plus the sinking fund balance of $1.19), and investment in leveraged lease of $23.10 would be removed from the asset side of the balance sheet. Calculation of the tax bill is as follows:

Original tax basis (Figure 7-2)	$102.00
Less: Depreciation plus amortization (Figure 7-2)	$101.00
Remaining tax basis	$1.00
Termination value (Figure 7-6)	$72.45
Less: Remaining tax basis	$1.00
Taxable income	$71.45
Taxes at 34%	$24.29

Note that the tax liability of $24.29 exactly reverses the deferred tax account and is exactly equal to the available cash balance.

Again, the lessor's previously booked earnings have been preserved. If all of the entries and reversing entries in the deferred tax account are ignored, it is easy to see that the lessor originally invested $22, booked $6.01 of pretax income, and received $4.90 in lessor's cash, leaving $23.10 ($22 plus $6.01 minus $4.90), which must be received to preserve earnings and return on the equity investment.

In the extreme case of a sale of the asset for the debt balance, the lessor would receive no pretax cash from the sale and would write off the $23.10 asset on its balance sheet. It would record an accounting tax benefit of $7.85 ($23.10 times 34 percent), resulting in an after-tax accounting loss of $15.25. The accounting tax benefit of $7.85 would reduce the deferred tax account to $16.44, which reflects income taxes payable by the lessor as follows:

Assumed sales proceeds (forgiven indebtedness)		$49.35
Original tax basis	$102.00	
Less: Depreciation plus amortization	$101.00	
Remaining tax basis		$1.00
Taxable income		$48.35
Taxes payable at 34%		$16.44

The lessor's after-tax accounting loss of $15.25 is exactly equal to the amount of the tax payment of $16.44 reduced by the cash available in the sinking fund of $1.20.

7.04 LESSEE PERSPECTIVES

The most important factors in structuring a lease financing are the goals the lessee is seeking to accomplish, the prioritization of those goals, and information concerning the lessee's expected future tax position. This information will guide the structure toward a lease that, from the lessee's point of view, is tax oriented, accounting oriented, or both. The size of the transaction and credit quality of the lessee are added considerations in determining whether the transaction is structured as a leveraged or unleveraged (single-investor) transaction.

Unleveraged transactions tend to be used for transactions that cannot either economically or practically support the added complexities of leveraged transactions. Smaller deals cannot support the relatively higher transaction expenses involved in a leveraged transaction and are often attractive as unleveraged transactions. Transactions for lesser credits are often easier to consummate as single-investor transactions because they do not involve subordination negotiations between the providers of funds, which increase in importance as the credit quality of the lessee declines. In addition, the lessee's goals may include structuring complexities that are easiest to accomplish with the fewest possible number of parties.

In the absence of these types of factors, transactions are generally structured as leveraged financings, for three reasons. First, for larger transactions, especially tax-oriented ones, the economics tend to be better. Second, the relative depth of the markets for leveraged financings compared to single-investor financings tends to push larger transactions into the leveraged markets. Third, from the lessee's point of view, leveraged transactions provide the most flexibility in choosing the funding sources.

Because in a leveraged transaction, the debt, which represents 60 percent to 85 percent of the financing, is nonrecourse to the lessor and is completely serviced from the rental payments, the lessee usually chooses the type of debt incurred. The loan under the lease and therefore the portion of rent that services the loan can be structured as fixed rate or floating rate and can be denominated in various currencies. U.S.-dollar-denominated loans can be raised in the U.S. public or private markets, in the Euromarkets, in the Japanese market, or in other markets. Foreign currency loans are typically raised in the local currency market. Available maturities vary from market to market.

The remainder of the lessee perspectives focus on tax-oriented leases because non-tax-oriented leases can be analyzed in the same fashion that other borrowings are analyzed.

[1] Lessee's Advantages in a Tax-Oriented Lease

The most attractive benefit of tax-oriented leasing for most companies is its low cost; the lessor under a true lease can pass through to the lessee the tax benefits of ownership of the assets, which the lessee otherwise may lose forever by purchasing rather than leasing. Among the other reasons companies prefer leasing to other financing alternatives are the following:

- *100 percent financing.* Leasing provides 100 percent financing (which may include shipping costs and capitalized interest during construction and/or acquisition), while alternative financings frequently require some equity contribution. In some circumstances where the fair market value of the asset exceeds its cost (e.g., for long-lead-time items in an inflationary environment), a lease financing may cover the full appraised value.

- *Diversification of lessee's investor base.* Since leasing involves investors that are different from the typical lending circle, it enables the lessee to tap into a broader investor base.

- *Elimination of future residual risk.* Leasing enables the lessee to transfer to the lessor the exposure to, or responsibility for, the future residual value risk or remarketing of the asset.

- *Cash flow improvement.* Lease payments typically provide the lessee with more favorable cash flows than loan payments during the initial period of the lease, since the payments are often weighted toward the later years.

- *On- or off-balance sheet accounting.* A lease can often be structured on or off balance sheet for financial accounting purposes, depending on the lessee's objectives.

- *Impact on book earnings.* Lease payments under a properly structured operating lease have less impact on book earnings in the early years than the combination of depreciation and interest expenses associated with the purchase and debt financing of the asset.

- *Financial covenants.* Depending on the terms in existing loans, a lease may provide the lessee with financing that otherwise may not be available to it.

- *Long terms.* Lessors are often willing to provide a longer-term commitment than other providers of capital. Leasing therefore may provide the lessee with longer-term financing than may be available from other sources.

- *Industrial revenue bond limits.* If costs of plant and equipment to be financed exceed the statutory limits of industrial revenue bonds, a lease can be used to keep the project within the bond limits.

The economic, tax, and accounting aspects of leases are relatively complex in comparison with straightforward loans; however, the potential for real cost savings and benefits from leasing can be very significant.

[2] Lease-Versus-Buy Analysis

[a] Methodology. The decision to acquire the use of an asset is different from the decision of how to finance it. The first is a capital-budgeting problem and involves an analysis of the possible revenues that can be generated from the asset, as well as its operating costs. The second is a financing decision involving only an analysis of the alternative cash flows created by various financing techniques after the decision to acquire the use of the asset has been reached. The textbook theory is that for capital-budgeting purposes the company's cost of capital is the appropriate discount rate to use in the analysis but that for financial decision making (such as deciding whether to lease or own) the appropriate discount rate is the company's debt rate. In practice, however, the appropriate discount rate to use in the lease-versus-own decision is controversial.

Some companies use their borrowing rate, but increasing numbers of companies are using their cost of capital. Companies using their debt rate argue that lease payments are contractual obligations and therefore use debt capacity in the same manner as an obligation to make loan payments. Even if the transaction is off balance sheet, financial analysts put these obligations back on the balance sheet for analytical purposes.

Believers in the appropriateness of cost-of-capital discounting are somewhat more skeptical of analysts' inclination and ability to adjust the income statement and balance sheets appropriately to capitalize off-balance sheet financings. In addition, they note that companies are often debt-constrained by financial covenants but are not constrained by operating leases, and therefore, the available alternative to lease financing is not debt but debt plus equity. Even if the company is not debt-constrained by financial covenants, lessors are often willing to provide 100 percent financing for assets when lenders are not because lessors are entitled to equity-type returns provided by the residual upside. This chapter does not intend to resolve this controversy, since the authors believe that the right theoretical answer is highly dependent on one's view of somewhat controversial premises.

Less controversial issues that must be resolved prior to doing any analysis are pretax versus after-tax analysis and IRR analysis versus a discounted cash flow (DCF) approach. Since true leasing involves transfer of depreciation tax benefits and because the payments made by the lessee have a different tax character from loan payments (that is, they are fully deductible), most people agree that an analysis of after-tax cash flow using after-tax discount rates is the appropriate methodology. If the lessee believes that it will be in a permanent non-tax-paying position, the after-tax analysis and the pretax analysis will yield the same results, and in these cases, pretax analysis is sometimes used. However, this lessee assumption is highly unusual, especially with the introduction of AMT. Except for certain non-U.S. lessees whose home jurisdictions treat U.S. leases as debt financings that are not subject to U.S. taxes, there are almost no lessees that can make a non-taxpayer-forever prediction.

Also, most lessees choose a discounted cash flow analysis over an IRR analysis. A DCF analysis is more appropriate because the choice between leasing and buying are mutually exclusive choices and because the duration and maturities of the two financing choices are almost always different. In other words, the lowest IRR may be a poor choice if it is a relatively short financing and cannot be repeated. For example, if a company had the choice between borrowing money at 1 percent for one year and borrowing at 2 percent for two years and, in each case, at maturity the company could only refinance at prevailing market rates, it would probably choose to borrow at the higher rate because there is more total benefit in the 2 percent transaction. Although not quite so extreme, the principle in analyzing the lease-versus-buy decision is the same.

One complicating factor in attempting to apply an after-tax present value analysis to the lease-versus-buy decision is determining the after-tax discount rate (even after a choice between cost of capital and cost of debt has been made). It is typical for a company to believe that it will have a changing tax position over the life of the lease. It may expect to be a nontaxpayer in some years, an AMT taxpayer in some years, and a full taxpayer in other years. As a result, the company expects its after-tax discount rate to vary. The leasing industry has developed a defeasance type of analysis, in which a hypothetical deposit takes into account these changes in the company's after-tax discount rate. The methodology is referred to as the equivalent loan method.

The equivalent loan method calculates the value of a hypothetical deposit that, after taking into account tax benefits available over the analysis period, is sufficient to cover all the cash outflows due under the lease or buy option. This deposit is assumed to accrue interest at the company's debt rate (or adjusted cost of capital) when it has a positive balance and is replenished by hypothetical borrowing at the company's debt rate (or adjusted cost of capital) when it is not sufficient to cover cash outflows. The analysis also takes into account the impact of the company's tax position on interest earnings on the hypothetical deposit balance and of any interest expense on the hypothetical loan.

In employing the equivalent loan method to the lease-versus-buy analysis, the company can use either the present-value approach or the future-value approach. In the present-value approach, an estimate of the asset's fair market value at the end of the analysis period is added to the lease-versus-buy analysis; that is, it is assumed that the asset is sold in the buy scenario or is purchased in the lease scenario at the estimated residual value amount. Given this residual input, the analysis produces the after-tax present values of the two scenarios, lease and buy. Alternatively, the company can solve for the future value of the asset at the end of the analysis period to produce the identical present-value cost to the company in both scenarios (breakeven residual). If the company expects the fair market value to be higher than the break-even residual value, buying is a better alternative. If, on the other hand, the fair market value is expected to be lower than the break-even residual value, leasing is a better alternative. Whichever approach the company employs, it must make an estimate of the future residual value of the asset to determine its optimal course of action.

If the lease contains a fixed-price purchase option either during the term of the lease or at the end of the lease term, this amount can be incorporated into the analysis. If the lease alternative incorporating the fixed price is the superior choice, a potential lessee who knows that he can acquire the property at a fixed price can ignore the uncertainty surrounding the expected future residual value because if the future residual value is higher than the fixed price, he can purchase the property for the fixed price, resulting in the lease alternative's still being the superior choice. If, however, the future residual value is lower than the fixed price, he can purchase the property for the future market value, in which case the lease alternative will be a better choice than that shown in the analysis.

If, on the other hand, the buy alternative is the superior choice after the fixed price is incorporated, the potential lessee must do sensitivity analysis if he believes that the fair market value of the property may be less than the fixed price. If he believes that the fair market value of the property at the end of the lease term is less than the fixed price, he anticipates purchasing the property for the future fair market value rather than for the fixed price. If the expected fair market value (which is less than the fixed price) were input in the lease-versus-buy analysis, the result might well be reversed.

In the following example, assume that the lease contains no fixed-price purchase option and, therefore, the analysis is performed as a break-even residual analysis. In doing this analysis, it is assumed that the lessee will purchase the asset at the end of the lease term at its fair market value. In solving for this break-even residual, the first step is to compute the size of the defeasance deposit necessary to defease all cash flows (including the initial flow representing the purchase of the asset) on the buy option. The second step is to calculate the purchase price at the end of the lease term for the lease option, which results in the same size of defeasance deposit on the lease option as on the buy option.

EXAMPLE: The following are assumptions used to generate buy and lease options for a lease-versus-buy analysis using the equivalent loan method.

Buy Option Assumptions

Tax attributes of ownership. Since TRA 1986 eliminated the investment tax credit, depreciation allowance is the sole tax attribute of ownership applicable for the buy side of any lease-versus-buy analysis. For presentation purposes, assume that the asset qualifies for a seven-year modified accelerated cost recovery system (MACRS) depreciation. In the after-tax analysis, a reduction in taxes generated by depreciation is a cash inflow to a U.S. taxpayer.

Loan parameters. Although many people like to assume that the buy option is financed by a loan, this analysis assumes that the buy option was financed with available cash. When discounting at the after-tax debt rate, financing with available cash and financing with a loan always yields the same result, since the present value of after-tax loan payments discounted at the after-tax debt rate always equals the original principal amount of the loan. The danger of financing the buy option with a loan is the trap of creating fixed cash flows using a fixed

FIGURE 7-7

Rent and Debt Schedule

Date	A Rent No.	B Rent	C Interest	D Principal	E Debt Service	F Lessor's Cash
12/30/1993	1	$ 4,000.0	$ 4,000.0	0	$ 4,000.0	0
6/30/1994	2	6,374.2	4,000.0	$ 2,374.2	6,374.2	0
12/30/1994	3	3,881.3	3,881.3	0	3,881.3	0
6/30/1995	4	6,492.9	3,881.3	2,611.7	6,492.9	0
12/30/1995	5	3,750.7	3,750.7	0	3,750.7	0
6/30/1996	6	6,623.5	3,750.7	2,872.8	6,623.5	0
12/30/1996	7	3,607.1	3,607.1	0	3,607.1	0
6/30/1997	8	6,767.2	3,607.1	3,160.1	6,767.2	0
12/30/1997	9	3,449.1	3,449.1	0	3,449.1	0
6/30/1998	10	6,925.2	3,449.1	3,476.1	6.925.2	0
12/30/1998	11	3,275.3	3,275.3	0	3,275.3	0
6/30/1999	12	7,099.0	3,275.3	3,823.7	7,099.0	0
12/30/1999	13	3,084.1	3,084.1	0	3,084.1	0
6/30/2000	14	7,290.2	3,084.1	4,206.1	7,290.2	0
12/30/2000	15	2,873.8	2,873.8	0	2,873.8	0
6/30/2001	16	8,653.2	2,873.8	5,779.4	8,653.2	0
12/30/2001	17	2,584.8	2,584.8	0	2,584.8	0
6/30/2002	18	10,094.8	2,584.8	5,737.1	8,321.9	$ 1,772.9
12/30/2002	19	2,297.9	2,297.9	0	2,297.9	0
6/30/2003	20	10,381.7	2,297.9	5,279.6	7,577.5	2,804.2
12/30/2003	21	2,034.0	2,034.0	0	2,034.0	0
6/30/2004	22	10,645.7	2,034.0	8,375.3	10,409.3	236.4
12/30/2004	23	1,615.2	1,615.2	0	1,615.2	0
6/30/2005	24	11,064.4	1,615.2	9,449.2	11,064.4	0
12/30/2005	25	1,142.7	1,142.7	0	1,142.7	0
6/30/2006	26	11,536.9	1,142.7	10,394.2	11,536.9	0
12/30/2006	27	623.0	623.0	0	623.0	0
6/30/2007	28	12,056.6	623.0	11,433.6	12,056.6	0
12/30/2007	29	51.3	51.3	0	51.3	0
6/30/2008	30	12,628.3	51.3	1,026.8	1,078.1	11,550.1
Total		$172,903.9	$76,540.3	$80,000.0	$156,540.3	$16,363.6

Note: Dollars in thousands.

debt rate and then performing a sensitivity analysis using various discount rates. It is not clear why it makes sense to discount debt payments at rates other than the debt rate.

Lease Option Assumptions

Lease rentals. For analytical purposes, assume that the rent schedules used are those in Figure 7-7. This leveraged lease pricing is still simplified but is more realistic than the simplified lease used thus far. The following are the primary pricing assumptions used to generate the rents contained in Figure 7-7:

Delivery	June 30, 1993
Asset cost	$100 million
Lease term	15-year base term with no interim term
Lease rental	Variable within 90–110 range; payable semiannually in arrears
Amount of loan	$80 million (80% of asset cost)
Debt rate	10%
Transaction expenses	0% of asset cost (most transaction expenses are financed by the lessor and include various fees involved in structuring the lease transaction but generally exclude certain legal fees and out-of-pocket expenses of lessee)
Lessor's yield	9.5% after tax
Lessor's booked residual	15% of asset cost
Fixed-price purchase option	None
Defeasance deposit rate	10% bond equivalent rate
Lessor's tax rate	34%
Lessor's tax year-end	December
Tax method	100% current taxpayer

[b] Decision Analyses. The results of lease-versus-buy analyses vary, depending on the forecast of the lessee's tax position. This forecast may include a different assumption each year as to whether the lessee is a full 34 percent taxpayer (regular taxpayer), a 20 percent AMT payer, or a nontaxpayer owing to anticipated net operating losses (NOLs). State tax considerations would also be relevant.

Figure 7-8 presents the after-tax cash flows of both the lease and the buy options assuming four scenarios of the potential lessee's tax position. Except for the different assumptions with respect to the potential lessee's tax position, all four scenarios are based on the same lease-versus-buy methodology and the same facts summarized in both the buy option and lease option assumptions. The lessee's tax positions, however, may change the depreciation schedule. One of the consequences of being in an AMT-paying position is that the depreciation schedule available for property eligible for seven-year MACRS deductions is a less favorable depreciation schedule. In scenario 1, "Forever Regular Taxpayer," the cash flows in the buy option are computed. There is only one cash outflow, of $100 million, representing an initial cash amount to purchase the asset and ensuing cash inflows representing the value of depreciation tax benefits. The value of these depreciation tax benefits reflect the company's tax position as a regular taxpayer. The initial deposit amount that will defease these after-tax cash flows is then calculated through a trial-and-error process. Because of the reductions in taxes generated by depreciation, the company is required to place an initial deposit of less than 100 percent of the cost of the asset, or $71,173,150. In this scenario, because the potential lessee's tax position is not changing during the lease term, the defeasance deposit can be approximated by subtracting the present value of the after-tax cash inflows at the after-tax discount rate from the initial outflow of $100 million. (However, because the analysis has been performed on a monthly basis and has taken into account monthly accrual of deposit earnings but quarterly estimated tax payments, discounting the after-tax cash flows in Figure 7-8 does not produce exactly the same result.)

Once the value of defeasance deposit for the buy option is determined, that amount

FIGURE 7-8

Lease-Versus-Buy Analyses: After-Tax Cash Flows

	Company Tax Position							
	Scenario 1: Forever Regular (34%) Taxpayer		Scenario 2: Forever AMT (20%) Payer		Scenario 3: NOLs Then Regular (34%) Taxpayer		Scenario 4: Forever Nontaxpayer	
	A	B	C	D	E	F	G	H
Year Beginning	Lease-Side After-Tax Cash Flow	Buy-Side After-Tax Cash Flow	Lease-Side After-Tax Cash Flow	Buy-Side After-Tax Cash Flow	Lease-Side After-Tax Cash Flow	Buy-Side After-Tax Cash Flow	Lease-Side After-Tax Cash Flow	Buy-Side After-Tax Cash Flow
1/1993	$ (2,628.0)	$(95,142.9)	$ (3,192.9)	$(99,062.5)	$ (4,000.0)	$(100,000.0)	$ (4,000.0)	$(100,000.0)
1/1994	(6,768.4)	8,326.5	(8,204.3)	1,835.9	(10,255.5)	0	(10,255.5)	0
1/1995	(6,760.6)	5,947.5	(8,194.8)	1,762.7	(10,243.7)	0	(10,243.7)	0
1/1996	(6,751.9)	4,248.2	(8,184.3)	1,698.6	(10,230.6)	0	(10,230.6)	0
1/1997	(6,742.4)	3,034.4	(8,172.8)	1,642.5	(10,216.2)	0	(10,216.2)	0
1/1998	(6,732.0)	3,034.4	(8,160.2)	1,616.4	(10,200.4)	0	(10,200.4)	0
1/1999	(6,720.5)	3,034.4	(8,146.2)	1,616.4	(10,183.0)	0	(10,183.0)	0
1/2000	(6,705.6)	1,517.2	(8,129.6)	1,616.4	15,520.2	34,000.0	(10,163.9)	0
1/2001	(7,414.3)	0	(8,988.8)	1,616.4	(7,414.3)	0	(11,238.0)	0
1/2002	(8,178.7)	0	(9,913.9)	1,616.4	(8,178.7)	0	(12,392.8)	0
1/2003	(8,193.8)	0	(9,932.2)	1,616.4	(8,193.8)	0	(12,415.6)	0

1/2004	(8,091.4)	0	(9,808.2)	1,616.4	(8,091.4)	0	(12,260.9)	0
1/2005	(8,055.8)	0	(9,765.2)	808.2	(8,055.8)	0	(12,207.2)	0
1/2006	(8,024.6)	0	(9,727.4)	0	(8,024.6)	0	(12,159.9)	0
1/2007	(7,990.2)	0	(9,685.7)	0	(7,990.2)	0	(12,107.9)	0
1/2008	(15,278.5)	0	(46,730.4)	0	(38,326.6)	0	(79,416.1)	0
1/2009	605.6	0	678.6	0	2,622.7	0	0	0
1/2010	432.6	0	651.5	0	1,873.3	0	0	0
1/2011	309.0	0	627.8	0	1,338.1	0	0	0
1/2012	220.7	0	607.1	0	955.8	0	0	0
1/2013	220.7	0	597.4	0	955.8	0	0	0
1/2014	220.7	0	597.4	0	955.8	0	0	0
1/2015	110.4	0	597.4	0	477.9	0	0	0
Total	$(118,917.0)	$(66,000.0)	$(170,579.7)	$(80,000.0)	$(134,905.3)	$(66,000.0)	$(239,691.8)	$(100,000.0)
Defeasance deposit	$71,713,150		$86,916,020		$78,691,900		$100,000,000	
Break-even residual	$7,273,279		$36,960,291		$31,497,957		$66,787,818	

Note: Dollars in thousands.

  The company purchases the asset at the end of the lease for the break-even residual in the lease side of the analysis, after which it depreciates the asset assuming seven-year MACRS. Note that in scenario 4, the company is assumed to be nontaxpayer forever; therefore, there is no value to the depreciation benefits available upon such purchase.

is treated as a known amount for calculations made with respect to the lease option. Given the defeasance deposit amount ($71,173,150) and the monthly after-tax cash flows resulting from the periodic lease payments, the break-even future residual value of the leased asset can be calculated. The calculation of the break-even residual takes into account that upon purchase of the asset at the end of the lease term, the company starts depreciating the asset using seven-year MACRS with the initial tax basis equal to the purchase price, thus receiving the tax benefits from depreciation at the 34 percent rate. Therefore, there are further cash inflows after the purchase of the asset at the end of the lease, representing tax reductions generated by depreciation. In scenario 2, the analysis for the forever AMT payer is the same as that for the forever regular taxpayer except for the following:

1. The value of depreciation tax benefits for the buy option is less in scenario 2 owing to the lower tax rate (i.e., 20 percent as opposed to 34 percent).

2. The depreciation schedule is a 12-year rather than a 7-year schedule as a result of the AMT rules.

3. The value of depreciation tax benefits for the lease option upon purchase of the asset at the end of the lease term is less in scenario 2 for the very same reason as described in items 1 and 2.

4. The after-tax cost of the periodic lease rental payments is higher owing to the lower tax rate.

Therefore, given less tax benefits offsetting the intial cash outflow, the intial defeasance deposit required in scenario 2 is $86,916,020 (which is greater than that in scenario 1). The break-even residual of $36,960,291 is also higher than that in scenario 1 because the changed tax rate and depreciation schedule have a greater impact on the defeasance deposit than on the cost of leasing.

In scenario 3, unlike scenarios 1 and 2, the NOL/regular taxpayer in the buy option will not be able to use the depreciation tax benefits in the initial seven years owing to NOLs. The value of the depreciation tax benefits will only be used when the company becomes taxable at 34 percent in the eight year. For simplicity, assume that the company could use up 100 percent of the value of the deferred depreciation tax benefits in the eighth year alone. (However, in all likelihood, the company would be able to use the benefits in installments over time.) The result is a defeasance deposit equal to $79,691,900. In the lease option, also owing to the company's NOL situation, the periodic lease rental payments will not generate tax reductions on a current basis for the first seven years. The value of the deferred tax reductions associated with the periodic lease rental payments will not be used until the company becomes taxable at 34 percent in the eighth year. As in the case of the buy option, 100 percent of the value of the tax reductions associated with the periodic lease rental payments was assumed to be taken in the eighth year. (The positive figure in 2000 in the lease option after-tax cash flows in Figure 7-8 represents the value of the deferred tax benefits associated with periodic lease rental payments for the first seven years offsetting the current rental expense in the eighth year). In the years after the company becomes a 34 percent taxpayer, the company will receive the same amount of tax benefits generated by the periodic rental payments as in scenario 1. The depreciation tax benefits associated with the purchase of the asset at the end of the lease, however, will be different from those in scenario 1 because of the different breakeven residual amount. The result is a break-even residual of $31,497,957.

In scenario 4, the forever nontaxpayer will not be able to use any tax benefits; therefore, in effect, the lease-versus-buy analysis will be a pretax analysis. In the buy option, the company will have the initial outflow of $100 million with no ensuing cash inflow that represents tax benefits from depreciation. In the lease option, the company will make periodic lease rental payments as well as a payment to purchase the asset at the end of the lease term without receiving the tax benefits from depreciation associated with the purchased asset. Therefore, the initial defeasance deposit in this scenario is equal to the asset cost. The break-even residual is the highest in this scenario ($66,787,818), thus making leasing undoubtedly more advantageous than buying.

As can be seen in the cash flows presented in Figure 7-8, the after-tax cash flows vary with differing assumptions of the lessee's tax-paying position. Although not visible from the figure, the lessee's tax payments on interest earned on the defeasance deposit and ability to use tax benefits on any borrowed amounts incurred in the defeasance deposit calculation also vary with the lessee's tax-paying position. Because of these factors, the break-even residual value varies.

The following are the results of the example of the break-even residual lease-versus-buy analysis in four different scenarios of the lessee tax position assuming that the lessee intends to purchase the asset at the end of the lease term:

Lessee's Tax Position	Break-Even Residual Value (as percentage of asset cost)
Example 1: Forever regular (34%) taxpayer	7.27
Example 2: Forever AMT (20%) payer	36.96
Example 3: Nontaxpayer for the first 7 years (NOL carryforwards) and regular taxpayer thereafter	31.50
Example 4: Forever nontaxpayer	66.79

As is evident, the break-even residual is lowest when the company is a full taxpayer and greatest when the company is a nontaxpayer. These break-even residual amounts represent the amount that the lessee can pay at the end of the lease term for the asset and be indifferent between leasing and buying. If the value of the asset at the end of the lease term is higher than the break-even residual amount, the asset should not be leased. As can be seen, when the lessee is expected to be a regular taxpayer, the buy is usually the better alternative, and when the company is expected to be other than a regular taxpayer, the lease is a relatively more attractive alternative.

Therefore, if the company expects the fair market value of the asset to be, e.g., 40 percent of the original asset cost at the end of the lease term, the company that is expected to be a regular taxpayer throughout the analysis period should buy the asset, take depreciation benefits of the asset over time, and retain the asset or, if it so desires, sell the asset for 40 percent. On the other hand, the company that is expected to be a nontaxpayer throughout the analysis period should lease the asset and, if it so desires, purchase the asset for 40 percent at the end of the lease. The company that is expected to be either the scenario 2 taxpayer or the scenario 3 taxpayer has a more difficult decision. It must be remembered that the lease-versus-buy analysis is only a tool in the decision-making process and is dependent on the many assumptions that were made in its development.

[3] Who Should Lease?

Based on the lease-versus-buy analyses described, companies most likely to be lessees in tax-oriented leases include the following:

- A company that currently owns equipment and is not generating sufficient income to offset depreciation generated from such equipment

- A start-up company that requires a heavy capital expenditure on equipment and does not expect to generate sufficient income to use depreciation benefits generated from such equipment efficiently

- A company that has accumulated a substantial amount of NOLs and cannot use such NOLs on a current basis

- A company that is acquiring equipment and expects to generate NOLs or be an AMT payer for an extended period.

[4] Lessee Lease Accounting

From an accounting point of view, most lessees are concerned with whether the lease is classified as an operating lease (and is therefore off balance sheet) or a capital lease (and is therefore on balance sheet) in accordance with SFAS No. 13. Whether the lease is a leveraged lease or a single-investor lease does not make any difference to lessees for accounting purposes.

Operating lease treatment for the lessee provides that the lessee does not record depreciation deductions relating to the asset and does not carry the physical asset on its balance sheet but periodically records rental expense on the profit and loss statement. Capital lease treatment for the lessee, on the other hand, provides that the lessee books the leased property under the capital lease (as adjusted for accumulated depreciation) and the obligation under the capital lease on its balance sheet and periodically records interest expense and depreciation expense on the profit and loss statement. Just as lessors prefer capital lease treatment, lessees prefer an operating lease for the same reasons: off-balance sheet treatment and a more favorable profit and loss profile. The same lease, however, can be classified as an operating lease for the lessee and as a capital lease for the lessor, thus providing both parties with favorable accounting results.

The other major issue for lessees under SFAS No. 13 relates to the amount of the rental expense recorded in each year after the operating lease determination has been made. In cases where the annual rent payments made by the lessee are not equal, SFAS No. 13 provides that for accounting purposes, they must be leveled "unless another systematic and rational basis is more representative of the time pattern in which use benefit is derived from the leased property." As can be seen in the rent schedule in Figure 7-7, the majority of market rent schedules are not level and are typically back-loaded. This occurs because lessors generally structure the rents to minimize their present value to the lessee. Back-loading the rent back-loads the recognition of taxable income by the lessor, thereby increasing the tax deferral in the lease and permitting a lower present value of rents. Because lessors optimize their rents in accordance with the guideline with respect to uneven rents, there are limits to the back-loading benefit. Optimized rents, therefore, typically vary within the range of 90 percent and 110 percent of the average rents during the lease term. In an operating lease, if rents are not level, lessees are required to prorate aggregate rents over the lease term (that is, an annual accounting expense equals the aggregate rents divided by the number of years in the lease term). The results of this rule, therefore, is that accounting rent expense often exceeds cash rent payments in the early years of the lease.

There is an accounting concern that only relates to lessees in sale-leaseback transactions involving real estate. A sale-leaseback transaction is a common practice in which the owner of the asset sells the asset to a lessor and leases it back. Companies contemplating a sale-leaseback transaction usually want to account for the leaseback as an operating lease. If the asset does not involve real estate, sale-leaseback transactions are solely governed by SFAS No. 13. The accounting for transactions involving real estate, however, is also governed by SFAS No. 98. For this purpose, the term "real estate" is interpreted very broadly and includes not only land and buildings but also anything that is, practically speaking, permanently attached to land or a building. For example, it is not practical to move a power plant and therefore a power plant is classified as real estate for accounting purposes.

SFAS No. 98 prohibits operating lease accounting (off-balance sheet financing) when a company that sells and leases back assets involving real estate retains substantial benefits and risks of the property being sold or has an interest in the property that continues after the lease term. If, in such a sale-leaseback, the seller/lessee has any type of purchase option, whether it is for fair market value or a fixed price, the lessee is not entitled to account for the transaction as an operating lease. Since most companies that contemplate sale-leaseback transactions desire to treat the transactions off balance sheet, this is a very important issue. Structures and techniques have been developed for lessees wishing to retain the benefits of a purchase option and accomplish their accounting goals that are beyond the scope of this chapter.

7.05 FACILITY LEASING

Another lease-structuring alternative available to the lessee is a facility lease. A facility is a property that consists of a group of items that function together as an integrated unit and are not intended for independent, commercial operation. For example, all of the items of equipment included in any assembly line can be viewed as a facility. When comparing equipment leasing with facility leasing, there are several issues of which the company should be aware.

[1] Lease Term and Economics

In an equipment lease, the lease term is based on the equipment's economic useful life. In a facility lease, the lease term is based on the facility's economic useful life. Typically, the overall facility has a longer economic useful life than some of its components. In general, the longer the lease term is, the better the lease economics are for the lessee. Therefore, the facility lease may provide the lessee with better economics.

[2] Administrative Burdens

The single facility lease, as opposed to a series of equipment leases, also imposes fewer administrative burdens on the lessee, which will be required to perform obligations under only one lease.

[3] Limited-Use Property

Certain components of a facility, if viewed as individual assets being leased, would constitute limited-use property and would not be eligible for an equipment lease. However, when such assets are included as part of a facility, they become financeable through a facility lease, because the facility as a whole is not limited-use property. An example is a component whose installed value is high but whose value when removed is negligible, either because the item is destroyed by removal or because any reinstallation cost is high relative to the value of the removed asset. As a separate item, the asset would not be leasable because it would be uneconomic for anyone other than the operator of the facility to use the component since it cannot economically be moved. However, because a facility could generally be used by many different operators, the component may be leased if it is included as part of a leased facility. The installation costs may also be included as part of the original cost of the facility.

[4] Economic Obsolescence

Most equipment leases permit the lessee to terminate the lease by paying an amount equal to termination value in the event that the leased equipment becomes economically obsolete. Unfortunately, such a termination may prove onerous and less cost efficient than if the lessee had not entered into the lease. As a practical matter, it is often easier to replace an obsolete component of a facility without the risk of adverse tax consequences than an item of equipment subject to a separate lease. Therefore, a facility lease provides the lessee with more operating and financing flexibility.

[5] Improvements and Modifications

Although issues relating to modifications and improvements are not unique to facility leases, they take on a heightened significance. Because of the longer term of the lease and because a facility is a more complex asset than individual items, it is more likely that an improvement or modification will be made to the leased asset in the case of a facility lease than in the case of a lease of an individual item. The IRS Guidelines contain relatively specific rules governing the lessee's financing of improvements to leased assets. According to the Guidelines, the lessee is allowed to make ordinary "maintenance and repairs" that are required under the lease. The difference between a repair and an improvement is sometimes difficult to ascertain because the determination is based on facts and circumstances. In general, repair is intended to maintain the property in good operating condition and does not add value to the property nor extend its economically useful life, while an improvement adds value to the property and may extend its economically useful life.

The Guidelines allow the lessee to make an improvement which is readily removable without causing material damage to the leased asset (severable improvements).

The Guidelines also allow the lessee to make an improvement that is not readily removable without causing material damage to the property (nonseverable improvements), provided

(1) At the commencement of the lease, no Nonseverable Improvement is required in order to complete the property for its intended use by the lessee;

(2) The furnishing of the cost of the Nonseverable Improvement does not constitute an "equity investment" by the lessee;

(3) The Nonseverable Improvement does not cause the leased property to become "limited use property"; *and*

(4) (x) The Nonseverable Improvement is furnished in order to comply with health, safety, or environmental standards of any government or governmental authority having relevant jurisdiction; *or*

    (y) The Nonseverable Improvement does not:

        (a) substantially increase the productivity of the leased property over its productivity when first placed in service by more than 25%;

        (b) substantially increase the capacity of the leased property over its capacity when first placed in service by more than 25%; or

        (c) modify the leased property for a materially different use; *or*

    (z) The cost of such Nonseverable Improvement (together with previously made Nonseverable Improvements other than these described in clause (x) above) does not exceed 10% of the original cost of the property.

As a practical matter, most of the improvements that the lessee makes may be characterized as severable improvements. Generally, lessees also refrain from making nonseverable improvements because such improvements become the lessor's property, and the lessee ends up paying twice for nonseverable improvements when it exercises a purchase option on the leased property at the end of the lease. In the event that the lessee cannot avoid making nonseverable improvements, those improvements more easily meet the criteria for permitted nonseverable improvements in the facility lease because of the size of the original cost of the property involved in the facility lease. This provides the lessee with more operating flexibility. In addition, although the lessee may be required to indemnify the lessor for adverse federal income tax consequences of making improvements, the actual federal income tax consequences to the lessor will be governed by the relevant case law, which may be less restrictive than the Guidelines.

7.06 PROJECT FINANCING

The terms "project financing" and "lease financing" are often used as if they were mutually exclusive. In fact and in practice, they are not. Lease financing refers to a legal-accounting structure rather than a credit structure. Project financing, in its purest form, is the antithesis of credit-based financing. Credit-based financing involves the corporate credit of the sponsor, the strength of its balance sheet, and the pledge of corporate cash flow to meet its obligations as a lessee in a lease or as a borrower under a credit agreement. A pure project financing, often referred to as nonrecourse financing, relies entirely on the project economics, contractual arrangements, and resulting cash flows as security for the financing. Should the project fail to generate sufficient cash flow to service the financing, the creditors cannot look to the credit of the project sponsor as a source of repayment. A failure to meet obligations can lead only to foreclose on the project assets and contracts.

Because the project sponsor does not assume the risks associated with a particular project, the key to a successful project financing is the allocation of risks to the various project participants through contractual arrangements. The financing provider evaluates the quality of these various contractual obligations. The typical project risks that are allocated among the participants relate to the construction of the facility, the contracts that are the source of the operating revenues, the procurement of fuel or other raw materials, the operation of the facility, and appropriate insurance arrangements. Thus, each project participant assumes risks appropriate to its role in the transaction. Occasionally, depending largely on the nature of the contractual arrangements for a particular business, the project sponsor might be called on to provide some additional security in support of the financing.

Historically, most projects were developed by small, private concerns, and the financing structure accordingly reflected their requirements and concerns. Financings for projects have been structured as partnerships between project developers and tax-oriented equity investors. Partnerships borrow from sophisticated long-term lenders the amount equal to the difference between the project cost and equity investment. The disadvantage of the partnership structure is that often accounting losses are recorded by the equity investors and project developers. Today, project developers tend to be major corporations that care about the accounting impact of a financing. Accordingly, many of these project developers are seeking ways to minimize accounting losses generated by partnership structures and are more frequently using lease financing to meet this objective. Tax-oriented equity investors have also recognized the favorable accounting effect of leasing in a project finance transaction.

The most common use of leasing in project financing has been in the energy field, where long-term contracts for the sale of energy output can be arranged with utilities or other users. Other applications of leasing to project financing include mining, paper pulp production, and other capital-intensive businesses, as well as commercial real estate.

7.07 CONCLUSION

Leasing is defined by complex sets of accounting and tax rules and may involve sophisticated economic analysis. It is, however, one of the most common financing methods available for a variety of assets in the United States and can provide very attractive financing for appropriately situated companies. Leasing has also been one of the most attractive investments available for equity investors.

Occasionally, the accounting profession considers overhauling the rules governing lease accounting for both lessors and lessees and from time to time has made some interpretative changes. Changing the rules with respect to lessees tends to have only a small impact on the number of transactions consummated, since the primary motivation of most lessees is economics, not accounting. Some rule changes affecting lessors, however, could have a significant impact on the supply of lease financing. For example, most current lessors would refuse to enter into leases if the expected result was that they would incur accounting losses in some years. To date, however, the accounting profession has not been willing to propose such significant changes affecting lessor accounting. Furthermore, because of the widespread impact on lessors and lessees alike and the possible economic impact on many capital-intensive industries, most market participants believe that such changes are likely to be politically opposed and will not happen any time soon.

Tax law changes can also significantly affect the volume and number of transactions. Except for the brief period during which TBTs and finance leases were permitted, the U.S. tax laws governing leasing have generally remained consistent. The basic leasing guidelines have been in place for more than 15 years. However, some tax law changes have affected the leasing market. For the most part, these changes have affected the tax benefits associated with particular assets (i.e., different depreciation schemes and investment credits), the value of the benefits (i.e., tax rate changes), and the increase in value that can be obtained by transferring the benefits (e.g., AMT). These types of tax law changes tend to be cyclical in nature, stimulating leasing activity at the same time as capital expenditures are stimulated. Even in the bottom part of the cycle, however, the leasing market has remained a very important source of capital and has adjusted to such tax law changes by prompting innovations in lease structures and/or reconfiguration of the equity investor base. As long as there are companies that cannot efficiently use the tax benefits of ownership on a current basis and companies that are profitable and seek efficient tax shelters and deferral and residual upside, there will be a leasing market, which will evolve around changing tax, economic, and accounting environments.

Chapter 8

Project Financing

RONALD A. ZANONI

JAMES F. LYNCH

8.01 INTRODUCTION

A growing number of companies are turning to project financing to fund capital equipment investments. A properly structured project financing undertaking may permit not only off-balance sheet financing but also off-credit financing. Risk allocation can also be facilitated through project financing (although it must be remembered that while passive investors,[1] which frequently supply the bulk of the capital, are prepared to assume some credit risks, they are reluctant to assume operating and other risks not premised on the ability of the parties to meet their financial obligations). Thus, in all but a few project financings, a reasonably complete network of credit support arrangements is required before financing can be consummated.

For the purposes of this chapter, "project financing" is defined as financing in which the value of the assets being financed and/or the contractual arrangements involved provide a major source of credit support. In other words, project sponsors do not commit their full corporate credit to support outside investors in the project but instead assume limited financial exposure in the event of project failure.

Although a number of business, legal, tax, accounting, and other questions must be addressed in the evaluation of potential project financing, the sponsors must make two fundamental decisions:

1. Should a project financing vehicle be employed and, if so, what type? Since the object is often to distance the project's financial obligations from the project's sponsors, a special-purpose vehicle is frequently used. The vehicle may take any one of several organizational forms (e.g., corporate, partnership, and trust). Tax effects, accounting objectives, risk allocations, and protection from unlimited liability are all considerations that will determine which form is employed.

2. What credit support arrangements should be put in place to provide financing with sufficient substance to attract the necessary capital? Rarely will the value of the assets alone be sufficient to support financing. Almost always, the sponsors and others will enter into contractual arrangements that, when taken together, assure the project of the necessary cash flow. The art of project finance lies in the design of these credit support arrangements.

8.02 CAPITAL SOURCES

[1] Analysis of Cogeneration Facility

To illustrate what is typically involved in developing a project financing package, a basic case is presented here that includes many of the elements commonly found when project financing for a cogeneration facility is put together. Cogeneration is a focal point for project financing. In fact, cogeneration, which is the sequential use of steam to produce electricity and thermally useful energy, has a long history in this country. As a result of federal legislation and implementing regulations, the number of cogeneration projects has increased and the electrical power industry has become much more competitive.

---

[1] Passive investors (which may be either equity or debt investors in a project) are those interested only in receiving a return on their investment, such as insurance companies purchasing the project's secured notes. Active investors are those that have a business interest beyond earning a stated return on investment, such as a vendor that expects to provide equipment to the project.

Engineering Company, a hypothetical firm in the basic case, is experienced in the design and construction of energy projects. Engineering Company has found (as have many of its competitors) that in order to obtain engineering assignments, it is required to make equity investments in projects and even to assume some responsibility for operations following the construction period. Unfortunately, Engineering Company has only limited capital to invest and may also be hampered by its inability to use all of the tax benefits that may be associated with ownership of cogeneration equipment fully and efficiently. (Under current law, these tax benefits include the right to claim accelerated depreciation, usually 150 percent declining balance for cogeneration equipment, and interest expense deductions. Investment tax credits and energy tax credits have been eliminated pursuant to the Tax Reform Act of 1986.) In addition, as a public company, Engineering Company is concerned with the accounting implications of its investment and is anxious to limit its credit exposure in any transaction. In this case, Engineering Company has approached Steam Host, another hypothetical firm, with a proposal to install a cogeneration facility at Steam Host's plant.

Steam Host manufactures chemical products at the plant involved. Two aged, gas-fired steam boilers have provided Steam Host with its process steam since the plant was placed into commercial operation in the 1950s. Utility, in whose service territory Steam Host's plant is located, has supplied the plant's electricity requirements to date. Engineering Company has proposed that the existing boilers be replaced with a cogeneration facility consisting of new gas-fired turbine-generator equipment. All of the steam would be supplied to Steam Host at a cost significantly below its current energy expenditures. In addition, the electricity would be sold to Utility. In its response to Engineering Company, Steam Host identified the following as its principal objectives:

1. It wants no responsibility for providing funding for the project; it is prepared, however, to provide the site for the cogeneration facilities at a nominal rent.

2. It is not prepared to enter into a steam purchase contract with a term longer than 10 years.

3. It wants its purchase obligation limited to a take-if-tendered arrangement; in other words, Steam Host does not want to be obligated to pay if, for any reason, steam is not supplied by the project.

4. It wants the flexibility to reduce its purchase commitment, although it is willing to commit to take and use enough steam to maintain the project's qualification under the Public Utilities Regulatory Policies Act (PURPA).[2]

[2] Active Equity Capital

Utility is a medium-sized, investor-owned electric utility company that has announced its willingness to enter into power purchase contracts with PURPA-qualified cogenerators. As is true of a number of such companies, Utility has organized a nonregulated subsidiary to serve as a vehicle for diversification investments. Utility cogeneration affiliates have become increasingly significant forces in the unregulated power market.

---

[2] This federal legislation exempts qualified cogeneration projects from regulation as public utilities and requires utilities to purchase electricity from qualified projects at the utility's avoided cost. "Avoided cost" is defined as the utility's marginal cost to produce electricity. A minimum steam usage is required to maintain the project's qualification under PURPA.

Investments in cogeneration projects are viewed as a way of redeploying assets into projects that have many of the same operational characteristics as the utility's plants while permitting more generous returns than are obtainable in regulated activities. Utility, therefore, is prepared to invest up to one half of the required equity (which is the current regulatory limit for such investments) in attractive cogeneration projects but will assume no direct responsibility for the repayment of the project's debt and insists on off-balance sheet treatment for the financing. It is and expects in the near future to be a full taxpayer; thus, it could use any available tax benefits more efficiently than Engineering Company. Utility is also interested in operating the facility, especially since it expects to provide base load generation.

Natural Gas Company has found itself with surplus gas supplies and is anxious to develop a market for them. By offering to participate in Engineering Company's project as an equity investor, it seeks to obtain a firm 10-year gas supply contract. Natural Gas Company is also concerned about the accounting treatment of its investment and is unwilling to take recourse responsibility for the project's debt. Natural Gas Company will benefit from participating in the project by securing a long-term customer for its gas and receiving its share of any available tax benefits.

Although Engineering Company, Utility, and Natural Gas Company will supply the active equity capital, other active equity investors also can be located. For example, additional equity might come from equipment vendors, companies interested in being awarded the construction contract, and transportation companies, i.e., virtually any type of firm that might profit from a direct business relationship with the project or from earning a relatively larger return associated with accepting the greater risk in the project's construction period. Such companies are generally prepared to invest (and thereby assume risk) in the early stages of a project's development. In one way or another, they provide the seed money that carries the project to the point where passive investors may commit funds. Generally, this is the point where a project has gained sufficient definition so that the equity investment's profitability and risk exposure can be clearly articulated. Passive equity sources are usually approached when the design engineering is well advanced, the major permits and the purchase power contracts are in hand, and the project sponsors are close to beginning procurement.

[3] Passive Equity Capital

Passive institutional investors, which seek investment opportunities with higher yields than those obtainable from alternative investments, provide capital for a range of financial and business enterprises. For example, finance companies have long been a source of such capital, although many of their investments are structured in a leasing format. The appetites of these companies for projects ebb and flow over time, depending on factors such as the profitability of the parent's core business and the status of the finance company's investment portfolio. Today, the unregulated subsidiaries of utility companies have also become quite active in seeking investments in alternative energy projects, and these power company affiliates are rapidly becoming the key institutional equity investors for cogeneration projects. As a result of the tax law changes that forced limited partnerships to be driven by economics rather than tax benefits, other passive institutional investors, such as insurance companies and pension funds, are taking an increased interest in cogeneration projects.

8.03 PROJECT FINANCING VEHICLE

If the three active equity investors—Engineering Company, Utility, and Natural Gas Company—structured their investments on an undivided interest basis, this would mean that each sponsor would be responsible for directly funding its share of the total project. Accordingly, sponsors frequently employ a project financing vehicle that owns the project and secures the financing. The form of the vehicle is determined by a number of legal, tax, and accounting issues.

[1] Corporation

Using a corporate vehicle has a number of advantages. The principles with respect to equity method accounting are clearly established.[3]

As long as each company has less than a majority interest and does not control the corporation through contractual arrangements, its investment is carried on a net basis (cost method of accounting for investments in subsidiaries) with no balance sheet recognition of project debt. Furthermore, the sponsors' status as shareholders may offer the best assurance that their exposure to liability for project debt and for such events as industrial accidents will be limited to their stock investments. However, the corporate vehicle has a major disadvantage when a project has substantial tax benefits: It is a taxpayer. Since no sponsor can consolidate a project corporation for tax purposes,[4] it cannot use a project's tax benefits to shelter its nonproject taxable income. Consequently, tax benefits can be effectively realized only to the extent that a project corporation can generate sufficient taxable income to absorb them. For this reason, multiparty projects are rarely structured in a project corporation format.

[2] General Partnership

A more common approach is the use of a general partnership format,[5] in which each sponsor indirectly, through a special purpose subsidiary, holds a general partnership interest. Properly structured, a general partnership vehicle is a pass-through for tax benefits. In other words, the partnership does not trap the benefits at the partnership level, but permits partners to take their pro rata shares indirectly. Thus, the partners need not wait until the project partnership generates sufficient taxable income from

---

[3] Generally accepted accounting principles affecting consolidation of related entities and equity method accounting are primarily set forth in Accounting Research Bulletin (ARB) No. 51, Accounting Principles Board Opinion (APB) No. 18, and Financial Accounting Standards Board Statement No. 94.

[4] Internal Revenue Code Section 1501 permits an affiliated group of corporations to file a consolidated federal income tax return in lieu of separate returns. But under Section 1504(a), as amended, a corporation is not considered a member of an affiliated group unless 80 percent of its total stock value (common and preferred) and at least 80 percent of the total voting power of its stock (common and preferred) is held within the group. Nonvoting preferred stock is excluded from consideration in the foregoing 80 percent tests only if it is nonconvertible, limited, and preferred with regard to redemptions and liquidations as well as dividends.

[5] The use of a grantor trust vehicle, not discussed in this chapter, is frequently employed in lease financing where the ownership is vested in parties other than the user of the asset. A trust is, in many ways, similar to a general partnership with respect to its tax characteristics.

its own operations to employ the project's tax benefits (as is the case with a corporate format). Although the applicability of equity method accounting is not as clear in the partnership format, the proposition that a general partner need record only the net investment on the balance sheet has support in accounting literature.[6] The principal difficulty with the general partnership vehicle is the legal principle that general partners have unlimited liability for partnership obligations. Accordingly, when a general partnership vehicle is chosen, it is wise for sponsors not to hold the general partnership interest directly. Rather, they should each organize a special-purpose subsidiary to hold that interest so that only the subsidiary's assets are exposed. This arrangement permits the pass-through of tax benefits to the sponsor level, since each sponsor can consolidate its subsidiary for tax purposes. Even though each subsidiary is also consolidated for accounting purposes, the project debt does not show on the subsidiary's balance sheet, since the subsidiary is employing equity method accounting for its partnership investment.

[3] Limited Partnership

Experience proves that the limited partnership format generally offers the most advantages for these types of investments. Off-balance sheet accounting, limited liability, and the efficient allocation of tax benefits can all be effectively realized if this vehicle is properly employed. In addition, a limited partnership interest is one that can be marketed at a later time to new investors that might be unwilling to take a general partnership position. In the Engineering Company case, where preliminary engineering and licensing are to be performed in the first 6 months and actual construction is to take place over the next 18 months, a project sponsor has a real need for the greater flexibility offered by a limited partnership. In 2 years, a sponsor's tax position or the tax laws may change, and it may wish to transfer its interest to a new investor that can make better use of the project's benefits. Further, once a project nears completion, its economic value increases, since the construction period risks are diminished. Thus, a project sponsor may be in a position to dispose of all or part of its interest at a price that exceeds its book value investment and thus realize a premium from the value added by the successful completion of construction. This can mean an immediate boost in earnings per share and also provide capital that can be used for other projects. For all of these reasons, the limited partnership is frequently the preferred project financing vehicle.

In the Engineering Company case, Cogeneration Company, a limited partnership project financing vehicle, was employed. Engineering Company, Utility, and Natural Gas Company (collectively the General Partners and individually a General Partner) would indirectly hold general partnership interests in Cogeneration Company through wholly owned subsidiaries. Utility, Natural Gas Company, and Passive Equity (collectively the Limited Partners and individually a Limited Partner) would directly hold the limited partnership interests issued by Cogeneration Company. Figure 8-1 illustrates these ownership arrangements. The remainder of Cogeneration Company's capital structure would consist of 10-year fixed-rate debt capital.

---

[6] See, e.g., American Institute of Certified Public Accountants Interpretation No. 2 of APB No. 18.

FIGURE 8-1

Ownership Arrangements of Cogeneration Company

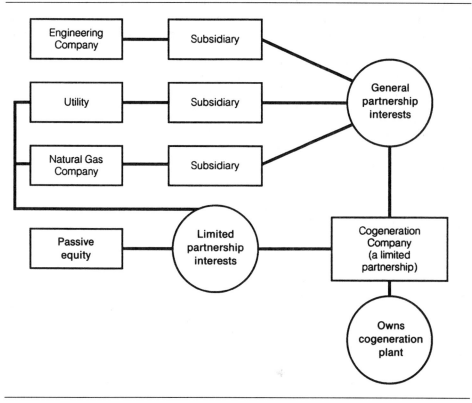

8.04 CREDIT SUPPORT NETWORK

Cogeneration Company has no real economic substance of its own. Although it owns the project while the project is under construction and in operation and the related equipment has some economic value, such value is not sufficient to support the debt investment required. Consequently, Cogeneration Company will rely heavily on contractual arrangements to provide a credit support network. Investors will review the project in its totality to be certain that there are no gaps in the contractual arrangements that would raise the risk of project failure to an unacceptable level. The project's risk profile is determined by different elements during construction and operation, but generally certain contractual arrangements are essential to obtain funding commitments from passive investors.

[1] Engineering and Construction Contract

The reputation of Engineering Company is critical. If the company has an excellent track record in the cogeneration area, lenders give greater credence to its projections.

Many project financings involve lump-sum, fixed-price contractual undertakings by developers such as Engineering Company. Frequently, these undertakings are further supported by performance bonds provided by insurance companies to augment or protect Engineering Company's balance sheet. The floating interest cost normally associated with the construction loan poses a further risk with regard to fixing in advance the total project cost. In the past, this risk was covered by building a contingency into the cost projection so that if the floating rate was 11 percent at the time of the initial borrowing, the project's guaranteed price might be calculated using a cost of construction funds several hundred basis points higher. Since many of these transactions are competitively bid, too high a projected interest cost might cause a bidder to lose the contract. Even where the construction lender insists on a floating rate, it is possible to fix the rate through the judicious use of interest rate hedging programs employing financial futures contracts. In this way, a contractor is in a position to reduce substantially interest rate risk when quoting a fixed-price, lump-sum contract.

[2] Vendor and Other Warranties

Once construction has been completed, investors have another fear: Suppose the switch is turned on and the project does not operate on an acceptable basis? This technological risk is ordinarily covered by a combination of vendor warranties, performance guarantees included in the construction contract, and, on occasion, efficacy insurance. In the case of Cogeneration Company, gas-fired combined cycle turbine technology is involved. This technology is well proven (there are hundreds of such facilities operating worldwide) and relatively free of technical risks. Consequently, standard warranties suffice. Where less-proven technology is involved, investors would insist on more extensive protection. If the perceived technological risk is too high, it may be impossible to finance a project without the sponsors' committing their full corporate credit. It is with first-of-a-kind technology that the concept of project financing may not be feasible.

[3] Natural Gas Supply Contract

Fuel is the project's largest operating cost item, representing 82.5 percent of cash operating expenses in the first year of full production. Under the gas supply contract, Natural Gas Company commits to provide the project with its fuel requirements at a price structured to limit the risk that operating costs may exceed operating revenues. This does not mean a flat gas price. Instead, under the supply contract, the cost of gas is adjusted to maintain a stated relationship to the price charged for the project's prime source of revenues, which is electricity sales. From the investors' perspective, the gas supply contract removes the risk that project operations (and therefore project cash flow) might be interrupted by the inability to obtain fuel at an acceptable price.

[4] Steam Supply Contract

Under this contract, Cogeneration Company agrees to supply Steam Host with a stated quantity of steam, meeting minimum criteria, at a stated price. The project's economics are relatively insensitive to the revenues realized from steam sales (that is, steam sales provide less than 6 percent of total revenues in the first full year of operation). Consequently, it is not essential to fix the escalation of the steam price. In order to secure the project assignment, Engineering Company's initial proposal to Steam Host calls for a steam price linked to movements in the Producer Price Index (PPI). There is another risk, however, which all parties may not be prepared to accept: the risk that the project might lose its PURPA qualification. To protect against this risk, Steam Host commits to use a certain amount of the project's steam production, or to cause another company to use it, over the 10-year contract. In a number of cases, a company in Steam Host's position insists on the ability to terminate the steam supply contract. This is acceptable, but only if Steam Host is prepared to pay a termination charge sufficient to protect the equity and debt investors' return.

[5] Power Sale Agreement

This is the critical revenue production item. For Cogeneration Company, power sales will provide 94.5 percent of the revenue stream in the first full year of production. As mentioned earlier, PURPA requires utilities to purchase the power production of qualified cogenerators at avoided cost. Some states have sought to encourage cogeneration by fostering attractive avoided cost pricing and have even published standard offer contracts that cogenerators can employ. More commonly, the power purchase contract is a negotiated arrangement with the utility involved. Cogeneration Company has negotiated an acceptable power purchase contract; its principal terms and conditions are as follows:

1. *Term*. 10 years.

2. *Quantity to be purchased*. Utility is obligated to purchase up to 1.8 million megawatt-hours per year, under a predetermined schedule, subject to availability.

3. *Price*. The price is strictly an energy charge; there is no capacity payment involved. The energy charge is $39.50 per megawatt-hour delivered.

4. *Utility's purchase obligation*. Utility's obligation is in the nature of a take-if-tendered commitment; in other words, if electric power meeting contract specifications were not tendered, Utility need not pay.

5. Standard force majeure provisions excuse nonperformance.

A number of other contractual arrangements are also commonplace. For example, Cogeneration Company enters into an agreement with Utility whereby Utility would act as operator of the project. Also, insurance policies covering contingent business interruption risks, casualty, personal liability, and so forth, are frequently required. The principal contractual relationships are illustrated in Figure 8-2.

8.05 PROJECT ECONOMIC ANALYSIS

For project financing to be viable, the project's cash flow must support the returns required by both debt and equity investors in the transaction. Since return on investment is generally commensurate with risk, equity investors command a higher return than lenders, and general partnership equity seeks a higher return than limited partnership equity. Logically, a project has two funding phases: (1) the construction period

FIGURE 8-2

Contractual Arrangements of Cogeneration Company

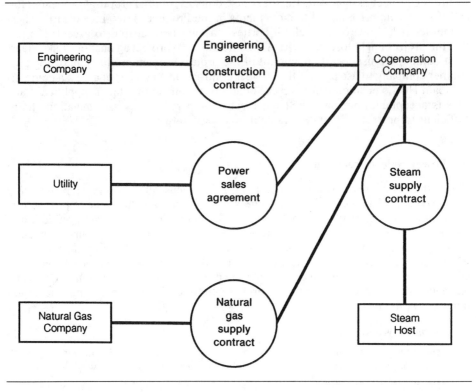

and (2) the operating period. Funding expenditures during the construction period are examined first. Then, three categories of permanent investment (debt, limited partnership equity, and general partnership equity), each with different risk character- istics and levels of return, are considered.

[1] Construction Period Analysis

The first step in evaluating a project's economic viability is to determine the project's all-in cost, or total project cost. This cost includes all hard (direct) costs, such as engineering, labor, and materials, and all soft (indirect) costs, such as financing-related charges (including interest and commitment fees) and the cost of financial guarantees or other credit support mechanisms.

    A construction drawdown schedule is usually supplied by the engineering firm that has designed the facility. For Cogeneration Company, the construction period, which includes a 6-month period for preliminary engineering and licensing and an 18-month physical construction period, is 2 years. Construction financing will be supplied by a commercial bank, which not only funds the construction costs but also funds the interest, fees, and other financing charges. Therefore, debt will fund 100 percent of

FIGURE 8-3

Total Project Cost

Month	Construction Drawdown	Commitment Fees	Interest	Total Financing Costs	Total Construction and Financing	Cumulative Funds Used	Unused Balance of Commitment
0	—	—	—	—	—	—	$110.00
1	$ 0.50	$0.05	$0.00	$0.05	$ 0.55	$ 0.55	109.45
2	0.50	0.05	0.00	0.05	0.55	1.10	108.90
3	0.50	0.05	0.01	0.05	0.55	1.65	108.35
4	0.50	0.05	0.01	0.06	0.56	2.21	107.79
5	0.50	0.04	0.02	0.06	0.56	2.77	107.23
6	0.50	0.04	0.02	0.07	0.57	3.34	106.66
7	1.50	0.04	0.03	0.07	1.57	4.91	105.09
8	2.00	0.04	0.04	0.08	2.08	7.00	103.00
9	2.00	0.04	0.06	0.10	2.10	9.10	100.90
10	2.00	0.04	0.08	0.12	2.12	11.22	98.78
11	4.00	0.04	0.09	0.13	4.13	15.35	94.65
12	4.00	0.04	0.13	0.17	4.17	19.52	90.48
13	5.00	0.04	0.16	0.20	5.20	24.72	85.28
14	5.50	0.04	0.21	0.24	5.74	30.46	79.54
15	6.00	0.03	0.25	0.29	6.29	36.75	73.25
16	8.00	0.03	0.31	0.34	8.34	45.08	64.92
17	10.00	0.03	0.38	0.40	10.40	55.49	54.51
18	11.00	0.02	0.46	0.49	11.49	66.97	43.03
19	9.00	0.02	0.56	0.58	9.58	76.55	33.45
20	8.00	0.01	0.64	0.65	8.65	85.20	24.80
21	7.00	0.01	0.71	0.72	7.72	92.92	17.08
22	6.50	0.01	0.77	0.78	7.28	100.20	9.80
23	3.50	0.00	0.84	0.84	4.34	104.54	5.46
24	2.00	0.00	0.87	0.87	2.87	107.41	2.59
Total	$100.00	$0.77	$6.65	$7.41	$107.41		

Note: Dollars in millions. Total hard costs = $100; commitment amount = $110; commitment fees = 0.5%; interest rate = 10%.

the cost during the construction period.[7] Construction period loans generally are made on a floating-rate basis, with the interest rate tied to industry standards, such as the commercial bank's cost of funds as evidenced by certificates of deposit or the London interbank offered rate.

It is important to ensure that the construction loan has sufficient capacity to provide funds for contingencies and fluctuations in interest rates. Since the construction loan requires the lender to pay fees that are tied to the size of the commitment, it is also wise not to oversize the construction loan, thereby unnecessarily increasing the financing charges.

Figure 8-3 shows a calculation of the total project cost given a construction draw-

---

[7] Sometimes lenders require a phase-in of equity during the construction period.

FIGURE 8-4

Sensitivity of Total Project Cost to Interest Rate

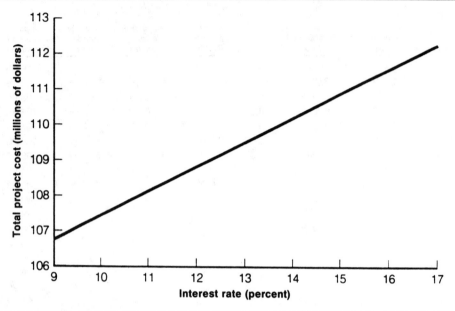

down schedule and an interest rate of 10 percent. Generally, construction loans are structured on a basis where interest is paid on funds that are drawn down and a commitment fee is charged on the unused balance of the commitment. The loan commitment has been sized so that it accommodates interest rates at a level of 14 percent throughout the construction period.

As Figure 8-4 shows, the total project is sensitive to the interest rate applicable during the construction period. If the interest rate is higher than projected, the total project cost increases accordingly, thereby requiring a larger amount of permanent financing.

In a project financing, the construction lender must be assured that the construction loan will be repaid from a combination of the equity investment and the proceeds from the issuance of long-term debt. Frequently, the borrower has the option to convert a portion of the construction loan to a term loan that extends into the operating period.

[2] Operating Period Analysis

For Cogeneration Company, the project's targeted capital structure is 20 percent equity and 80 percent debt. The proportions of equity and debt are determined after analyzing the project economics; the greater the level of income that can be contractually assured, the greater the amount of debt that the project can support on a nonrecourse basis. Since the debt is nonrecourse to the equity, the lender must look solely to the project's cash flow for its repayment. The equity investors receive their return from excess cash flow (i.e., after payment of debt service) from the project, the project's tax benefits, and any residual value of the asset.

FIGURE 8-5

Sources of Permanent Capital for Cogeneration Company

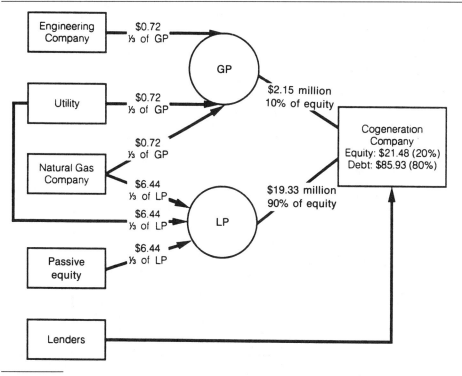

Note: Dollars in millions. GP = general partners; LP = limited partners.

Figure 8-5 describes the capitalization of Cogeneration Company at the outset of project operation. The capitalization equals $107.41 million (or the total construction cost) and consists of 20 percent equity representing $21.48 million, and 80 percent debt representing $85.93 million. Of the equity portion, the general partners invest $2.15 million, which is commensurate with their 10 percent share, and the limited partners invest $19.33 million, which is commensurate with their 90 percent share. (For the sake of simplicity, this analysis does not cover working capital, which is normally financed with commercial banks through a separate lending facility.)

The limited partnership vehicle best accommodates the needs of each party by providing an investment opportunity that properly allocates risks and returns. As general partners, Engineering Company, Utility, and Natural Gas Company are responsible for running the business of Cogeneration Company. The limited partners—Natural Gas Company, Utility, and Passive Equity—equally own the limited partnership interests. The general partners have a 10 percent interest and the limited partners have a 90 percent interest in all taxable income and cash distributions until the limited partners have received cash distributions on a cumulative basis that equal their cash investments. When that milestone is reached, the general partners will receive 50 percent and the limited partners will receive 50 percent of all future income and cash distributions of Cogeneration Company.

FIGURE 8-6

**Allocation of Cash Distribution and Taxable Income Among
Project Participants**

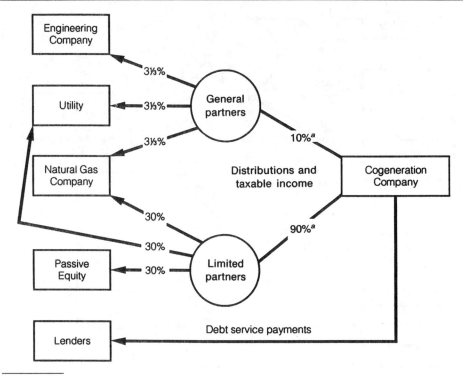

^a The allocation of 10 percent to the limited partners and 90 percent to the general partners changes to a 50:50 allocation after the limited partners receive cash distributions that equal their original investment of $19.33 million.

Figure 8-6 describes the flow of cash distributions and income from Cogeneration Company to project participants.

[3] Project Economics

The project's main source of revenues is its power sales agreement with Utility. Cogeneration Company will provide Utility with firm power for a period of 10 years. The price for each megawatt-hour of electricity sold to Utility will be contractually defined prior to the funding of construction; therefore, the electricity revenues can be predicted with some certainty in advance, since the power output is known and the operating performance of similar plants is well documented. A secondary source of revenues is the steam sale contract with Steam Host. These revenues are also contractually determined at a fixed dollar amount per thousand pounds of steam and escalated over time in accordance with the PPI.

FIGURE 8-7

Operating Arrangements of Cogeneration Company

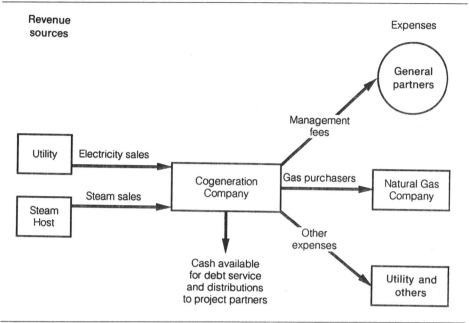

The project's operating costs are also contractually determined. Natural Gas Company will provide a 10-year gas supply at a price fixed at the time the contract is signed but adjusted over time in order to track the price received for the project's electricity. The general partners will manage the business operations of Cogeneration Company during the 10-year period for a fee that is fixed at the start of operations and that escalates over time in accordance with the PPI. Utility will operate, repair, and maintain the facility for a fee that is included in the operating expense. Engineering Company has guaranteed the output of the plant and will provide assurances that the facility will be able to meet specific production levels.

The parties to the contractual arrangements are creditworthy entities that are able to support their promises of performance with their own financial guarantees or outside insurance. The project's technology involves little risk, and Cogeneration Company carries insurance against calamities and catastrophic events. Since the project's revenues and expenses are contractually determined and established with a high degree of certainty in advance of project start-up, the net cash flow that the project will generate is therefore equally certain.

Figure 8-7 describes the operating arrangements of Cogeneration Company, which provide the project cash flow available for debt service and for distribution to the partners.

Cash flow projections are derived from the prices and volumes of the project's steam and electricity production, minus the operating and other expenses (including the cost of natural gas) incurred. Price assumptions for the project are shown in Figure 8-8; Figure 8-9 shows the corresponding cash flow projections.

FIGURE 8-8

Assumptions for Operation of the Facility

	Initial Price	Contractually Established Escalation Factor	Volume		
			Capacity	Maximum Annual	Projected Annual (90% Utilization)
Production					
Electricity	$41.50/MWH	6% annually	225 MWH	1,971,000 MWH	1,773,900 MWH
Steam	$3.50/1,000 pounds	PPI	150,000 PPH	1,314 B P	1,183 B P
Consumption					
Natural gas	$3.30/M BTU	6% annually	1.78 M BTU/hour	15.59 B BTU	14.03 B BTU

Note: Total operating and other expenses are $9,830,000/year. Total operating and other expenses include operating and maintenance expenditures, insurance, local taxes, and management fees paid to the general partners. The fees to the general partners are designed to produce a pretax profit to the general partners equal to 3 percent of gross revenues. All components of operating and other expenses except the management fee are escalated by PPI, assumed to be 5 percent per annum. Because the management fee is tied to gross revenues, its escalation reflects rates applicable to electricity and steam. MW = megawatts; MWH = megawatt-hours; PPH = pounds per hour; B P = billion pounds; BTU = British thermal units; M BTU = million BTUs; B BTU = billion BTUs.

FIGURE 8-9

Income and Cash Flow From Operation of the Facility

	Revenues		Expenses		Income and Cash Flow From
Year	Electricity	Steam	Natural Gas	Other	Operations
1	$ 73.62	$4.14	$46.31	$ 9.83	$21.62
2	78.03	4.35	49.09	10.34	22.95
3	82.72	4.56	52.03	10.88	24.36
4	87.68	4.79	55.16	11.45	25.86
5	92.94	5.03	58.47	12.05	27.45
6	98.52	5.28	61.97	12.68	29.14
7	104.43	5.55	65.69	13.35	30.93
8	110.69	5.82	69.63	14.04	32.84
9	117.33	6.12	73.81	14.78	34.86
10	124.37	6.42	78.24	15.55	37.00

Note: Dollars in millions.

[4] Analysis of Lender's Position

Given the strength of the project's contractual arrangements, lenders can rely on a secure cash flow stream for debt repayment. A significant risk that must be addressed, however, relates to the volatility of interest rates. The construction period is generally financed on a floating-rate basis. If long-term rates rise during this period and, at the time the project begins operation, the cost of long-term debt is significantly higher than originally projected, the project's cash flow may not support the loan that is outstanding during the operating period.

This problem can be handled in several ways. One option is to convert the portion of the construction financing that is not repaid from equity proceeds into a floating-rate term loan; permanent fixed-rate financing can then be delayed until a more favorable interest rate environment prevails. In this case, the project would probably maintain an interest reserve fund, possibly funded from equity. If interest rates rise, the reserve fund is drawn down; if interest rates fall, the fund is replenished. Financing a 10-year project on a floating-rate basis can be very risky and the loan will probably require refinancing with fixed-rate, long-term debt as soon as long-term interest rates decline.

Another alternative to handle fluctuating interest rates is the use of financial futures at the beginning of the construction period to hedge against a rise in long-term interest rates. Thus, if interest rates rise during the construction period, the value of a short position in a futures contract also rises. The proceeds from the futures contract are then used to reduce the principal amount of fixed-rate borrowing at the end of the construction period. In this way, for example, Cogeneration Company's debt service during the operating period can remain at a level that keeps the project's economics viable from the lender's point of view.

Finally, a method that is increasingly popular involves certain lenders that are willing at the outset to set a fixed rate on long-term financing that can be drawn down a certain number of months later. Such programs may be expensive, but project sponsors benefit from the certainty of the level of operating period debt service at the beginning of the operating period.

Although the lender generally has a lien on a project's assets, especially in the case of a fixed site facility, their value alone will not give the lender sufficient security to advance funds. Instead, lenders must look to the net cash flow under the contractual arrangements for their assurance of repayment.

One measure of the security of a loan is the debt service coverage ratio. As part of the economic analysis, the project's annual net cash flow is compared to the debt service requirements under the loan. Figure 8-10 shows a simplified version of a debt service coverage ratio calculation. The cash flow available for debt service is equal to the project's net cash flow from operations prior to distributions to the limited or general partners.

The precise debt service coverage ratio that a lender requires varies from project to project. The sample case in Figure 8-10 is strong enough economically to attract capital, since the project's operating cash flows are projected to cover debt service 1.5 times in the first year and 2 times on average over the debt term, using reasonably conservative assumptions. The debt service shown in Figure 8-10 is calculated on a fixed-rate basis; if the loan were at a floating rate, the lender would pay strict attention to the maximum level of interest the project could support at any time during the operating period.

[5] Return to Limited Partnership Equity

The limited partners do not receive a contractually defined cash flow as do the project's lenders. The limited partners' return arises from cash distributions, tax attributes of the project, and residual value. Usually, the limited partners make a commitment to

FIGURE 8-10

Debt Service Coverage

Year	Cash Flow Available for Debt Service	Debt Service			Coverage Ratios	
		Interest	Principal	Total	Interest	Total
1	$21.62	$9.32	$ 5.06	$14.38	2.32	1.50
2	22.95	8.74	5.64	14.38	2.63	1.60
3	24.36	8.11	6.27	14.38	3.00	1.69
4	25.86	7.40	6.98	14.38	3.49	1.80
5	27.45	6.61	7.77	14.38	4.15	1.91
6	29.14	5.73	8.65	14.38	5.09	2.03
7	30.93	4.75	9.63	14.38	6.51	2.15
8	32.84	3.66	10.72	14.38	8.97	2.28
9	34.86	2.45	11.93	14.38	14.23	2.42
10	37.00	1.10	13.28	14.38	33.64	2.57

Note: Dollars in millions. Principal = $85.93 million; term = 10 years; interest rate = 11 percent; 20 level semiannual payments of principal and interest.

the construction lenders to invest a stated percentage of the project's capital upon completion of construction. This commitment, made prior to the initial drawdown under the construction loan, is necessary to obtain the construction financing.

The project's cash flow is first used to pay the lenders. The portion that remains is divided between the limited partners and the general partners on a basis whereby the limited partners receive 90 percent of the taxable income and cash distributions until they have received an amount in cumulative cash distributions that equals their investment in the project; after that point, they receive 50 percent.

Figure 8-11 calculates the after-tax cash flow that the limited partners can expect to receive from the Cogeneration Company project. Figure 8-12 describes the calculation of taxes paid by the limited partners (which appears under "Allocated Taxes Paid" in Figure 8-11).

The timing of the limited partners' funding of their investment is important in the determination of their rate of return. Before construction starts, the limited partners commit to fund a portion of the total project cost (i.e., repay a portion of the construction loan) at the time the facility is placed in service. A liberal approach to the limited partners' investment would analyze their return on equity as though the inception of the investment period occurs at the time of funding, just prior to project operation, and not at the time the commitment is made, which would occur at the beginning of the construction period.

It can be argued, however, that this approach is inaccurate and tends to overstate the return because it does not account for the funding obligation that exists throughout construction. A more conservative approach would assume that the investment is made as the plant is under construction. Thus, the limited partners increase their investment as the construction loan increases. The limited partners count as equity investment the percentage of the construction loan that represents the percentage of the total project cost that the limited partners have agreed to fund. In the case of

FIGURE 8-11

After-Tax Cash Flow to the Limited Partners

Year	Cash Flow From Operations	Less Debt Service	Cash Available for Distribution to All Partners	Cash Distributed to Limited Partners		Allocated Taxes Paid	After-Tax Cash Flow
				%	$		
Construction							
−1	—	—	—	—	—	—	—
0	—	—	—	—	—	—	—
Operation							
1	$21.62	$14.38	$ 7.24	90	6.52	$1.26	$5.26
2	22.95	14.38	8.57	90	7.71	2.02	5.69
3	24.36	14.38	9.98	90	8.98	2.80	6.17
4	25.86	14.38	11.48	50	5.74	2.02	3.72
5	27.45	14.38	13.07	50	6.54	2.50	4.04
6	29.14	14.38	14.76	50	7.38	3.01	4.37
7	30.93	14.38	16.55	50	8.28	3.54	4.74
8	32.84	14.38	18.46	50	9.23	4.09	5.14
9	34.86	14.38	20.48	50	10.24	4.64	5.60
10	37.00	14.38	22.62	50	11.31	5.24	6.07

Note: Dollars in millions. The cash flows associated with the project occur throughout the year and the timing of the cash flows is very important in terms of accurately defining the project's return. For simplicity and clarity of presentation, however, in this figure and in the following figures and analyses it has been assumed that cash flows occur discretely at the end of each year. No such simplifying assumption would be made, however, when the investment community actually prices project equity.

The facility qualifies for 20-year 150 percent declining-balance (switching to straight-line) depreciation against all of the hard costs of the project, which are assumed to equal $100 million. The remaining soft costs are depreciated on a straight-line basis over 10 years.

Cogeneration Company, it is 18 percent. The net cash flow from these two approaches is shown in Figure 8-13.

In Figure 8-14, four methods have been used to analyze the return associated with this investment: (1) the net present value (NPV) at several discount rates; (2) a present value index (PVI); (3) the internal rate of return (IRR); and (4) a simple payback of investment.

[6] Return to General Partners

The three active equity investors, Engineering Company, Utility, and Natural Gas Company, have equal shares of the general partnership interest. The general partners invest 10 percent of the equity in Cogeneration Company and, until the limited partners receive cumulative cash distributions equal to their cash investment, the general partners receive a 10 percent allocation of partnership taxable income and losses, tax credits, and cash distributions. In the early years, the general partners will not receive a major portion of their return from this investment; however, the general partners will receive fees for managing the business of the partnership that produces a pretax

FIGURE 8-12

Taxes Paid by the Limited Partners

| | Items Applying to Partnership as a Whole | | | | Allocation to Limited Partner | | |
| Year | Cash Flow From Operations | Deductions | | Taxable Income | % | Taxable Income | Taxes Paid [a] |
		Depreciation	Interest				
Construction							
−1	—	—	—	—	—	—	—
0	—	—	—	—	—	—	—
Operation							
1	$21.62	$8.19	$9.32	$ 4.11	90	$ 3.70	$1.26
2	22.95	7.62	8.74	6.59	90	5.93	2.02
3	24.36	7.09	8.11	9.16	90	8.24	2.80
4	25.86	6.59	7.40	11.87	50	5.93	2.02
5	27.45	6.14	6.61	14.70	50	7.35	2.50
6	29.14	5.72	5.73	17.69	50	8.85	3.01
7	30.93	5.33	4.75	20.85	50	10.43	3.54
8	32.84	5.09	3.66	24.09	50	12.04	4.09
9	34.86	5.09	2.45	27.32	50	13.66	4.64
10	37.00	5.09	1.10	30.80	50	15.40	5.24

Note: Dollars in millions.

[a] Taxes paid are calculated by multiplying the "Taxable Income" column by the 34 percent tax rate to arrive at the tax liability.

profit equal to 3 percent of project revenue. Figure 8-15 shows the after-tax cash flow that the general partners can expect to receive from the project.

Like the limited partners, the general partners will commit to fund their 10 percent interest at the beginning of the construction period, and the total return on that investment can be calculated by analyzing the net after-tax cash flow. Figure 8-16 shows the net cash flow associated with the investment according to the liberal and conservative approaches discussed previously.

As with the analysis for limited partners, the return associated with general partners' investments can be analyzed in a number of ways. Figure 8-17 uses the liberal and conservative approaches to calculate the NPV, PVI, and payback for this investment.

[7] Return to Equity Investors

Each of the equity investors has a different motivation for participating in the project, and their investment returns reflect these motivations.

Passive equity receives an attractive return on its cash investment and is able to limit its risk with respect to Cogeneration Company by holding only the limited partnership interest. The return to the passive equity investor is calculated from its pro rata share of the net after-tax cash flow to all limited partners (for example, one third of the taxable income and cash distributions is allocated to passive equity as a one-third participant in the total limited partnership equity). Figure 8-18 provides a summary of results for the passive equity investment.

FIGURE 8-13
Net After-Tax Cash Flow to the Limited Partners

Year	Liberal Approach			Conservative Approach		
	After-Tax Cash Flow	Equity Investment	Net After-Tax Cash Flow	After-Tax Cash Flow	Equity Investment	Net After-Tax Cash Flow
Construction						
−1	—	—	—	—	$ 3.51	$ (3.51)
0	—	$19.33	$(19.33)	—	15.82	(15.82)
Operation						
1	$5.26	—	5.26	$5.26	—	5.26
2	5.69	—	5.69	5.69	—	5.69
3	6.17	—	6.17	6.17	—	6.17
4	3.72	—	3.72	3.72	—	3.72
5	4.04	—	4.04	4.04	—	4.04
6	4.37	—	4.37	4.37	—	4.37
7	4.74	—	4.74	4.74	—	4.74
8	5.14	—	5.14	5.14	—	5.14
9	5.60	—	5.60	5.60	—	5.60
10	6.07	—	6.07	6.07	—	6.07

Note: Dollars in millions.

FIGURE 8-14
Analysis of Return on the Limited Partners' Investment

Discount Rate	Liberal Approach		Conservative Approach	
	NPV	PVI[a]	NPV	PVI[a]
0	$31.48	2.63	$31.48	2.63
7.5%	14.41	1.80	14.17	1.78
10.0	10.78	1.61	10.46	1.58
12.5	7.81	1.45	7.42	1.42
15.0	5.38	1.32	4.92	1.28
17.5	3.37	1.20	2.84	1.17
20.0	1.70	1.11	1.11	1.07
IRR		23.1%		21.9%
Payback		3.6 years		3.6 years

Note: Dollars in millions.
[a] Calculated by dividing the present value of the after-tax cash flow by the present value of the equity investment.

FIGURE 8-15

After-Tax Cash Flow to the General Partners

Year	%	Allocation to General Partners		Management Fees	Taxes Paid [a]	After-Tax Cash Flow [b]
		Taxable Income	Cash Distributions			
Construction						
−1	—	—	—	—	—	—
0	—	—	—	—	—	—
Operation						
1	10	$ 0.41	$ 0.72	$2.33	$0.93	$2.12
2	10	0.66	0.86	2.47	1.06	2.27
3	10	0.92	1.00	2.62	1.20	2.42
4	50	5.93	5.74	2.77	2.96	5.55
5	50	7.35	6.54	2.94	3.50	5.98
6	50	8.85	7.38	3.11	4.07	6.42
7	50	10.43	8.28	3.30	4.67	6.91
8	50	12.04	9.23	3.50	5.28	7.45
9	50	13.66	10.24	3.70	5.90	8.04
10	50	15.40	11.31	3.92	6.57	8.66

Note: Dollars in millions.

[a] Taxes paid are calculated by taxable income for the partnership by allocating the proper amount of taxable income to the general partners, adding the management fees, and multiplying this sum by 34 percent to arrive at the tax liability.

[b] The after-tax cash flow equals cash distributions to the general partners plus the management fees less taxes paid.

Engineering Company holds one third of the general partners' interest in Cogeneration Company. Its return, therefore, arises from this investment and from its share of the revenues that the general partners receive for managing the project. Engineering Company receives one third of the income, fees, and cash distributions that the general partners as a group receive. Figure 8-19 provides a summary of Engineering Company's return on its investment in the partnership.

Utility and Natural Gas Company each hold a one-third share in the general partners' interest in Cogeneration Company and a one-third share of the limited partnership interest as well. The return to these parties is calculated by combining the net after-tax cash flow of these holdings. Figure 8-20 describes the cash flow that each would expect. Figure 8-21 provides a summary of the returns to Utility and Natural Gas Company on their respective investments in Cogeneration Company.

[8] Residual Value

The analysis so far has not included the project's residual value, but most likely the plant would retain some value after the 10-year steam and electricity contracts expire. Since the useful life of such assets is well in excess of 10 years, the actual equipment that composes such a project can be sold after the contract term. The equipment will

FIGURE 8-16

Net After-Tax Cash Flow to the General Partners

Year	Liberal Approach		Net After-Tax Cash Flow	Conservative Approach		Net After-Tax Cash Flow
	After-Tax Cash Flow	Equity Investment		After-Tax Cash Flow	Equity Investment	
Construction						
−1	—	—	—	—	$0.39	$(0.39)
0	—	$2.15	$(2.15)	—	1.76	(1.76)
Operation						
1	$2.12	—	2.12	$2.12	—	2.12
2	2.27	—	2.27	2.27	—	2.27
3	2.42	—	2.42	2.42	—	2.42
4	5.55	—	5.55	5.55	—	5.55
5	5.98	—	5.98	5.98	—	5.98
6	6.42	—	6.42	6.42	—	6.42
7	6.91	—	6.91	6.91	—	6.91
8	7.45	—	7.45	7.45	—	7.45
9	8.04	—	8.04	8.04	—	8.04
10	8.66	—	8.66	8.66	—	8.66

Note: Dollars in millions.

FIGURE 8-17

Analysis of Return on the General Partners' Investment

Discount Rate	Liberal Approach		Conservative Approach	
	NPV	PVI	NPV	PVI
0	$53.68	25.99	$53.68	25.99
7.5%	30.66	16.34	30.84	16.12
10.0	25.80	14.21	25.78	13.96
12.5	21.84	12.44	21.80	12.16
15.0	18.60	10.96	18.55	10.67
17.5	15.93	9.71	15.87	9.41
20.0	13.71	8.66	13.64	8.35
IRR		NA		NA
Payback		1.1 years		1.1 years

Note: Dollars in millions.

FIGURE 8-18

Analysis of Return on Passive Equity

Discount Rate	Liberal Approach		Conservative Approach	
	NPV	PVI	NPV	PVI
0	$10.49	2.63	$10.49	2.63
7.5%	4.80	1.80	4.72	1.78
10.0	0	1.61	3.49	1.58
12.5	0	1.45	2.47	1.42
15.0	1.79	1.32	1.64	1.28
17.5	1.12	1.20	0.95	1.17
20.0	0.57	1.11	0.37	1.07
IRR		23.1%		21.9%
Payback		3.6 years		3.6 years

Note: Dollars in millions.

FIGURE 8-19

Analysis of Return to Engineering Company

Discount Rate	Liberal Approach		Conservative Approach	
	NPV	PVI	NPV	PVI
0	$17.89	25.99	$17.89	25.99
7.5%	10.22	16.34	10.21	16.12
10.0	8.60	14.21	8.59	13.96
12.5	7.28	12.44	7.27	12.16
15.0	6.20	10.96	6.18	10.67
17.5	5.31	9.71	5.29	9.41
20.0	4.57	8.66	4.55	8.35
IRR		NA		NA
Payback		1.1 years		1.1 years

Note: Dollars in millions.

probably have the greatest value if the integrity of the project were maintained and the project were either sold to another party or operated in accordance with new or renewed steam and electricity contracts. Because the debt is repaid over the initial 10-year operating period, all of the cash flow from the project after the tenth year flows to the limited and general partners. The cash flow that the project will produce after the steam and electricity contracts expire will strongly influence the purchase price of the plant. Although the actual residual value will only be known at the time the contracts expire, the sensitivity analysis of various residual values can indicate

FIGURE 8-20

Net Cash Flow to Utility and Natural Gas Company (Conservative Approach)

	Net After-Tax Cash Flow From/to		
Year	Limited Partners Position	General Partners Position	Total Net After-Tax Cash Flow
Construction			
−1	$(1.17)	$(0.13)	$(1.30)
0	(5.27)	(0.59)	(5.86)
Operation			
1	1.75	0.71	2.46
2	1.90	0.76	2.66
3	2.06	0.81	2.87
4	1.24	1.85	3.09
5	1.35	1.99	3.34
6	1.46	2.14	3.60
7	1.58	2.30	3.88
8	1.71	2.48	4.20
9	1.87	2.68	4.55
10	2.02	2.89	4.91

Note: Dollars in millions.

FIGURE 8-21

Analysis of Return to Utility and Natural Gas Company

Discount Rate	Liberal Approach		Conservative Approach	
	NPV	PVI	NPV	PVI
0	$28.39	4.96	$28.40	4.97
7.5%	15.03	3.26	14.94	3.11
10.0	12.19	2.87	12.08	2.72
12.5	9.88	2.55	9.75	2.39
15.0	7.99	2.28	7.83	2.12
17.5	6.43	2.06	6.24	1.90
20.0	5.14	1.86	4.92	1.71
IRR		39.7%		37.2%
Payback		2.7 years		2.7 years

Note: Dollars in millions.

FIGURE 8-22

After-Tax Proceeds From Sale of the Project

Percentage of Original Total Project Cost	Gross Proceeds	Less Taxes[a]	Net After-Tax Proceeds
0	—	—	—
25	$26.85	0	$26.85
50	53.71	$ 2.80	50.91
75	80.56	11.93	68.63

Note: Dollars in millions.

[a] All proceeds less the undepreciated amount of the original project cost (equal to $45.5 million) are taxed as ordinary income.

FIGURE 8-23

Analysis of Effect of Residual Value on Returns of Each Equity Investor in the Partnership (Conservative Approach)

	Residual Value		NPV Inclusive of Residual Value					
	Percentage of Original Total Project Cost	After-Tax Proceeds to Party	0%	7.5%	10%	15%	20%	IRR
Passive equity	0	—	$10.49	$ 4.72	$ 3.49	$ 1.64	$0.37	21.9%
	25	$ 4.48	14.97	6.74	5.05	2.60	0.97	24.3
	50	8.49	18.98	8.55	6.46	3.46	1.51	26.0
	75	11.44	21.93	9.88	7.49	4.10	1.91	27.1
Engineering	0	—	17.89	10.21	8.59	6.18	4.55	NA
Company	25	4.48	22.37	12.23	10.16	7.15	5.15	NA
	50	8.49	25.68	13.73	11.32	7.86	5.60	NA
	75	11.44	28.63	15.06	12.35	8.49	5.99	NA
Utility or Natural	0	—	28.40	14.94	12.08	7.83	4.92	37.2
Gas Company	25	8.95	37.35	18.98	15.22	9.75	6.13	38.8
	50	16.97	44.00	21.99	17.55	11.18	7.02	40.7
	75	22.88	49.91	24.65	19.62	12.45	7.82	40.7

Note: Dollars in millions.

the project's potential upside. Figure 8-22 describes the after-tax proceeds arising from the sale of the project[8] after the 10-year contracts expire, given various levels of residual value.

The proceeds from the sale of the asset (or residual cash flow, if the partnership

---

[8] In residual value analysis, the sale of the project is often used as a surrogate for the residual value of the facility because of its conceptual simplicity. If Cogeneration Company were to continue to operate the project after the 10-year contracts expire, the residual value in year 11 would be the NPV of the after-tax cash flow from year 11 until the end of the useful economic life of the project. The approach that uses the after-tax NPV in year 11 would be the same as that using the after-tax proceeds from a sale of the project in year 11.

continues to operate the facility) are divided among the general and limited partnersaccording to the ratio described in the partnership agreement; under the agreement in the case of Cogeneration Company, the general and limited partners each receive 50 percent. This residual benefit enhances the return to each party.

Figure 8-23 describes the effect of the residual value on each party in Cogeneration Company.

8.06 CONCLUSION

The credit support network fashioned for project financing is based on a series of indirect mechanisms. If the parties supplying such support were instead to provide direct support (i.e., a direct financial commitment recorded on their corporate balance sheets), the risks associated with investments in the project would be more readily understood by investors, which would then charge less for their money.

Despite the potentially higher financing charges, project financing is attracting increasing interest for a number of reasons:

- *Reduces and properly allocates risk.* Project financing mechanisms can be fashioned to shift risk to parties in the best position to bear it. Thus, engineering companies can shoulder the construction and design risks, fuel suppliers can be responsible for the project's fuel supply, and so forth.

- *Minimizes credit impact.* The contractual arrangements that define the project provide sufficient credit support for the debt financing so that direct financial commitments from the project sponsors are usually not required. This preserves a sponsor's debt capacity for other uses. As rating agencies have become more sophisticated in analyzing complicated project financings, it has become possible to obtain rating agency recognition of the benefits related to this reduced financial exposure.

- *Allows greater leverage.* The contractual arrangements can also support greater leverage than is normally found in a corporate capital structure, thus allowing equity in project financing to be more leveraged, thereby realizing a higher equity return. Since debt carries a lower cost than equity, the more leveraged structure also reduces the project's cost of capital.

- *Achieves accounting benefits.* Although it is less important than the previous considerations, the ability to obtain off-balance sheet accounting has a strong appeal to certain public companies. The accounting profession, however, seems to be expanding disclosure requirements, so the benefits have become less and less tangible.

- *Minimizes impact of restrictive covenants.* The accounting treatment may still be important, however, in the application of restrictive covenants contained in a project sponsor's existing debt instruments and even its charter.

The revision of existing tax laws or accounting rules could have significant effects on the use of project financing techniques. Regardless of changes that may occur in the accounting and tax arenas, however, project financing techniques should continue to offer to those considering capital equipment investments an important alternative means of attracting much-needed external funds.

Chapter 9

Venture Capital

WILLIAM B. GARTNER

WILLIAM D. BYGRAVE

9.01   OVERVIEW

Most venture capital companies are involved in financing of new (or young) companies that have the possibility of rapid growth. Venture capitalists provide both the capital and the managerial expertise to seed first-stage companies (businesses that need additional capital to initiate or expand commercial manufacturing and sales). They also provide the capital and managerial expertise to expand second-stage companies (businesses that are already producing a product and making sales that need additional capital for expansion), as well as to effect management buyouts (MBOs) and leveraged buyouts (LBOs) in situations where the venture capitalist expects to earn significant returns within a five-year period. Venture capitalists share in the upside potential of their investments through equity or through debt instruments with equity opportunities.

The financing of high-growth companies is, however, just one aspect of venture capital. Another distinguishing characteristic of most venture capital investments is that venture capitalists take active rather than passive roles in their investments. More than two thirds of a venture capitalist's time is devoted to working with those companies in his or her portfolio. Although venture capitalists are not generally seeking hands-on involvement, they are likely to be directly involved through the company's board of directors and are likely to stipulate specific performance objectives as part of a financing deal through management covenants. In addition, venture capitalists are not indiscriminate investors. They do not take chances in risky new ventures. Rather, each venture capital deal is carefully structured so that the investment can provide a potential growth company with the needed resources to achieve rapid growth and profitability.

Venture capital deals are designed (through commitment letters, investment agreements, and loan covenants) to reward performance and penalize failure. In order to continue to acquire further rounds of financing for future growth, current management must achieve performance objectives. Entrepreneurs who can meet their plan objectives are likely to realize significant financial rewards when the company is taken public, sold, or refinanced. Those who fail to meet the growth benchmarks specified in their plan objectives are likely to lose their jobs and hold significantly fewer or no shares in a restructured organization.

Over the past 20 years, the venture capital industry has been significantly influenced by legislation, tax policy, and the public's interest in the initial public offering (IPO) market. The purpose of this chapter is to describe the venture capital industry: the types of venture capital investors, sources of venture capital funds, venture capital disbursements, rates of return on venture capital funds, international venture capital, and companies that are likely to acquire venture capital, plus the deal-making process by which entrepreneurs seek, negotiate for, and acquire capital from venture capitalists. Specific attention is given to the activities that entrepreneurs undertake to acquire venture capital. Particular attention is focused on the business plan as a financing proposal. In addition, the criteria venture capitalists use to evaluate business plans are explained, along with the methods for pricing a venture capital investment and typical ways in which venture capital investment is structured.

9.02   CURRENT VENTURE CAPITAL INDUSTRY

The venture capital industry is a recent source of financing for growing companies. The industry has been greatly influenced by government legislation and tax policies, as well as by the public's fickle enthusiasm for IPOs. While such modern-day precursors of the venture capital industry as J.H. Whitney & Company, American Research Development, and the Rockefeller Family and Associates were investing in growth companies in the 1950s, the Small Business Investment Act of 1958 laid the foundation for the current private venture capital industry. During the 1960s, with funds that were leveraged with loans from the Small Business Administration (SBA), over 700 small business investment companies (SBICs) were formed to finance small businesses. These SBICs were the training ground for many individuals who later went on to start private venture capital companies.

Many SBICs were started as subsidiaries of banks. However, the compensation structure for most investment managers in bank-owned SBICs did not reward risk taking or recognize the long-term, high-risk/high-return nature of venture capital investments. By the end of the 1960s, many SBIC investment managers saw private venture capital partnerships as a more flexible and financially remunerative way to fund high-growth ventures. The SBIC industry was a government-sponsored and -regulated industry that required each SBIC to provide detailed reports on its investment activities. An SBIC's use of government loans made it necessary for most investments to be low-risk debt instruments that required firms to generate immediate cash flow to pay a rate of return sufficient to pay back the yearly interest owed by the SBIC on its borrowed funds. Investment managers of bank-owned SBICs realized that a general partner in a venture capital limited partnership could earn substantially more (through the 20/80 general partner–limited partner split on the fund's capital gains) than could a bank employee. By 1967, less than 300 SBICs remained in business.

Although many private venture funds generated high returns from an active new issues market in 1969 (nearly 700 companies with a net worth of $5 million or less raised over $1.4 billion), sources of investment for new venture funds nearly vanished as the maximum capital gains tax was raised from 25 percent to 49 percent. Because of the high tax rates, most of the 1970s can be characterized as a time when little money was raised for new venture capital funds. (See Figure 9-1.) As the U.S. economy staggered through a series of oil price shocks and recessions coupled with a lackluster IPO market, many venture funds gravitated toward later-stage financings and more conservative short-term investments. Ironically, some venture capitalists were targeting their investments toward innovative new growth companies that would eventually spawn new industries and subsequently provide phenomenal returns when these companies were taken public (e.g., Sevin Rosen's investments in Compaq and Lotus, Kleiner Perkins's investment in Tandem Computers, and Arthur Rock and Company's investment in Apple).

Changes in government legislation (the Employee Retirement Income Security Act of 1974 "prudent man rule," which allowed pension funds to invest in venture capital) and tax policies (a reduction of the capital gains tax from 49 percent to 28 percent) in the late 1970s set the stage for an avalanche of capital into the venture capital industry. From a low of $10 million in 1975, venture funds raised over $4.1 billion in 1987. A robust IPO market enables many venture capital firms to harvest their maturing investments by selling their stock at very high earnings multiples. The opportunity to sell stock in the public market at these high multiples enables venture capital firms to generate high rates of return on their portfolios. On average, venture funds that were started in the late 1970s generated yearly compounded rates of return of over 35 percent. Funds started during the 1980s have not demonstrated such high returns. During the 1990s, over $1 billion has continued to flow into the venture capital industry each year, as shown in Figure 9-1.

FIGURE 9-1

Capital Commitments to Independent Private Venture Capital Firms (1974–1992)

Source: Venture Economics

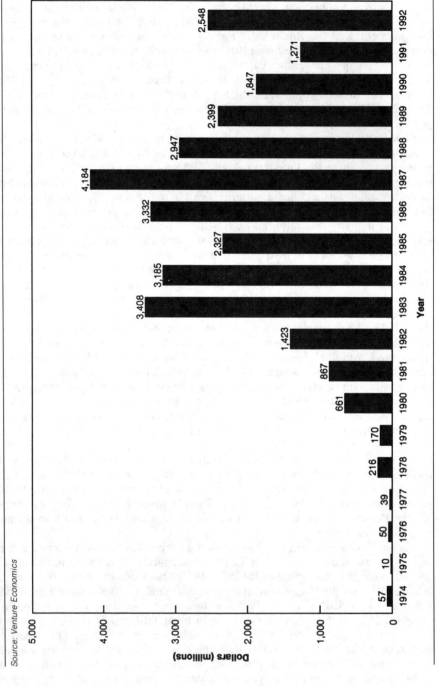

9.03 VENTURE CAPITAL INVESTORS

There are three major types of companies that provide venture capital: private companies, SBICs, and companies owned by large corporations.

[1] Private Venture Capital Firms

The firms with the most capital to invest are independent private venture capital firms. Over 200 such firms exist. Although some venture capital firms are publicly held or are owned by banks, venture capital companies are usually run as limited partnerships, in which the venture capitalist acts as a general partner and typically raises from $5 million to $100 million from pension funds, insurance companies, and wealthy investors. A small amount of the fund is used for salaries and expenses in managing the fund, but most is made available for investments. The general partner typically retains 20 percent of the profits once the fund has returned the limited partners' original investment.

There are no general rules regarding when a venture capital company begins to raise money to form another limited partnership, but the industry trend suggests that venture capital companies begin to raise money for their next limited partnership once 50 percent of the funds from the current partnership are invested. The usual rule is that the remaining 50 percent of the current fund is used for further investments in companies already in the partnership's portfolio and for a few additional investments in new companies.

Understandably, venture capitalists want to begin earning their 20 percent share of the fund's returns as well as begin new funds as quickly as possible, so they look for investments that can grow significantly within a five-year period. Venture capitalists with a good track record of achieving significant growth in the value of the partnerships they manage are likely to attract the highest-quality new ventures. Just as investors want to invest in a fund that will achieve high rates of return, entrepreneurs seek the legitimacy that results from being picked by a venture capitalist who has a history of choosing winners. The better its record, the more successful a venture capital company will be in attracting both resources for additional limited partnerships and entrepreneurs most likely to achieve impressive growth.

A limited partnership fund has a life of 5 to 10 years, after which time the fund is dissolved and any remaining assets in the limited partnership (cash, stocks, debt instruments, and stock options and warrants) are distributed to the partners. Returns to the venture fund take place through (1) taking companies in the fund portfolio public; (2) selling companies in the fund portfolio to larger companies for cash or publicly traded securities; or (3) buyouts in which the portfolio company buys back the fund's shares in it. Therefore, one important standard that the venture capital company looks for in making an investment is how it will exit from the investment. A company may have a good chance for growth and profitability, but if venture capitalist determines that the company is not likely to go public, be acquired by a larger organization, or amass the resources to cash out the venture capitalist, he or she is unlikely to make an investment.

[2] Small Business Investment Companies

About 300 SBICs are supported by the federal government to make investments in smaller U.S.-based companies (SBICs leverage their equity with loans from the SBA). An SBIC must have a minimum of $1 million in equity investment and can borrow $4 for every $1 of equity. Since an SBIC must pay interest on the money provided by the SBA, most investments made by an SBIC will be debt investments. The interest from the SBIC's investments is used to pay the interest that the SBIC owes the SBA. Therefore, the returns to SBICs are mostly from options to own equity tied to the debt investments. For example, an SBIC might invest in a company by using a 15 percent convertible debenture with conversion privileges to purchase 40 percent of the company's equity after 10 years. Interest on the debenture is used to pay the interest on money borrowed from the SBA. After 10 years, if 40 percent of the company's shares are worth more than the value of the debenture, the SBIC converts the debenture into shares of the company. Otherwise, the SBIC asks the company to cash out the debenture. Much like private venture capital companies, SBICs are looking for companies that can provide significant growth and profitability so that their debentures can be converted into equity having a much higher value than the debenture.

In 1969, the SBIC program was expanded to increase the number of investments made in minority-owned companies through minority enterprise small business investment companies (MESBICs). Over 100 MESBICs provide debt and equity to small businesses that are at least 51 percent owned by socially or economically disadvantaged persons.

[3] Corporate Venture Capital Firms

Many large corporations have venture capital subsidiaries (e.g., IBM, General Motors, Gillette, Tektronix, and Monsanto). These subsidiaries are regular parts of the corporation, and it is estimated that corporate venture capital firms managed over $2.5 billion in capital in 1991. A corporate venture capital company often has goals beyond that of earning a substantial return from its investment. Common reasons for the existence of venture capital subsidiaries in major corporations are that investments in new ventures provide a window on new technologies, new markets and products, a partnership to eliminate a potential competitor, potential acquisition candidates, and a vehicle for acquiring entrepreneurial talent for the corporation's other divisions.

9.04 STAGES OF VENTURE CAPITAL INVESTMENT

Investment can occur at various times in a company's life, from preincorporation to well after the company is established. In most cases, the earlier an investment is made, the higher the rate of return and percentage of the company the venture capitalist requires.

[1] Seed Financing

The beginning of a venture is the seed stage. In this stage, the entrepreneur usually has nothing more than a nebulous idea for beginning a new company and needs financing to realize the concept. Typically, resources for the seed stage come to the entrepreneur from family and friends. The major challenge of the seed stage is to demonstrate the idea's viability and potential profitability. Seed financing supports an entrepreneur in the development of a business idea and the generation of a business plan, in conducting limited research and development (R&D), and in the formation of a management team. It may initially cost as little as $10,000 or as much as $100,000. Few venture capitalists provide entrepreneurs with seed financing, although some firms (such as Zero Stage Capital) have developed funds solely to support companies needing seed capital.

[2] Research and Development Financing

Current legislation provides for the creation of R&D limited partnerships that can be structured to finance product and process development for new as well as more mature companies. Investors in an R&D limited partnership receive tax write-offs for their investment as well as a share of later profits. Typically, the funds provided by R&D limited partnerships are expensed by the company using the fund, and these expenses can be claimed as a loss by the investors. Many R&D limited partnerships generate returns for the investors by claiming royalties on sales or savings generated by the R&D expenditures. For example, an R&D limited partnership formed to provide funds for a company to develop a patentable bacteria might receive a royalty payment of 10 percent of future sales.

[3] Start-Up Financing

Start-up financing is provided to get companies launched, i.e., to demonstrate that a company has a viable product and market demand. These funds are provided after most of the management team is in place and the company is continuing to develop its products and generate sales. Usually, the company has been in business for less than a year. Start-up financing is provided for product development and marketing and completing the management team.

[4] Going-Concern Financing

[a] **First-Stage Financing.** Resources are provided at this stage to going concerns that have all aspects of the business in place (e.g., a management team, a technology, a product, and a defined market). Such companies need additional capital to initiate or expand commercial manufacturing and sales.

[b] **Second-Stage Financing.** In second-stage financing, resources are provided to expand a company that is producing a product and making sales but is probably not showing a profit and has negative cash flow.

[c] **Mezzanine or Bridge Financing.** A company expecting to go public within six months to a year may use bridge financing (debt or an additional equity investment) to continue the company's growth during the time the company prepares to go public.

In some cases, bridge financing is also used to restructure equity and debt for the company. By the time a company has reached the stage where it is large enough to go public, it may have had a number of rounds of financing. Bridge financing allows restructuring of the ownership of the company, consolidating all of the different types of shares that may have been issued into one type of share. Often bridge financing is used to purchase shares of former managers or early investors wanting to liquidate their positions.

[d] MBO and LBO Financing. In this stage, resources are provided to acquire a business from a public or privately held company in which the operating management will hold a significant interest.

9.05 SOURCES OF VENTURE CAPITAL FUNDS

While there have been some changes in the year-to-year percentage participation of various venture capital investor groups, what is particularly striking is the growth in total capital committed by all investor groups. (See Figure 9-2.) Although pension funds have become the largest source of capital for investment in venture capital funds since changes in government regulations have allowed them to invest, other groups continue to contribute a similar percentage of total capital. It would seem reasonable to expect that while the amount of capital provided by pension funds increased, the amount of capital provided by the other investor groups would remain at previous levels, making pension funds the dominant source of funding. Instead, each investor group continues to increase total contributions to venture funds, and, while pension funds are an important source of venture capital investment, they have not taken on an overwhelming role in funding the venture capital industry. In fact, no major changes in investment patterns are discernible from Figure 9-2.

9.06 VENTURE CAPITAL DISBURSEMENTS

With the tremendous growth in capital flowing into the venture industry, there has been much speculation about whether a significant change has taken place in how the funds have distributed this money. For example, analysts should consider whether this increase in capital has led to a diversification of venture funds into all sections of the United States and whether increased capital has led to a diversification in the types of industries in which venture capitalists have typically invested (e.g., away from high technology). Analysts should also consider whether venture capitalists are continuing to invest in seed and start-up companies or whether these companies are too small for investment by funds with such large amounts of capital.

[1] Geographical Investment Patterns

Venture capitalists have tended to invest the majority of their funds in California (primarily Silicon Valley in Northern California) and the Northeast (Massachusetts's Route 128), as show in Figure 9-3. Traditionally, about 60 percent of all venture capital is invested in high technology companies. These two high technology areas have developed a symbiotic and synergistic effect between venture funds and emerging technology companies that has fueled many start-up firms, which has led to increasing levels

FIGURE 9-2

Capital Commitments to Independent Private Firms Only

Source: Venture Economics

	1981	1982	1983	1984	1985	1986	1987	1988	1989	1990	1991	1992
Total Capital Committed												
Pension funds	$200	$474	$1,070	$1,085	$767	$1,672	$1,632	$1,355	$863	$980	$571	$1,060
Foreign	90	188	531	573	548	361	544	401	312	129	140	283
Individuals and families	201	290	715	467	303	392	502	249	144	203	153	280
Corporations	142	175	415	463	274	350	460	324	480	129	51	84
Insurance companies	132	200	410	419	154	348	628	277	312	166	64	370
Endowments and foundations	102	96	267	178	181	209	418	341	288	240	292	471
Total	$867	$1,423	$3,408	$3,185	$2,327	$3,332	$4,184	$2,947	$2,399	$1,847	$1,271	$2,548
Total Capital Committed												
Pension funds	23%	33%	31%	34%	33%	50%	39%	46%	36%	53%	45%	42%
Foreign	10	13	16	18	23	11	13	14	13	7	11	11
Individuals and families	23	21	21	15	13	12	12	8	6	11	12	11
Corporations	17	12	12	14	12	10	11	11	20	7	4	3
Insurance companies	15	14	12	13	11	10	15	9	13	9	5	15
Endowments and foundations	12	7	8	6	8	6	10	12	12	13	23	18
Total	100%	100%	100%	100%	100%	100%	100%	100%	100%	100%	100%	100%

Note: Dollars in millions.

FIGURE 9-3

Venture Capital Disbursements by State (Percentage of Dollar Amount Invested)

	1982	1983	1984	1985	1986	1987	1988	1989	1990	1991	1992
California	45	47	44	44	38	39	40	36	24	42	35
Massachusetts	11	11	13	13	14	11	11	15	18	21	23
	56	58	57	57	52	50	51	51	52	63	58
Others	44	42	43	43	48	50	49	49	48	37	42
Total	100	100	100	100	100	100	100	100	100	100	100

of new venture capital investments, which has led to additional start-up firms, and so on.

Research by Bygrave (1988) supports this conclusion. His study of the investment networks of venture capital firms describes a highly interconnected set of relationships between venture capital firms in these two high-technology regions. Bygrave found that syndicated investments are very high between venture capitalists in these two regions who specialize in highly innovative technology companies, while syndicated investments in less-innovative technology companies are more geographically dispersed. In other words, high technology–oriented venture capital funds continue to focus the majority of their investments in high technology firms located in California and Massachusetts.

What Figure 9-3 does not show is the geographical spread of venture funds into nearly all regions of the United States. While the category encompassing all other states has not grown in relative percentage amounts, the total dollar amount of new investments has enabled the start-up of venture funds in most major metropolitan areas of the United States. Even so, in both total dollars invested and percentage amounts, venture capital remains a predominantly bicoastal phenomenon.

[2] Industry Investment Patterns

The information in Figure 9-4 indicates that venture capitalists are directing their investments away from computer hardware (e.g., 36 percent of the total dollar amount invested in 1982 versus 14 percent in 1991), electronics, and industrial products toward other emerging technologies (for example, biotechnology received 3 percent of the total dollar amount invested in 1982 versus 8 percent in 1991) and consumer products.

[3] Company Stage Investment Patterns

With such a large influx of investment into the venture capital industry during the 1980s and with the formation of venture capital limited partnerships in the $50 million to $100 million range, there has been some concern as to whether such large funds can afford to invest in very small companies in the seed and start-up stages. Overall,

FIGURE 9-4

Venture Capital Disbursements by Industry

Source: Venture Economics

	1981	1982	1983	1984	1985	1986	1987	1988	1989	1990	1991
Percentage of Dollar Amount Invested											
Communications	11%	10%	13%	15%	16%	16%	14%	14%	15%	16%	14%
Computer software and services	30	6	7	11	10	10	10	10	11	16	25
Computer hardware	—	36	39	29	25	19	13	13	11	11	13
Medical	6	6	9	8	10	12	12	13	14	17	11
Consumer products	5	5	7	7	7	9	17	13	11	10	10
Other products and services	10	7	5	7	6	11	11	15	14	13	6
Electronics	12	14	10	13	14	13	9	9	8	7	10
Biotechnology	7	3	3	2	5	4	6	8	8	8	8
Industrial products and services	9	7	4	6	6	4	6	5	7	1	2
Energy-related products and services	10	6	3	2	1	2	2	1	1	1	1
Total	100%	100%	100%	100%	100%	100%	100%	100%	100%	100%	100%

FIGURE 9-5

Venture Capital Disbursements by Financing Stage

Source: Venture Economics

	1981	1982	1983	1984	1985	1986	1987	1988	1989	1990	1991
Percentage of Dollar Amount Invested											
Seed	2%	2%	3%	3%	2%	2%	2%	2%	4%	3%	4%
Start-up	22	15	11	12	10	16	11	11	9	7	6
Other early stage	18	22	19	18	12	17	16	19	15	17	22
Expansion (second and third)	44	51	55	54	60	44	47	48	47	52	54
LBO or acquisition	14	7	9	9	11	17	19	19	21	18	4
Other	—	3	3	4	5	4	5	1	4	3	10
Total	100%	100%	100%	100%	100%	100%	100%	100%	100%	100%	100%

the figures on company stage investment patterns, shown in Figure 9-5, indicate that seed and start-up companies continue to receive about the same percentage of the total pool of venture capital investments as in earlier years. Since 1982, about 2 percent to 3 percent of the total capital invested in companies has been devoted to seed investments, while a declining percentage (22 percent in 1981 versus 6 percent in 1991) has been devoted to start-up companies.

9.07 RATES OF RETURN ON VENTURE CAPITAL FUNDS

[1] Expected Returns on Venture Capital Investments

As a rule, venture capitalists expect to make 5 times their money within 5 years, or a compounded annual rate of return of 38 percent. Other rates of return that are often given by venture capitalists include 3 times their money in 3 years (44 percent annual return), 4 times their money in 4 years (41 percent), 5 times their money in 3 years (71 percent), 7 times their money in 5 years (48 percent), and 10 times their money in 5 years (58 percent). A venture capitalist's expected rate of return for a specific investment varies based on the venture capitalist's perception of (1) the company's stage of growth; (2) the previous track record of the entrepreneurs managing the company; (3) the company's prospects for significant sales growth and profits; (4) the attractiveness of the company's industry; and (5) any competitive advantages that suggest that the company can sustain future growth and profitability. Like any investor, the venture capitalist wants to generate the highest returns possible for the lowest perceived risks, but in almost all cases, the funding of new companies is perceived to be very risky, so venture capitalists seek much higher rates of return than corresponding investments in established publicly traded companies would require.

In general, seed and start-up stage investments often require expected compounded annual rates of return over 50 percent; first-stage financings require 40 percent to 60 percent returns; second-stage financings require 25 percent to 50 percent returns; bridge financings require 20 percent to 40 percent returns; and buyouts require 25 percent to 50 percent returns. The lowest expected rate of return for any venture capital investment will not be less than 20 percent, and this would be for investments in companies that are perceived as risk-free, that is, those demonstrating a history of continual growth and profitability with no major changes in this picture for the future.

[2] Actual Returns on Venture Capital Investments

Determining the rate of return for a venture capital fund is difficult. Most venture capital funds are privately held limited partnerships that do not publicly distribute information on their financial performance. In addition, the long-term nature of most venture capital investments in emerging growth companies and the 10-year life of most partnerships make interim valuations of fund portfolios difficult to ascertain.

Venture capital funds are typically set up as limited partnerships with a 10-year defined term, which can often be extended. Extensions of a limited partnership are negotiated between the general partners and the limited partners. In most cases, a partnership is extended if a number of companies in the partnership's portfolio can still benefit from the venture capitalist's involvement. These companies might be in the process of being taken public or sold. When a partnership is disbanded, all of its assets (e.g., cash, stock, warrants, options, and debt instruments) are distributed to members of the partnership.

In most partnerships, the general partners receive an annual management fee of 2 percent to 3 percent of the paid-in capital, and the general partner's share of the profits is typically 20 percent, with the other 80 percent going to the limited partners. In the formation of a new fund, the limited partner provides the committed investment over several installments (known as takedowns) over the first two to three years. General partners usually send quarterly reports and financial statements to the limited partners; the limited partners can use these statements to calculate their share of the book value of the partnership, known as the partnership's residual value. The residual value is the uninvested capital in the partnership and the partnership's share of the estimated value of the portfolio companies in which the partnership has invested.

When a portfolio company goes public, the limited partner may receive its share of the stock in that company, called a disbursement, although the general partner may hold the stock for a period within the partnership before distributing it. A disbursement of stock is usually valued by the partnership at the price per share at the time of the public offering. When the stock carries restrictions on its sale, its price is often discounted by 20 percent to 30 percent. In addition to stock, the limited partners may receive other disbursements such as cash dividends from the sale of portfolio companies through corporate acquisitions, company stock buybacks, or liquidations. As mentioned earlier, venture capital partnerships typically do not distribute information on their financial performance. However, limited partnerships have information on takedowns, disbursements, and residuals from which rates of return can be generated.

With the increase in institutional investors (especially pension funds) in venture capital limited partnerships, more emphasis has been placed on developing methods for determining a venture fund's residual value. Institutional investors have also been more willing to share the financial information that they have received from their venture capital general partners. Venture Economics began building a data base on venture capital rates of return in 1985 based on information provided by institutional investors. A number of analysts have used this data base to conduct studies to determine the rates of return for venture capital funds. In order to place these results in the proper context, analysts review previous research on venture capital rates of return and try to assess the likely effects of the IPO market and corporate acquisitions on venture fund performance.

In a review of earlier studies of venture capital rates of return, Bygrave et al. (1989) found that returns varied from 11 percent (Faucett's 1971 study of 14 publicly held venture capital companies)[1] to 27 percent (Martin and Petty's 1983 study of the rates of return from 1974 to 1979 of the stocks of 11 publicly held venture capital companies). Most earlier studies of venture capital funds found that normal rates of return tended to average in the high teens (e.g., Bessemer Securities' reported achievement of a 17 percent rate of return from 1967 to 1974 and Hambrecht and Quist's report of a 15 percent rate of return over several years through 1972), but these figures were anecdotal and unsubstantiated reports of rates of return by the venture capitalists themselves (Poindexter).[2] Poindexter surveyed 270 venture capital firms about their rates

---

[1] R.B. Faucett, "The Management of Venture Capital Investment Companies," Master's Thesis, Massachusetts Institute of Technology, 1971.

[2] J.B. Poindexter, "The Efficiency of Financial Markets: The Venture Capital Case," Ph.D. Dissertation, New York University, 1976.

FIGURE 9-6

Holding Periods and Realized Gains by Exit Method

Source: Venture Economics, Venture Capital Journal (Aug. 1988), p. 13

Exit Method	Average Holding Period[a] (Years)	Average Cost	Average Proceeds	Multiple
IPO	4.2	$ 814	$5,804	7.1
Acquisition	3.7	988	1,699	1.7
Company buyback	4.7	595	1,268	2.1
Secondary sale	3.6	715	1,431	2.0
Liquidation	4.1	1,030	198	0.2
Write-off	3.7	961	—	—

Note: Dollars in thousands.

[a] "Holding period" refers to time elapsed between initial date of investment and date of final exit.

of return. The 59 firms that responded estimated their rates of return to range from 35 percent to −40 percent, with an average of 13.3 percent.

[3] Venture Capital Investment Exit Patterns

The performance of a venture capital fund depends on its ability to sell companies in its portfolio at significantly higher multiples of what was originally invested. In 1988, Venture Economics conducted a study on the realized gains for different types of exits (IPO, acquisition, company buyback, secondary sale, liquidation, and write-off) from venture fund portfolios. Venture Economics studied 443 portfolio companies in 26 venture capital funds (which were started between 1970 and 1982) that exited these funds. As shown in Figure 9-6, on average venture capital funds generate their greatest returns by taking companies in their investment portfolios public. Firms that were taken public returned over 7 times their original investment, compared with a return of less than 2 times the original investment for firms that were sold as acquisitions. Venture Economics also found that 96 percent of IPOs provided realized gains for venture capital portfolios, while only 59 percent of the acquisitions provided positive gains. Since the average holding period for all exit methods is at least 3.7 years, it is difficult to evaluate a venture fund's portfolio performance until its fourth or fifth year. Another implication of these results is that venture funds are likely to generate high rates of return only when they can take companies public in an active IPO market. Yet, as subsequent tables show, the IPO window opens infrequently.

One interesting phenomenon shown in Figure 9-6 is the similarity in average holding periods for "winners" and "losers." Companies that eventually are liquidated or written off (losers) are held just as long in venture capitalists' portfolios as the winners, and venture capitalists continue to pour money into the losers at levels much higher than the investments that are made in winners. The average investment in a liquidated firm ($1 million) and a write-off ($0.96 million) was higher than the average investment in an IPO ($0.81 million).

FIGURE 9-7

Venture-Backed IPOs (1978–1992)

Source: Venture Economics

Year of IPO	Number of Companies	Median Age of Company (Years)	Total Amount Offered	Average Offering Size	Median Offering Size	Average Offering Valuation
1978	10	9	$ 91.0	$ 9.1	$ 6.9	$ 32.4
1979	12	9	104.5	8.7	7.5	34.1
1980	27	6	420.5	15.6	10.5	97.2
1981	68	5	770.3	11.3	10.1	53.1
1982	27	3	548.7	20.3	13.0	87.9
1983	121	4	3,031.3	25.1	16.2	116.0
1984	53	5	743.1	14.0	11.2	65.9
1985	47	3	843.3	17.9	15.2	69.7
1986	98	5	2,128.2	21.7	16.3	86.7
1987	81	5	1,839.5	22.7	17.6	85.1
1988	36	5	788.5	21.9	17.0	91.8
1989	39	5	996.0	25.5	16.5	100.0
1990	42	6	1,196.7	28.5	23.8	109.3
1991	121	6	3,833.0	31.7	27.0	116.8
1992	151	6	4,420.3	29.3	23.4	98.4

Note: Dollars in millions.

The market's receptiveness to venture-backed IPOs in the 1980s was erratic but much more favorable than in the late 1970s. (See Figure 9-7.) Of major significance was the explosion of IPOs that occurred in 1983. Funds started in the late 1970s benefited significantly during this short period when the public was extremely receptive to IPOs. This cycle appears to be repeating itself, as the IPO window opened in 1991 with over $3.7 billion invested and then moved toward closing in the last half of 1992 after $4.4 billion was invested in 151 IPOs.

Figure 9-8 shows the number of venture-backed companies that were acquired from 1982 to 1992. As might be expected, increases in acquisitions tend to be inversely related to the IPO market. As the IPO market for venture-backed companies continues to decline, the number of acquisitions of venture-backed companies continues to increase.

In summary, any discussion about the rates of return on venture capital must recognize that (1) venture capital funds have long-term investment horizons that are supported by 10-year limited partnership agreements; (2) on average, a company in a venture fund portfolio takes 4 to 5 years to blossom into a winner that can be harvested or to turn into a loser; (3) taking a venture-backed company public generates significantly higher returns than any other exit option; and (4) the IPO market in the early 1980s and 1990s provided an opportunity for many venture funds to take an extraordinary number of companies public.

FIGURE 9-8

Acquisitions of Venture-Backed Companies (1982–1992)

Source: Venture Economics

Year	Number of Acquisitions	Average Valuation of Deals
1982	40	$86.0
1983	49	55.7
1984	86	57.7
1985	101	41.0
1986	90	50.8
1987	113	41.3
1988	106	52.1
1989	101	71.3
1990	76	33.7
1991	65	36.8
1992	69	23.4

Note: Dollars in millions.

[4] Early and Long-Term Rates of Return

A study by Bygrave, Fast, Khoylian, Vincent, and Yue (1989) on the early rates of return of 131 venture capital funds in the Venture Economics data base yielded some controversial results about the performance of funds that were started during the early 1980s, compared with funds started in the late 1970s. The findings of this study suggest that the rates of return of venture capital funds, on average, declined during the mid- to late 1980s.

The Venture Economics data base used for this analysis contained approximately 15 percent of all new venture capital committed to private funds for the period 1971–1978, 43 percent for 1979–1980, and 50 percent for 1981–1982. For the funds started from the beginning of 1978 through the end of 1984, the analysis by Bygrave et al. found that the average internal rate of return (IRR) for all funds peaked in 1980 at about 32 percent. Except for 1983, when a rate of return of 29 percent was achieved, rates of return have steadily declined, so that by 1985 the average rate of return had fallen to less than 10 percent. Since the rate of return for a venture fund is heavily influenced by its age and when it was founded, Bygrave et al. used the data base to generate comparisons on these two dimensions. When the venture funds were grouped by the year in which they were started (see Figure 9-9), Bygrave et al. found that the rates of return were higher the earlier a fund was started across each year of the analysis. Funds started in 1978 and 1979 began with high rates of return and continued to outperform funds started later on a year-to-year basis.

When venture funds were grouped according to age and compared according to the date that each fund was started (see Figure 9-10), the study found that at any given age, the earlier a fund was started, the higher its rate of return (with the exception of

FIGURE 9-9

IRRs of Funds by Calendar Year, Grouped by Year Fund Started

Source: W.D. Bygrave, N. Fast, R. Khoylian, L. Vincent, and W. Yue, "Early Rates of Return of 131 Venture Capital Funds Started 1978–1984," Journal of Business Venturing, Vol. 4 (1989), p. 100

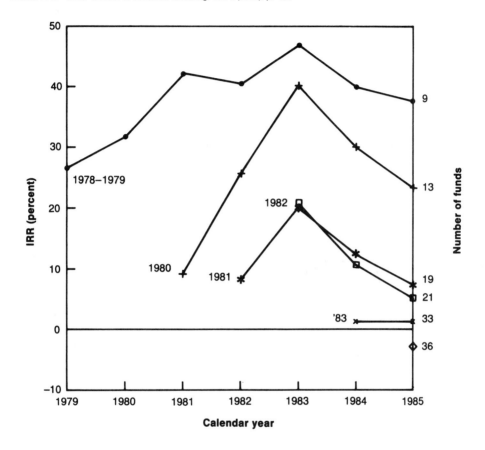

Note: Labels are years funds started.

the 1981 and 1982 funds at an age of one year). For both the age and time analyses, differences in the rates of return were highly significant statistically for each of the years (1981–1985) and for each age (three-year-old and five-year-old funds); that is, funds started earlier outperform funds started later even when the age of the fund is held constant. In addition, when Bygrave et al. compared the performance of the three-year-old and five-year-old funds (see Figure 9-11), they found that the median return for the older funds was much higher than for the younger funds (25 percent versus 13 percent). Thus, on average, rates of return on all venture capital funds

FIGURE 9-10

IRR of Funds by Age, Grouped by Year Fund Started

Source: W.D. Bygrave, N. Fast, R. Khoylian, L. Vincent, and W. Yue, "Early Rates of Return of 131 Venture Capital Funds Started 1978–1984," Journal of Business Venturing, *Vol. 4 (1989), p. 101*

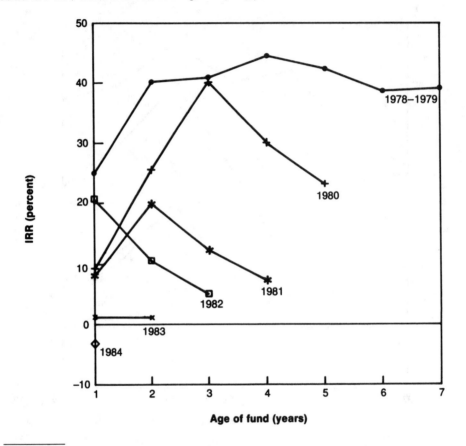

Note: Labels are years funds started.

steadily declined during the 1980s. In addition, funds started during the 1980s did not achieve the same rates of return as funds started in prior years.

In a more comprehensive study of the rates of return of venture capital funds by Venture Economics (summarized in the *Venture Capital Journal* of August 1989) analyzing 197 funds formed from 1970 through 1987 (which represents about 42 percent of the funds established during this time and accounts for 65 percent of the capital under management), Venture Economics found results similar to those found by Bygrave et al. Funds formed from 1977 through 1979 generated median rates of return by year 5 of over 35 percent. Returns for funds started in these years were significantly better than for funds formed earlier or later. (See Figure 9-12.) This study suggests that the IPO market in the early 1980s enabled venture funds to take companies public at earlier

FIGURE 9-11

Distribution of IRRs: All Three-Year-Old and Five-Year-Old Funds

Source: W.D. Bygrave, N. Fast, R. Khoylian, L. Vincent, and W. Yue, "Early Rates of Return of 131 Venture Capital Funds Started 1978–1984." Journal of Business Venturing, *Vol. 4 (1989), p. 102*

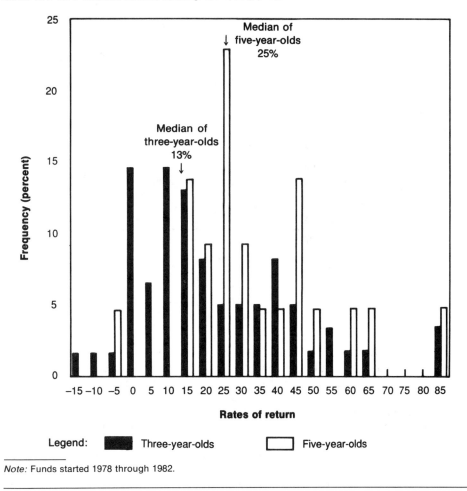

Note: Funds started 1978 through 1982.

ages and at higher valuations. The IPO market between 1980 and 1984 benefited all funds started in the 1970s:

> Funds started between 1970 and 1976 reported a capital-weighted average IRR of 21% and distributed, on the average, 4.6 times their paid-in capital by the end of the partnership's life. Three quarters of those distributions were paid out between 1980 and 1984, when 296 venture-backed initial public offerings occurred.[3]

___

[3] *Venture Capital Journal* (Aug. 1989), p. 12.

FIGURE 9-12

Year 5 Total Value of Venture Fund Capital

Source: Venture Economics. Venture Capital Journal *(Aug. 1989), p. 12*

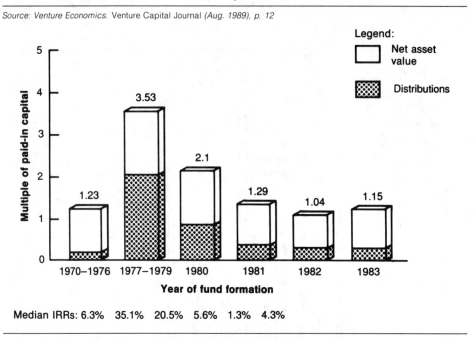

Median IRRs: 6.3%   35.1%   20.5%   5.6%   1.3%   4.3%

This Venture Economics report found that funds started in the early 1970s took until their seventh year to return 100 percent of their paid-in capital to their limited partners, but by the tenth year these funds distributed three and one-half times their original paid-in capital.

Venture capital rates of return are highly dependent on the IPO market for extraordinary gains. A high rate of return for a particular venture capital fund is a function of timing (when the IPO window opens) and the maturity of the fund; that is, the rate of return depends on the length of time for which the investment is held as well as on the multiple for which the investment is sold. The declining rates of return in venture capital in the late 1980s were more heavily influenced by a lackluster IPO market than by such factors as the growth in the total pool of venture capital (too much money chasing and too few good deals) or the lack of experience of many of the venture capital fund managers (too few experienced venture capitalists managing too much money).

If previous patterns of behavior in the IPO market continue to hold true in the future, interest in purchasing the shares of new companies will increase when investors see that some IPOs have generated significant gains in their aftermarket share prices. When investors see that IPOs can generate significant returns, they are more receptive to taking the risk of purchasing these shares. What occurs in the IPO marketplace is that many companies that were not able to go public in earlier years because the IPO window was closed—interest in buying shares in new companies was low—are now ready to "go public"; that is, these companies are poised for significant growth, because of a solid management team and years spent in developing new markets and technologies, which can be fueled by an infusion of new equity. Investors that purchase shares in these companies often see spectacular gains in their share prices (e.g., Apple Computer, Tandem Computer, Compaq, Lotus, and Microsoft). However, as the IPO market expands as more companies are taken public, the quality of each company in relation to the value of its IPO share price (as measured by its price/earnings (P/E) multiple) begins to fall.

In a hot IPO market, many companies are taken public that have little chance of generating the earnings growth indicated in their IPO P/E multiple. When a company fails to achieve its expected earnings growth, its aftermarket share price falls. The investor in that IPO usually ends up taking a loss on that investment and usually is less inclined to purchase subsequent IPOs. When losses on IPOs occur for the majority of investors in the market, interest in purchasing subsequent IPOs declines; the IPO window closes. In time, when memories of these losses fade or when new investors to the IPO market appear, and when IPOs generate returns higher than their initial IPO share prices—when IPOs are sold at "reasonable" P/E ratios—the IPO window opens and the investment cycle repeats itself. It is when a hot IPO market occurs that participants in the venture capital industry are able to harvest their portfolio companies and generate high rates of return for their investors.

9.08 INTERNATIONAL VENTURE CAPITAL

Venture capital is no longer a phenomenon that is found only in the United States; however, the structure and focus of the venture capital industry in other countries (e.g., types of investors and investments, exit opportunities, tax policies, and government regulations and incentives) are typically very different from those in the United States.

Within the last decade, venture capital funds have been started in all of the industrialized countries of the world, although most of the growth in capital commitments has occurred in countries that have emphasized tax and regulatory policies to promote new public equity markets. Estimates by Venture Economics appearing in Figure 9-13 show worldwide venture capital commitments by geographical region as well as for selected countries in those regions. This table includes a wider variety of capital types than what is normally considered venture capital in the United States. Information on the U.S. venture capital industry usually does not include capital commitments to specialist buyout firms such as Kohlberg Kravis and Roberts, while the venture capital commitments to funds in other countries do include such investment types.

Two estimates of U.S. capital commitments for comparative purposes are offered in Figure 9-13. Total new capital commitment to traditional venture capital companies (nonbuyout firms) in the United States was $2.9 billion in 1988, while there were over $4.1 billion worth of new capital commitments to European venture funds in 1988. These figures indicate that more capital was raised in Europe than in the United States. However, if all forms of venture capital, including capital committed to buyout firms, in the United States were considered, over $14 billion was raised in 1988.

The United States has been the major beneficiary of an international interest in venture capital. From 1980 through 1988, over 14 percent ($3.2 billion) of the capital committed to U.S. venture capital funds came from foreign investors (as shown in Figure 9-1). Aside from the returns from these investments, many foreign investors have gained knowledge about the venture capital process. Many foreign companies,

FIGURE 9-13

International Venture Capital Commitments and Capital Pools

Source: Venture Economics, Venture Capital Journal *(Dec. 1989), p. 10*

	New Capital (1988)	%	New Capital (1987)	%	Pool (1988)	%	Pool (1987)	%
North America					**By Country**			
United States	$ 2,900	35	$ 4,200	46	$31,140	54	$29,020	58
Canada	438	5	738	8	2,585	4	2,123	4
Total	$ 3,338	40	$ 4,938	54	$33,725	58	$31,143	62
Europe								
United Kingdom	$ 2,273	27	$ 1,189	21	$11,531	20	$ 9,257	19
France	773	9	599	7	3,247	6	2,473	5
Netherlands	292	4	113	1	1,472	3	1,180	2
Italy	280	3	134	1	1,033	2	752	2
Germany	173	2	361	4	763	1	590	1
Belgium	40	1	65	1	653	1	613	1
Spain	107	1	64	1	516	1	409	1
Rest of Europe	242	3	324	3	1,326	2	1,084	2
Total	$ 4,180	50	$ 3,549	39	$20,541	36	$16,358	33
Asia and Pacific Rim								
Australia	$ 125	1	$ 60	1	$ 774	1	$ 649	1
Japan	544	7	419	5	2,224	4	1,680	3
Rest of Asia and Pacific Rim	85	1	35	0	130	0	50	1
Total	$ 754	9	$ 514	6	$ 3,128	5	$ 2,379	5
Rest of World								
Total	$ 100	1	$ 60	1	$ 350	1	$ 250	0
Total Worldwide	$ 8,372	100	$ 9,061	100	$57,744	100	$50,130	100
					By Region			
United States	$14,150	72	$ 7,200	60	$43,890	62	$30,520	59
North America	$14,588	74	$ 7,938	66	$46,475	66	$32,643	63
Europe	4,180	21	3,550	29	20,540	29	16,360	32
Asia and Pacific Rim	754	4	514	4	3,128	4	2,380	5
Rest of world	100	1	60	1	350	1	250	0
Total Worldwide	$19,622	100	$12,062	100	$70,493	100	$51,633	100

Note: Dollars in millions.

such as the U.K. National Coal Board Pension Funds, became direct investors in U.S. venture-backed portfolio companies.[4] Because of the number of foreign investors boasting successful track records in the U.S. venture capital industry, the number of countries significantly changing tax and regulatory policies toward emerging companies, and the globalization of technology, the venture capital industry slowly expanded into all of the industrialized countries.

In a review of venture capital in Western Europe, Tyebjee and Vickery (1988) outlined four factors that influence a country's venture capital industry: (1) the size of its technology sector; (2) its culture of entrepreneurship; (3) the financial markets for new companies; and (4) public policy initiatives. These factors are useful in the evaluation of the venture capital industries in various countries.

After the United States, the United Kingdom has the second-largest venture industry in the world. Many observers of international venture capital investing believe that the United Kingdom's long history of public equity markets and a strong tradition of enforcing property rights has fostered a foundation for venture capital investments. The ability to take privately held emerging growth companies public seems to be the most important incentive for venture capital investors. The Unlisted Securities Market (USM), which was founded in 1981 and is similar to the OTC market in the United States, is the primary exit vehicle for venture capital investments, although corporate acquisitions are also an important way of realizing investments. Dozens of new companies went public in the 1980s on the USM, which has fueled interest from the London Stock Exchange in IPOs as well. The United Kingdom also offers tax breaks to individuals making investments in young companies. U.K. venture capitalists have traditionally invested all over the world but have emphasized investment in the United States. However, trends indicate that U.K. venture capitalists are shifting their investment focus from the United States to other European countries in line with the changes in the Common Market in the 1990s.

In France, banks are the primary source of venture capital (providing both debt and equity to companies), accounting for 35 percent of venture fund commitments in 1988. Corporate investors contributed 13 percent, foreign investors contributed 14 percent, and 25 percent came from pension funds and government agencies. In 1983, the French instituted the Seconde Marche, the second market, similar to the U.S. OTC market. Along with tax deductions for long-term capital gains on venture capital investments, the ability to generate high returns by taking companies public has made France home of the third-largest venture capital industry.

The Netherlands have instituted policies similar to those of the United Kingdom and France that have resulted in a burgeoning venture industry. In 1982, the Netherlands launched the Parallel Market, an OTC market for new publicly listed securities. Government policy has also spurred investments in new ventures; the government rebates 50 percent of the losses incurred by investors in government-approved venture capital funds.

Countries that have not been able to sustain a viable new issues market for emerging companies have not fostered a strong venture capital industry. This is not to say that these countries do not foster the growth of emerging businesses; many countries support these businesses through government grants, incentives for individuals to use their personal savings, and corporate ventures. Venture capital, however, is not a major source of funds for emerging businesses in these countries. For example, West

---

[4] *Venture Capital Journal* (Nov. 1984).

Germany had the largest economy in Western Europe even prior to its unification with East Germany, but Germany's venture industry is less than one tenth the size of the United Kingdom's. The equity markets in Germany are not a traditional source of capital. German companies prefer to use banks as sources of long-term capital rather than equity, and banks foster close relationships with firms as well. In fact, funding for venture capital firms in Germany has come primarily from banks and major corporations.

Even if a country encourages investments in emerging growth companies, the opportunity to take these emerging companies public appears to be a major incentive for venture capital investment. Despite Belgium's significant tax incentives for new technology-oriented companies and their investors and a readily available pool of capital from the government for investment in new companies (government agencies were responsible for 71 percent of all 1988 capital commitments in venture capital funds in Belgium), the difficult listing requirements for the Belgium OTC market have limited the number of companies that have gone public. With corporate acquisitions as the primary exit vehicle for venture capitalists, the prospects of generating large returns on a venture investment appear meager, and the venture capital industry remains very small.

In 1983, the Australian government initiated the management and investment companies (MIC) program, which enabled investors to deduct 100 percent of investments made in licensed venture capital companies. As with the SBIC program in the United States, many venture capitalists left these companies to start funds without the government regulation (and without benefit of the investor tax deduction). A licensed MIC can invest only in technology- and export-oriented companies, which then must be approved by the government's licensing board. Since the 1987 stock market crash in Australia, which discouraged many Australian investors from purchasing IPOs, corporate acquisitions have been the primary way in which venture capitalists exit their investments.

In Japan, the venture capital industry has focused on established privately held companies that can be taken public. Japan has established an emerging OTC market for small companies with less stringent listing requirements than those of the Tokyo Stock Exchange. However, Japan has placed less emphasis on supporting emerging companies. The lack of a mobile labor market in Japan has made it nearly impossible to start independent emerging growth companies. Without a labor force willing to leave jobs with established companies, the ability of emerging companies to grow becomes a problem not of lack of capital but of lack of labor.

According to the 1988 new capital commitments for each country, the most significant factor enabling venture capital to flourish in a particular country was the institution of a U.S.-type OTC equities market in new securities. The largest venture capital industries belong to countries with emerging second-tier security markets: the United Kingdom, France, Japan, and the Netherlands. Just as in the United States, venture capitalists need an exit opportunity that can yield high returns for their long-term venture investments.

9.09 ENTREPRENEUR'S SEARCH FOR CAPITAL

Of the estimated 600,000 companies that are started in the United States each year, fewer than 1,000 qualify to receive venture capital (about 0.15 percent). Even companies with the possibility of achieving high growth and profits have only a meager chance of receiving venture capital: It is estimated that for every 100 business plans submitted to a venture capitalist, fewer than 5 are seriously considered for funding, and only 2 are likely to be funded. The likelihood of finding capital, however, appears to be much higher. The results of studies by Bruno and Tyebjee (1981, 1983, 1985) on high technology entrepreneurs who were denied funding by a venture capitalist indicate that 33 percent of the entrepreneurs who are initially turned down by a venture capitalist eventually go on to raise funds. (On the other hand, Bruno and Tyebjee found that more than 30 percent of the firms that were denied funding by a venture capitalist had gone out of business.) Taken together, these studies of an entrepreneur's chances of receiving venture capital are somewhat ambiguous. From the perspective of the individual venture capitalist, the chance of an entrepreneur's getting venture capital is very slim (2 percent), but from the perspective of the entrepreneur, the chance of receiving venture capital after a number of tries is much higher (33 percent). However, all of the studies indicate that the acquisition of venture capital is a difficult process and very time-consuming, with most successful searches for venture capital taking 2 to 8 months to complete.

Venture capitalists invest with the expectation of high returns. Yet, even after careful screening and evaluation and with the financing and management expertise provided by the venture capitalist, most venture capital deals fail to achieve the high returns expected. Of the 5 to 10 companies a venture fund may have in its portfolio, the 1 or 2 stars that achieve at least a 50 percent compounded annual return must balance the returns from the total losses and the "living dead" (companies that continue to exist but have no possibility of providing an adequate return on investment to the venture capitalist), so that the overall portfolio might earn a rate of return of 25 percent.

[1] Strategies for Acquiring Venture Capital

Most venture capitalists suggest that the entrepreneur seeking capital first use a venture capital directory (such as *Pratt's Guide to Venture Capital* or any of the other directories from the National Venture Capital Association (NVCA), the National Association of Small Business Investment Companies, and so forth) in order to identify 5 to 10 venture capital companies that might be interested in the type of deal offered by the entrepreneur (based on, e.g., the amount of financing, stage of financing, type of industry, and geographical location). The entrepreneur can either use an intermediary who can arrange an introduction to the venture capitalist, approach the venture capitalist in writing with a brief letter and a 2- or 3-page summary of the business, or simply make a blind telephone call. The purpose of the initial contact (through any of the 3 avenues) is to determine whether the venture capitalist is interested in evaluating a business plan. For a variety of reasons, most inquiries for submitting a business plan are turned down. These reasons include the following:

- The business is in the wrong industry.
- The business is in the wrong location.
- The amount of financing required is too high.

- The amount of financing is too low (it takes as much work to evaluate and monitor a $100,000 investment as it does for a $1 million investment).

- The management team is inadequate.

- The venture capitalist is currently occupied in arranging another deal.

Between 20 percent and 40 percent of proposal inquiries actually result in the submission of a business plan for evaluation.

The studies by Bruno and Tyebjee on the experiences of entrepreneurs searching for capital for their high technology companies indicate that the median amount of time spent searching for financing is between 4 and 5 months. Twenty percent of the entrepreneurs surveyed required more than 8 months, and 20 percent required 2 months or less. Equity financing required an average of 6.7 months to acquire, while debt financing required an average of 5.2 months. A period of 6 months was required to arrange a venture capital deal (the same amount of time needed for dealing with noninstitutional investors or private individuals). On average, firms gave up 45.1 percent of their equity to outside investors for financing. Average equity amounts obtained by investors in the first 3 rounds of financing were 31.5 percent, 19.7 percent, and 10.2 percent, respectively. For less than 5 percent of equity, firms raised an average of $22,000; for 5 percent to 50 percent of equity, the average amount raised was $246,000; and for more than 50 percent of equity, the average amount raised was $4.7 million. Requests for financing that involved giving up equity received over 20 percent more capital than requests for debt financing.

In a survey of the most active venture capital companies in 1981, Timmons, Fast, and Bygrave (1983) found that the average amount of an initial investment by a venture capital company was $813,000 and that the amount of equity given up for this investment varied. Brophy's 1981 study of the NVCA found that the average amount of an initial investment by all venture capital companies was $597,000. The amount of equity given up for this level of investment was not provided. However, the amount of equity given up by the entrepreneur is usually a function of the company's stage of growth.

A general rule suggested by many venture capitalists is that the venture capitalist will ask for 50 percent to 90 percent of the equity in seed and start-up stages when putting in all of its funds and 10 percent to 50 percent for investments in first, second, and further financings. The percentage of equity received depends on the ratio of the amount of funds invested to the total amount already invested, the experience and abilities of the management team, and the potential of the venture for growth and profits.

Most entrepreneurs are likely to submit their business plans to three to five venture capitalists, although a business plan submitted to too many venture capitalists is likely to acquire the reputation of being "used goods." According to Bruno and Tyebjee (1981, 1983), entrepreneurs were likely to say that the reason for being denied venture capital was a characteristic of the venture, while venture capitalists were more likely to mention deficiencies in the venture's management.

[2] Evaluating Proposals for Venture Capital Financing

Every study of the venture capital decision-making process has found that the primary criterion for determining whether a venture will be successful is the quality of the management team. The business plan is one of the primary methods for evaluating the management team. It is a comprehensive guide to all aspects of the venture and provides the venture capitalist with an overview of management's ability to address all of the important issues necessary for expanding the firm.

The results of a number of studies to determine the criteria venture capitalists use to analyze venture proposals found that venture capitalists evaluate the following four areas: management, finances, industry attractiveness, and competition.

The primary reasons why venture capitalists deny funding to a venture are weak management, low market potential, and, to a lesser extent, product feasibility, form of financing, the presence of a similar investment in their portfolio, and competition. Yet, good management remains the main concern of the venture capitalist in evaluating a business plan. Confronted with the choice of a first-rate management team with a less than first-rate idea and a second-rate team with a first-rate idea, the venture capitalist would choose the venture with the first-rate management team. New ventures need entrepreneurs, individuals with the commitment, skills, and abilities to develop and build the venture into a substantial and profitable business. In addition, because venture capitalists seek to provide management with guidance as well as financing, the ability of the entrepreneur to work with the venture capitalist is an important criterion.

[a] **Management.** Of primary concern are the background, skills, and abilities of the top management team who will develop the venture. The venture capitalist evaluates the entrepreneur's previous successes in business, as well as his or her current and future ability to develop and product the product, generate sales, acquire and control resources, and build an organization.

[b] **Finances.** Financial considerations include the growth rate of the venture in terms of sales, costs, and profits, as well as future prospects for cashing out of the deal. The venture is judged on its financial riskiness and its ability to provide substantial returns to the investor. Among the financial aspects of the business plan given careful attention are the growth potential of the venture; potential profit margins; the risk of losing the investment; avenues for getting out of the investment through going public, a merger and acquisition, or a cash buyout; and the terms of the deal. Venture capitalists are looking for win-win investments, i.e., investments where both the venture capitalist and the entrepreneur can earn substantial returns from the partnership. No venture capitalist is going to invest in a company if the returns to the investor are meager relative to the risk involved. Conversely, a venture capitalist does not want to invest if the returns to the entrepreneur are so low that few incentives exist for the entrepreneur to devote the substantial effort required to expand the business and make it profitable.

[c] **Industry Attractiveness.** Venture capitalists also evaluate the features of the market in which the firm is seeking to compete. The possibility for a firm's profitability and growth depend to a large extent on the characteristics of the industry the firm is entering. A venture capitalist is concerned with the market's total size, its potential for growth, the number and strength of other firms in the industry, government regulations, possible substitutes for the industry's products and services, the characteristics of the industry's customers and suppliers, and the threat of other entrants. Trendy, new industries are often more likely to attract venture capital investment, and it is not

uncommon for such industries to go through a boom-and-bust cycle of venture capital investment when venture capitalists finance numerous new companies only to see most of these start-ups fail when the marketplace becomes saturated with too many new firms and too few innovative ideas. New ventures in industries that have peaked often have difficulty attracting venture capital, even though all other aspects of the deal are sound.

[d] Competitive Advantage. The venture must indicate a potential for sustained future growth and profitability. Particularly important is a unique feature that demonstrates that the venture can be a successful competitor, such as (1) a unique product, technology, location, or distribution system; (2) special access to raw materials; (3) particularly impressive employees, sales force, or marketing strategy; and (4) patent production. The financial statements show that a venture provides value through growing sales and profits, and the venture capitalist wants to see how this value is generated. A venture capitalist wants to know what makes a venture special and whether these features can be easily duplicated by other competitors. Profitable ventures involve firms that have a competitive advantage that is sustainable over the long run.

9.10 BUSINESS PLAN

The systematic presentation of all of the crucial information needed to start a new venture comes through the development of a business plan. The business plan used for the acquisition of venture capital has a particular orientation that is different from one designed for other activities, such as business, strategic, and operational planning. First, in the development of a business plan for a new venture, entrepreneurs are dealing with the unfamiliar. As part of the process of planning the new venture, entrepreneurs must demonstrate an aptitude for confronting the new and for acquiring the information necessary to decision making. Second, new venture planning must recognize that a venture has many different facets, some internal (production, employees, products, and plant and equipment) and others external (customers, suppliers, competitors, and government regulations).

New ventures are very complex and involve many key aspects; consequently, a framework is required to define and coordinate these many pieces. Besides helping the entrepreneur obtain financing, the business plan provides a road map to keep the entrepreneur on track in establishing the business by helping him or her take care of the hundreds of details that are part of developing and expanding a business, as well as outlining the critical issues for business success and establishing objectives to be met.

The sample business plan framework that appears in Appendix 9.1 is similar to most other business plan frameworks. Business plan guides are generally available free of charge from most public accounting firms, local SBA offices, and most major banks as well. Of the many business planning guide books available, books by Gladstone (1983), Mancuso (1985), Rich and Gumpert (1985), and Timmons (1990) are particularly helpful for guiding entrepreneurs through the business planning process. Whatever the format, however, the general ideas a business plan must convey are found in Appendix 9.1.

9.11 PRICING A VENTURE CAPITAL DEAL

The value of venture capitalists' investment in a company is based on the venture capitalists' perceived value for the total company. Their share of the venture is based on their estimation of a reasonable return for the risk involved in investing in the venture. Venture capitalists take a comprehensive approach to determine what the company might be worth in five to seven years. The total value of a company is usually based on the net present value (NPV) of future cash flows or on a multiple of future earnings. The discount rates used and multipliers to be used are determined by a number of factors that generally influence the venture capitalist's determination of the company's value, such as downside risk, upside potential, and exit opportunities.

[1] Downside Risk

While everyone, including entrepreneurs, investors, buyers, suppliers, and employees, who participates in the development of a venture expects it to succeed, many ventures do fail. The venture capitalist recognizes this possibility for failure and attempts to account for the downside risks of the investment in a number of ways. One of the primary ways the venture capitalist comes to terms with the possibility of losing an investment is insuring that in the event of failure, the entrepreneur suffers financially as well. An entrepreneur with his or her own money at stake is likely to pursue every possible strategy for turning around a failing company. Most venture capitalists require the entrepreneur to put up a sizable amount of the entrepreneur's total financial assets as either collateral for the venture capitalist's investment or a direct investment in the company. The venture capitalist may, for example, ask the entrepreneur for a second mortgage on the entrepreneur's house.

The venture capitalist would also like to protect the investment by structuring the deal as either preferred stock or as a loan with stock options or warrants so that in case of liquidation, the venture capitalist has first claim to the assets. Some investments are also tied to specified assets such as machinery, land, or buildings so that, in the event of bankruptcy, the venture capitalist can realize some return. For example, the venture capitalist might fund a venture with a collateralized note with warrants. If the venture declares bankruptcy, the venture capitalist is able to claim the property or machinery. If the venture grows, the venture capitalist will be able to exchange the note for shares in the successful company.

As in any financial investment, the less risk the investor perceives, the lower the rate of return the investor requires. By reducing downside risk, the venture capitalist is more willing to reduce the percentage of the company required for the venture capitalist's investment.

[2] Upside Potential

Venture capitalists want to know how much money they will make and how long it will take to make it. Any evaluation of such returns is based on NPV. Obviously, the venture capitalist wants to earn a great deal of money quickly, rather than later on; as indicated earlier, the rule for many venture capital investments is 5 times the investment in 5 years. Another safe assumption is that venture capitalists would like to earn the amount of their initial investment for every year, although the longer the investment remains outstanding, the lower the rate of return (e.g., 3 times in 3 years yields 44 percent; 10 times in 10 years yields 26 percent).

The more confidence the venture capitalist has in the entrepreneur's predictions for future earnings, the less risky the investment is perceived to be. In most cases, this is reflected in the stage of financing. Newer companies, such as start-up and first-stage companies, are perceived to be riskier than later-stage companies, so the rates of return required for investment are higher. The ability of the entrepreneur to convince the venture capitalist of the venture's future earnings potential is primarily based on the business plan and the entrepreneur's past experiences in growing companies, although strong persuasive skills are helpful in determining the venture capitalist's perceptions. The venture capitalist's familiarity with the company's overall health plays a part in establishing a company's future earnings potential.

[3] Exit Opportunities

Venture capitalists expect to get their investment back plus a substantial return and then move on to other investment opportunities. As mentioned earlier, most venture capitalists set up their investment portfolios as limited partnerships. Venture capitalists seek to return the principal to the limited partners as soon as possible so that they can begin to enjoy their 20 percent share of the capital gains in the fund. In determining a company's value, venture capitalists also want to know how they can remove themselves from the deal.

In most cases, the venture capitalist expects the company to go public. Investing in a company that will go public has two advantages. First, the investment becomes liquid once the stock is publicly traded. A venture capital company can exit during or after the IPO by sellings its shares (barring any restrictions based on federal and state security laws or the corporate charter). Second, a publicly traded company has a P/E ratio, so the venture capitalist can determine the value of the company based on that multiple. Privately held companies are much more difficult to value, which usually results in a lower valuation. Indeed, liquidity commands a substantial premium. It is fair to say that most venture capitalists expect to take the companies they invest in public or to sell their shares to large corporations willing to pay either cash or their own publicly traded securities. Entrepreneurs expecting to keep their companies private find it difficult to raise venture capital.

In some instances, it is impossible to take a company public (e.g., because the company is in the wrong type of industry for a fairly valued IPO or because the total value of the company might be too small to warrant an IPO); such companies have to provide other means for venture capitalists to get out their principal and their expected return. One way is to sell the venture to a larger corporation. Barring this alternative, the venture capitalist may ask for an earnout agreement in which the venture capitalist's investment will be bought out by the company itself at a prearranged price. For example, a venture capitalist might invest $250,000 for 100,000 shares in a company with which he or she might enter into an agreement stipulating that he or she can either sell the 100,000 shares back to the company for a guaranteed price of $1 million in 5 years or sell the shares to the public if the company is taken public (in which case the 100,000 shares might be worth $2 million). In either case, through a guaranteed buyout or through going public, the venture capitalist is able to earn the required rate of return.

[4] Pricing Example

Given the various issues involved in pricing a company, the valuation of a venture is very subjective and is always arrived at through much interpretation and negotiation. Assume, for example, that a company is projecting after-tax profits of $500,000 in 5 years and needs a $250,000 investment in order to expand its production capacity and increase its sales force. A venture capitalist, after looking over the business plan, might feel that the profit estimate is too high and arrive at a figure of $400,000 after-tax profit in 5 years. Further, the venture capitalist might determine that companies in this particular industry are likely to sell for a P/E multiple 5 years from now of between 8 and 10. He would thus estimate the total value of the company in the fifth year as follows:

$400,000 \times (8 \text{ to } 10) = \$3,200,000 \text{ to } \$4,000,000$

In addition, the venture capitalist in this situation feels that the amount of risk for investing in this company requires a 50 percent compounded annual rate of return. An investment of $250,000 would therefore be worth $1,898,437 at the end of 5 years, and the share of the company requested by the venture capitalist would consequently be between $1,898,437/$4,000,000 and $1,898,437/$3,200,000 (i.e., between 47 percent and 59 percent of the company).

An equation for determining the venture capitalist's share of ownership in the company for this example would be

$$E = \frac{I(1 + RR)^N}{N\text{th PAT(PEM)}}$$

where:

E = venture capitalist's percentage ownership

I = venture capitalist's investment

RR = venture capitalist's compounded rate of return

N = number of years the venture capitalist expects to hold the investment before cashing out

Nth PAT = after-tax profit that venture is expected to generate in year venture capitalist plans to cash out

PEM = P/E multiple at which company might be valued in Nth year

Using this model, the venture capitalist's calculation is as follows:

$$E = \frac{\$250,000(1 + 0.5)^5}{\$400,000(8)} = \frac{\$1,898,437}{\$3,200,000} = 59\%$$

Each figure, of course, is subject to negotiation. Even small changes in projected earnings, the amount of the investment, the P/E multiple, and the annual rate of return required can affect the percentage of the company the venture capitalist will require. For instance, a reduction in the venture capitalist's rate of return to 40 percent would change the venture capitalist's share of the company to 42 percent. If the P/E multiple is renegotiated at 10 rather than 8, the venture capitalist's share would change to 47 percent from 59 percent.

Entrepreneurs often assume unrealistic valuations for their companies. For example, an entrepreneur with a strong product idea, no management team, and the bare outlines of a business plan might think that a $100,000 investment is worth 10 percent of the company. This, however, represents a valuation of $1 million, which is likely to be viewed as somewhat excessive for a company without sales, a product, or a track record. An investor would have to see considerable upside potential in this entrepreneur's $1 million idea. Yet, venture capitalists rarely invest solely in ideas but in entrepreneurs who can develop and expand a business. Some venture capitalists have in fact put up to 100 percent of the capital for a new venture and have taken less than 30 percent of the total equity in return, but such investments are usually made to entrepreneurs with track records. In most seed investments, the entrepreneur is likely to give up 80 percent to 95 percent or more of the company's equity.

The valuation of the venture capitalist's investment is also affected by how the deal is structured and by the type of investment and the terms and conditions under which the investment is made.

9.12 STRUCTURING A VENTURE CAPITAL DEAL

Accounting for upside potential, downside risk, and exit opportunities often requires a complex financing structure that minimizes the venture capitalist's risks while still offering good opportunities for significant rewards. Venture capitalists are not passive investors; rather, venture capitalists see themselves as partners working together with the entrepreneur to generate growing sales and profits. Most venture capital investments are designed to facilitate this working partnership. Potential entrepreneurs are often under the mistaken impression that as long as they retain more than 50 percent of the shares of voting stock, they will be able to control their companies. In most cases, however, the number of shares owned by each side is essentially meaningless when it comes to making decisions about company operations.

The structure of a venture capital investment provides the venture capitalist with a sufficient degree of control over operations to insure that the financial returns promised by the entrepreneur are generated. At the same time, venture capitalists do not invest in companies with the expectation of being involved in the day-to-day operations of the business. They generally structure their investments so that the entrepreneur has considerable leeway in running the company as long as the performance targets specified in the business plan and the investment agreement are met or surpassed. However, most venture capital investments are structured so that when the entrepreneur fails to meet the promised performance goals, control of the company shifts to the venture capitalist. Structuring the financing, then, is a crucial aspect of acquiring venture capital funds.

[1] Commitment Letters and Investment Agreements

A venture financing is usually conducted in two stages. In the first stage, the venture capitalist offers a commitment letter that provides a broad outline of the proposed deal between the venture capitalist and the entrepreneur. If the entrepreneur agrees in general to the terms offered in the commitment letter and is willing to continue negotiations, an investment agreement is drawn up. In this second stage, the investment agreement defines the specific terms under which a venture capitalist will make an investment in the company. Many aspects of the commitment letter and the investment agreement are identical. In fact, some venture capitalists do not offer a commitment letter at all but draw up the investment agreement based on the oral understanding that both sides have reached.

Each of these documents is a legal business plan specifying the company's goals for the future and providing for specific actions and remedies under both good and bad scenarios. The commitment letter and investment agreement can be quite lengthy and may appear to be so much legal boilerplate, but these agreements should be carefully reviewed by both the entrepreneur and a lawyer with experience in writing and negotiating investment agreements. Covered in these documents are four general issues: (1) the terms of the investment; (2) representations and warranties; (3) covenants and undertakings; and (4) closing conditions.

[a] Terms of the Investment. The agreement specifies the type of securities offered, the amount and price of the securities, and the collateral. Guarantees and subordination (for debt), conversion privileges, and time limits are also specified.

[b] Representations and Warranties. Even though the venture capitalist will have thoroughly researched and studied the company before making an investment, there is still a need for the company to provide full disclosure of many of the details of its operations. Among these details are financial statements (both audited and unaudited) prepared under generally accepted accounting principles; proof that the company meets all legal requirements for doing business at federal, state, and local levels; any pending litigation that may affect the company's operations; owned (tangible and intangible) assets; any insider transactions or financial relationships with other outside investors; proof of compliance with federal and state corporate and securities laws; prior employment contracts of the company's founders and employees with their previous employers; and any other information that may influence the ability of the company to meet the terms of the investment agreement.

[c] Covenants and Undertakings. This agreement also specifies what the company will try to achieve (or refrain from doing) in the future. If the venture capitalist already has control of the board of directors, the number of covenants will probably be kept to a minimum. In situations where control of the company is held by the entrepreneur, the covenants can be extensive. While covenants and undertakings are typically associated with debt instruments, venture capitalists also use covenants and undertakings with equity investments as a way of controlling and monitoring the activities of the entrepreneurs operating the venture.

Many of the affirmative covenants found in an investment agreement make obvious business sense. Common among these covenants are warrants that the company will do the following:

- Pay all lawful taxes and assessments
- Pay all trade debt and the interest and principal on debt securities
- Maintain and repair plant and equipment
- Purchase insurance for plant and equipment and for key officers and employees
- Protect proprietary rights such as patents and trade secrets

Other affirmative covenants to help the venture capitalist manage the investment may be those that do the following:

- Guarantee the venture capitalist access to the company's facilities, books, and records
- Provide timely financial reports and operating statements
- Require advance approval from the venture capitalist for operating budgets and the purchase of plant and equipment
- Offer representation or attendance at all company board meetings
- Specify that the company will meet certain financial benchmarks

In addition, in debt or equity investments, as in many loan covenants stipulated by bankers, the venture capitalist will ask that the company maintain certain levels of cash, working capital, net worth, and so forth.

Negative covenants relate to actions that the company agrees not to undertake without the approval of the venture capitalist, such as selling stock or securities, providing dividends, merging or selling the company, selling key assets, increasing indebtedness, and entering into contracts in excess of a specified dollar amount.

Venture capitalists also require other rights in the areas of registration and future financings. They may demand registration rights that would in effect provide them with the right to ask the company to go public at any time (although such power would rarely be invoked because of the expense of going public). When the company does go public, the venture capitalist often has piggyback registration rights and marketing rights that obligate the company to register and market the venture capitalist's shares at the same time as it does the company's. Venture capitalists often have the right to participate in future financings so that their initial investment are not be diluted when additional capital is raised.

[d] Closing Conditions. In order to complete a venture capital financing, other conditions must be met as well. Some issues in finalizing a deal are legal opinions for the investor and the company; employment, noncompete, and stock registration agreements; and elections and resignations of members of the board of directors.

[2] Types of Investment Securities

A number of creative methods have been used by venture capitalists to finance entrepreneurial companies. In general, however, three types of investment securities are most common: common stock, convertible preferred stock, and debt with conversion privileges or warrants.

[a] Common Stock. The most straightforward way a venture capitalist can participate in financing a venture is through the purchase of common stock. Common stock provides a direct equity investment. Common stockholders can elect members to the board of directors of the firm and share in both the upside and downside potential of the venture.

The major problem with common stock is its failure to protect the investor's downside risk adequately: In a liquidation, common stockholders have the last claim on the assets of the venture. Because even the best investments made by the venture capitalist have some chance of failure, it is preferable that venture financings be structured to minimize downside risk.

[b] Convertible Preferred Stock. The primary advantage of convertible preferred stock is its ability in case of liquidation to claim assets of the venture before the common stockholders while still providing the opportunity to share in the equity gains of common stock through the conversion privilege. Convertible preferred stock is often designed to provide a minimum rate of return through the payment of dividends, which may be cumulative or noncumulative. Most convertible preferred stock carries the same voting privileges as common stock, based on the number of common stock shares to which the preferred share can be converted.

[c] Subordinated Debt With Conversion Privileges or Warrants. Debt securities are used by venture capitalists who need to receive a current return on their investment. This is often the case for SBICs, which must make interest payments on funds they borrowed from the SBA to make the investment. Subordinated debt holders would have claims to the assets of the venture that take priority over those of both preferred and common stock holders but not over those of other debt holders, such as banks and trade creditors. Subordinated debt holders would not have voting rights in the venture, so venture capitalists influence the company in other ways, such as by voter proxy agreements and affirmative and negative covenants. Most subordinated debt carries privileges to convert the debt into common stock at a later date or warrants that can be exercised to purchase common stock. Thus, subordinated convertible debt (with additional ancillary agreements and covenants) provides the best of both worlds; it minimizes downside risk and provides some current return while providing the opportunity to share in the upside potential of the venture as well.

The type of debt or equity instrument to be used is a matter of negotiation between the entrepreneur and venture capitalist. Issues to be considered by both parties include the financing requirements of the venture, the stage of the venture, the ability of the venture to make interest and principal payments, the rates of return and payback of the principal, and interest or capital gain expected by the venture capitalist. Sometimes the selection of a particular financing vehicle is made because of the particular preference of the venture capital company to have only one type of investment.

[3] Antidilution Provisions

Obviously, the venture capitalist wants to protect the value of the investment made in the venture. One way of insuring full value is through antidilution provisions in the investment agreement. This practice is commonly called the full ratchet. The basic idea of these provisions is that the total value of the investment made by the venture capitalist never declines, no matter how much the shares of the stock are worth. If the price of the stock declines, the venture capitalist is given more shares of stock until the total number of shares equals the original investment made. Antidilution provisions prevent situations where the original investor has purchased shares at prices higher than subsequent investors. (In general, one's assumption would be that subsequent investors would have to pay more for their shares because the venture's success has driven up the price of the shares.) Antidilution provisions come into play when additional equity is acquired by the venture. In situations where the stock price of the venture remains above the stock price sold to the venture capitalist or no additional shares of stock are sold, the full ratchet is not enforced. However, in situations where the venture has to sell an additional round of equity at a stock price lower than the stock price originally paid by the venture capitalist, the entrepreneur experiences the full ratchet.

Consider the following example. An entrepreneur raises $1 million from a venture capitalist for 25 percent of the company's equity at $10 per share; the venture capitalist owns 25 percent (100,000 shares) and the entrepreneur owns 75 percent (300,000 shares). For some reason, however, the venture does not perform as well as expected (e.g., development of the product takes longer than anticipated, sales take longer to develop, and product costs are higher), and the venture needs an additional $500,000 in order to continue operations. The entrepreneur might assume that because some progress has been made in the venture's development, additional shares can be sold at $10 per share. In that case, the entrepreneur would expect the venture capitalist to buy 50,000 shares at $10 per share, so that the venture capitalist owns 33.3 percent (150,000 shares) and the entrepreneur owns 66.7 percent (300,000 shares). Thus, the entrepreneur's share of the equity goes from 75 percent to 66.7 percent because of the additional 50,000 shares. If the shares can be sold at $10, the entrepreneur would lose little in this transaction. However, a scenario such as this is unlikely. It is rare that an entrepreneur who does not meet his or her projections can raise capital at the original share price. The entrepreneur is more likely to sell shares at much less than $10, probably at around $2.50 per share, and, once shares are sold at less than $10, the full ratchet takes effect. The shares originally sold to the venture capitalist also become valued at $2.50 per share. In order to match the original investment of $1 million (100,000 shares at $10 per share), the venture capitalist must receive 400,000 shares at $2.50 per share (the full ratchet). If the venture capitalist purchases the $500,000 in additional equity, the ownership of the company changes dramatically. The venture capitalist now owns 66.6 percent (600,000 shares), while the entrepreneur's 300,000 shares represent only 33.4 percent.

From the venture capitalist's perspective, the full ratchet is a fair method of compensating the investor for the failure of the entrepreneur to expand the venture and raise the value of the original shares. From the entrepreneur's perspective, two lessons are apparent. First, the entrepreneur should always try to raise more money than he or she thinks will be needed, so that if the venture does not perform as expected, there will be a cushion of resources to fall back on. Second, the entrepreneur should try to meet the promised performance goals, so that when additional resources are required, the price of the original shares will be higher (because the firm is performing as expected) than they were originally. Sales of additional rounds of equity at prices lower than those paid by the original investor trigger antidilution provisions that are very much to the disadvantage of the entrepreneur.

9.13 CONCLUSION

The use of venture capital can be an important factor in helping ventures grow rapidly. Often, the infusion of equity into a new company helps bring other sources of funding into the venture as well (such as bank loans and commercial credit). An investment by a venture capitalist is an important sign of legitimacy for a fledgling venture, indicating an informed belief that the new company will grow rapidly and earn significant return within five to seven years.

Venture capital involves more than providing funds to risky, new, and growing businesses. The venture capitalist is a partner with the entrepreneur. Even though the legal and financial details of a venture capital financing may seem overly complex and even unfair (the affirmative and negative covenants may appear to the entrepreneur to be ways to eliminate any risk to the venture capitalist), the venture capitalist is just as concerned about expanding and developing the company as the entrepreneur. No investment agreement can be structured to provide large financial returns in a failing venture. In addition, venture capitalists can provide expertise and advice in finding key people for the management team, knowledgeable consultants, and thoughtful and perceptive advisers for the board of directors. By coupling funding with support and advice, the venture capitalist plays an important and crucial role in building future Fortune 500 companies.

Suggested Reading

Brophy, D.J. "Venture Capital Investment, 1981." *Frontiers of Entrepreneurship Research.* Wellesley, Mass.: Babson College, 1981, pp. 246–280.

Bruno, A., and T. Tyebjee. "The Entrepreneur's Search for Capital." *Journal of Business Venturing,* Vol. 1 (1985), pp. 61–74.

———. "The One That Got Away: A Study of Ventures Rejected by Venture Capitalists." *Frontiers of Entrepreneurship Research.* Wellesley, Mass.: Babson College, 1983, pp. 289–306.

———. "Venture Capital Decision Making: Preliminary Results From Three Empirical Studies." *Frontiers of Entrepreneurship Research.* Wellesley, Mass.: Babson College, 1981, pp. 281–320.

———. "The Structure of the Investment Networks of Venture Capital Firms." *Journal of Business Venturing,* Vol. 3 (1988), pp. 137–157.

———. "Syndicated Investments by Venture Capital Firms: A Networking Perspective." *Journal of Business Venturing,* Vol. 2 (1987), pp. 139–154.

Bygrave, W.D., N. Fast, R. Khoylian, L. Vincent, and W. Yue. "Early Rates of Return of 131 Venture Capital Funds Started 1978–1984." *Journal of Business Venturing,* Vol. 4 (1989), pp. 93–105.

Gardner, Jr., W.F. "Venture Capital Financing: A Lawyer's Checklist." *Business Lawyer* (Jan. 1971), p. 997.

Gladstone, D.J., *Venture Capital Handbook.* Reston, Va.: Reston Publishing Co., 1983.

MacMillian, I.C., R. Siegel, and P.N.S. Narasimha. "Criteria Used by Venture Capitalists to Evaluate New Venture Proposals." *Journal of Business Venturing,* Vol. 1 (1985), pp. 119–128.

Mancuso, Joseph R. *How to Write a Winning Business Plan.* Englewood Cliffs, N.J.: Prentice-Hall, Inc., 1985.

Martin, J.P., and W.P. Petty. "An Analysis of the Performance of Publicly Traded Venture Capital Companies." *Journal of Financial and Quantitative Analysis,* Vol. 18 (1983), pp. 401–410.

Pratt, Stanley E., and Jan K. Morris, eds. *Pratt's Guide to Venture Capital Sources.* Wellesley, Mass.: Capital Publishing Co. (updated yearly). (Available from Venture Economics, 16 Laurel Avenue, Box 348, Wellesley Hills, Mass. 02181.)

Rich, Stanley R., and David E. Gumpert. *Business Plans That Win $$$.* New York: Harper & Row, 1985.

Roberts, E. "Business Planning and Start-Up in High Technology Companies." *Frontiers of Entrepreneurship Research*. Wellesley, Mass.: Babson College, 1983, pp. 107–117.

Stewart, M.D. "Venture Capital: Semi-Industry." *Venture Capital*. Publication 44-1092. New York: Practising Law Institute, 1973, p. 29.

Testa, Richard J. "The Legal Process of Venture Capital Investment," *Pratt's Guide to Venture Capital Sources,* Stanley Pratt and Jan K. Morris, eds. Wellesley, Mass.: Capital Publishing Co., 1984, pp. 57–67.

Timmons, J.A. *New Venture Creation,* 3rd ed. Homewood, Ill.: Richard D. Irwin, 1990.

Timmons, J.A., N. Fast, and W.D. Bygrave, "The Flow of Venture Capital to Highly Innovative Technological Ventures." *Frontiers of Entrepreneurship Research*. Wellesley, Mass.: Babson College, 1983, pp. 316–334.

——. "Seed and Start-Up Venture Capital Investment in Technological Companies." *Frontiers of Entrepreneurship Research*. Wellesley, Mass.: Babson College, 1984, pp. 1–17.

Tyebjee, T., and L. Vickery. "Venture Capital in Western Europe." *Journal of Business Venturing,* Vol. 3 (1988), pp. 123–136.

Venture Economics. *Trends in Venture Capital*. Wellesley Hills, Mass., 1981–1992.

Venture Economics. *Venture Capital Journal*. Wellesley Hills, Mass., 1982–1992.

APPENDIX 9.1 SAMPLE FRAMEWORK FOR A BUSINESS PLAN

1. Executive Summary. This brief summary of the facts of the business should be usable by itself and should highlight key points from the other sections of the plan.

2. Description of the Proposed Business
   - What business are you going to enter?
   - Exactly what products or services will be sold?
   - What are the uses, features, and key benefits of your products or services?
   - Who will be the primary customers of your products or services, and why will they buy?

3. Description of the Products or Services
   - What is the current stage of development (idea, prototype, or ready for sale), and what remains to be done?
   - What features of your products or services (e.g., patents or design) give them an advantage or disadvantage over the competition?

4. Description of the Market
   - What is the approximate size of the total potential market for your kind of product or service? Identify your sales area and the total dollar sales for the past, present, and future.
   - Are there several kinds of products or services that compete for the same business or for the same customers?
   - Who are your major competitors? List them in order of the share of the market. How do they compete (price, quality, or innovation)? What are their strengths and weaknesses? What are their profits? How do they operate? Which are growing most rapidly? Which are the most aggressive? Which are having problems?
   - How does your product or service fit into the existing marketplace? Can you price the product or service competitively and still make a profit? Why?
   - What share of the market will you be able to acquire?

5. Marketing Strategy
   - What methods will you use to sell and distribute your products or services (sales representatives, direct sales, or distributors)?
   - How will you bring your product or service to the attention of potential customers?
   - What are the costs of selling, distribution networks, and advertising?

6. Production Plan
   - What are the major difficulties (such as equipment, labor skills, special operations, and suppliers) in the manufacture of the product or delivery of the service?
   - How will you overcome these difficulties? Estimate time and money needed to do so.

7. Personnel Strategy
   - What key managerial skills and expertise in functional areas does the proposed venture need to succeed? What are the critical tasks that have to be accomplished?
   - Who will perform these tasks (founders, employees, or others)?

- Why are you in business? What in your previous experiences gives you the knowledge needed to run your business?

8. Financial Plan
    - Sources and use of funds* (How much initial capital will be required to start the business? How much additional funding will be required? When? Where is the money coming from? Where is it going?).
    - Capital equipment list** (list of depreciable assets).
    - Pro forma balance sheets.***
    - Pro forma income statements.*
    - Pro forma cash flow statements.*
    - Break-even analysis.**

9. Conclusions
    - What are the major risks and problems, and what will you do to minimize them?
    - What is the strength of business in brief?

10. Supporting Material
    - Backup material to support statements in previous sections.
    - Short biographies of key personnel or their resumes.

---

* Should be prepared monthly.
** Should be prepared yearly.
*** Should be prepared quarterly.

Chapter 10

Corporate Valuation

BRADFORD CORNELL

10.01 INTRODUCTION

Corporate valuation or appraisal[1] is a strange blend of science and art. Ideas developed by financial economists, such as the efficient market hypothesis, the weighted average cost of capital, and discounted present value, play a key role in corporate valuation. Corporate valuation, however, is based on more than financial economic theory. In fact, some valuation approaches, such as those based on analyzing accounting statements or on comparisons with purportedly similar companies, make virtually no use of modern finance. Too often, finance theorists dismiss the work of practicing appraisers as ad hoc application of rules of thumb, while practicing appraisers and managers dismiss the work of finance theorists as esoteric and irrelevant. The fairest assessment is that both views are wrong. Financial models have not developed to the point where they can be applied without practical experience and judgment, and appraisers who attempt to proceed without any understanding of finance theory are sure to go astray.

    There are a host of practical situations in which a company must be appraised. For instance, every state requires railroads and utilities operating within the state to be appraised each year for the purpose of assessing property taxes. Appraisals are commonly required for estate tax purposes and in divorce proceedings. Initial public offerings (IPOs) require accurate appraisals for proper pricing of new securities. If the offering price is too high, the offer will fail; if the offering price is too low, the issuing company will not receive full value for the securities sold. Regulatory policy is also related to valuation. One way to interpret public utility regulation, for example, is to say that regulators attempt to set rate of return on equity so that the value of a utility's shares equals the value of the assets financed by sale of equity. Finally, the growing popularity of employee stock option plans has greatly increased the need for annual appraisals.

10.02 FAIR MARKET VALUE

Before the procedures used to appraise companies are discussed, it is necessary to determine exactly what is being valued. While the goal of an appraisal is to estimate the fair market value of a company, there are two ambiguities in the phrase "fair market value of a company." What is meant by "fair market value," and what is meant by "a company"? The Internal Revenue Service (IRS), in its Revenue Ruling 65-193, defines "fair market value" as

> the price at which the property would change hands between a willing buyer and a willing seller when the former is not under any compulsion to buy and the later is not under any compulsion to sell, both parties having reasonable knowledge of relevant facts. Court decisions frequently state, in addition, that the hypothetical buyer and seller are assumed to be able, as well as willing, to trade and be well informed about the property and concerning the market for such property.

The IRS's rational buyer–rational seller rule has become the standard in the appraisal profession.

    When the asset being appraised is a corporation, the property that the hypothetical

---

[1] The terms "valuation" and "appraisal" are used interchangeably throughout this chapter.

rational buyer and seller are trading consists of the claims of all of the company's security holders. .This includes the value of outstanding common stock, preferred stock, bonds, and privately held debt such as bank loans. Confusion can arise because there are numerous corporate acquisitions in which all of the securities do not change hands. For example, a company may have a fair market value of $300 million, of which $200 million represents the market value of the common stock and $100 million represents the market value of a bank loan. In one possible transaction, a buyer may purchase the stock for $200 million and assume the bank debt. Thus, the company appears to change hands for a price of $200 million. However, this does not mean that the value of the company is $200 million, because only the common stock was purchased for that price. The bank retains a claim on a portion of the company's cash flow that has a market value of $100 million, so the total value of the company remains $300 million.

In short, what appraisers are trying to value is the aggregate fair market value of all of a company's securities, not just the equity. This seems to suggest an appraisal procedure in which the values of the company's debt, preferred stock, and common stock are estimated and added to arrive at the value the firm. While this is an ideal approach when it is applicable, it is often not feasible because some of the company's securities are not traded in a public market. Under such circumstances, the best approach is generally to estimate the entire value of the firm in one step rather than to estimate the value of each class of security separately and add the values.

Of course, there are situations in which the appraiser is interested exclusively in valuing one class of securities issued by the firm, such as the common stock. Even in this case, however, it is often better to value the total firm and then to allocate the total value among the various classes of securities rather than to attempt to value the equity directly. Valuing the entire firm as a unit makes it easier to deal with issues like control premiums, minority discounts, and discounts for nonmarketability in a consistent fashion.

10.03 APPROACHES TO VALUATION

Four appraisal approaches are used widely in practice. The first approach is the stock-and-debt approach, which amounts to adding the market values of a company's outstanding securities. Its theoretical foundation is the efficient market hypothesis, which states that the prices of publicly traded securities accurately reflect the true underlying value of the company. Although the stock-and-debt approach can be applied directly only to a limited number of companies whose securities are publicly traded, it serves as an input for appraisals based on direct comparisons.

The second approach makes use of the balance sheet. The simplest balance sheet valuation procedure is to add the book values of the company's outstanding securities. The problem with this procedure is that it equates the historical values of assets and liabilities, as recorded by accountants, with their market values. Because book and market values frequently diverge, appraisers typically adjust the balance sheet entries with the goal of more accurately estimating market values.

The third approach appraises a company on the basis of comparisons with similar or comparable companies whose value is known, either because the comparable company was recently sold or because it can be valued using the stock and debt approach. The direct comparison approach, which is sometimes referred to as the direct capitalization approach, consists of calculating ratios such as market value to earnings for the comparable companies and then multiplying the ratios by the appraisal target's earnings. The term "direct comparison" is used in this chapter because capitalization is often confused with discounting (which has nothing to do with this approach).

The fourth and final approach to appraisal is projecting the future cash flows that a company will earn for its security holders and then discounting those cash flows to present value. This approach, called the discounted cash flow (DCF) approach, is based on the assumption that no matter what product a company produces, investors hold its securities because they expect those securities to produce future cash payouts for them. The more cash expected to be received, the sooner the cash is expected to be received, and the lower the rate of discount, the more highly investors will value the company's securities.

10.04 STOCK-AND-DEBT APPROACH

When the securities of a company being appraised are publicly traded, there is a straightforward valuation procedure: Add the market values of all of the outstanding securities. This procedure has been dubbed the stock-and-debt approach by property tax appraisers. It is also occasionally referred to as the market approach because it is based on observation of the market prices of the firm's securities.

The valuation of Monsanto, a diversified chemical company, provides an example of the stock-and-debt approach. On December 30, 1990, Monsanto had short-term outstanding debt with a market value of $582 million and long-term outstanding debt with a market value of $1.652 billion. The company also had 164,394,194 shares of common stock outstanding. At the closing price of 48¼ on December 30, these shares had a market value of $7.932 billion. Adding the market value of the debt to the market value of the equity gives a total value of $10.166 billion for Monsanto. (The value of the preferred shares is also added if the company has preferred stock outstanding.)

Although the stock-and-debt approach is straightforward, debate has arisen over what prices to use when the securities, particularly the equity, are valued. Because of the volatility of stock prices, some appraisers advocate using an average of recent stock prices, rather than the price of the stock on the lien date (the day on which the appraiser is attempting to estimate value). Depending on the length of the average employed, this can have a marked impact on the calculated value. Averaging is often used by state ad valorem tax appraisers. In some cases, security prices may be averaged over a period extending backward in time a year or more from the lien date. The rationale for averaging is that an average of past prices is a more reliable indicator of a company's true underlying value than the current stock price.

This view is contradicted by the efficient market hypothesis, which states that securities prices reflect all publicly available information regarding a company's true underlying value.[2] If this is true, securities prices change because new information

---

[2] This is the semistrong form of the efficient market hypothesis. The weak form states that security prices reflect all historical price and volume information, while the strong form states that securities prices reflect all information. When appraisers refer to the efficient market hypothesis, however, they invariably mean the semistrong form.

arrives.[3] Consequently, averaging makes no sense. The correct securities prices to use to value a company are the market prices on the lien date, because those prices reflect all public information available at that time. Averaging earlier prices, which are based on past information, reduces the accuracy of the appraisal. Furthermore, the more volatile security prices are, the less appropriate it is to average them, because the high volatility indicates rapid arrival of new information, so that historical prices are significantly out of date.

The foregoing assumes, of course, that the efficient market hypothesis is true. That is a subject of considerable debate. Although the evidence provided by Fama (1970, 1991) in his two classic review papers generally supports the view that the equity market is efficient, there is countervailing evidence. Among the more highly publicized work that raises questions about market efficiencies are papers by the following writers:

- Banz (1981), who shows that small firms tend to earn abnormally high returns
- Keim (1988), who reports that returns are abnormally large in January, particularly for small firms
- Shiller (1981), who argues that stock prices are too volatile to be consistent with market efficiency
- Summers (1986), who points out that traditional tests of market efficiency have little power against a variety of alternative hypotheses

However, from the standpoint of appraisal practice, the importance of the academic debate regarding market efficiency should not be exaggerated. The key question is not whether the market is perfectly efficient but rather whether there is a procedure that an appraiser can use to produce valuations that are more accurate than market prices. There is no evidence to indicate that such is the case. After all, if appraisers had the ability to consistently identify undervalued or overvalued securities, they could make vast fortunes by becoming professional investment managers. Furthermore, market valuations are objective in the sense that they are unrelated to the reasons that an appraisal was requested. The work of appraisers, on the other hand, reflects their own views and biases and may also reflect the goals of the client that is paying for the appraisal.

From a practical appraisal standpoint, therefore, it is reasonable to assume that the efficient market hypothesis holds. Thus, if all of a company's securities are publicly traded, the simplest and most accurate way to appraise the company is to add the market values of the outstanding securities.

Unfortunately, most valuation assignments do not involve appraising publicly traded firms. More commonly, a manager wants to know the value of a subsidiary or a privately held firm, while an investment banker wants to know the value of a company that is about to go public. It appears that under such conditions, the stock-and-debt approach is of little value, but this is not entirely true. The stock-and-debt approach still plays a key role as an input into direct comparison appraisals. As described later in this chapter, a commonly employed method for valuing companies whose equity is not publicly traded as well as divisions and subsidiaries of publicly traded companies

---

[3] More precisely, unexpected security price changes are due to the arrival of new information. Because expected price changes are small over short periods for most corporate securities, actual changes and unexpected changes are virtually identical.

is to calculate ratios, such as the price/earnings (P/E) ratio, for comparable firms and then to apply those ratios to the appraisal target. This procedure pushes the appraisal problem back one step. To calculate the ratios, it is necessary to value the comparable firms. The preferred solution to this problem is to find comparable companies that have publicly traded securities so that the stock-and-debt approach can be applied.

10.05 BOOK VALUE APPROACHES

The most straightforward approach to valuing a company is to rely on the information provided by the balance sheet. There are two ways the balance sheet information can be used to appraise a firm. First, the book values of investor claims, including debt, preferred stock, and common stock, can be added directly. Second, the net assets can be added and liabilities other than investor claims deducted.

The obvious weakness of the balance sheet approach is that the book values of assets and liabilities reported on the balance sheet by accountants may not equal their market values. Because book values are based on historical cost, they fail to take account of factors such as inflation and obsolescence that will cause book value and market value to diverge. In addition, there are valuable assets such as a firm's organization capital that are not reported on the balance sheet. The most striking evidence of the weakness of an unadjusted balance sheet approach is the sharp divergence between book value per share of common stock and market value per share of common stock for many publicly traded companies. For instance, at year-end 1990, Monsanto had a book value per share of $24.93, while the market value of the stock was $48.75. In the case of Microsoft, the market value was over five times the book value at the end of 1990.

In spite of factors such as inflation and obsolescence, it is not always necessary to abandon the book value approach. In some situations, book values can be adjusted to approximate market values more accurately. The most common adjustments are replacing the book values of a company's assets by estimates of the replacement cost or by the liquidation value of those assets. Such adjustments have two drawbacks. First, it is often difficult to determine whether adjusted book values are accurate estimates of market value. Second, the adjustment process typically fails to take proper account of assets such as organizational capital that do not appear on the balance sheet.

Appraising a company based on unadjusted book value literally amounts to reading a balance sheet. For example, Figure 10-1 presents the balance sheet as of June 30, 1989 for Forms Engineering Company (FEC), a small printing company located in the Los Angeles area. The balance sheet shows that FEC had three classes of investors: owners of the notes, preferred stockholders, and common stockholders. In FEC's case, the notes represent bank loans.

From the balance sheet, the value of the firm can be calculated directly by adding the book values of the investor claims or indirectly by adding net assets and subtracting current liabilities (other than debts owed to investors) and deferred taxes. Both methods, the investor claims approach and the asset-liabilities approach, are illustrated in Figure 10-2. The claims of investors include FEC's short-term notes, long-term notes, preferred stock, and common stock. Adding these items gives an estimated value of $6,177,898. Only the claims of investors are included in the valuation, however; claims

FIGURE 10-1

FEC Balance Sheet for Fiscal Year Ending June 30, 1989

Cash	$ 383,168	Accounts payable	$ 510,258
Accounts and notes receivable	2,885,742	Accrued commissions	78,934
Inventories	933,087	Accrued payroll	101,475
Tax claim receivable	117,318	Accrued vacation pay	157,838
Prepaid income taxes	80,386	Employee benefit plan	20,330
Prepaid expenses	6,961	Notes payable	581,146
Deposits	43,244	Other liabilities	35,496
Deferred income taxes	47,136	Current liabilities	$1,485,477
Current assets	$4,497,042	Notes due after one year	$1,768,929
Leasehold improvements	$ 169,015	Deferred income taxes	227,682
Machinery and equipment	6,166,997	Total	$1,996,611
Office equipment	141,868	Total liabilities	$3,482,088
Automotive	162,683		
Computer equipment	201,807	Preferred stock	$1,055,580
Total	$6,842,370	Common stock paid in capital	58,000
		Retained earnings	2,714,243
Accumulated depreciation	(4,029,501)	Total shareholder equity	$3,827,823
Net property and equipment	$2,812,869		
		Total liabilities and shareholder	
Total assets	$7,309,911	equity	$7,309,911

FIGURE 10-2

Balance Sheet Valuation

Investor Claims Approach		Asset-Liabilities Approach	
Notes payable	$ 581,146	Total assets	$7,309,911
Notes (due after one year)	1,768,929	Current liabilities (less notes	
Preferred stock	1,055,580	payable)	(904,331)
Common stock and retained		Deferred income taxes	(227,682)
earnings	2,772,243	Total	$6,177,898
Total	$6,177,898		

of trade creditors and employees, such as accounts payable, accrued payroll, and accrued commissions, reflect accrued costs of operation, not investments in the firm.

Deferred income taxes are also excluded because they are not investor claims. Deferred taxes arise because the IRS allows companies to use accelerated depreciation for tax purposes, while reported earnings are based on straight-line depreciation. A simple example illustrates how this leads to a deferred tax. Assume that a company with earnings of $500,000 before depreciation and taxes buys a new machine which costs $1 million and has a 10-year life. Although the straight-line depreciation is $100,000 per year, the company employs accelerated depreciation for tax purposes and writes off $200,000 in the first year. If the tax rate is 40 percent, the company will owe $120,000 in taxes the first year. (The tax due equals the earnings of $500,000 minus the depreciation of $200,000 times 40 percent.) However, if the firm reports earnings based on straight-line depreciation of $100,000, the apparent tax due will be $160,000 ($500,000 minus $100,000 times 40 percent). The company accounts for this discrepancy by showing $120,000 as the tax paid and by adding $40,000 to deferred income taxes.

Deferred tax is an appropriate name because as the asset ages, accelerated depreciation falls below straight-line depreciation and taxes paid rise relative to apparent taxes due, so that tax deferrals eventually become negative and the deferred tax account for that asset falls. By the end of the asset's life, the deferred tax account for that asset is back to zero. Of course, total deferred taxes for a company may continue to rise if the firm is buying other new assets, but the contribution of the older asset to deferred taxes must eventually turn negative. Thus, the benefit of accelerated depreciation is not that it reduces taxes but that it postpones them.

If tax rates remain constant, the same total tax is paid over the life of an asset but less is paid at the beginning and more is paid at the end. To the extent that this deferral is valuable, it will cause the market value of equity to rise above the book value because benefits of the deferral are not included on the balance sheet.

The deficiencies of the book value approach are most easily seen by looking at the indirect calculation of value. Because current liabilities have short maturities, their book value will be close to their market value. Thus, the accuracy of a book value appraisal depends on how well the net book values of the assets approximate their market values. There are three reasons why the book value of a company's assets commonly diverge from their market value. First, inflation drives a wedge between the current value of an asset and its historical cost less depreciation. Second, technological change renders some assets obsolete before their depreciable life ends. Third, assets may be combined in such a way that their value as part of a going concern exceeds the sum of their values as individual entities. That is, the firm may have specialized organizational capital that adds to value but does not appear on the balance sheet.

[1] Adjusted Book Value Approaches

Adjusted book value approaches attempt to reduce the discrepancy between the reported book value and the market value of a company's assets. One common adjustment is to substitute an estimate of the replacement cost of the assets for the historical cost. Although the earning power of an asset is unlikely to be related to the historical net cost of the asset, particularly if the asset is old, it is more likely to be related to the current replacement cost.

Unfortunately, there is disagreement among appraisers and economists regarding how to measure replacement cost. One possibility is to use a price index, such as the consumer price index (CPI), to convert dollars in the year the asset was purchased to current dollars. Using a price index in this fashion, however, fails to take obsolescence into account. It also fails to reflect changes in the prices of specific assets. For example, the prices of computer equipment, for a given level of processing power, fell dramatically during the years 1985–1990 despite increases in the CPI. A better approach, therefore, is to adjust each asset separately to reflect its own replacement cost today. If done properly, such an adjustment takes both inflation and obsolescence into account because both factors influence the cost of replacing assets today.

Defining "replacement" is no easy task. Even for relatively stable goods, like railroad cars and steel, new products incorporate enhancements and improvements that differentiate them from earlier models. Thus, substituting a new asset for an old one represents an upgrade as well as a replacement. In other words, the substitution includes both an element of replacement and an element of new investment. For more rapidly evolving goods, such as computers, distinguishing replacement from new investment requires a good deal of judgment because new products typically offer features not available on earlier models.

Even if "replacement" can be defined unambiguously and the price of the replacement is known, the replacement cost approach still fails to take account of organizational capital. Corporations exist because they make it possible to combine assets and people in such a fashion that the value of the whole exceeds the sum of the parts. Appraisals based on replacement cost ignore this value-creating synergy. Therefore, they fail to account for that element of value that leads to the formation of a corporation in the first place.

A related adjustment similar in spirit to using replacement cost is using liquidation value. If the assets trade on an active secondary market, as with diesel trucks, liquidation prices equal secondary market prices. Unfortunately, secondary markets do not exist for many corporate assets such as AT&T's copper phone lines or Union Pacific's rail system. Consequently, the appraiser must attempt to estimate the hypothetical price at which such assets could be sold. Although trade publications may aid in the estimation of a hypothetical price in some situations, the appraiser must often rely on management's estimates of liquidation value.

If it is assumed that liquidation values can be estimated, this approach suffers from the same deficiency as replacement cost adjustment: It ignores the value of organizational capital. Only in rare circumstances, such as bankruptcy, will the value of the firm fail to exceed the liquidation value of the assets.

[2] Book Value Appraisal as a Reasonable Estimate of Fair Market Value

The bottom line is that book value appraisals are reasonable only in special situations. Regulated utilities are an example of a special case in which book values appraisal approaches may produce a reasonable estimate of fair market value. Regulatory authorities typically attempt to insure that utilities, including gas and electric companies, earn a fair rate of return on their rate base, where the rate base is defined as the net book value of the company's assets. This ties the future earning power of the company, and therefore the value of the company, to the net book value of its assets. However, even in the case of utilities, net book value and market value may diverge. Regulations are not perfect nor are they completely binding, so utilities often earn more or less than their true cost of capital. In addition, investors may believe that regulation will change in the future or that the utility has opportunities for future growth.

In general, situations in which book value approaches are applicable are rare because organizational capital, which the book value approach ignores, is an important source of value for most going concerns. In this respect, book value approaches to appraisal are particularly inappropriate for high technology or service firms that derive much of their value from organizational capital. The only way to value organizational capital is treat the business as a going concern, but that requires a different approach to valuation.

10.06   DIRECT COMPARISON APPROACHES

Economic theory and common sense agree that similar assets should sell at similar prices. Therefore, a straightforward way to value an asset is to find an identical or at least closely comparable asset that has changed hands between a reasonably informed buyer and seller. The implication that the value of the asset being appraised equals the sale price of the comparable asset works well in real estate: If there are five similar houses on a block and one sells, the appraised values of the other four equal the sale price.

Even in real estate, however, differences in scale make it difficult to find properties that are directly comparable. If house A sold for $200,000 but is only half the size of house B next door, it would be a mistake to appraise house B for $200,000. The solution to the scale problem is to make the comparison on a per-unit basis in terms of ratios. For instance, if house A is 2,000 square feet, the selling price comes to $100 per square foot. If house B is 4,000 square feet and square footage is closely related to value, house B should be appraised at $400,000.

As the example illustrates, the direct comparison approach, adjusted for differences in scale, involves two quantities: a value indicator and an observable variable that is related to value. For direct comparisons to be possible, data on both the value indicator and the observable variable must be available for the comparable asset, and data on the observable variable must be available for the appraisal target. In the real estate example, the value indicator is the price of the house and the observable variable is the number of square feet. The ratio of the price of the house to the number of square feet is calculated for the comparable houses that sold recently and multiplied by the number of square feet in the house being appraised.

Expressing the direct comparison approach in mathematical terms yields further insight into how it works and the assumptions on which it depends. The critical assumption on which the direct comparison approach depends is that the ratio of V, the value indicator, to x, the observable variable, for the appraisal target equals (at least approximately) the ratio of V to x for the comparable firms, as shown in Equation 10.1.

$$\frac{V(\text{target})}{x(\text{target})} = \frac{V(\text{comparables})}{x(\text{comparables})} \tag{10.1}$$

If Equation 10.1 holds, the appraisal procedure is trivial. Solving Equation 10.1 for the unknown variable, the value indicator for the appraisal target, gives

$$V(\text{target}) = x(\text{target}) \left[\frac{V(\text{comparables})}{x(\text{comparables})} \right] \tag{10.2}$$

Equation 10.2 works for any observable variable x, as long as the ratio of V to x is constant across firms, as shown in Equation 10.1. For instance, x could be the number of paintings in a house. If the relation between the price of a house and the amount of artwork it contains is relatively constant across houses, the direct comparison approach based on art will produce an accurate appraisal. The problem is that there are people who live in expensive homes and do not like art. For these homes, Equation 10.1 breaks down and the direct comparison approach will not produce a reasonable appraisal. For this reason, a critical step in applying the direct comparison approach is choosing observable variables, x, that have a consistent relation to value, V. In general, the best way to do this is to find x variables that economic theory indicates will be causally related to value. In the case of a house, square footage is a good candidate because larger houses tend to sell for higher prices. In the case of a company, variables such as cash flows and earnings are good choices because the ultimate sources of value are the net benefits received by investors.

[1] Selecting Comparable Companies

There are two obstacles to overcome when valuing companies by direct comparison. First, sales of corporations are relatively rare. Therefore, it is typically difficult to find sales of comparable companies to serve as the basis for comparisons. Second, and more important, the concept of a comparable company is nebulous. Corporations are complex entities characterized by a wide variety of traits. Which traits must be similar for two companies to be deemed comparable?

The first problem can be overcome by using data for publicly traded firms. Although entire companies rarely change hands, minority positions in publicly traded companies, as represented by ownership of the firm's stock and debt, are bought and sold daily. These comparable publicly traded firms can be valued by applying the stock-and-debt approach.

With respect to the second problem, from a valuation standpoint all companies produce the same product—cash. Whether the company is in steel, biotechnology, or computers, its value to potential buyers is determined by the cash flows it is expected to generate. Ideally, therefore, comparability should be defined in terms of the statistical properties of the anticipated cash flow stream. Applying this definition, two firms are comparable if the correlation between their expected future cash flows is high.

Unfortunately, this definition of comparability requires forecasting cash flows many years into the future. One of the prime reasons for the popularity of the direct comparison approach is that application of Equation 10.2 does not require cash flow forecasts. If cash flow forecasts are necessary to select comparables companies, this rationale for using the direct comparison approach is undermined. Furthermore, if cash flow forecasts are available for the appraisal target, the value of the firm can be calculated directly by discounting the forecast cash flows to present value, so that it is not necessary to search for comparable companies.

For the direct comparison approach to be useful, there must be a way to identify comparable companies without developing detailed cash flow forecasts for each firm. One common solution is to rely on industry classifications. The assumption behind this approach is that if two companies are in the same industry, their cash flows will react to similar market forces and therefore will be highly correlated. In support of the view that comparability can be assessed at least in part by relying on industrial classification, the IRS, in Revenue Ruling 59-60, states:

> In selecting the corporations for comparative purposes, care should be taken to use only comparable companies. Although the restrictive requirement as to comparable corporations specified in the statute is that their lines of business be the same or similar, yet it is obvious that consideration must be given to other relevant factors in order that the most valid comparison possible will be obtained.

Industry classifications are typically defined in terms of Standard Industrial Classification (SIC) codes, published in the U.S. government's *Standard Industrial Classification Manual*.

As the IRS ruling makes clear, however, industrial classification alone provides only a rough estimate of comparability. For instance, IBM and AST Research, which are both computer companies, share the same four-digit SIC code, 3573. Nonetheless, the companies are of vastly different sizes, have different capital structures, make largely different products, have distinct management philosophies, and have markedly disparate corporate histories.

Pratt[4] reports that in *Tallichet v. Commissioner* and in *Estate of Victor P. Clarket,* the tax court recognized that in addition to industrial classification, comparability should also be measured, in terms of, among other things, the following:

- Products
- Capital structure
- Depth of management
- Personnel experience
- Nature of competition
- Earnings
- Book value
- Credit status

One excellent source of information on comparability is securities analysts' reports. In addition to offering a wealth of data about the target company, these reports often contain a detailed list of comparable firms. In some cases, the list of comparables is accompanied by a discussion of the economic factors that led the analyst to conclude that the companies were comparable. Analyst reports are available from the firms that employ the analysts and from a variety of public sources. For example, Investext, which is available through Dow Jones News Retrieval, maintains a relatively complete database of both current and historical analyst reports.

Investment research companies such as Standard & Poor's, Moody's, and Value Line also prepare economic reports on a large number of firms. These reports generally identify comparable firms as part of the analysis. In addition, investment research firms are beginning to distribute their analysis on floppy and optical disks. If analyst reports and independent investment studies are not available, the appraiser should seek the aid of an industry expert in developing the appraisal. An industry expert can provide valuable information not only regarding potential comparable companies but also in developing forecasts regarding the appraisal target's future profitability and cash flow.

In addition, the appraiser has the option of asking the target's managers which firms they see as most comparable to their own and why. The advantage of such direct questioning is that the target's managers, on the basis of firsthand experience, should be excellent judges of comparability. The problem is that target managers may also have an interest in determining the final appraised value, and this may cloud their judgment regarding comparability.

Finally, financial ratio analysis can also be used to assess comparability. Although ratio analysis is typically presented in the context of measuring financial performance,

---

[4] Shannon Pratt, *Valuing a Business* (Homewood, Ill.: Business One Irwin, 1990).

two comparable companies should also be expected to have similar financial ratios. As described by Shapiro,[5] financial ratios are generally divided into four categories:

1. *Liquidity ratios.* These measure the quality and adequacy of current assets to meet current liabilities as they come due. Examples of liquidity ratios are the current ratio (current assets/current liabilities) and the quick ratio (current assets − inventories/current liabilities).

2. *Activity ratios.* These measure the efficiency with which the firm is using its resources. Examples of activity ratios include the gross profit margin (gross profit/net sales) and inventory turnover (cost of goods sold/inventories).

3. *Leverage ratios.* These measure a firm's ability to service its debt. Key leverage ratios include times interest earned (earnings before interest and taxes (EBIT)/annual interest expense) and the debt-to-equity ratio (total debt/market value of equity).

4. *Profitability ratios.* These measure management's effectiveness as indicated by the returns on sales, assets, and owners' equity. Commonly used profitability ratios are the gross profit margin (gross profits/net sales) and the operating profit (EBIT/net sales).

Analysis of the financial ratios is particularly useful as a check on comparability. Suppose that the appraiser has selected a group of comparable companies based on industry analysis, examination of analyst reports, and discussions with management. Presumably, those comparable companies should have financial ratios similar to each other and similar to those of the appraisal target. If one or two comparable companies are found to have significantly different financial ratios, they can be deleted from the sample. If the comparable firms as a group have widely divergent ratios, the appraiser should look for other potential comparable companies with financial ratios more similar to those of the target.

[2] Use of Price/Earnings Ratios

One of the most common applications of the direct comparison approach is the valuation of the equity of a firm on the basis of an analysis of P/E ratios. P/E valuations are frequently used by investment banks when evaluating potential acquisitions, spin-offs, and restructurings. An example of the P/E valuation procedure is presented in Figure 10-3. The example is based on the spin-off of a transportation company by a conglomerate firm.

The comparables chosen by the investment bank in Figure 10-3 were selected because they were in the same industry as the appraisal target. Ratios were calculated as of December 1992 using both actual earnings for 1992 and estimated earnings for 1993. (The analysis was performed in early 1993.) Estimated earnings are often used in place of actual earnings because they are less variable. The problem with actual earnings is that they reflect year-to-year fluctuations in profitability that may not be permanent and therefore may have little affect on value. Because analysts cannot anticipate such random year-to-year fluctuations, estimated earnings are based more on assessments of long-term trends. As a result, estimated earnings tend to vary less over time and from company to company. For this reason, ratios based on estimated earnings are often considered to be more reliable.

---

[5] Alan C. Shapiro, *Modern Corporate Finance* (New York: Macmillan, 1989), pp. 731–759.

FIGURE 10-3

P/E Analysis for Spin-Off of Major Transportation Company as of December 1992

Comparable Company	Ratio of Equity Value to 1992 Earnings	Ratio of Equity Value to 1993 Estimated Earnings
T1	17.8	16.7
T2	12.3	11.8
T3	15.0	14.3
T4	15.8	16.5
T5	28.6	31.0
T6	15.1	14.4
T7	21.5	21.7
T8	53.0	50.5
T9	16.7	16.0
Average excluding T5 and T8	16.3	15.9
Median	16.7	16.5

Implied Values of Appraisal Target's Equity[a]

	Estimated Value Using 1992 Earnings of $218 Million	Estimated Value Using 1993 Estimated Earnings of $269 Million
Average multiple	$3,557	$4,281
Median multiple	$3,641	$4,439

[a] Dollars in millions.

The P/E ratios presented in Figure 10-3 reveal that two of the companies, T5 and T8, had P/E multiples that significantly greater than those of the others. For this reason, the investment bank chose to drop both companies before calculating the average P/E ratio. (They were not dropped in the calculation of the median because the median is not significantly affected by their inclusion.) Dropping "outliers" is not uncommon because P/E ratios are meaningless for companies with small or negative earnings. If a company's earnings are close to zero, its P/E ratio will be huge and including it in the average will bias the entire appraisal. An alternative to dropping the companies is recalculating the ratios for the entire sample using "normalized" earnings. However, such a procedure does not appear promising in this case, because the ratios for T5 and T8 are just as anomalous when calculated using estimated earnings as they are when calculated using actual earnings.

Once the appropriate ratios, in this case the average and the median, have been selected, the equity value of the target firm is estimated by multiplying the ratios by the actual earnings and estimated earnings of the target firm. For instance, the estimated 1993 earnings for the target company are $269 million. Multiplying this number by the 15.9 average P/E calculated using estimated earnings gives a value of $4.281 billion for the equity. The estimated value of the equity ranges from $3.557 billion and

$4.439 billion, depending on the whether the average or the median, and the actual or estimated earnings, are employed.

Although the investment bank chose to apply average and median ratios, there is another option. Rather than treating all of the companies retained in the sample identically, which is what using the average or median does, comparability can be assessed and the most comparable companies can be given greater weight. The drawback of this approach is that it opens the door to data mining. By employing the average and median, the investment bank in the example is less likely to be accused of cherry picking in order to reach a particular conclusion.

Although the use of P/E multiples provides one illustration of the direct comparison approach, it is not the only nor necessarily the best way in which direct comparisons can be developed. As the next section demonstrates, in many situations price per share is not the most appropriate value indicator and earnings per share is not the most appropriate financial variable.

[3] Choosing the Observable Financial Variable and the Value Indicator

As noted at the outset, for the direct comparison approach to provide an accurate estimate of value, the ratio of the value indicator to the observable variable, V/x, must be approximately the same for the comparable firms and the appraisal target. Because the variability of V/x depends critically on the choice of V and x, the two variables must be carefully selected.

From a logical standpoint, the financial variables most likely to produce a constant V/x ratio are those that economic theory predicts will be closely associated with the value of the firm. Because the ultimate source of corporate value is cash produced for security holders, financial variables that measure potential payouts, such as earnings and cash flow, are obvious potential choices for x. In addition, variables that indirectly measure the earning power of the firm, such as sales and book value of equity, are also possible choices.

When selecting appropriate financial variables, the appraiser can turn to the data for help. If a group of comparable companies has been identified, the variability of the V/x ratio across the comparables can be calculated for several choices of x. If the ratio is found to vary substantially for a given x, such as cash flow, the choice of x is probably a poor one. How can the appraiser confidently conclude what the V/x ratio will be for the target firm if the comparable firms all have markedly different ratios?

In the analysis of variation in V/x as an aid in the choice of the proper measure of x, there is an important caveat to keep in mind. In some cases, variability in the V/x ratio may result not from a poor choice of the observable variable but because of short-term aberrations in the data. For instance, suppose that earnings are selected as the observable variable, x. Reported earnings in a given year may be affected by short-term aberrations such as realizations of capital gains or losses, new product introductions, strikes, and foreign exchange fluctuations. In such situations, variation in the V/x ratio can often be mitigated by adjusting the financial data to reduce or eliminate the impact of the aberration. For instance, replacing the current value of x by a five-year average may eliminate most of the variation in the V/x ratio.

Although adjusting the data may reduce variation in the V/x ratio, the adjustment process introduces another source of possible error and bias. For this reason, it is wise to include in the list of financial variables some that do not require adjustment because they are less subject to short-term aberrations or manipulation by target management. On this score, total sales, which is less volatile and less subject to manipulation, may be superior to earnings or cash flow. For instance, partnerships, such as law firms and consulting practices, are commonly valued as multiples of annual revenues rather than as multiples of earnings or cash flow. Because the costs incurred by partnerships are subject to a good deal of discretion, the reported earnings reflect managerial decisions that often vary substantially across otherwise comparable firms. For that reason, appraisers have found that total revenue, which is much less subject to discretionary alterations, is a more reliable indicator of value. Similarly, actors and screen writers generally ask that their bonuses be tied to a motion picture's gross receipts rather than its earnings because studios have a good deal of leeway in defining costs. As a result, pictures with large gross sales often end up producing virtually no net earnings.

The selection of financial variables also depends on the relationship between the comparables and the company being appraised. Suppose the appraisal target and its comparables are similar in all dimensions except capital structure. Some companies have a great deal of debt, while others have none. In this case, the ratio of earnings to firm value across the comparables will vary substantially because companies with more debt have greater interest expense and are therefore riskier. Increasing risk causes a firm's cost of capital to rise and thereby reduces the ratio of value to earnings. On the other hand, earnings before interest, depreciation, and taxes (EBIDT) is independent of the amount of debt and therefore should be relatively constant across firms. Thus, EBIDT is typically a more appropriate choice for the financial variable if otherwise comparable firms have different capital structures.

Although the appraiser has some discretion when choosing a financial variable, it must be matched with an appropriate value indicator. If a gross indicator such as EBIDT is selected, it should be matched with total firm value. On the other hand, if the appraiser decides to use the value of equity (price per share) in the numerator, the denominator should measure the earnings or cash flow available to the equity holders, net of interest and preferred dividends (net earnings). For example, in the P/E analysis presented earlier, price per share was used as the value indicator. If price per share and net earnings are used to estimate the V/x ratio, the result of the analysis is an estimate of the value of equity, not the total value of the firm. The debt and preferred stock must be appraised separately in the calculation of the total value of the firm.

The view that broader measures of income are more appropriate is supported by the work of Miller and Modigliani,[6] who, in two classic papers, presented convincing arguments that show that the value of the firm depends little, if at all, on the firm's capital structure. Therefore, the ratio of total firm value to a gross measure of income, such as EBIDT, should be similar even for firms with different capital structures. This is important because otherwise comparable firms may have divergent capital structures. Applying a P/E ratio observed for these comparable companies will result in a misleading appraisal. Using ratios derived from gross measures, such as total firm value and EBIDT (as opposed to net earnings), corrects this mistake.

---

[6] F. Modigliani and M.H. Miller, "The Cost of Capital, Corporation Finance and the Theory of Investment," *American Economic Review*, Vol. 43 (June 1958), pp. 261–297; M.H. Miller, "Debt and Taxes," *Journal of Finance*, Vol. 32 (May 1977), pp. 261–275.

[4] Adjusting Financial Data

As noted previously, variation in the V/x ratio can be reduced by careful adjustment of the financial data. A simple example illustrates the potential importance of such adjustments. Suppose that the average P/E multiple for a sample of comparable companies is 12. Assume further that during the last fiscal year the company being appraised lost $10 million. Naive application of the direct comparison approach leads to the nonsensical conclusion that the firm has a negative value because the company lost money in the previous year. However, it is unlikely that the $10 million loss represents the company's normal earnings. (If the $10 million loss is normal, the comparable companies are not truly comparable. Truly comparable companies would also be losing money consistently and therefore would also have negative P/E ratios.) The fact is that good companies can have bad years. Ford Motor Company, for example, lost money for several years, but the firm was never worthless.

For the direct comparison approach to work properly, the ratios and the financial variables to which they are applied must not be based on aberrant data. There are two basic reasons why a firm's financial data may be considered abnormal. First, the company may use accounting practices that are not standard in the industry, or it may make significant accounting adjustments. Loan write-downs by banks illustrate the extent to which accounting adjustments can affect financial variables. Current regulations give banks a good deal of leeway in deciding when to realize losses on problem loans. As a result, some banks carry questionable loans at book value until the problem becomes so critical that a huge write-down is required. When the write-down is taken, earnings plunge. For example, Citibank reported losses of nearly $3 billion in one quarter owing to a massive write-down of foreign loans. A direct comparison appraisal of Citibank based on that quarter's earnings would clearly be misleading.

Second, short-term economic conditions may be such that current performance does not reflect the firm's underlying earning power. For example, an automaker may lose money during a recession, a computer manufacturer may experience a decline in sales preceding the introduction of a new machine, and a hotel chain's profits may fall while a major building is being renovated. Under such circumstances, direct comparisons based on current financial data will produce erroneous appraisals.

Procedures for adjusting financial data to mitigate the impact of aberrations fall into two general categories. One approach is to apply statistical techniques. For instance, calculating five-year averages is a simple statistical procedure that is commonly employed. The second approach is to study the economics of the firm and make the adjustments directly. For example, a bank's earnings may be recalculated to take account of a large write-down. It is also possible to combine the two approaches.

[a] Statistical Techniques for Adjusting Financial Data. The statistical approach to adjusting financial data is appealing because it is based on mechanical rules that are easy to apply and are less reliant on the appraiser's judgment. Furthermore, analysis of the economic and financial events that caused the aberrations is not required.

The goal of a statistical adjustment is to reduce variation in V/x by smoothing the financial data used to measure x. To see how the adjustment process is supposed to work, consider a hypothetical appraisal of Bank Zero with earnings as the financial variable. Although the example is developed for banks, the points illustrated are not unique to banks. The same considerations apply to most other companies with appropriate definitions of the variables.

FIGURE 10-4

Appraisal of Bank Zero

Year	Bank Zero (Appraisal Target) EBIDT	Comparable Banks				Average of Comparables
		Bank One EBIDT	Bank Two EBIDT	Bank Three EBIDT	Bank Four EBIDT	
1988	$1,200	$1,600	$3,500	$1,000	$1,800	
1989	1,700	2,500	4,600	1,500	2,700	
1990	1,200	2,000	(4,000)	1,100	(2,500)	
1991	1,500	(2,400)	4,500	1,300	2,800	
1992	(2,000)	1,800	4,000	(1,600)	2,400	
Five-year average	$720	$1,100	$2,520	$660	$1,440	
Estimated market value (under stock-and-debt approach)		$11,000	$23,184	$6,930	$15,552	
Market value/earnings (based on current EBIDT)		6.1	5.8	(4.3)	6.5	3.51
Market value/earnings (based on five-year average)		10.0	9.2	10.5	10.8	10.13

Implied value based on analysis using current-year data = 3.51 × −2,000 = −$7,020

Implied value based on five-year average data = 10.13 × 720 = $7,294

Note: Dollars in millions.

Earnings data for Bank Zero and its four publicly traded comparables, Banks One, Two, Three, and Four, are presented in Figure 10-4 for the five years from 1988 to 1992. Because of lending problems in the last three years, all five banks were forced to write off a significant number of loans. Owing to divergent management philosophies, however, the timing of the write-offs differed across banks. Bank Two and Bank Four wrote off bad loans at the first sign of trouble, while Bank Zero and Bank Three waited until the last possible moment. Bank One took an intermediate position. The earnings of each bank reflects its decision regarding write-offs. All of the banks report profits in every year except during the year of the write-off.

Figure 10-4 also reports the current market value for each of the comparable banks, derived from application of the stock-and-debt approach, the ratio of market value to current EBIDT and the ratio of market value to five-year average EBIDT. (For banks, the interest included in EBIDT is interest on bank capital, not interest payable on deposits.) The ratios of market value to EBIDT in 1992 are difficult to interpret because of Bank Three's write-off, which makes its ratio negative. The negative ratio for Bank Three also drags down the average of the market value/EBIDT ratio for all of the comparable banks. Eliminating Bank Three from the sample fails to solve the problem because the appraisal target, Bank Zero, also reported a loss in 1992 owing to loan write-offs. Applying a positive market value/EBIDT ratio to Bank Zero's negative earnings results in a negative estimate of market value.

Replacing current EBIDT with five-year averages solves both problems. First, the ratio of market value to five-year average EBIDT is close to 10 for all of the comparable banks. Second, averaging replaces the negative EBIDT for Bank Zero with a positive number. Multiplying the average market value/EBIDT ratio for the comparable banks (calculated with a five-year average EBIDT) by Bank Zero's five-year average EBIDT produces a reasonable estimate of market value.

The five-year averages reported in Figure 10-4 are simple arithmetic averages. Some appraisers prefer to use weighted averages that place more weight on recent observations. One common choice is a sum-of-the-years'-digits method similar to that employed in depreciation accounting. If five years of data are available, for example, the numbers 1 through 5 are added to give 15. The current year is then given a weight of $\frac{5}{15}$, the previous year a weight of $\frac{4}{15}$, and so forth. It should be noted that weighting is not always appropriate. In the Bank Zero example, for instance, weighting would be a mistake because it places the banks that wrote off bad loans in more recent years at a disadvantage.

In deciding whether to use a weighted average, it should be kept in mind that the goal of the averaging process is to reduce variation in the V/x ratio. However, the appraiser is not free to experiment with dozens of weighted averages to see which leads to the smallest variation in V/x across the comparable firms. Such a procedure reduces variation in V/x by definition, but the reduction is apt to be spurious. The weights should be chosen on the basis of ex ante economic analysis, not random experimentation. Only if the appraiser has sound reasons for believing that current information will produce more reliable V/x ratios should current data be given greater weight in the calculation of the averages.

In the valuation of Bank Zero, using a five-year average improves the accuracy of the appraisal because it distributes the impact of the loan write-off over five years. This distribution is more consistent with economic reality. Although the loan losses are recognized in one fell swoop, the loan problems undoubtedly developed slowly. Rather than having four highly profitable years and one year with large losses, each of the banks probably experienced five years of mediocre profitability. In an efficient market, the market value of the banks reflects this underlying economic reality. Therefore, there is a closer association, across banks, between market value and five-year average earnings than between market value and current earnings.

If the appraiser chooses to use statistical procedures to adjust the comparable firms' financial variable, the same adjustment must be applied to the appraisal target's financial variable before it is multiplied by the ratio. For example, if a ratio is developed by dividing market value by five-year average earnings for the comparable firms, the resulting ratio must be multiplied by the five-year average earnings of the target.

In the application of statistical techniques, the distinction between smoothing and normalizing must be kept in mind. Some techniques, such as five-year averaging, are designed simply to smooth the data; they are not intended to approximate current levels of the financial variable under normal circumstances. For instance, the five-year averages reported in Figure 10-4 are not necessarily good estimates of normalized 1992 earnings for any of the banks. Other techniques, such as regression analysis, can be used to estimate the normalized levels of the financial variables as well as to smooth the data. This distinction between smoothing and normalizing is not critical in the context of the direct comparison approach because the goal of the adjustment is only to make the V/x ratio more consistent across firms. As long as the comparable firms and the appraisal target data are smoothed in the same fashion, a fair appraisal will result even if the smoothed data represent normalized values.

[b] Direct Adjustment of Financial Data. Whereas statistical adjustments are based largely on mechanical rules, direct adjustment of the data requires identifying the source or sources of aberrations and then deciding on the appropriate adjustments. For example, suppose that the appraiser decides to adjust the Bank Zero financial data to reflect normal operations instead of the aberrations that caused the $2 million loss. This requires both isolating the unique events that led to the loss and recalculating what the financial results would have been had the unique events not occurred. If the aberration is based on an accounting decision, such as Bank Zero's decision to write off bad loans, the relevant financial variables must be recalculated with accounting conventions that more accurately mirror economic reality.

Because normalizing the financial statement requires identifying the unique factors that affect individual companies, the process is largely case specific. There are no general rules that can be laid down regarding how the data ought to be adjusted. This raises the specter of bias because the appraiser must determine what adjustments are required and how they are to be applied. Nonetheless, there are several standard situations that are worth reviewing and rules of thumb that are helpful in dealing with complex cases.

If the sole source of aberration is the application of nonstandard accounting conventions, the adjustment process is conceptually straightforward, although frequently it is computationally tedious. The income statement and balance sheet for the appraisal target and the comparable companies must all be stated in terms of the same accounting conventions. For example, if most of the companies under consideration use last-in, first-out (LIFO) inventory accounting, the books of the few companies that use first-in, first-out (FIFO) accounting must be restated in terms of LIFO before V/x ratios are computed.

When the source of the aberration is a onetime change in accounting numbers, such as a loan write-off or realization of a capital gain, the adjustment process is more complex. Consider the case of Bank Zero, discussed earlier. Because Bank Zero's loan write-off led to losses in the appraisal year, the direct comparison approach cannot be used unless the earnings data are adjusted. But which bank's earnings should be adjusted and for what years? Furthermore, how large should the adjustments be?

One possibility is to adjust the earnings of Bank Zero and Bank Three by eliminating the impact of the write-offs those banks took in 1992. However, eliminating the 1992 write-offs overstates the profitability of Bank Zero and Bank Three relative to the banks that took write-offs in earlier years. A solution more consistent with economic theory is to recalculate each bank's balance sheet and income statement, marking all of the loans to market in every year. This procedure eliminates the lumpiness of the write-off because the market value of the loans should change slowly. More important, marking loans to market should lead to a closer association between financial variables, such as earnings and cash flow (calculated using market values), and the market value of the banks, because in valuing the banks' securities investors will look at the market value of the loans. Consequently, recalculating the balance sheet and income statement with market values for the loans should reduce variation in the V/x ratio across banks.

In this respect, the Bank Zero example illustrates a more general principle. A major goal of the adjustment process should be to restate accounting variables so that they more accurately reflect their economic counterparts. In the case of Bank Zero, restating loans to reflect their market value turns the accounting measure of earnings into true economic earnings. As another example, companies often report large profits associated with the sale of assets or the closing of divisions. However, the economic events that led to the sale or closing do not occur at the date of sale or closure but are spread over prior years. Therefore, the adjustment process should distribute the reported gain or loss over the years in which it was actually realized in order to reflect true economic conditions.

Aside from accounting aberrations, the most common source of deviations in the financial variables is abnormal performance. The problem with defining "abnormal performance" is that a bad year in the eyes of management may be a good year in the eyes of the firm's critics. For instance, it is not uncommon for makers of computer software to attribute a bad year to the costs of introducing a new product while critics claim that the problem is customer dissatisfaction with the new product. Nonetheless, it is indisputable that there are circumstances in which a firm's current performance fails to reflect its long-term earning power. In those situations, an adjustment is required.

Adjusting financial data to mitigate the impact of short-term variations has a long history in economics. The most famous example, which is directly applicable to valuation, is the consumption function. One of the key relations in macroeconomic models is that between national consumption and national income. Early macroeconomic models assumed that consumption was a linear function of income. Unfortunately, the data were inconsistent with this assumption. Consumers spent a larger fraction of their income during recessions and a smaller fraction of their incomes during expansions. In work for which he was cited when receiving the Nobel Prize, Milton Friedman offered an explanation for this observation. Consumers plan to spend a constant fraction of their "permanent" income. By "permanent income," Friedman meant long-term normal income for the year in question. In years when actual income is above the long-term average, consumers add to savings. In years when income is below average, savings are reduced. Thus, the relation of current income to consumption varies from year to year, even though the ratio of permanent income to consumption is virtually constant.

Friedman's work applies to valuation because the relation between earnings (or cash flow) and market value is similar to the relation between national consumption and national income. In valuing a company, the market looks to the firm's long-term earning power. Therefore, the ratio of current earnings to value will be high when current earnings are above normal and low when current earnings are below normal. This variation in the ratio, which invalidates the foundation on which the direct comparison approach is based, can be reduced by substituting normal or permanent earnings for current earnings. The difficulty is in determining what normal earnings are in a given year. An approach suggested by Friedman is to use a weighted average or regression analysis, as discussed earlier. Another possibility is to rely on analyst and investment company reports. When dissecting a company's earnings record, analysts typically discuss whether earnings in a given year are abnormal. They also provide forecasts of the following year's earnings and state whether they expect it to be normal. If the future year is expected to be normal, an average of analysts' forecasts for the next year can be used as the financial variable, x, in the construction of the V/x ratios. Recall that the analysts' forecasts were used by the investment bank to construct P/E ratios for the transportation companies reported in Figure 10-3.

In many situations, however, the company and its comparables are not publicly traded or are not widely followed, so analyst reports are unavailable. In such cases, appraisers must turn to management or apply their own judgment to decide whether the financial variables used in the ratio analysis are normal and, if they are judged to be abnormal, to determine how they should be adjusted. Bias is a clear danger; therefore, when adjustments are based on management input, a careful explanation is required.

10.07 DISCOUNTED CASH FLOW APPROACH

The DCF approach attempts to value directly the benefits that accrue to investors from their participation in the company. The strength of such an approach is that it can be applied in virtually any situation. If future cash flows to investors can be predicted, the DCF value can be applied.

The DCF approach to appraisal involves three interrelated steps. First, a detailed item-by-item cash flow forecast is developed. Second, because firms have an indefinite life, at some point the cash flow forecasting must cease and the continuing value of the firm must be estimated using a simplified procedure. Finally, the firm's weighted average cost of capital (WACC) must be estimated in order to discount the predicted cash flows and the continuing value to present value.

The starting point for a DCF appraisal is a forecast of future cash flow. A simple analogy illustrates why it is cash flow, not accounting earnings, that is the ultimate source of value for investors. Consider a buyer who purchases all of a company's outstanding securities, including any privately held debt and bank loans. On the day following the purchase, the buyer opens a bank account to handle all company-related transactions. Every receipt is deposited in the account, and all company payments other than original expenditure to purchase the firm are deducted from the account. (An automatic overdraft provision is available in case withdrawals exceed deposits.) The account is used for no other purpose. At the end of the first year of business, the balance in the account represents funds that the buyer can withdraw from the business and spend. (If the balance is negative, it represents the funds that the buyer must put into the account to cover the overdrafts of the business.) Assume that the buyer does withdraw the funds so that the bank balance is reset to zero by the start of the second year. In that case, the balance at the end of the second year represents the spendable cash generated in year 2. It is clear that each year's ending balance represents funds that the buyer can withdraw and spend. Because value is ultimately derived from spendable cash, the value of the firm to the buyer is determined by this sequence of year-end bank balances. But these year-end balances are precisely the company's annual net cash flows. Therefore, the value of a business can be estimated by forecasting future cash flows and discounting them to present value.

[1] Calculating Cash Flow

As the bank account analogy illustrates, calculating cash flow amounts to tracking the dollars that flow into and out of a company. Cash flows, not accounting earnings, are the ultimate source of value. There are three major distinctions between cash flow and accounting earnings. First, accountants attempt to record revenue, or book sales, when the funds are earned, such as when a product is shipped or a service is performed. Unfortunately, there can be a substantial difference between the time when a product is shipped and the time when the bill is paid. Cash flow does not occur until the bill is paid. Of course, the same is true of cash outflows, because the firm can also postpone payment of its own bills. On balance, therefore, the lag between the time receipts and costs are booked and the time when cash is received or paid has little impact on net cash flow.

Second, accountants distinguish between current and capital expenditures. Whereas current expenditures are expensed, capital expenditures are depreciated over time. The rationale for this procedure is that the original capital expenditure should be written off against earnings as the capital equipment is used up in the production of income. From a cash perspective, however, the outflows occur when the expenditure is made, not as the equipment is used up. Whereas accounting profits are stated net of depreciation, cash flow is calculated net of capital expenditure. Because capital expenditure rarely equals depreciation, a wedge is driven between accounting earnings and cash flow. (In a perfectly static world in which there is no growth and no inflation and economic deterioration equals accounting depreciation, depreciation equals its capital expenditures and accounting earnings equal cash flow. However, this is not the world in which we live.)

Third, accountants keep track of special reserves, such as those for deferred taxes and bad loans. When reserves are altered—e.g., when a bank increases its reserve for bad loans—accounting earnings are affected, but there is no impact on cash flow because moving entries from one account to another does not involve payment or receipt of cash. When Citibank increased its reserve for bad loans by $3 billion, earnings fell a like amount, but cash flow was unaffected because the increase in reserves did not alter the rate at which Citibank was collecting or paying its bills. (This ignores taxes. If the write-off leads to lower tax payments, cash flow will rise.)

[2] Complications in Calculating Cash Flow

To undo accounting conventions and get back to the dollars that flow into and out of a company, a cash flow statement must be constructed from the income statement and the balance sheet. The procedure for constructing a cash flow statement is best illustrated by working through a detailed example. Before the example calculations, however, there are several complications that need to be addressed.

[a] Payments to Investors and the Interest Tax Deduction. There are two exceptions to the rule that cash flow equals the difference between the dollars that flow into a company and the dollars that flow out. First, payments to security holders are not deducted because they are accounted for by the discounting process. The return to investors is reflected in the firm's WACC. Therefore, deducting payments to investors from the cash flow stream to be discounted is double counting. Put another way, the goal of a DCF analysis is to estimate the value of the stream of payments that the investors that purchased the firm can expect to receive and then to discount that stream to present value using the average rate of return required by investors. In this context, the purchasers of the firm include all investors, not just stockholders. Returning to the bank account example for an all-equity-financed firm, suppose that the owner of the company paid the entire balance of the bank account out to himself as a dividend. If the cash flow stream were measured net of payments to investors, the net cash flow each year would be zero, implying that the firm had no value. However, the firm is clearly valuable to the owner because it provides him with spendable cash each year. In fact, the value of the firm to the owner is the present value of the spendable cash flow stream. This cash flow stream is precisely the same as the funds available for disbursement to investors.

With respect to interest payments, this introduces another complication: What happens to the interest tax deduction? Federal tax rules and the tax laws in most states allow companies to deduct interest payments in the calculation of taxes due. If interest payments are not considered to be a cash outflow, what happens to the interest tax deduction? It is also included in the WACC by calculating the cost of debt on an after-tax basis. Because interest payments are deductible, the after-tax cost of debt is lower than the before-tax cost. This reduces the WACC. To avoid double counting, therefore, the interest tax deduction is not accounted for in the cash flow calculation. Instead, taxes due are computed as if the firm were all equity financed. For this reason, the cash flow that is calculated in this manner is often referred to as debt-free cash flow.

[b] Nonrecurring Cash Flows. Another complication involves extraordinary items. The value of the firm can be thought of as arising from two sources: the cash flow produced by normal operations and extraordinary cash flows from nonrecurring events as shown in Equation 10.3.

$$\text{Total value of firm} = \text{present value of operating cash flow} \qquad (10.3)$$
$$+ \text{ present value of extraordinary cash flow}$$

Extraordinary cash flows include income from sales of assets, revenues from discontinued operations, payments to settle outstanding lawsuits, and other nonrecurring sources and uses of cash. In the calculation and forecasting of cash flow, it is usually a good idea to treat extraordinary items separately. Including extraordinary items with operating cash flow makes trends in operating cash flow more difficult to spot and to project.

Separating the two sources of cash flow is also advisable because they may entail varying degrees of risk. The WACC measures the cost of financing the firm's normal operations. If the risk of the extraordinary cash flows is not equal to the risk of normal operations, a different discount rate should be used to discount the extraordinary cash flows to present value. In practice, however, a separate discount rate is rarely used. Only if nonrecurring cash flow accounts for a significant fraction of the firm's value is it worthwhile to attempt to calculate a separate discount rate. For example, if a firm plans to downsize by selling off several divisions in future years, the receipts from those sales should be forecast and discounted separately. Whether a different discount rate is used depends on whether the appraiser believes that the receipts from the sales are more or less risky than normal cash flow from operations.

There is another reason why a separate discount rate generally does not have to be calculated for extraordinary income: Most extraordinary cash flows have a short horizon, and many occur only in the current year. Therefore, they are not sensitive to small changes in the discount rate.

[c] Income From Excess Marketable Securities. Cash flows produced by excess marketable securities should also be separated from normal operating cash flow. Because every firm must hold some cash and marketable securities as part of its normal operations, the income from these normal holdings is included as part of the cash inflow from operations. However, some companies use cash and marketable securities as a repository for excess funds. For example, at one point IBM built up over $5 billion in cash and marketable securities before deciding to use the excess funds to buy back its own stock. These unusually large holdings of securities constitute an investment that is distinct from the cash held to facilitate normal operations.

Excess marketable securities can be valued as part of the overall firm by simply including the income from the securities as a component of the total cash flow. The problem with this approach is that the income from marketable securities is less risky than the revenue produced by normal operations. For this reason, it is appropriate to discount the income from excess marketable securities at a lower rate than the company's cost of capital. As a result, excess cash and marketable securities should be valued separately, as shown in Equation 10.4.

Total value of the firm = present value of cash flow operating   (10.4)
                                    + market value of cash and excess marketable securities

Fortunately, the discounting process can usually be avoided because the market and book values of cash and marketable securities are generally equal. Therefore, excess marketable securities can be valued by deducting an estimate of the company's required normal holdings from the cash and marketable securities reported on the balance sheet. The only difficult issue is determining the level of cash and marketable securities required for normal operations, so that the excess is defined properly. The FEC example discussed subsequently illustrates this problem.

[d] Deferred Taxes. As noted earlier, the provision for income taxes reported on the income statement will not equal taxes paid in cash if different depreciation methods are used for reporting purposes and tax purposes. To calculate cash flow, the appraiser must "undo" deferred tax accounting and get back to taxes paid in cash. This is accomplished by deducting the change in deferred tax, which is included in the provision for income taxes but is not paid in cash, from the income tax provision. The change in deferred taxes is deducted from the taxes calculated on a debt-free basis. Fortunately, for most companies the change in deferred tax on a debt-free basis equals the change in deferred tax computed from the balance sheet because the increase in deferred tax depends solely on depreciation. The change in deferred tax equals the added depreciation available in a given year (owing to accelerated depreciation methods) times the effective tax rate.

[e] Leases. The fact that there are two types of leases leads to confusion as to how they should be treated. Capital leases are those that transfer ownership of the asset to the lessee. All other leases are operating leases. The treatment of operating leases is straightforward. The lease payment is an operating expense that is included in the cost of goods sold or selling and administrative expenses. Therefore, the lease payment is automatically deducted in the computation of cash flow.

When a lease is capitalized, the present value of the lease payments (at the interest rate implicit in the lease) is added to both the company's fixed assets and its liabilities. Therefore, capital leases should be treated like other forms of debt. Rather than deducting the lease payments from cash flow, the payments are treated as disbursements to investors and included as an element of debt in the firm's WACC.

It is also possible to capitalize operating leases. In that case, the market value of the lease, which equals the present value of the lease payments, is added to both the assets and liabilities of the company. The lease payments are then treated as disbursements to investors. In most cases, however, capitalizing operating leases unnecessarily complicates the appraisal process without adding accuracy. Unless operating leases account for a large fraction of the company's assets, it is more practical to treat them as operating expenses.

[f] Pensions. Because pension costs are included in the cost of goods sold or selling and administrative expenses, an adjustment to the cash flow calculation typically is not required. An exception arises when a pension fund is significantly underfunded or overfunded. In that case, future cash flows associated with the pension fund will differ from those reflected in the current cost of goods sold. These added costs or benefits must be taken into account in the forecasting of future cash flow.

In some cases, underfunded or overfunded pension funds can have a significant impact on the value of the firm. For instance, when Kaiser Industries was involved in a battle for corporate control, one of the assets suitors sought most aggressively was the firm's overfunded pension plan.

[3] Forecasting Cash Flow

Corporate value is based on future cash flow, not historical cash flow. The appraiser's task, therefore, is to produce a predicted cash flow statement, which begins with the present year and extends into the future. That task involves understanding the company, its products, and its customers well enough to forecast the income statement and the balance sheet for up to ten years into the future.

Unfortunately, financial economics provides no set rules on how such forecasts are to be constructed. Cash flow forecasting is as much in the domain of industrial economics, accounting, statistics, and management science as it is in the domain of finance. It also requires a good deal of judgment and practical experience. Perhaps it is for these reasons that financial valuation models based on DCF begin with the assumption that cash flow forecasts are given. Whatever the explanation, only general issues related to forecasting cash flow are discussed here.

[a] Forecasting Sales. At the core of any cash flow forecast lies a sales forecast. Sales are a measure of the company's overall economic activity. All other sources and uses of cash, including production costs, capital expenditures, and interest income, are related, either directly or indirectly, to sales. The first problem an appraiser faces, therefore, is developing a sales forecast. Unfortunately, this is also likely to be the most difficult task.

Consider, for instance, the task of forecasting sales for the PS/2 line of personal computers when IBM introduced them in 1987. A reasonable sales forecast would have to take account of at least the following factors:

- The technical capabilities of the IBM machines in relation to current and future competitors. These capabilities include the power of processor, the storage capacity of the disk drives, and the speed of the data bus.
- The software available for the IBM machines compared with competing machines.
- The ease with which third-party products could be used on the IBM machines.
- The opportunity to expand or improve the IBM machines compared with competing computers.
- The extent to which customers would be willing to pay a premium for the IBM name.
- The relative pricing of the IBM machines compared with competing machines and the general sensitivity of the market to price.

IBM no doubt considered these and many other factors in its decision to release the PS/2 line. Nonetheless, the company was disappointed. Buyers decided that the features provided by the PS/2 machines were not sufficiently innovative or that they could get more computing power for their money by buying clones of IBM's old line of computers rather than the new PS/2s. Furthermore, IBM's name carried less weight than the firm had hoped, and the market proved to be more price sensitive than IBM had estimated. To make matters worse, third-party producers chose to support IBM's old line and its clones more actively than the PS/2s. All of these factors resulted in a sharp fall in IBM's market share and thus a decline in profitability. As a result, the value of the division turned out to be less than an appraisal based on 1987 forecasts would have indicated. As the stock market became aware of this fact, IBM's stock price dropped significantly in inflation-adjusted terms.

Though the PS/2 line was new, IBM did have a history of making personal computers. In some situations, such as when valuing start-up companies, appraisers must develop sales forecasts without the benefit of history. Consider, for example, litigation that arose over the valuation of a proposed instant sign franchising company. The franchise company went bankrupt following the collapse of negotiations with a venture capital firm. The franchise company then sued the venture capital firm on the ground that its business had been destroyed by the failure of the venture capitalist to provide necessary financing. Putting aside the legal merits of the claims, the economic question that arose in the litigation was, What would have been the value of the franchise company if the financing had been provided? To estimate the value of the firm, business valuation experts for both sides used the DCF approach and agreed on the discount rate. Nonetheless, the resulting appraisals differed by 2,500 percent. One expert predicted a dynamic "McDonald's-like" future for the instant sign business, with sales and outlets doubling every few years. The other foresaw stagnant sales for a struggling company sandwiched between instant printers and home computer users. This difference in sales forecasts alone accounted for virtually all of the twenty-five-fold discrepancy.

[b] Six Rules of Cash Flow Forecasting. Both the IBM and instant printing examples illustrate the first maxim of cash flow forecasting:

1. *The sales forecast is generally the most critical element of a cash flow forecast.* Changes in a sales forecast often lead to dramatic changes in value. The examples demonstrate that sales forecasting generally requires a detailed knowledge of the company being appraised, including, among other things, the industry in which the company operates; the products the company produces; the relationship of the company with its customers, suppliers, and servicers; and the nature of the company's competition.

   Because sales forecasting is difficult, the process is subject to potential abuse, depending on the goal of the appraiser. In the instant sign printing example, the two appraisers were able to reach dramatically different conclusions by making different assumptions regarding future sales growth. Whenever possible, historical data, either for the firm or its industry, should be examined to assess the reasonableness of the sales forecasts.

The second rule of cash flow forecasting is as follows:

2. *The sales forecast should be consistent with the firm's historical performance and the historical performance of the industry.* While it is always possible that a company will develop in unexpected ways so that the future does not resemble the past, this is not the

best way to bet. Appraisals based on forecasts that depart markedly from historical patterns are suspicious. In particular, predictions of dramatic turnarounds should be viewed with skepticism. One useful warning is "Beware of hockey sticks." "Hockey sticks" arise when historical sales are flat or declining, but future sales are predicted to take off. Therefore, plotting historical sales and forecast sales against time results in a chart that looks like a hockey stick. Hockey stick forecasts are a simple way for an appraiser to create value out of thin air. Consequently, if a turnaround is predicted, all of the actions necessary to produce the expected success should be specified.

Another way for an appraiser to create value is to assume that a company will grow faster than other firms in its industry for a sustained period. Such sustained growth implies that the appraisal target will eventually become the dominant firm in the industry. This is usually not a reasonable assumption and leads to the third rule:

3. *The sales forecast and the forecasts for the items that depend on sales must be internally consistent.* Once a sales forecast has been developed, it is often relatively easy to forecast other cash flows, because those other flows are related to and dependent on the level of sales. Even other cash flow items for which predictions are not derived directly from the sales forecast must still be consistent with the sales forecast. For instance, rapid growth in sales can rarely be achieved without significant capital expenditures and a buildup of working capital. Therefore, appraisals that forecast a rapid rise in sales without an associated increase in capital spending should be viewed with suspicion. In addition, costs must bear a reasonable relation to sales. The tendency to assume that increased volume will naturally lead to lower per-unit costs should be resisted unless the appraiser can find convincing evidence that such is the case. Assuming that costs per unit will inevitably fall as sales rise is one way to produce a hockey stick forecast for net cash flow.

The advent of the electronic spreadsheet makes it less likely that checking for consistency will detect faulty appraisals. With a computer, any appraisal can easily be made internally consistent. If the appraiser's goal is to produce a high or low value, that can be done without introducing any inconsistencies by building a cash flow model on an electronic spreadsheet and then adjusting the key assumptions, such as the sales growth rate, until the desired value is achieved. In this way an internally consistent but still biased appraisal can be produced.

Interest rates, and therefore the cost of capital, reflect expectations regarding future inflation. For an appraisal to be consistent, the same inflation forecast must be incorporated in the cash flow forecasts, leading to the next maxim:

4. *The cash flow forecast must reflect the same expected inflation rate implied by the discount rate.* Saying that the cash flow forecast must reflect expected inflation does not mean that every revenue and expense item should be adjusted upward each year by exactly the same percentage. In a dynamic economy, the prices of some goods and services will rise more quickly than inflation, while the prices of others lag behind. Furthermore, some items, such as depreciation, are contractually fixed in terms of nominal dollars and do not vary with inflation at all. The point is that the expected rate of inflation should be taken as the baseline assumption around which price variation occurs. For example, if the expected rate of inflation implied by interest rates is 5 percent, all prices that are not fixed in nominal terms should be assumed to grow at 5 percent unless specified information to the contrary is available.

Although a DCF model involves many assumptions, all assumptions are not created equal. Some, such as the assumed choice of depreciation method, may have a minor impact on value, while others, such as the assumed growth rate in sales, almost invariably have a major impact on the final appraised value.

5. *Employ sensitivity analysis to isolate assumptions that have the largest impact on the cash flow forecasts. The rationale for those key assumptions should then be double-checked.* Because it highlights the assumptions on which the cash forecasts are most critically dependent, sensitivity analysis is a valuable tool for assessing a cash flow forecast. Once the key assumptions have been isolated, their rationale can be reviewed.

The best way to perform sensitivity analysis is to reduce the cash flow forecast to an electronic spreadsheet model. This procedure not only facilitates sensitivity analysis but also forces the appraiser to specify the quantitative relations between the various elements of the cash flow forecast. Once the spreadsheet has been developed, the assumptions can be altered and the impact on future cash flow is recalculated automatically.

Whereas sensitivity analysis is useful for isolating key assumptions, it is not of much help in determining whether a given set of assumptions is reasonable. For instance, the sensitivity analysis may make it clear that the growth rate in sales is a key assumption without offering much insight as to the correct growth rate.

6. *Compare the DCF value indicator with the value indicators produced by other approaches.* A DCF model and the cash flow forecasts on which it depends can be assessed directly by comparing the DCF value indicator with value indicators produced by alternative appraisal approaches. If the DCF indicator is significantly different from the alternative value indicators, the critical assumptions isolated by the sensitivity analysis should be reviewed carefully. In conducting the review, the appraiser should determine what alterations of key assumptions are necessary to bring the DCF value indicator into line with the other indicators. This will help the appraiser understand whether a discrepancy exists between the DCF model and competing approaches. Without such knowledge, it is difficult to know whether the DCF approach or the alternative approaches are on stronger footing and which should be given greater weight in making a final judgment as to the value of the firm.

Although comparison with other approaches is an excellent method for evaluating DCF models, it is least applicable when it is needed most. If the company being appraised is a publicly traded firm with a long history, such as IBM, a DCF appraisal can be checked against both stock and debt and direct comparison valuations. However, the cash flow forecasts for publicly traded firms with long histories are also likely to be relatively uncontroversial. Conversely, if the appraisal target is small and privately held and has virtually no history, as with the instant printing franchise, it is impossible to do a stock-and-debt appraisal and difficult to find comparables for a direct comparison appraisal. It is in this situation, when the most weight must be placed on the DCF approach, that the cash flow forecasts are likely to be the most controversial. Without an historical record, appraisers are freer to peer into their crystal balls and come up with radically different views regarding the future of the company and its industry.

[c] Sample Cash Flow Forecast. Figure 10-5 presents a simple cash flow forecast for FEC as of July 1, 1992. It shows the historical data for 1992 as well as forecasts for the next seven years. The choice of the seven-year forecasting horizon is discussed below.

The sales forecast was provided by the company's chief financial officer. Though

FIGURE 10-5
Predicted Cash Flows for FEC (1993–1999)

	1992 (Actual)	1993	1994	1995	1996	1997	1998	1999
Sales revenue (from management schedule)	$15,243,196	$17,857,709	$20,694,227	$23,504,090	$26,374,409	$29,075,149	$31,780,591	$33,446,530
Cost of goods sold (70% of sales)	(11,796,820)	(12,500,396)	(14,485,959)	(16,452,863)	(18,462,086)	(20,352,604)	(22,246,414)	(23,412,571)
Depreciation (from management schedule)	(756,526)	(720,000)	(1,020,000)	(975,000)	(895,000)	(880,000)	(950,000)	(910,000)
Administrative expense (16.5% of sales)	(2,240,719)	(2,946,522)	(3,414,548)	(3,878,175)	(4,351,778)	(4,797,400)	(5,243,798)	(5,518,677)
Income from operations	$ 449,131	$ 1,690,791	$ 1,773,721	$ 2,198,052	$ 2,665,545	$ 3,045,145	$ 3,340,380	$ 3,605,282
Normal interest on securities[a]	26,822	31,422	36,413	41,358	46,408	51,160	55,921	58,852
Debt-free taxable income (EBIT)	$ 475,953	$ 1,722,213	$ 1,810,134	$ 2,239,410	$ 2,711,953	$ 3,096,305	$ 3,396,301	$ 3,664,134
Taxes (40% total tax rate)	(190,381)	(688,885)	(724,054)	(895,764)	(1,084,781)	(1,238,522)	(1,358,520)	(1,465,653)
Increase in deferred taxes (based on capital expenditures)	51,378	14,750	79,854	29,865	21,654	14,987	31,000	28,750
Net operating profit after adjusted tax	$ 285,572	$ 1,033,328	$ 1,086,080	$ 1,343,646	$ 1,627,172	$ 1,857,783	$ 2,037,780	$ 2,198,480
Depreciation add-back	756,526	720,000	1,020,000	975,000	895,000	880,000	950,000	910,000
Increase in working capital (19% of change in sales)	(266,597)	(496,757)	(538,939)	(533,874)	(545,361)	(513,141)	(514,034)	(316,528)
Capital expenditures (from management schedule)	(153,519)	(50,000)	(3,450,000)	(150,000)	(175,000)	(225,000)	(650,000)	(375,000)
Net cash flow	$ 621,982	$ 1,206,570	$(1,882,858)	$ 1,634,772	$ 1,801,811	$ 1,999,643	$ 1,823,746	$ 2,416,952

Note: Figures are rounded.

[a] The normal holdings of cash and marketable securities are assumed to maintain the same ratio to sales as the ratio that applied in 1992. The yield on those securities is forecast to average 7 percent.

it is common for appraisers to rely on management sales forecasts, this should not be done naively, because frequently managers have axes to grind that can bias the sales forecasts provided.

Once a sales forecast has been developed, operating costs must be estimated and deducted. Operating costs include the cost of goods sold, administrative and selling expenses, and depreciation. The estimates for the cost of goods sold and the selling and administrative expense shown in Figure 10-5 are based on historical average ratios for the industry.

The depreciation forecast includes future depreciation on equipment purchased prior to July 1, 1992 and still in service on the lien date as well as depreciation on anticipated new investments. New investments are assumed to be made in accord with the company's capital spending plan. In conjunction with the sales forecast, the chief financial officer, in consultation with the president, estimated what new equipment would be required to assure that future production could keep pace with future sales.

Two entries, extraordinary items and earnings on security investments, distinguish operating income from debt-free taxable income. Extraordinary items do not appear in Figure 10-5 because FEC has not had and does not expect to have extraordinary income or expenses. However, even if such items existed, they should probably be excluded from the cash flow forecast and valued separately. As discussed previously, mixing nonrecurring items with normal operating income and expenses makes cash flow more difficult to forecast.

With regard to income from marketable securities, FEC expects to hold only marketable securities that it needs to assure that the firm has sufficient liquidity to meet short-term contingencies. The interest income from investments for any future year is calculated by multiplying the ratio of cash holdings to sales in 1989 by the sales forecast for the year in question and then applying an interest rate of 7 percent.

Because there are no extraordinary items, adding predicted interest income to operating income gives debt-free taxable income. Debt-free taxable income also equals EBIT net of extraordinary items. EBIT measures the earning power of the firm prior to the making of payments to the government, to investors, to purchase new equipment (net of depreciation), and to add to working capital.

For simplicity, FEC is assumed to face a total tax rate, both state and federal, of 40 percent. Applying that rate to the debt-free taxable income gives FEC's predicted provision for income taxes, shown in Figure 10-5. The income tax provision exceeds taxes paid in cash because FEC is a growing company that expects to take advantage of accelerated depreciation. This leads to rising deferred taxes. The annual increase in deferred taxes represents the fraction of the provision for income taxes that is not paid in cash. To arrive at cash tax payments, an estimate of future increases in deferred taxes must be deducted from the provision for income taxes.

Subtracting cash taxes paid yields net operating profit after adjusted taxes (NOPAT). There are three items that distinguish NOPAT from cash flow: depreciation, changes in working capital, and capital expenditures. First, depreciation is added to NOPAT because it was deducted in the calculation of taxable income, but it is not a cash expense. Second, the expected increase in working capital is deducted. In the case of FEC, working capital is assumed to equal 19 percent of future sales, so the change in working capital is 19 percent of the change in sales. Finally, capital expenditures are deducted to arrive at net cash flow. The capital expenditure forecasts are based on the company's financial plan mentioned earlier. The capital expenditures are "lumpy" at the start of the seven-year forecasting interval because FEC is still making periodic large investments in new equipment to expand production.

[4] Selecting the Terminal Horizon

Because the life of a firm is indefinite, at some point the cash flow forecasting must cease and a simplified model must be used to estimate the continuing value of the firm. The key criterion for selecting the terminal horizon for the cash flow forecasts is that by the time the terminal date is reached, the firm should have arrived at an equilibrium state in which it is no longer evolving rapidly and growth is relatively smooth and predictable.

To estimate the continuing value of the firm, the appraiser must make two interrelated decisions: selecting the terminal date and deciding what valuation model to apply at the terminal date. The decisions are interrelated because the procedure used to estimate the continuing value defines what is meant by the firm's "equilibrium state," which, in turn, defines the terminal date.

Two popular models for estimating the continuing value are the direct comparison model and variants of the constant growth model. The constant growth model is based on the assumption that in equilibrium at the terminal date, the growth in the firm's real (inflation-adjusted) cash flow is at a constant level that is maintained indefinitely. Given the assumption of constant real growth in cash flow, the continuing value at the terminal date is calculated from the formula

$$\text{Continuing value at time } t = \frac{E(\text{NCF}_{t+1})}{\text{WACC} - [(1 + g)(1 + \pi) - 1]} \tag{10.5}$$

where:

t = end of the forecasting horizon

$E(\text{NCF}_{t+1})$ = normalized cash flow expected during the period $t + 1$, equal to the normalized cash flow for the year ending on the terminal date multiplied by $[(1 + g)(1 + \pi) - 1]$

g = long-term real growth in cash flow

π = expected inflation rate impounded in the WACC

For the constant growth model to be applicable, explicit cash flow forecasts are required up to the point where the real growth rate in cash flow becomes constant. Unfortunately, for many firms, particularly recent start-ups and high technology enterprises, it may take 20 years or more for growth rates to fall to a constant level. Rather than abandoning the growth model under such circumstances, it is often possible to extend it in a straightforward manner. Specifically, individual cash flows are forecast up to an equilibrium point where the cash flow growth becomes predictable though not necessarily constant. That predictability is then used to forecast the trend in cash flow without developing an item-by-item cash flow forecast.

The direct comparison approach relies on a less stringent definition of "equilibrium" to define the terminal date. Rather than requiring that growth in cash flow be constant, the direct comparison approach requires that the firm be a mature member of its industry so that it can be valued by applying ratios derived from established publicly traded firms.

It may seem as if it would be extraordinarily difficult to find companies today that are comparable to what the appraisal target is expected to become in the future.

However, the reverse can be true for small and rapidly growing companies. It is often easier to find companies comparable to what the firm is likely to become than to find companies comparable to the firm it its current condition. For example, Genentech and Biogen are both biotechnology firms, but their products are evolving so rapidly that it is unclear how comparable the firms are today. This is a common problem that arises when the value of a company depends heavily on its growth opportunities. Because growth opportunities are intangible and because they involve products that are yet to be produced, it is difficult to determine whether one set of growth opportunities possessed by one firm is comparable to a related set possessed by another firm. As firms mature, their cash flows come to depend more on proven products and assets in place and less on intangible opportunities. As a result, comparability is easier to assess. For example, it is not difficult to determine that Ford and General Motors are comparable.

Once ratios have been derived from the comparable firms, the continuing value is calculated by applying the ratios to the forecast financial data at the terminal date. In applying the ratios, care should be taken to assure that the terminal year's financial forecast is not anomalous. For example, if the firm is expected to sell off a major division in the terminal year, normalized financial statements should be developed as discussed earlier.

[5] Selecting a Discount Rate

The appropriate rate for discounting the forecast cash flows and continuing value back to present value is the firm's WACC. Estimating the WACC involves two interrelated steps:

1. The after-tax cost of capital is estimated for each class of securities that the firm issues.

2. The WACC is calculated by weighting each of the individual financing costs to reflect the firm's target capital structure. For example, if the capital structure target is 60 percent equity and 40 percent debt, the weights are 0.6 and 0.4.

The steps are interrelated because the financing cost depends on the capital structure. The more leverage a firm employs, the higher its cost of both debt and equity. As long as the firm's target capital structure weights and present capital structure weights are approximately equal, this does not cause a problem. Financing costs can be estimated under current conditions. However, in situations in which the current capital structure is seen to be anomalous, it cannot be assumed that financing costs will remain unchanged as the firm moves toward its long-term capital structure. The financing costs must be calculated under the same leverage assumption that defines the long-term capital structure weights.

In this vein, a unique problem arises in the valuing of companies using the DCF approach. For example, assume that a company is financed by a combination of debt and equity and that the value of the debt equals its book value. In that case, the value of the equity equals the value of the firm minus the value of the debt. The value of the firm, in turn, equals the net present value of the cash flow forecasts and the continuing value discounted at the WACC. Unfortunately, the WACC depends on the value of the equity, since it depends on the capital structure weights. As a result, the capital structure weights and the value of the firm must be calculated simultaneously. Cornell (1993) describes an iterative procedure for doing this.

One way to avoid the complications introduced by the iterative procedure is to assume that the financing costs and the capital structure weights for the firm are approximately equal to industry averages. If this assumption is made, it should be checked when the appraisal is finished. If the capital structure weights calculated using the appraisal are significantly different from the assumption, the iterative procedure must be employed.

10.08 ADJUSTING THE APPRAISED VALUE FOR CONTROL PREMIUMS AND MARKETABILITY DISCOUNTS

[1] Control Premiums

There are a number of reasons why a controlling block of securities may be worth more on a pro rata basis than a minority position. Among the benefits of control are the following:

- Power to elect directors and appoint management
- Power to determine cash payouts on common shares
- Power to decide what investments are undertaken and how those investments are financed
- Power to manage free cash flow and set perquisites
- Freedom to choose when to sell or liquidate the company

These control benefits may drive a wedge between the value of a controlling interest and a minority position. The problem facing the appraiser in dealing with the wedge is twofold. First, it must be determined whether a wedge exists. If there is evidence of a wedge, its size must be estimated. Second, the appraiser has to decide whether to increase a value indicator to reflect a control premium or to reduce the value indicator to reflect a minority discount. That decision depends on the nature of the company being appraised and on the appraisal approach that was employed to arrive at the value indicator.

In appraisal practice, it is common to assume that control is valuable and that a wedge exists. Accordingly, many appraisers automatically move to the next step of estimating the magnitude of the wedge. The standard procedure for estimating the size of the wedge is examining data on control transactions. For instance, based on data provided by W.T. Grimm, the average premium paid in 134 control transactions during the period 1980–1987 was 41.5 percent.[7] Grimm calculates the premium as the percentage difference between the stock price of the target company five business days before the receipt of a bid and the price paid by the acquiror. Because takeover bids are often partially anticipated, the price of the target company's stock five business days before a bid may already reflect the possibility of a bid. To the extent that a bid is anticipated, Grimm's calculation understates the value of control. Nonetheless, the 41.5 percent premium calculated by Grimm is consistent with results obtained by investment banks that measure the premium as the percentage difference between the stock price six weeks before a bid was received and the price paid by the acquiror.

Academic studies have employed a different definition of "premium." The most

---

[7] W.T. Grimm, *Mergerstat Review* (Chicago: W.T. Grimm and Company).

commonly used estimate is the change in the stock price of the target, net of market-related movements, during a specified period surrounding the first announcement of a takeover bid. For instance, one study examines the net change in the target's stock price from 20 trading days prior to the first bid until consummation of the transaction. Jensen and Ruback report that average premiums are on the order of 20 percent for mergers and 30 percent for tender offers.[8]

Viewed from the other side, a premium of 41.5 percent translates into a discount of 29 percent $(1 - 1/(1 + 0.415))$ for shares that do not convey control compared with shares that do. This calculation makes it clear that the minority discount is just the mirror image of the control premium.

While it is common in appraisal practice to apply a control premium or a minority discount, this may be an error. Both research in finance and common sense support the proposition that a buyer is willing to pay more than the market price for a controlling interest in a company only when the buyer believes that the future cash flow of the company, and therefore the value of the company, can be increased once it is under the buyer's control. Thus, in situations where control transactions occur, it follows that the buyer expects to be able to enhance after-tax cash flow. It does not follow that potential buyers believe that a controlling block of every company is worth 45 percent more than the market price. More likely, the reverse is true. The fact that most companies do not receive takeover bids at premiums above the market price indicates that investors believe that the shares of those companies are not worth significantly more than the market price. Otherwise, someone would make a bid. For this reason, it would be misleading to assume that the wedge between the value of control and the value of a minority interest in companies that are not takeover targets is 45 percent. In fact, the wedge would be zero for companies that potential acquirors would not change in any way. At a minimum, there is no basis for concluding that the size of the wedge for a particular company equals the historical average of premiums paid in recent mergers and takeovers. Those transactions occurred because acquirors saw a potential for adding value that probably does not exist in the case of a typical company.

To determine the appropriate control premium (or minority discount) for a company that is not a takeover target, information on how a new owner might be able to add value to the firm is required. Research on the market for corporate control[9] suggests a variety of ways in which the transfer of control may lead to increased cash flow and enhanced value, including the following:

1. *Synergy.* If the target firm has specialized resources that could be more profitably employed in combination with another firm, the value of the firm as part of a larger organization should exceed its value on a stand-alone basis.

2. *Inefficient management.* If the firm's management is inefficient or incompetent, replacing current management will increase cash flow and enhance value. Examples of inefficient

---

[8] M.C. Jensen and R.S. Ruback, "The Market for Corporate Control: The Scientific Evidence," *Journal of Financial Economics*, Vol. 11 (Apr. 1983), pp. 5–50.

[9] Papers on the subject include M. Bradley, A. Desai, and E.H. Kim, "The Rationale Behind Interfirm Tender Offers: Information or Synergy," *Journal of Financial Economics*, Vol. 11 (Apr. 1983), pp. 183–206; M. Bradley, A. Desai, and E.H. Kim, "Synergistic Gains From Corporate Acquisitions and Their Division Between the Stockholders of Target and Acquiring Firms," *Journal of Financial Economics*, Vol. 21 (May 1988), pp. 3–40; M. Jensen, "Agency Costs of Free Cash Flow, Corporate Finance, and Takeovers," *American Economic Review*, Vol. 76 (May 1986), pp. 326–329; S. Kaplan, "Management Buyouts: Evidence on Taxes as a Source of Value," *Journal of Finance*, Vol. 44 (Sept. 1989), pp. 611–632.

management include excessive investment in projects that fail to earn their cost of capital, inability to cut costs and employment where necessary, and unwillingness to shed inefficient bureaucracy.

3. *Excess perquisite consumption.* If managers consume excessive perquisites, reducing the perquisites will increase cash flow. Although some perquisites are required to provide incentives, there are clear abuses. For example, when Ross Johnson was chairman of RJR Nabisco, he maintained 27 country club memberships and had a fleet of corporate jets at his beck and call, all at company expense.[10]

4. *Tax benefits.* If there are tax benefits that can be realized by a corporate control transaction, a takeover will increase cash flows to shareholders at the expense of the government. For instance, a firm with several years of losses and no turnaround in sight may have to merge with a more profitable company to take advantage of the tax losses. In this situation, the control premium represents the cost of buying the tax loss.

If none of these factors are present and if the appraiser can see no other reason why the transfer of control would lead to higher cash flow and greater value, there is no reason to make a significant adjustment to a value indicator to take account of a control premium. Put another way, if the appraiser cannot identify what a buyer of the appraisal target would change to increase cash flow, there is no reason to assume that a control premium exists.

If the appraiser concludes that a wedge does exist between the value of a minority position and the value of a controlling block, the next step is deciding whether to add a control premium or deduct a minority discount from the value indicators produced by the various approaches. The decision depends on whether the value indicator, prior to the adjustment, is interpreted as an estimate of a controlling interest or a minority position in the firm. That, in turn, depends on the approach that was used to derive the value indicator.

In some cases, the decision is easy. For example, the value indicator produced by the stock-and-debt approach, which is based on the prices at which minority positions trade in the market, clearly reflects the value of a minority position. Similarly, the direct comparison approach values a minority position if the comparables are appraised by the stock-and-debt approach. To value a controlling interest, an estimate of the control premium must be added. Conversely, if sales of entire companies are used to value the comparables, the direct comparison approach values a controlling interest. Consequently, a discount must be deducted to value a minority position.

The DCF approach is more ambiguous. On the one hand, it can be interpreted as valuing a controlling interest because the cash flows are forecast for the entire company. On the other hand, it can be argued that the forecast represents the cash flows current management is expected to produce. New management might be able to produce greater cash flows by taking advantage of the factors discussed earlier. In that case, it would be proper to add a control premium to the DCF value. Despite this ambiguity, DCF appraisals are most often interpreted as reflecting the value of a controlling interest in the firm.

The book value approach suffers from the same ambiguity. Because the balance sheet reflects the value of the entire firm, it is usually interpreted as representing a controlling interest. However, new management may choose to alter the balance sheet

---

[10] Bryan Burrough and John Helyar, *Barbarians at the Gate* (New York: Harper & Row, 1990).

by selling assets or recapitalizing the firm, so it cannot automatically be assumed that the book value will remain unchanged.

[2] Marketability Discounts

Investors purchase securities in a company not because they want to own securities but because they want to increase the spendable cash that they will have available in the future. If the securities are not publicly marketable and thus cannot easily be resold, they will be worth less to the investor because they cannot be converted to cash quickly without a significant discount in price. If the nonmarketable securities do not represent a controlling position, the investor will have no control over when the securities are to be registered and thus become marketable.

In appraisal practice, a marketability discount is generally not applied to fixed-income securities because these securities are held by long-term investors and because the securities offer a periodic fixed payment that reduces the need to sell them before maturity. In the case of equity, however, nonmarketable shares are assumed to be a good deal less valuable than marketable shares because of the empirical evidence of the pricing of restricted shares. In an early study, the Securities and Exchange Commission found that discounts for letter stock issued by companies that traded on the New York Stock Exchange and the American Stock Exchange and in the over-the-counter market were approximately 25 percent.[11] Follow-up studies summarized by Pratt (1990) and Cornell (1993) report discounts of at least this magnitude.

Another measure of the marketability discount is the difference between the price paid for shares in private transactions before a company goes public and the price at which such shares would have traded if the company were public. By definition, this discount cannot be observed directly. However, it is possible to observe the prices at which privately held shares traded prior to a public offering and compare them with the IPO price. Cornell reports that studies of the price differential find differences of 25 percent or more.

Controlling shareholders always have the option of overcoming the nonmarketability problem by taking the company public. From their standpoint, therefore, the discount for lack of marketability should not exceed the flotation costs as a percentage of the value of the equity. If the discount exceeds flotation costs, a controlling shareholder would choose to take the company public. If there is no controlling shareholder, minority shareholders have an incentive to organize and to pressure management to take the company public when the discount significantly exceeds flotation costs. Consequently, another way to estimate the discount for lack of marketability is to calculate the costs of going public.

The most comprehensive study of flotation costs was performed by Smith (1977), who reports costs ranging from about 20 percent to 25 percent of the value of the issue for small issues down to 3 percent to 5 percent of the value of the issue for large issues. The fact that these numbers are smaller than the discounts found in the studies of transactions involving restricted shares is a puzzle.

Given the state of current research, the safest conclusion to draw is that the appropriate marketability discount is at least on the order of magnitude of the cost of going

---

[11] *Discounts Involved in Purchases of Common Stock,* Securities and Exchange Commission, Institutional Investor Study Report (Washington, D.C.: 1971).

public. It may be greater if shareholders are anxious to trade and there are impediments to going public, such as entrenched management.

10.09 DETERMINING THE FINAL VALUE INDICATOR

Once the appraiser has estimated the value of the firm using the approaches described previously and has made necessary adjustments, the last hurdle is putting all the information into a final value indicator. One possible way to aggregate the individual indicators produced by each of the approaches is to calculate an average or weighted average. Such predetermined weighting schemes have little to recommend them other than a quasi-scientific appearance. The problem is that an appraisal approach that provides useful information about the value of one company may provide almost no information about the value of another company. While there are no hard-and-fast rules, there are several guidelines that are worth mentioning:

- As noted earlier, the book value approach to appraisal is likely to be of limited use. Except in unique situations where the earning power of a company is tied to its book value by regulation (as is the case with public utilities), book value and market value are not likely to be correlated in a reliable fashion.

- A stock-and-debt value indicator, when it can be calculated, should generally be given the greatest weight. Unlike the other appraisal approaches, which are based on the forecasts and judgments of accountants and appraisers, the stock-and-debt value indicator reflects the market's assessment of the value of the company. For this reason, it is not excessive to give the stock-and-debt approach a weight of 100 percent if all of the company's securities are publicly traded.

- The accuracy of the direct comparison approach depends on the ability of the appraiser to find comparable companies whose values are known or can be estimated accurately by straightforward techniques such as the stock-and-debt approach. If the issue of comparability becomes murky, or if the comparables must be appraised by a less reliable technique, the weight placed on the direct comparison approach should be reduced accordingly.

- The virtue of the DCF approach is that it can be applied in nearly any appraisal context. The drawback is that it depends on the appraiser's forecasts of future cash flows and estimates of the cost of capital. In situations where there is a long history on which to base cash flow forecasts and market data on which to base estimates of the cost of capital, a good deal of confidence can be placed in the DCF approach. However, the DCF approach is easily abused, particularly when applied to new companies or in novel situations. In such circumstances, value can be created out of thin air by optimistic forecasting. Therefore, the weight applied to a DCF forecast should be directly proportional to the confidence that can be placed in the cash flow forecasts.

Although these general guidelines provide direction, any information that leads the appraiser to believe that one approach or another produces a more accurate estimate of value should be considered. Because each company has unique characteristics that affect its value and may or may not be picked up by a particular valuation model, appraiser judgment is required to arrive at a final value indicator. Impeding that judgment by enforcing an averaging scheme that does not take account of the peculiarities of the individual case generally results in less accurate appraisals.

Suggested Reading

Banz, R.F. "The Relationship Between Return and Market Value." *Journal of Financial Economics*, Vol. 9 (Jan. 1981), pp. 3–18.

Bradley, M., A. Desai, and E.H. Kim. "The Rationale Behind Interfirm Tender Offers: Information or Synergy." *Journal of Financial Economics*, Vol. 11 (Apr. 1983), pp. 183–206.

———. "Synergistic Gains From Corporate Acquisitions and Their Division Between the Stockholders of Target and Acquiring Firms." *Journal of Financial Economics*, Vol. 21 (May 1988), pp. 3–40.

Cornell, B. *Corporate Valuation: Tools for Effective Appraisal and Decision-Making*. Homewood, Ill.: Business One Irwin, 1993.

Fama, E.F. "Efficient Capital Markets: A Review of Theory and Empirical Work." *Journal of Finance*, Vol. 25 (May 1970), pp. 383–417.

———. "Efficient Capital Markets: II," *Journal of Finance*, Vol. 46 (Dec. 1991), pp. 1025–1075.

Jensen, M.C. "Agency Costs of Free Cash Flow, Corporate Finance, and Takeovers." *American Economic Review*, Vol. 76 (May 1986), pp. 326–329.

Jensen, M.C., and R.S. Ruback. "The Market for Corporate Control: The Scientific Evidence." *Journal of Financial Economics*, Vol. 11 (Apr. 1983), pp. 5–50.

Kaplan, S. "Management Buyouts: Evidence on Taxes as a Source of Value." *Journal of Finance*, Vol. 44 (Sept. 1989), pp. 611–632.

Keim, D. "Stock Market Regularities: A Synthesis of the Evidence and Explanations," *Stock Market Anomalies*, Elroy Dimson, ed. Cambridge: Cambridge University Press, 1988.

Miller, M.H. "Debt and Taxes." *Journal of Finance*, Vol. 32 (May 1977), pp. 261–275.

Modigliani, F., and M.H. Miller. "The Cost of Capital, Corporation Finance and the Theory of Investment." *American Economic Review*, Vol. 43 (June 1958), pp. 261–297.

Pratt, Shannon. *Valuing a Business*. Homewood, Ill.: Business One Irwin, 1990.

Shapiro, Alan C. *Modern Corporate Finance*. New York: Macmillan, 1989.

Shiller, R.J. "Do Stock Prices Move Too Much to Be Justified by Subsequent Changes in Dividends?" *American Economic Review*, Vol. 71 (June 1981), pp. 421–436.

Smith, C. "Alternative Methods of Raising Capital: Rights Versus Underwritten Offerings." *Journal of Financial Economics*, Vol. 5 (Dec. 1977), pp. 273–308.

Summers, L.H. "Does the Stock Market Rationally Reflect Fundamental Values?" *Journal of Finance*, Vol. 41 (July 1986), pp. 591–601.

Index